CW00968515

A HISTORY
of the
PORT TALBOT RAILWAY & DOCKS COMPANY
and the
SOUTH WALES MINERAL RAILWAY COMPANY

Volume 2: 1894–1971

Nos 5, 6 and 8 tips on North Bank of Port Talbot Docks,
looking west. June 1923.   *BR/OPC*

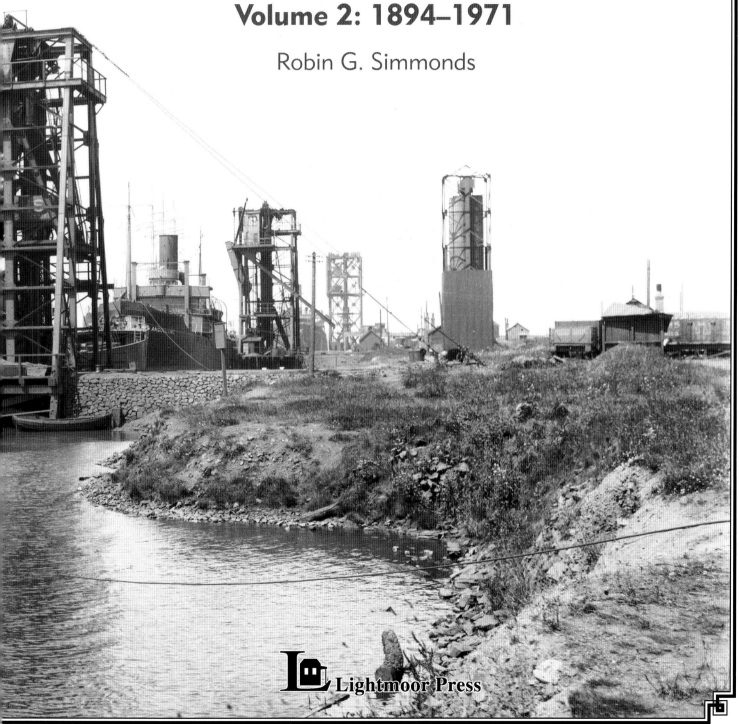

A HISTORY
of the
PORT TALBOT
RAILWAY & DOCKS COMPANY
and the
SOUTH WALES MINERAL RAILWAY COMPANY
Volume 2: 1894–1971

Robin G. Simmonds

Lightmoor Press

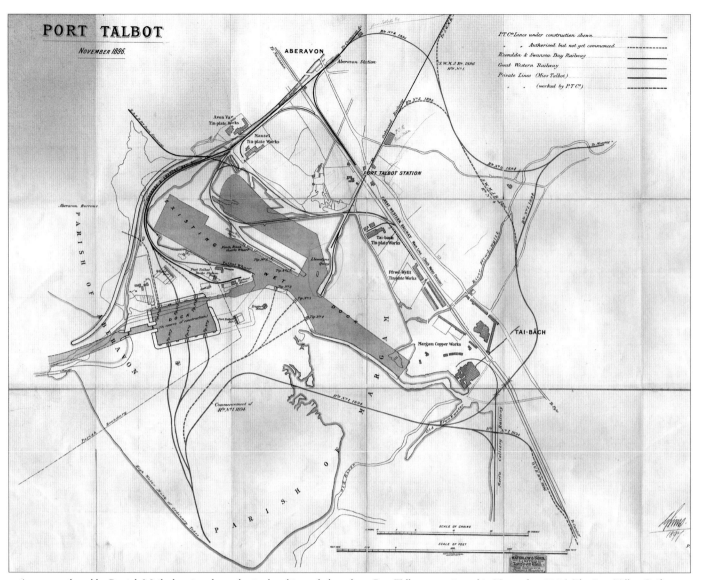

A map produced by Patrick Meik showing the authorised and intended works at Port Talbot as envisaged in November 1896. The Port Talbot Railway 1894 and Ogmore Valleys Extension Railway 1896 were constructed as shown, as were the South Wales Mineral Railway Junction Railway 1896 lines apart from Railway No. 4, but Central station is only pencilled in, although not in its final position, and the railway to it is absent. The troublesome crossing of the Oakwood Railway over the Great Western Railway main line is adjacent to Port Talbot station. In the dock area the course of the training wall is apparent along the right bank of the River Avon, but otherwise the final layout bore little relation to what is depicted. The Old Dock is shown connected via the old lock to the New Dock. Meik's proposal to cut through from the New Dock to the Old Dock is shown dotted. The resulting Island to the north of the erstwhile Port Talbot Inn was eventually removed. The existing tips, Nos 5 and 6, are on North Bank, but of the others, only Nos 7–10 were erected, becoming Nos 1–3 and 7. Also shown are the old hydraulic power station on North Bank and the new one east of the New Dock. The shallow area of sea south of Margam Copper Works and Railway No. 1 1894 and the pre-1837 course of the River Avon was gradually reclaimed and later became part of the site of the Abbey Works. *Author's collection*

© Robin G. Simmonds and Lightmoor Press 2013
Designed by Nigel Nicholson
British Library Cataloguing-in-Publication Data. A catalogue
record for this book is available from the British Library
ISBN 9781 899889 79 2
All rights reserved. No part of this publication may be reproduced, stored in a retrieval
system or transmitted in any form or by any means, electronic, mechanical, photocopying, recording or otherwise,
without the written permission of the publisher

LIGHTMOOR PRESS
Unit 144B, Lydney Trading Estate, Harbour Road, Lydney, Gloucestershire GL15 5EJ
www.lightmoor.co.uk
Lightmoor Press is an imprint of Black Dwarf Lightmoor Publications Ltd.
Printed by Berforts Information Press, Eynsham, Oxford.

Contents

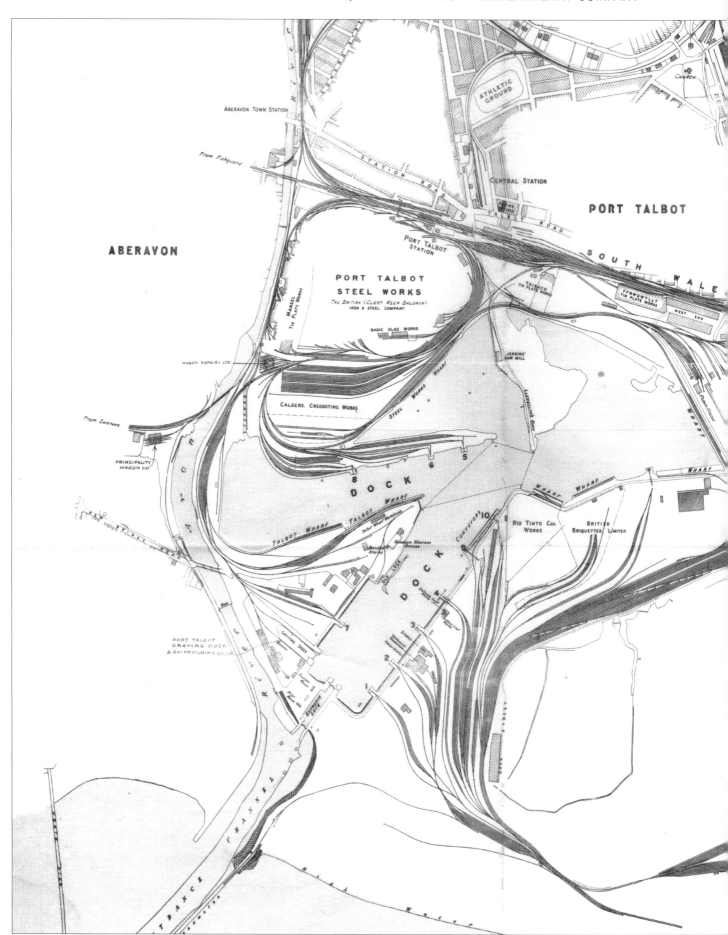

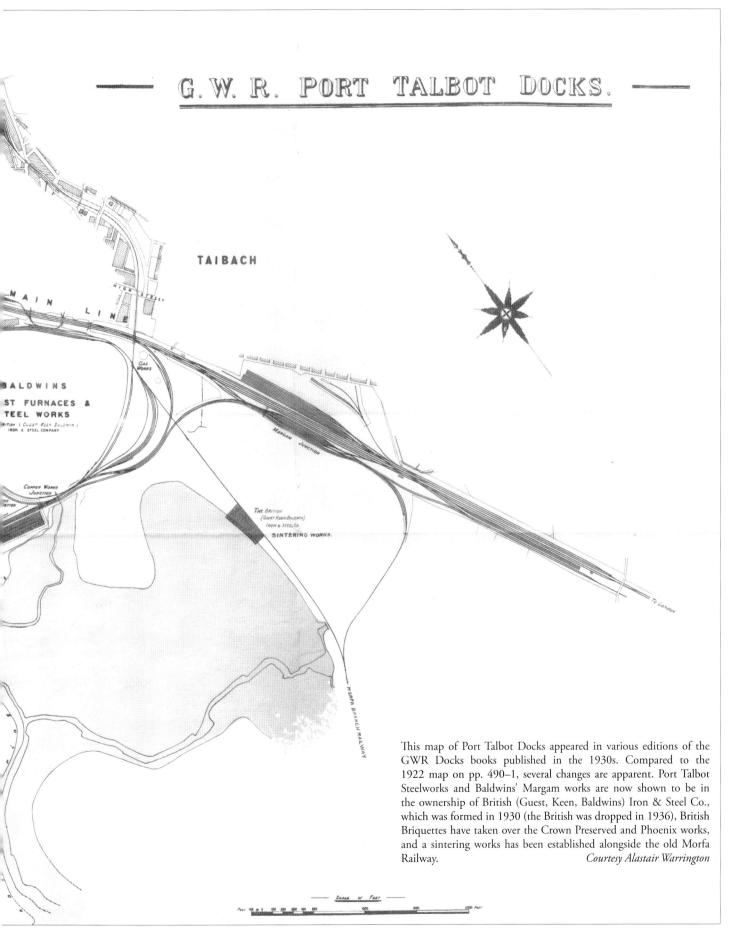

G.W.R. PORT TALBOT DOCKS.

This map of Port Talbot Docks appeared in various editions of the GWR Docks books published in the 1930s. Compared to the 1922 map on pp. 490–1, several changes are apparent. Port Talbot Steelworks and Baldwins' Margam works are now shown to be in the ownership of British (Guest, Keen, Baldwins) Iron & Steel Co., which was formed in 1930 (the British was dropped in 1936), British Briquettes have taken over the Crown Preserved and Phoenix works, and a sintering works has been established alongside the old Morfa Railway. *Courtesy Alastair Warrington*

Introduction to Volume 2

SPELLINGS

The spelling of place names always causes difficulties when writing accounts of Welsh railways. Throughout, this work uses the Anglicised spellings which predominated during the principal period it covers. Likewise, money is expressed in pounds (£), shillings (s) and pence (d), and distances in miles (m), furlongs (f) and chains (ch).

SOURCES

This history is based on primary sources, most of which are held by The National Archives (TNA): Public Record Office (PRO) at Kew. Other primary sources consulted were the Parliamentary Archives (PA), the National Library of Wales, Penrice & Margam Collection (NLW P&M), the National Museums & Galleries of Wales (NM&GW), Glamorgan Record Office (GRO), West Glamorgan Archive Service (WGAS), the Science Museum Library (SML) and Wiltshire & Swindon History Centre (W&SHC). These primary sources are complemented by contemporary newspapers, particularly *The Cambrian*, an online index for which is held by WGAS, and *The London Gazette*, which is fully available online. Background information on industrial developments in and around Port Talbot and the neighbouring valleys has been obtained from accounts written by local historians, as noted in the references.

Information on distances and dates has been obtained from the series of *Track Layout Diagrams of the Great Western Railway and BR Western Region* by R A Cooke. The sections consulted were 49A *Tondu Branches*, 50A *Neath to Port Talbot*, 50B *Margam to Bridgend* and 51 *Port Talbot & Cymmer Branches*.

All significant courses of action taken by the PTR&D and the SWMR were authorised by their boards of directors, and their Minute Books (TNA: PRO RAIL 574/1–5 and RAIL 639/1–3 respectively) provide the basis of this history of the companies during their independent existence. To avoid the lists of references becoming even longer, allusion to these Minutes Books is limited to citations of dates in the text, which is sufficient to identify them. Otherwise, references are collected at the end of each chapter.

ACKNOWLEDGEMENTS

I should like to acknowledge the help of all those who have contributed in various ways and without whose input this history could not have been written. In addition, thanks are due to Colin Chapman, Michael Hale, John Lyons, Harold Morgan, Ian Pope, Arthur Rees, Paul Reynolds, Roy Evans, Jason Jarvis, Damian Owen and members of the Welsh Railways Research Circle. Special thanks are due to Alastair Warrington for the loan of the GWR Property Plans which appear in Chapter 21, and to Nigel Nicholson who designed these two volumes.

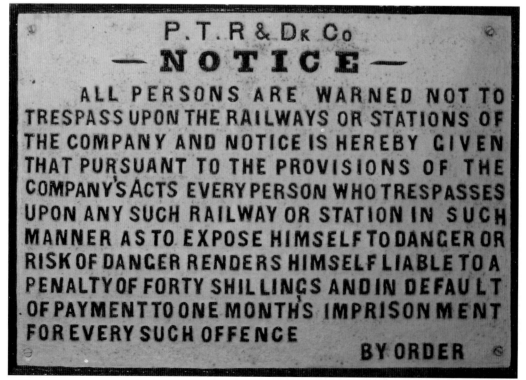

There were two versions of the PTR&D's trespass notice. This longer version, which is preserved at Didcot, bore the companies initials, unusually written P.T.R & Dk Co, whereas the other, shorter, type carried the company's name in full.
Author's collection

11

The Port Talbot Railway and
the South Wales Mineral Railway, 1908 to 1922

1894 RAILWAYS

The first aspect of the PTR's operations addressed by the Officers' Conference[1] was the economic working of coal trains. It proposed to improve this by extending certain station loops to accommodate longer trains and by providing additional locomotive power. The directors approved this course of action provided the costs incurred were not a charge to the PTR&D's capital account. Consequently the officers decided at their May 1909 meeting that the loops at Bryn, East End and Maesteg were to be extended to accommodate 35-wagon trains. This turned out to be a remarkably inexpensive operation, costing £8, £76 and £107 respectively, the low cost at Bryn presumably being for only moving a signal. Both East End and Maesteg loops were extended by July 1909.[2] Related to this, heavy trains were stopped at Duffryn sidings as from May 1909 and a pilot service worked traffic thence to the docks. This change in operating procedure resulted in only four engines being required to work between Duffryn and the collieries on the main line, plus one pilot engine between there and the docks, doing ten double trips as apposed to twelve with the large engines. In order to reduce delays, the GWR agreed to take empty wagons from the docks to Tondu via the OVER or via Pyle and the Porthcawl Branch as was most convenient. Later, in 1914, it was agreed that PTR engines could work to Tondu via the OVER and Cefn Junction for purposes of clearing traffic from Tondu for Port Talbot Docks, provided the enginemen were competent to do so. These engines and men were also cleared to assist GWR trains from Port Talbot to Cefn Junction.

In order to provide additional locomotive power, seventy-seven GWR engines in total were allocated to Duffryn Yard at various

GWR No. 3121 as built in May 1905 and as allocated to Duffryn Yard from 21st November 1907 to 27th March 1909. This engine was renumbered 5121 in May 1929 and withdrawn in October 1948. *Author's collection*

dates between 1907 and 1922,[3] a figure which includes five that were sent there twice, Nos 1024, 1651, 2746, 4504 and 4517. Not surprisingly, thirty-seven (50 per cent) were of various classes of 0-6-0 tank engine in both saddle and pannier tank forms. The longest resident of any was No. 1145, which arrived in January 1910 and was still there at the grouping. The next largest group consisted of seventeen 0-6-0 tender engines, which would have had little utility on the PTR but were presumably used by the GWR for services on its main line. The same remark must apply to 2-2-2 No. 381. The most likely explanation for the presence of 0-4-2 tank engine No. 535 in 1908–9 is as cover while the regular passenger engine No. 36 was at Swindon Works.

Nine of the '4500' Class of 2-6-2 tank engines were allocated to Duffryn Yard between 1908 and 1922, two of them, Nos 4504 and 4517, twice. No. 2177, later 4516, arrived as early as March 1908 and was another long-time resident, not departing until May 1916. The GWR officers noted that these engines were able to haul much greater loads than the PTR's 0-6-0 tank engines. Consequently the '4500' Class and the PTR 0-8-2T types were confined to goods and mineral working, although the former were also used for passenger trains once clearances had been increased at Aberavon R&SB station. Although less powerful than Hertz would have wished for, they were well up to the needs of the PTR. Four of the '3100' Class of 2-6-2 tank engines, including the prototype No. 99, and three of the slightly larger and more powerful '3150' Class were sent to Duffryn Yard, a first group of four between 1907 to 1909, and a second group of three from 1919 onwards. The cylinders of No. 3179 fouled the platforms at Bryn, Maesteg, Garth and Lletty Brongu when tested in June 1909, which resulted in the class being withdrawn until the clearances had been improved so that the GWR maximum loading gauge could be adopted.

Although allocated to Duffryn Yard for three months in 1912, No. 2158 was actually on loan to North's Navigation Collieries and worked North's trains on the PTR between the colliery connections at Maesteg and Cwmdu. No doubt brought about by the wartime situation, four Barry Railway Class 'F' 0-6-0 saddle tank engines loaned to the GWR were shedded at Duffryn Yard from March 1917 to December 1919. The number of GWR engines allocated to Duffryn Yard gradually crept up, from eighteen on 1st January 1915 to twenty-five on 1st January 1922.

MAIN LINE
The only significant new works on the 1894 main were a loop and new station at Cwmdu. Otherwise, piecemeal improvements were made. Maesteg signal cabin was raised in June 1908 to provide a dry locking room – which hitherto had been prone to flooding –

Engine No. 1621 of the '1076' Class was one of the large number of GWR locomotives allocated to Duffryn Yard in the pre-grouping period, being there from 19th April 1915 to 25th February 1923. This engine was built with a saddle tank in May 1880, converted to pannier tanks in 1922, and withdrawn in January 1932.

Author's collection

and to give the signalman a better view.[4] To bring the PTR into line with GWR practice, GWR instructions for working inclines were introduced. Stop boards were provided at Bryn, East End, West End, Blaenavon Junction and Duffryn No. 1 Down home signal for the Dock Branch, and also near Penstar Colliery siding on the SWMJnR.[5] The line between Duffryn Junction and Maesteg was relaid in stages between December 1912 and March 1915, this time with GWR material.[6] During this period the signalling and interlocking were improved, and long-burning lamps and distant signal repeaters were introduced. Tonygroes Junction was relaid in May 1911.[7] The R&SBR rearranged the connections from its engine and carriage sheds to the Down R&SBR and PTR lines respectively at Aberavon, this work being completed by 16th October 1912.[8] At the same time the signalling was improved to better protect trains passing to and from the PTR. Refuge spurs were laid in at the upper ends of the Up loops at Tynyffram, Bryn and West End; these last works were reported as having been completed by 20th November 1911, but not inspected until March 1912.[9] The flooring of Aberavon Viaduct was renewed in 1913,[10] and the timbers of the bridges carrying the Dock Branch over Margam Road and the GWR main line were renewed in 1916.[11] During the First World War the lines between Duffryn and Copper Works junctions, and those between Tonygroes Junction and Central station and Aberavon Junction were relaid as opportunity arose.[12] The level crossing gates at Chapel of Ease and Doctor's Crossing

were replaced by standard GWR types in 1921.[13] The wooden footbridge at the latter place, which dated from 1900, was replaced by GWR lattice type in 1922.[14]

Many of the original buildings were built on timber bases. Bryn station building and Tonygroes signal cabin deteriorated over the years and were lifted and placed on brick foundations.[15] Likewise Maesteg goods office was renewed in 1920.[16] In April 1908 Maesteg UDC applied for a footbridge to be erected across the line south of the station to connect the newly built Salisbury Road with the main part of the town. Miss Talbot agreed to contribute towards its construction and negotiations opened on the basis of each party paying one-third of the cost. The council at first declined to pay any portion, but relented when Major Traherne, the local landowner, agreed to contribute £50 to its share. The lattice footbridge, which was built by the GWR,[17] was completed in June 1910.

The capacity of the line between Duffryn and Maesteg was always of concern. In 1909, and again in 1920, the company made arrangements with the Margam Estate that it should have first call on any land that might be required in the Duffryn Valley for doubling the line. The nearest to this came to being achieved was in February 1920 when the directors noted that an additional passing loop was urgently needed at West End. Approval was given in November 1920 for this third line, capable of holding a 35-wagon train, at an estimated cost of £3,964, but the idea was not pursued, possible because absorption into the GWR was imminent. One putative scheme that would have put more traffic on the line was a 1911 suggestion for a connection between the PTR and the GWR at Maesteg, presumably running from east to north.

During the First World War the company allowed the land alongside the tracks to be used for growing food; they also offered the rails between Lletty Brongu and Pontyrhyll as scrap steel, although this offer was not taken up.

CWMDU AND GARTH 1908–1913
At the Board meeting held on 18th March 1908 the general manager reported that North's Navigation Collieries were about to sink a new pit – which became known as St. John's Colliery[18] – at the site of the old Cwmdu Colliery in Cwm Du; the colliery company had submitted an application to lay a line of rails about a mile in length on the railway company's property from North's existing junction at Maesteg to a proposed junction, at the 9 milepost, to the new colliery sidings. At their next meeting on 15th April the directors resolved that, subject to the GWR's approval, North's be offered running powers over the company's railway from the site of their new pits to the existing sidings and junction at Maesteg, subject to the payment of a toll to be agreed upon. The Consultation Committee confirmed that a private line would not be entertained and authorised Lowther to negotiate a running powers agreement over PTR, charging a nominal rate per ton upon any coal traffic. In

May 1908 the directors agreed to a temporary siding connection at 9m 21ch,[19] a quarter of a mile further on than the later permanent connection, to enable the site to be reached via an old tramroad. This connection was not reported to, or inspected by, the Board of Trade despite it being on a passenger carrying line, and was presumably removed once the permanent connection at 9m 1ch was operational. North's agreed to pay 1d on every ton hauled by them, plus the cost of a loop and 50 per cent of the cost of construction and maintenance of the necessary signal box which was provided by the GWR.

At first it was proposed to install the new loop, 250 yards long overall and signalled for two-way working, near milepost 8,[20] but this was not proceeded with and nothing was done for two years. Excavations for a loop between the 8¾ and 9 mileposts and sidings for North's commenced in September 1910.[21] The proposed layout was submitted to the Board of Trade for its provisional sanction in October 1910, which was granted on 23rd November, the running powers agreement with North's having been sealed on 16th November. North' siding connection at 9m 1ch was installed and the new loop completed in July 1911.[22] The loop was brought into use on 19th November 1911,[23] but the other works were not finished and brought into use until December 1911.[24] The cost was divided £3,648 to North's Navigation Collieries and £560 to the PTR. On 8th December 1911 the PTR was obliged to write to the

Lattice footbridge over the PTR main line south of Maesteg station, looking north. This bridge was erected by the GWR in 1910 at the point where the loop commenced. *GRO*

A view from Heol Fain level crossing, Cwmdu, on 4th February 1950, with the PTR main line to Pontyrhyll curving round to the right and North's sidings ahead. These too curved to the right and terminated in a headshunt out of sight. Originally these sidings were connected only to the main line, the direct connection in the foreground to the goods loop being added in 1912/13.

WRRC collection

Board of Trade pointing out that the works, although in use, had not yet been inspected.

The new loop could hold fifty-three wagons and initially was worked in the usual way, that is, as separate Up and Down lines. North's connection was not off the loop but rather off the main line at 9m 1ch, just the other side of Heol Fain level crossing. In October 1912 the Officers' Conference approved a direct connection from the goods loop to North's sidings so that shunting could be performed clear of the running line. The interchange sidings consisted of a fan of five loops which curved through almost ninety degrees and merged into a short headshunt on an embankment. From this a single line ran back for about one mile at an average gradient of 1 in 30 up to St. John's Colliery.

Garth station building was destroyed by fire on 21st May 1911. This station was not in the best position and a site near North's new sidings at Cwmdu was considered to be more convenient for the replacement. Both North's and Elder's collieries were in favour of this suggestion.[25] Nevertheless, the GWR proceeded to make plans for a new station at Garth. At first the new station was to be provided with two platforms but, when it was realised that passenger trains

A view of Cwmdu from Heol Fain level crossing on 23rd March 1962. The direct connection from the goods loop to the interchange sidings is to the right. The Up over-run siding referred to in the Board of Trade Inspector's report is prominent in the left foreground. The station building appears to be in good condition despite having been closed to passengers for thirty years.

Courtesy C H A Townley

262

ABOVE: GWR No. 2158 photographed alongside Cwmdu signal box, probably in 1912 during the time the engine was on loan to North's Navigation Collieries.
Author's collection

BELOW: Looking from Cwmdu towards Maesteg on 13th July 1959. The left-hand track was regarded as the main line, the other being a bidirectional goods loop. Connections for Bryn Rhyg, which closed in 1933, were laid in at the far end of the loop.
Courtesy H C Casserley

would not cross there, an amended plan with a single platform was eventually produced in February 1912, the estimated cost being £2,200. In the meantime, Maesteg UDC had in December 1911 requested a small station with goods yard at Cwmdu.[26] Cleaver submitted to the Board of Trade a proposed layout consisting of two sidings on the Up side with a trailing connection from the Down loop line via a diamond crossing, a third siding on the Down side behind the new signal box, and a platform on the Down line only. It was proposed to work passenger trains through the platform line only, all others being Up and Down through the loops in the usual way. The Board of Trade would not sanction this scheme, and to get round the objections the PTR proposed that no mineral traffic would run between Maesteg and Cwmdu or between Cwmdu and Garth when a passenger train was running.

Before this could be resolved, in February 1912 Lowther submitted the ultimate plan which omitted the goods yard and sidings altogether and provided for separate Up and Down passenger and goods lines with a 300-foot platform on the Down passenger line, for an estimated cost of £2,010. The scheme was provisionally sanctioned on 12th February 1912. Col Turbervill, the landowner, offered the necessary land free of charge provided the PTR made the roadway to the new station, estimated to cost £150. Work commenced immediately[27] and the station was opened on 9th June 1913,[28] although the works were not inspected until 2nd October 1913. To prevent over-runs, short catch sidings were put in at the Garth end of the passenger line and the Maesteg end of the goods line.

BETTWS AND WEST END

Garth was not the only building destroyed by fire. Bettws station and platform suffered this fate on 6th January 1910. The platform was renewed by 12th February and a new station building, this time clad in corrugated iron,[29] was completed in March 1910.[30] West End signal cabin was destroyed by fire on 8th June 1911, possibly caused by signal lamps bursting while being lit.[31] A temporary cabin was provided to enable trains to pass with minimal delay. A standard GWR design was promptly ordered from Reading Signal Works and was reported to have been completed and in working order by 15th July 1911.[32] As a consequence of this fire, ten signal lamp huts were provided throughout the railway.

DUFFRYN JUNCTION AND SIDINGS

A short siding holding fifteen wagons was added to the existing two on the Up side at Duffryn Junction in October 1912, and one of these was extended in March 1914. The permanent way siding was relaid for traffic purposes in June 1917.[33] A short shunting neck

West End of Tunnel signal box on the PTR was destroyed by fire on 8th June 1911 and was replaced by a standard GWR design, seen here nearing completion.
Author's collection

Two views of the interior of the new (1911) West End of Tunnel signal box. The smartly turned out signalmen are (*left*) Charlie Grange and Dan Davies, and (*right*) Charlie Davies. *Author's collection*

was added to the south end of Duffryn Sidings in January 1914 to avoid engines blocking Doctor's Crossing. The cripple siding there was extended, the work being completed in April 1914.[34] Duffryn No. 3 signal cabin, which controlled the crossing at the south end of the sidings, was renewed and enlarged and the new cabin brought into use in November 1918.[35] A sixth storage siding was approved in March 1920, but not laid until circa 1923.

DUFFRYN YARD

It seems that at first the GWR intended to continue to carry out heavy repairs to engines at Duffryn Yard. Two boiler trolleys were provided in May 1908, but in December 1911 the directors note that they had been sold back to the GWR as the bulk of the repairs were by then carried out at Swindon. Similarly, a wheel turning lathe was sold to the GWR in June 1919 for £500, even though a new engine hoist had been installed in 1914. Due to the increasing numbers of engines being stabled at Duffryn Yard it became necessary to provide additional inspection pits, one in 1910 and three more in 1913, and to extend two others. The shed layout changed little during this period, the principal alteration being the provision of a connection from the coaling road to the turntable road, also in 1913. All the pointwork was relaid in 1915.[36] An undisclosed rearrangement was under consideration in 1919, but

was deferred by the Officers' Conference in October 1920 and further improvements were not made until 1931.

One proposal that would have affected the future of Duffryn Yard came in February 1911 when it was reported to the directors that the GWR and R&SBR were contemplating a central running shed at Aberavon Seaside station. It was suggested that the PTR should join this scheme, and the directors resolved to offer facilities to this end provided no increase in capital was necessary. This proposal was considered by the GWR Officers' Conference in July 1911, but a year later it concluded that there was insufficient reason for making provision for PTR engines at the proposed shed.

PROPOSED PORT TALBOT JOINT STATION

Further changes were in prospect in June 1912 when the general manager reported to his directors on negotiations between the GWR, R&SBR and PTR regarding a central station at Port Talbot. The proposals became public in November 1913 when the GWR published the Parliamentary Notice for its 1914 Bill,[37] for which the engineer was William Grierson.[38] This omnibus Bill *inter alia* sought powers to make railways, deviations, widenings and alterations at Port Talbot and Aberavon, including Railway No. 7 at Margam. Most significant was Deviation and Widening No. 2, a double line carrying the R&SBR main line over the GWR main line, which

ABOVE: PTR 0-8-2T No. 20 forms the backdrop to this photograph of the Duffryn Yard, Port Talbot, enginemen and firemen improvement class, circa 1911. By this time the engine had lost the PTR's armorial device from the cabside. Albert Hertz, the locomotive superintendent from 1908 to 1922, is seated behind the board directly beneath the signal.
Courtesy Arthur Rees

BELOW: No doubt inspired by the Safety Movement instigated in 1913 by Felix Pole, assistant to the general manager of the GWR, ambulance classes were held at regular intervals across the GWR. This view shows the GWR/PTR Duffryn Yard ambulance class of 1914 at Port Talbot Central station. Albert Hertz is seated sixth from the left.
Author's collection

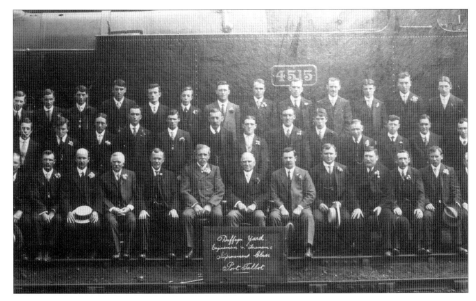

A later Duffryn Yard enginemen and firemen improvement class. No. 4515 was a 2-6-2 tank engine built in 1907 and originally numbered 2176. The first thirty engines of what became the '4500' Class, Nos 2161–2190, were renumbered in December 1912, giving an earliest date for this photograph. No. 2176/4515 was allocated to Duffryn Yard from 1st March 1911 to 15th April 1916. Although not apparent in this view, this engine was unique in having a sloping bunker, a feature which lasted until 1927. The position of the number plate is also unusual, and it was later moved to the usual place on the bunker. This time Albert Hertz is seated six from the left, behind the board. *Courtesy Arthur Rees*

commenced near Aberavon Seaside station and terminated at Corlanau, a distance of 1m 9ch. Railway No. 8 was a quarter mile long double line connection from this deviation railway to join the GWR main line just north of Port Talbot station. Also included were the necessary short deviations to the PTR's Aberavon Branch, Talbot Wharf Branch, North Bank Branch, the Oakwood & South Side Railway (O&SSR), and to the R&SBR's Port Talbot Dock Branch. After much amendment the Bill gained the Royal Assent on 31st July 1914.[39] The joint PTR/R&SBR station was envisaged to be sited on the newly elevated R&SBR line, replacing the old Aberavon station.

The First World War prevented this scheme being put into effect. The war period saw greatly increased industrial production, particularly of steel, with corresponding increased demands made of the railways. Following the termination of hostilities the chairman and officers of the GWR discussed informally with the Minister of Transport and his officials the new works considered necessary, which resulted in a Memorandum on New Works in South Wales.[40] The total estimated cost was £10,653,000, of which £5,300,000 was accounted for by a new combined rail and road bridge over the River Severn near Chepstow. Of the other nineteen schemes listed, two directly concerned the PTR and the R&SBR and two

Duffryn Yard shed staff 1920, grouped round a GWR '4500' Class 2-6-2 tank engine. The following are said to be present: driver Peter Jewell (standing front left); fireman J Collard; steam raiser W Lee (sitting); engine cleaners W Watkins and J Johnson (sitting), E John, S Short and T Coombes (standing); shed turner H Bath; store keeper E Curtis. *Author's collection*

the GWR at Margam, and these were given high priority. The Memorandum outlined three schemes at Margam to cope with the existing congestion, which was expected to increase once the developments at Port Talbot were completed. These were:

- a junction between the GWR and the PTR and the doubling of the OVER from Margam Moors to Margam East, estimated £21,000,
- an Up loop on the GWR from Margam East Junction to Margam Moors, estimated £17,000,
- additional sidings and a mileage yard at Margam Junction, estimated £92,000.

The fourth scheme revived the deviation and other works at Port Talbot authorised by the GWR's 1914 Act. In addition, it proposed to move Port Talbot station westward so that it could be connected by a stairway to the new high-level R&SBR station into which PTR trains would run, all three served by combined station offices. The final part of this scheme was the doubling of the R&SBR between Cwmavon and Velindre, powers for which had been obtained in that company's 1914 Act,[41] and the probable closure of Port Talbot Central station. The estimated cost of these works was £586,000. This memorandum was considered by the GW directors in March 1920, when they agreed that it should be submitted to the Minister as a formal statement of the company's proposals. The post-war years were not the time for such grandiose schemes, although the GWR main line between Port Talbot and Margam was quadrupled and Margam mileage sidings and goods yard were opened in 1921.

OGMORE VALLEYS EXTENSION RAILWAY

The May 1903 agreement with the GWR provided *inter alia* that the latter company would route all its traffic from the Llynvi and Garw valleys and other points east of Tondu, destined for Port Talbot and westward, via the OVER.[42] At its second meeting, on 5th May 1908, the Joint Consultation Committee of Directors[43] decided that in order to economise on the use of engines some trains previously running over the PTR between Garth, Maesteg and Margam via Duffryn Junction were also to be routed over the GWR via Tondu, Cefn Junction and the OVER. To accommodate these trains, running loop sidings at Waterhall Junction and refuge sidings and a running loop at Margam were authorised, at estimated costs of £2,250 and £1,000 respectively.

WATERHALL

The running line and existing loop at Waterhall had been slewed in March 1908 so as to give more room between them for guards and shunters.[44] Work on the three new loops, which were situated to the north of the existing lines and were each about 200 yards long, started in June 1908,[45] the permanent way being completed in February 1909.[46] The original estimate did not provide for the necessary signalling and an additional expenditure of £887 required approval. A standard GWR signal cabin to replace the original was

Permanent way gang at Margam East circa 1911 with the PTR Dock Branch bridge in the background. *Author's collection*

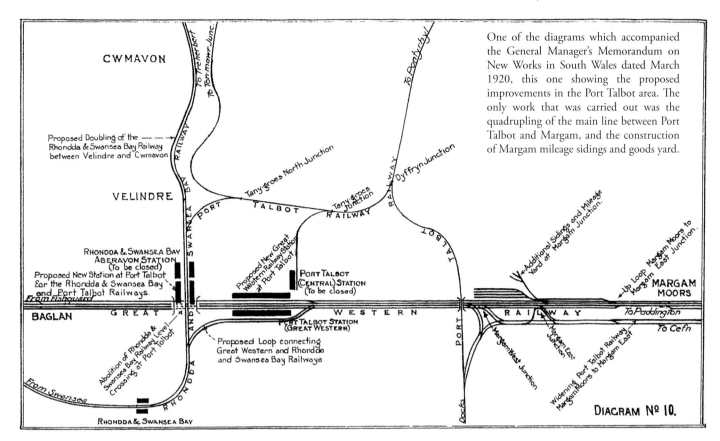

One of the diagrams which accompanied the General Manager's Memorandum on New Works in South Wales dated March 1920, this one showing the proposed improvements in the Port Talbot area. The only work that was carried out was the quadrupling of the main line between Port Talbot and Margam, and the construction of Margam mileage sidings and goods yard.

ordered from Reading Signal Works in January 1909[47] and erected about halfway along the loops. The new works were brought into use in the week beginning 19th April 1909.[48] In order to allow longer trains to stand there, one of the crossovers at Waterhall was moved 345 feet in May 1910 by the unusual practice of sliding it over the track pulled by a locomotive.[49]

MARGAM

The work at Margam for the GWR consisted of three refuge sidings trailing off the Down main line. A running loop was put in on the OVER alongside these sidings and was brought into use on 14th May 1909.[50] As with Waterhall, the required signalling, which was worked from the nearby Margam East box, was not included in the estimate and the expenditure of an additional £210 was authorised.

FURTHER IMPROVEMENTS

Some relief was obtained in February 1909 by the introduction of an electric occupation key for Cribbwr Fawr Colliery siding, thereby preventing the five and a half mile section between Margam and Waterhall being blocked by shunting there. Nevertheless, considerable delays in working traffic between Port Talbot and Tondu were reported in June 1910. In addition to coal for shipment arriving via the OVER, Margam Junction was the only convenient point of access to Port Talbot Docks for traffic originating either east or west on the South Wales main line. The directors of the PTR, in February 1907 and again in February 1909, had called upon the GWR to increase its siding accommodation at Margam for its own traffic. At its meeting in August 1910 the GWR Officers' Conference decided to recommend the provision of additional sidings at Port Talbot Docks,[51] alterations at Margam Junction, and

an extension of the accommodation at Waterhall Junction and at the nearby Aberbaiden Colliery.

MARGAM JUNCTION AND COPPER WORKS JUNCTIONS

The directors approved the extensive alterations at Margam Junction, which affected both the PTR and the GWR, in May 1911. The GWR installed a Down goods loop alongside the three sidings put in in 1909, the entrance controlled by a new Margam East signal box. The old East box was closed and replaced by a new Margam Middle signal box a short distance eastwards. These works were brought into use in June 1912. The PTR directors noted in September 1912 that the GWR was to lay down two sidings on the company's land at Margam. The first of these was an extension of the new Down goods loop from Margam Middle to Margam West which came into use in May 1913. The second was a parallel loop from Margam Middle to the west end of the exchange sidings with the PTR, with the necessary alterations at both ends. The work on the PTR consisted of incorporating the 1909 running loop on the OVER into an extension of the double line from Copper Works Junction to Margam Middle, giving a total length of just over one mile. This work was done by the GWR, but as it was deemed to be solely for the convenient and economical working of the Port Talbot Docks traffic, the cost of £1,758 was debited to the PTR. Finally, the connection from the OVER to the GWR laid in in 1903[52] was replaced by a full double junction. The works on the PTR were brought into use in June 1912.

WEST CURVE

Although these improvements at Margam benefitted traffic arriving from the east via the OVER or the GWR, trains to and from the

A view looking north on 22nd June 1921 from Margam Middle (later East, then Middle again) signal box. On the far left is the double line OVER snaking round Margam exchange sidings before heading off to Waterhall Junction. To the right of the exchange sidings are the GWR Down goods loop, Down main, Up main and Up goods loop. A second Up goods loop and the nine-road Margam Up Yard had been brought into use in April 1921. Further to the right is the unfinished four-road Margam goods and coal depot which came into use in August 1921. The PTR bridge over the main line is visible in the far distance.

NM&GW

ABOVE: The works associated with the new West Curve at Margam were completed in 1917 and the track layout was essentially unchanged when this view looking east was taken on 30th April 1946, just before the wholesale alterations necessary for the new Abbey Steelworks. Prominent is the second Copper Works Junction signal box, erected in 1914, which contained sixty-four levers. Running behind the signal box is a siding connection for Margam Steelworks. From left to right, the double tracks are the PTR line to Duffryn Junction, the West Curve and the OVER heading for Margam Sidings. In the centre distance are the reception sidings for the steelwork's gasworks/coke ovens, the gasholder for which is visible on the left.

Author's collection

BELOW: The view in the opposite direction to the one above, also taken on 30th April 1946, looking towards the end of the Dock Branch, some 64ch distant. This quadruple track section was arranged as Down Slow, Down Fast, Up Fast and Up Slow lines, with what looks like a train of iron ore hopper wagons on the Down Slow line. On the left are the sidings of No. 6 grid (No. 7 in the GWR's renumbering), with the double track O&SSR on the right heading across Margam Wharf towards the Old Dock. The dilapidated building is the electric power station erected in 1914 which had fallen into disuse following the arrangements made by the GWR to obtain electricity from Margam Steelworks. The only vehicular access to the south side of the docks was via the Military Road which crossed the main lines in the centre of this view. Originally this road approached the crossing from Taibach behind the photographer, but during the construction of Margam Steelworks was diverted to run alongside the O&SSR on Margam Wharf.

Author's collection

west had to be reversed there, causing congestion, delays and extra expense. In December 1912 the directors approved a proposal to build a double line connection between the GWR main line and the PTR docks line to permit direct running of trains from places west of Margam to the docks. The estimated cost was £13,699, shared equally between the two companies. Groundwork was in hand by May 1913,[53] although the layout was amended in December 1913 to allow for the Margam Steelworks then being planned.[54] The double line OVER from Copper Works Junction to Margam was slewed southwards by about 50 yards to enable the new curve to be built to a reasonable radius. These two lines made a double junction and continued to a second such junction with the line to Duffryn Junction – which itself was doubled for about 350 yards in that direction – and continued to join the original double line into the dock area. The final piece of the jigsaw was a short length of double track connecting the slewed OVER to the second pair of lines into the dock area which had been completed in July 1913.[55] This work commenced in September 1914[56] and completed the quadrupling of the line from Copper Works Junction to the dock head. The west curve and deviation of the OVER were authorised retrospectively as Railway No. 7 of the GWR's 1914 Act.

The PTR's portion of the new junctions and other works in the vicinity of Copper Works Junction was completed in February 1915.[57] It appears that by June 1915 the new curve was sufficiently far advanced to be used in an unfinished condition, as the GWR Officers' Conference noted that it was proving beneficial with a greater freedom in the movement of trains and a consequent saving of time, and was money well spent. A new standard GWR signal box replacing an old cabin was erected on a more appropriate site at Copper Works to work the plethora of new junctions there. The new works at Copper Works Junction were brought into use on 23rd August 1915, although completion of the junction of the new curve with the GWR main line was then in abeyance pending other alterations at that point.[58] The PTR directors noted in January 1916 that the curve was to be completed forthwith despite the cessation of capital works due to the war, although the whole was not completed until September 1917. The new junction, which was situated under the bridge carrying the PTR's 1894 railway to the docks over the GWR, was worked by Margam West signal box which had been re-sited nearby on the Up side. The Board of Trade provisionally approved all these works affecting the GWR main line in June 1911, subject to them being inspected when complete.[59] Formal

Derailment on the incline leading from the SWMJnR down to Ynysdavid sidings off to the left of the view. The breakdown crane, presumably from Neath, is standing on the main line. The R&SBR boundary fences are in the immediate foreground and the small group of people (who look as if they might be the bride and her family going to a wedding, see detail, left) is crossing the junction of the private sidings leading to Cwmmawr and Oakwood Collieries. Wagons visible include on the extreme left Llew. Howells, Argoed Colliery, Pontrhydyfen and on the right a Bute wagon, two Llwynon wagons from the Neath valley and part of a Hedleys wagon. This photograph is undated but might be of the incident which occurred on 31st July 1920 and was reported to the directors on 15th September. *Courtesy Peter Sims*

Derailment at the bottom of Ynysmaerdy Incline, Briton Ferry. The date is unknown but may be the incident reported in the local press on 20th August 1904 when a coupling broke, although on that occasion only four wagons were said to be involved and all were "broken into splinters". The nearest vehicle could be one the Glyncorrwg Colliery Co.'s three covered goods wagons. *Courtesy Peter Sims*

inspection seems not to have taken place, possibly being overlooked because of the war. Completion of the West Curve meant that the Morfa Railway hereabouts crossed two pairs of double tracks on the level. Increased use of the Morfa Railway by Baldwins for access to the slag tips required the crossings to be properly signalled in 1921.

Waterhall and Aberbaiden

The work at Aberbaiden Colliery consisted of an extension of the shunting loop by about 350 yards, estimated to cost £1,407, and was put in hand at once. Two additional sidings, a loop and a shunting spur on the south side of the running lines at Waterhall and extending over the old coke works site – estimated at £4,396 – were not commenced until May 1911.[60] Both sets of works were in use by January 1912.[61] As an estimated £1,500 worth of these benefitted Mill Pit, Aberbaiden and Ton Phillip collieries, in March 1911 their owners agreed with the PTR directors to pay 4% per annum (£20 each) on this sum from the time the work was completed. An electric train staff instrument was placed at Aberbaiden Colliery siding connection in 1920 so that the main line could be used while the three collieries' sidings were being shunted. The additional tracks at Waterhall made the pre-existing pedestrian crossing over them near Bryndu goods siding impracticable to use. A replacement footbridge was agreed in May 1912 and in use in September 1913,[62] the cost of £500 being shared equally between Miss Talbot, Penybont UDC and the PTR. The final improvement at Waterhall Junction came in 1921 when the scissors crossover put in in 1897 to connect the new OVER and the C&PR[63] was replaced by single crossing facing Margam Junction.[64]

Newlands Loop

In June 1920 the GWR recommended that a crossing loop was necessary between Margam and Waterhall Junction to facilitate the working of the OVER, the costs of which were estimated at £4,886. The Cribbwr Fawr Collieries Ltd was required to pay for this loop and was offered a rebate of 7½ per cent on its monthly carriage account. This was unacceptable, and the rebate was settled at 10 per cent in July 1920.[65] The permanent way for the Newlands Loop, which extended from 3m 36ch to 3m 62ch on the OVER, was completed in August 1921.[66] The whole of the work, including a new signal cabin at the centre of the loop between the lines, was brought into use on 4th December 1921[67] but, remarkably, not inspected until February 1928.[68]

Pyle Branch

The Pyle Branch saw very little traffic after Marshall Stonehouse abandoned their slag operation at Cefn in 1914. The sidings at Pyle, which were used mainly by the GWR, had become unsafe and were gradually renewed, this task being completed in June 1915.[69]

South Wales Mineral Junction Railway

As elsewhere, relaying the railways proceeded piecemeal. The top end of the Blaenavon Branch was renewed in 1907[70] and the bridge over the River Gwenffrwd there strengthened so that engines could work up to the dead end.[71] The "bad portion" of the Whitworth Branch was relaid in 1916,[72] but rest of the branch was not completed until September 1920.[73] The lower part of the SWMJnR was relaid in 1920.[74] A staff apparatus had been placed

Another view of the derailment at the bottom of Ynysmaerdy Incline.
Author's collection

at Blaenavon Junction on the SWMJnR to facilitate the working of traffic off the Blaenavon Branch. This short-lived block post, which was housed in the former Cefn Ironworks cabin,[75] was brought into use in September 1907,[76] but closed by the GWR in November 1909 because of a lack of traffic. The staff post at Ynysdavid, which was provided with signals in 1909,[77] was converted to a ground frame in 1916,[78] reinstated as cabin in 1920,[79] and reverted to a ground frame in 1926. In August 1908 Margam UDC applied for a footbridge to be constructed over the SWMJnR at Tyr Ynys near Cwmavon which would afford pedestrians bound for Taibach a more direct route. Once the existence of a right of way had been established this was agreed to, provided the council paid one half of the estimated cost of £250. As at Maesteg the council at first declined to make any contribution towards this cost, but eventually agreed to do so in April 1911. The bridge was commenced forthwith[80] and completed in October 1911.[81] By 1912 Pontrhydyfen Viaduct was showing fractures and other signs of weakness due to poor drainage.[82] Repairs started in March 1912[83] to strengthen the rail supports and modify the drainage arrangements. During the First World War the rails between Incline Top and Tonmawr were offered to the Government as scrap metal, but the offer was not taken up.

SOUTH WALES MINERAL RAILWAY

GLYNCORRWG

When the PTR took over the working of the SWMR, the facilities at Glyncorrwg – which was described on the 1899 edition of the 1:2500 Ordnance Survey as a goods station – consisted of the main line plus two loop sidings, off one of which ran a short siding which crossed the River Corrwg Fechan to reach the engine shed. Castle Street crossed two of the lines on the level near the northern end of the loops and in earlier times also crossed a short line leading up to exchange sidings for Welsh Main Colliery, the connection for which had been made in June 1875.[84] Glyncorrwg UDC's application for a footbridge at this level crossing in November 1912 was not entertained as the council would not contribute towards the cost. The council likewise declined to share the cost of a pair of gates estimated to cost £50. Glyncorrwg UDC returned to the subject in December 1912 and this time involved the Board of Trade,[85] claiming that the greatly increased population of the village justified a footbridge rather than crossing gates. Lowther refuted the council's arguments, pointing out that for some time past only one engine

was shunting at Glyncorrwg each day, usually between 12 noon and 2 pm, passing over the crossing five or six times. He confirmed that when Ynyscorrwg Colliery was fully working, the new connection for which also passed over the level crossing, there would be complete protection for the public. After much correspondence, Lowther informed the Board of Trade in May 1913 that it had been decided to erect gates and provide a proper person to work them. The council was still not satisfied, but had to be content with gates and the GWR officers confirmed in May 1914 that these would be provided as part of the plan to adapt the line for passenger service. The First World War then intervened and nothing was done until March 1921 when it was reconfirmed that gates would be provided. These were awaiting delivery in December 1921[86] and erected in 1922, together with a crossover facing the Tonmawr direction to provide a short run round loop at the platform. Both were inspected in October 1926.[87] An additional siding was laid in in 1913 and later converted to a loop. The three loops were extended by about 150 yards in 1922. Glyncorrwg had a small goods shed served by a siding off one of the loops. To deal with increasing local traffic a short mileage siding was provided in 1912 adjacent to the later platform.

CYMMER

The connection at the 9½ milepost on the SWMR with the Llynvi & Ogmore Railway (L&OR) was opened in July 1878[88] and worked by a ground frame. Some time later a passing loop holding thirty-five wagons was put on the SWMR and connected to the L&OR line by a short loop holding twelve wagons.[89] Storage sidings holding nineteen and thirty-two wagons were provided on the Up and Down sides respectively of the junction. No traffic facilities were provided until a 114-foot platform was erected in 1918 in conjunction with the Cymmer–Glyncorrwg passenger service. In October 1913 the GWR officers proposed that additional siding accommodation should be provided at Cymmer to cope with the increasing traffic. The estimated cost of £3,620, to be divided equally between the SWMR and the GWR, suggests that extensive works were envisaged. This idea was revived after the First World War – by which time Nantewlaeth Colliery on the SWMR, one mile towards Glyncorrwg, was in production – and the scheme was reconsidered in conjunction with a plan to work full loads through to Barry docks; this turned out to be not practicable, and a modified scheme for increased exchange siding accommodation was

The Court Sart area of Briton Ferry in post-grouping days, with a GWR train from the Neath direction passing over the flying junction opened in 1914 in conjunction with Swansea District Line scheme. Above the train are the sidings at the western end of the SWMR which connected to the ex-R&SBR at Neath Junction near Neath engine shed. *Author's collection*

proposed at an estimated cost of £2,675. In the event nothing was done at Cymmer and the layout remained unchanged until eventual closure. Instead, the loop sidings at Glyncorrwg were extended and Glenavon Garw Collieries Ltd, the owners of Nantewlaeth Colliery, put in additional sidings there in 1925.

INCLINE

The deviation railway authorised by the 1907 Act to eliminate Ynysmaerdy Incline was never constructed. In September 1909 Lowther reported that arrangements had been made by which a local GWR engine would work at the foot of the incline for two hours per day, thereby dispensing with one SWMR engine, a saving of £943 16s 0d per annum. By May 1910 very little traffic was using the incline and the GWR Officers' Conference decided to cease working it entirely as from 1st June 1910, traffic thereafter being worked via the SWMJnR. This decision provoked Briton Ferry UDC to complain to the Board of Trade in July 1910 that no steps had been taken under the Abandonment of Railways Act 1850.[90] The Board replied that it had no statutory powers to intervene in the matter, which could only be determined by the Court of the Railway & Canal Commissioners. Any hope of reinstating the incline disappeared in August 1912 when the iron bridge carrying the line over Neath Road at Briton Ferry was removed owing to its bad state of repair. The directors decided in November 1916 that one mile of rails on the disused incline should be taken up for use elsewhere.[91] The material, including the brake drums and old bridge, was taken by rail to Duffryn Yard[92] and sold to the GWR for £1,939 2s 2d. Thus a short loop near the old engine shed at the top of the incline became the western terminus of the SWMR. The

disused water tank at the incline top was moved to Tonmawr to provide additional water storage there.

BRITON FERRY

Following the closure of Ynysmaerdy Incline the SWMR Co. had very little use for its lines at Briton Ferry although it retained ownership of them until the grouping. The branch to Briton Ferry dock was realigned and relaid to provide room for additional sidings and later running loops for the GWR main line to the west of Briton Ferry station.[93] The line and sidings between the bottom of the incline and the junction with the R&SBR at Neath Junction were realigned in conjunction with the GWR's new flying junction at Court Sart in December 1914.

In February 1912 the directors of the PTR learned that the Glyncorrwg Colliery Co. had, without reference to them or the SWMR, sublet the building at Briton Ferry it was using as wagon shops to the North Central Wagon Co. of Rotherham. The site had started life in 1872 as a patent fuel works which the SWMR Co. had erected, equipped and then contracted with a John Deere to make the fuel. This business seems not to have been a success and circa 1890 the works were leased to the Briton Ferry Mineral Water Co.; then, in 1907, they passed to the Glyncorrwg Colliery Co. which used them for its wagon repairs. This work was continued by the North Central Wagon Co., whose lease was dated 30th September 1911 and terminated, with its successor Wagon Repairs Ltd, in 1935. The company's engine shed at Briton Ferry dating from 1877 was closed in June 1910 along with the incline and was leased in September 1918 to the Glyncorrwg Colliery Co. for wagon repairs, presumably as a replacement for its earlier works.

NOTES

1. See Volume 1, Chapter 8.
2. TNA: PRO RAIL 1057/1528/135.
3. TNA: PRO RAIL 254/65–80; see also Appendix 11.1.
4. TNA: PRO RAIL 1057/1528/124.
5. TNA: PRO RAIL 1057/1528/135.
6. TNA: PRO RAIL 1057/1528/148, 151, 182.
7. TNA: PRO RAIL 1057/1528/153.
8. TNA: PRO MT 6/2164/2.
9. TNA: PRO MT 6/2083/3.
10. TNA: PRO RAIL 1057/1528/181.
11. TNA: PRO RAIL 1057/1528/206.
12. TNA: PRO TAIL 1057/1528/207, 223, 235.
13. TNA: PRO RAIL 1057/1528/252, 253.
14. TNA: PRO RAIL 1057/1528/254, 1057/2554.
15. TNA: PRO RAIL 1057/1528/124, 227.
16. TNA: PRO RAIL 1057/1528/247.
17. A Vaughan, *A Pictorial Record of Great Western Architecture* (Oxford Publishing Co. 1977), p. 225.
18. Lewis, *Coal Industry*, pp. 119–26.
19. TNA: PRO RAIL 574/40.
20. TNA: PRO MT 6/2226/1.
21. TNA: PRO RAIL 1057/1528/146.
22. TNA: PRO RAIL 1057/1528/155.
23. TNA: PRO RAIL 1057/1528/159.
24. TNA: PRO RAIL 1057/1528/160.
25. TNA: PRO RAIL 1057/1528/154.
26. TNA: PRO MT 6/2226/1.
27. TNA: PRO RAIL 1057/1528/165.
28. TNA: PRO RAIL 1057/1528/176.
29. TNA: PRO RAIL 1057/1528/139.
30. TNA: PRO RAIL 1057/1528/140.
31. TNA: PRO RAIL 1057/1528/154.
32. TNA: PRO RAIL 1057/1528/155.
33. TNA: PRO RAIL 1057/1528/216.
34. TNA: PRO RAIL 1057/1528/182.
35. TNA: PRO RAIL 1057/1528/231.
36. TNA: PRO RAIL 1057/1528/200.
37. *The London Gazette*, 21 November 1913.
38. PA HL/PO/PB/3/plan1914/G4.
39. 4 & 5 Geo. 5 c.cvii.
40. TNA: PRO RAIL 267/323.
41. 4 & 5 Geo. 5 c.xxv.
42. See Volume 1, Chapter 6.
43. See Volume 1, Chapter 8.
44. TNA: PRO RAIL 1057/1528/121.
45. TNA: PRO RAIL 1057/1528/124.
46. TNA: PRO RAIL 1057/1528/131.
47. TNA: PRO RAIL 1057/1528/130.
48. TNA: PRO RAIL 1057/1528/133.
49. TNA: PRO RAIL 1057/1528/143.
50. TNA: PRO RAIL 1057/1528/134.
51. See Chapter 13.
52. See Volume 1, Chapter 6.
53. TNA: PRO RAIL 1057/1528/175.
54. See Chapter 14.
55. See Chapter 13.
56. TNA: PRO RAIL 1057/1528/186.
57. TNA: PRO RAIL 1057/1528/191.

58. TNA: PRO RAIL 1057/1528/197.
59. TNA: PRO MT 6/1993/2.
60. TNA: PRO RAIL 1057/1528/153.
61. TNA: PRO RAIL 1057/1528/161.
62. TNA: PRO RAIL 1057/1528/178.
63. See Volume 1, Chapter 5.
64. TNA: PRO RAIL 1057/1528/249.
65. TNA: PRO RAIL 574/60.
66. TNA: PRO RAIL 1057/1528/253.
67. TNA: PRO RAIL 1057/1528/255.
68. TNA: PRO MT 29/84 p. 38.
69. TNA: PRO RAIL 1057/1528/195.
70. TNA: PRO RAIL 1057/1528/117.
71. TNA: PRO RAIL 1057/1528/121.
72. TNA: PRO RAIL 1057/1528/208, 209.
73. TNA: PRO RAIL 1057/1528/245.
74. TNA: PRO RAIL 1057/1528/241.
75. See Volume 1, Chapter 5.
76. TNA: PRO RAIL 1057/1528/115.
77. TNA: PRO RAIL 1057/1528/134.
78. TNA: PRO RAIL 1057/1528/203.
79. TNA: PRO RAIL 1057/1528/244.
80. TNA: PRO RAIL 1057/1528/153.
81. TNA: PRO RAIL 1057/1528/158.
82. Cleaver, 'Alterations and Improvements', p. 118.
83. TNA: PRO RAIL 1057/1528/163.
84. TNA: PRO RAIL 639/8.
85. TNA: PRO MT 6/2481/10.
86. TNA: PRO RAIL 1057/1528/255.
87. TNA: PRO MT 29/83 p. 246.
88. See Volume 1, Chapter 1.
89. TNA: PRO RAIL 253/409.
90. TNA: PRO MT 6/1906/6
91. TNA: PRO RAIL 639/3.
92. TNA: PRO RAIL 1057/1528/212, 213, 216.
93. TNA: PRO RAIL 1057/1528/145, 146.

APPENDIX 11.1: GWR ENGINES ALLOCATED TO DUFFRYN YARD 1907–1922

GWR No.	Class	Type	To Duffryn	From Duffryn	Notes
3121	3100	2-6-2T	22/11/07	27/3/09	
2177	4500	2-6-2T	6/3/08	13/5/16	later 4516
1722	1854	0-6-0T	7/3/08	6/11/09	
1728	1854	0-6-0T	14/3/08	18/6/10	
1096	Standard Goods	0-6-0	28/3/08	15/8/08	
1206	Standard Goods	0-6-0	28/3/08	15/8/08	
2800	2721	0-6-0T	28/3/08	27/2/09	later 2700
3151	3150	2-6-2T	28/3/08	27/2/09	
3179	3150	2-6-2T	28/3/08	9/7/09	
2178	4500	2-6-2T	3/4/08	26/10/09	later 4517
99	3100	2-6-2T	10/4/08	23/3/09	later 3100
1733	1854	0-6-0T	16/4/08	8/10/09	
2021	2021	0-6-0T	15/5/08	10/9/10	
329	322	0-6-0	15/7/08	13/8/10	
535	517	0-4-2T	4/8/08	17/7/09	
339	322	0-6-0	12/8/08	25/2/11	
1651	1076	0-6-0T	25/1/09	4/11/11	
2165	4500	2-6-2T	10/3/09	9/7/09	ex-R&SBR 31, later 4504
2166	4500	2-6-2T	11/3/09	9/7/09	ex-R&SBR 32, later 4505
777	Standard Goods	0-6-0	4/6/09	14/8/09	
1145	1076	0-6-0T	14/1/10		
2074	2021	0-6-0T	14/1/10	22/3/13	
2045	2021	0-6-0T	20/8/10		
116	Standard Goods	0-6-0	6/1/11	1/1/12	
1019	1016	0-6-0T	13/1/11	14/6/13	
1616	1076	0-6-0T	13/1/11		
2038	2021	0-6-0T	27/1/11	2/11/12	
2176	4500	2-6-2T	1/3/11	15/4/16	later 4515
1569	1076	0-6-0T	22/4/11	8/6/18	
1182	1076	0-6-0T	29/5/11	12/4/19	
2746	2721	0-6-0T	5/7/11	1/11/13	
499	Standard Goods	0-6-0	12/8/11	1/11/13	
2158	2021	0-6-0T	20/4/12	13/7/12	on loan to North's

GWR No.	Class	Type	To Duffryn	From Duffryn	Notes
1651	1076	0-6-0T	24/4/12	17/4/15	
46	Standard Goods	0-6-0	2/10/12	12/6/15	
666	Standard Goods	0-6-0	29/10/12	30/9/15	
4517	4500	2-6-2T	14/12/12	26/6/15	
381	378	2-2-2	4/2/13	30/9/15	
2014	850	0-6-0T	21/4/13	14/2/15	
1638	1076	0-6-0T	14/6/13	7/7/17	
1696	1661	0-6-0T	9/7/13	14/4/17	
1024	1016	0-6-0T	11/10/13	19/1/18	
596	Standard Goods	0-6-0	16/10/13	26/10/15	
2746	2721	0-6-0T	13/4/14		
1621	1076	0-6-0T	19/4/15		
4504	4500	2-6-2T	21/4/15	27/10/17	
2369	2361	0-6-0	30/9/15	8/6/18	
2372	2361	0-6-0	2/10/15	27/2/21	
2375	2361	0-6-0	25/10/15	26/10/18	
964	1076	0-6-0T	12/4/16		
4544	4500	2-6-2T	12/4/16	-/-/20	
4554	4500	2-6-2T	12/4/16	-/-/20	
2309	Dean Goods	0-6-0	22/11/16	20/1/17	
Barry 129	F	0-6-0ST	5/3/17	15/12/19	
Barry 137	F	0-6-0ST	5/3/17	25/11/19	
Barry 72	F	0-6-0ST	6/3/17	30/8/19	
Barry 133	F	0-6-0ST	6/3/17	30/8/19	
1601	1076	0-6-0T	4/4/17	-/-/20	
2366	2361	0-6-0	23/6/18	10/9/22	
2370	2361	0-6-0	18/9/18		
1024	1016	0-6-0T	26/10/18	18/6/22	
1285	1076	0-6-0T	2/4/19	18/6/22	
1732	1854	0-6-0T	2/4/19		
1611	1076	0-6-0T	7/5/19		
947	1076	0-6-0T	17/5/19		
1236	1076	0-6-0T	8/6/19		
3126	3100	2-6-2T	11/6/19	5/11/22	
3132	3100	2-6-2T	23/6/19		
1264	1076	0-6-0T	3/11/19		
1648	1076	0-6-0T	17/11/19		
1641	1076	0-6-0T	12/12/19		
1883	1854	0-6-0T	16/12/19		
4527	4500	2-6-2T	27/1/20		
3162	3150	2-6-2T	23/2/20		
4501	4500	2-6-2T	30/8/20	5/11/22	
1818	1813	0-6-0T	14/12/20		
2362	2361	0-6-0	8/3/21		

Notes:
To Duffryn Yard; actual date.
From Duffryn Yard; end of 4 week period.
Periods at Swindon Works omitted if locomotive returned to Duffryn Yard.

Construction of the New Dock, circa 1897. The new lock in the left background appears to be nearly finished. The 1837 entrance channel, lock and Old Dock remained in use during the work. This view was taken before work started to connect the New Dock to the Old Dock, essentially by blocking the old entrance channel and cutting through below and to the right of the photographer's feet. Not removed then was the projecting area of land in the left centre of this view which became known as the Island. *NLW*

12

Port Talbot Docks, 1895 to 1922

PEARSON'S CONTRACT

As with the railway part of their contract, Messrs Pearson were given notice on 21st February 1895 to start work on the New Dock within three weeks, thereby fixing the completion date as defined in the contract as 14th March 1898.[1] The engineer for this part of their contract was Frederick Hopkinson,[2] later Sir Frederick Hopkinson.[3] On 12th March, Pearson's applied for permission to place a temporary swing bridge over the existing lock so as to get access to the site. This was approved provided it did not interfere with the traffic of the Old Dock. Before much work could be done it was necessary to demolish the Port Talbot Inn, a long-established hostelry[4] situated about 150 yards south-east of the old lock near the site of the future tip No. 4. In February 1895 the lessees were given one year's notice to quit. A new site for a hotel south of the R&SBR's Docks station was approved by the directors in April 1895. The Port Talbot Property Co. Ltd, a short-lived company registered in April 1895 and wound up in January 1899,[5] signed an agreement in June 1895 to build the new Port Talbot Docks Hotel.

The license was assigned to Messrs Truman, Hanbury, Buxton & Co. Ltd in March 1898.[6]

Initially Pearson's work consisted mainly of excavation of the lock chamber and dock, which were both dredged somewhat smaller than shown on the Deposited Plans, and repairs to the existing south breakwater. This work proceeded without problems, except that Pearson's had to be reminded occasionally that it was necessary to keep the entrance to the Old Dock clear of obstruction. In August 1896 the engineers recommended that the new dock gates should be operated by direct acting hydraulic rams, at an additional cost of £1,500.[7] This modification to the original design was approved and became Pearson's Contract G.[8] The expenditure incurred was approved by the directors at their meeting in January 1899, except that the cost of the temporary plant needed for working the gates whilst the hydraulic machinery was being installed was debited to Messrs Armstrong.

Pearson's contract also called for the construction of a new north pier, which was situated about half a mile to the north-west of the new lock. This pier headed approximately south-westwards,

R&SBR signal box on the site of Port Talbot Docks station, with the Docks Hotel behind, 23rd March 1962.   *Courtesy C H A Townley*

such that the distance between its end and the end of the south breakwater extension provided an entrance to the channel about 250 yards wide. The north pier was constructed of timber framing with a rubble filling, similar to the existing south breakwater, which Pearson's were required to strengthen by driving new piles between the existing main piles. To access the site, Pearson's made use of Vivian's sand siding which joined the R&SBR near the site of the future Seaside station. Construction of the north pier proceeded without any major problems and was reported to be practically completed by August 1898.[9] The directors had agreed in October 1895 that this pier might be used as a promenade pier, but nothing practical towards this end could be done at the time. The engineer reported in September 1899 that Aberavon Corporation proposed to extend the pier landwards by 120 feet,[10] which was agreed to provided none of the pier was used as a landing place. The net receipts for the pier's use were divided equally between the PTR&D, Aberavon Corporation and Lord Jersey, the landowner, and a tripartite agreement to this effect was eventually sealed on 16th April 1902.[11]

Although completion of the New Dock was at least two years away, the directors discussed at their meeting on 4th October 1895 the usability of the existing dock when the works were finished. The engineer, Patrick Meik, was instructed to prepare plans showing how the New Dock could be still further utilised for coal shipments. The first proposal was for lengthening the New Dock so as to increase its area from 9 to 16 acres, and at the Board meeting on 15th January 1896 Pearson's tender to carry out this work for £60,000 was accepted, although the contract was not signed until 21st October 1896, presumably when it was feasible to start this work.[12] In June 1896, Meik proposed that the length of the lock should be increased from 400 to 450 feet and the depth by 2 feet. The width of the lock entrance remained at 60 feet but its capacity was increased by a "lie-by" 315 feet long by 50 feet wide. Pearson's quoted £12,080 for this work, but with extras the tender price of £14,400 was accepted, and included constructing the outer lock gates to a revised specification. Again the contract was delayed, this time to 25th November 1896.[13] Meik's final proposal was that the New Dock should be cut through to the existing dock. Hitherto it been envisaged that vessels would reach the Old Dock via the old lock. This cut was agreed to, and on 17th February 1897 Pearson's tender of £25,380 was accepted, Contract K. It was stipulated that all three contracts were to finish simultaneously with the opening of the New Dock. The directors declined to entertain a request from Pearson's for an extension for completing the new cut. As nothing but traffic from coal tips was to be provided for in the New Dock no expensive dock walls were built. The dock sides were sloped at about 30 degrees and faced with copper slag.

At the half-yearly meeting held on 17th February 1897 Col Wright explained that the depth of the lock and the size of the dock had been increased with the money the company had in hand, and the earning capacity of the dock would consequently be larger than originally contemplated. Sixty per cent of the excavation for the dock had been completed, the wall of the lock and entrance were half finished, and the piers were progressing favourably.[14] Despite this public display of confidence, the directors at their meeting on 22nd April instructed Meik to write to Pearson's complaining of the slow progress of the work.

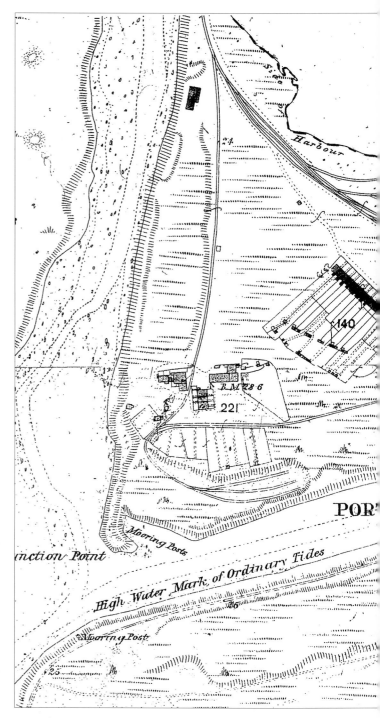

Further progress was announced in the report for the half-year ending 30th June 1897. Excavation of the dock had reached 70 per cent of the total required, the masonry and gates were two-thirds finished, and the piers were being proceeded with rapidly. The capacity of the New Dock had been considerably increased to 23 acres by incorporating the entrance channel to the Old Dock, and combining it with the Old Dock of 90 acres. All the water area would be available for large ships, and as trade developed all that would be required would be to dredge the Old Dock and erect additional tips.[15] Again, the directors were privately dissatisfied with the state of the works and in September the secretary wrote to Pearson's, this time specifically regarding the progress of the south breakwater extension.

A portion of the 1876 1:2500 Ordnance Survey, reduced by 50%, showing the state of Port Talbot Docks following the improvements made in 1874–76. Fortuitously, the locks were surveyed while the temporary bridge and track across them was still in position to allow the contractor access to the south side of the dock. It is possible that Pearson's used the same site for their temporary bridge in 1898. The extensive track on the improved Cwmavon Wharf was used exclusively by the English Copper Co. The PT Co.'s traffic was dealt with on New Wharf, later known as North Bank, and Messrs Byass used Llewellyn's Quay.

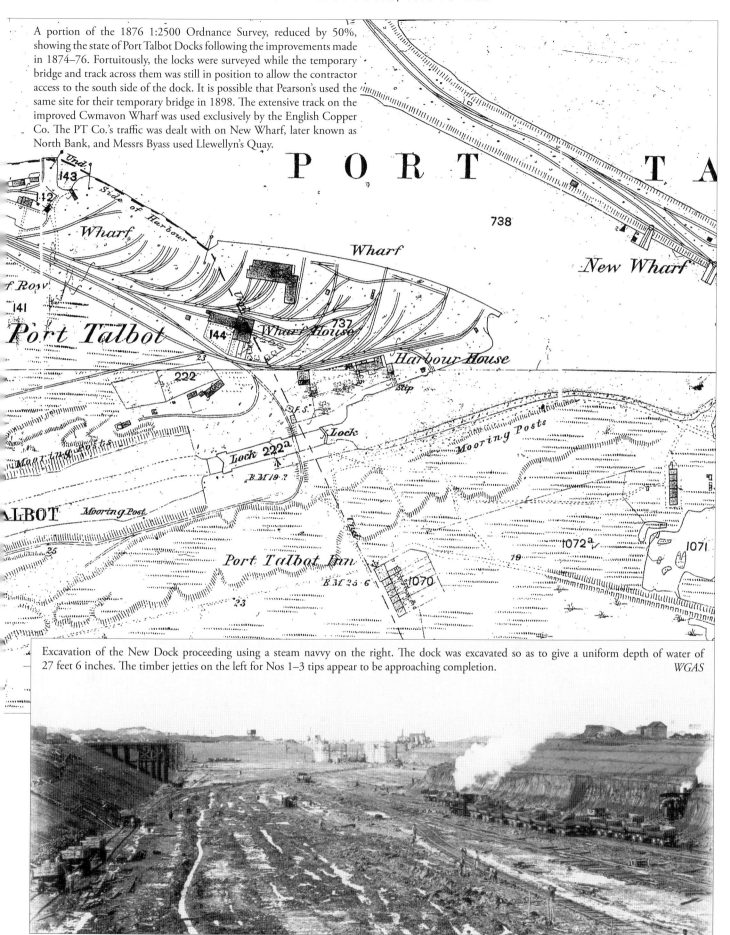

Excavation of the New Dock proceeding using a steam navvy on the right. The dock was excavated so as to give a uniform depth of water of 27 feet 6 inches. The timber jetties on the left for Nos 1–3 tips appear to be approaching completion.   *WGAS*

Early stages in the construction of the new lock viewed from inside the New Dock, circa 1896.
The lie-by which increased the lock's capacity is visible in the right centre.   *NLW*

In fact the shareholders had been given a misleading impression of the rate of progress with the piers. Work on the construction of the south breakwater extension had stopped on 31st March 1896 after about one-third had been built to a concrete design, owing to the foundations being in sand rather than the clay expected.[16] A change of design was required and it was not until 18th August that Messrs Messant & Matthews, consulting engineers, reported in favour of a rubble base with a sloping block superstructure. Instructions to carry out these recommendations were given two days later. The new design required the establishment of a blockyard and the construction of a Goliath crane capable of lifting 20 tons at 50 feet radius. The first sloping block was laid in October 1897, the interval having been spent in preparing for the new system of construction. Six hundred feet of pier were built in the two years to October 1899, leaving only forty feet to complete thereafter.

The shareholders heard good and bad news at the half-yearly meeting held on 16th February 1898. The New Dock was approaching completion and water was likely to be let in within the next month. It would then take three to four months to complete the entrance from the channel and to remove the dam dividing the New Dock from the Old Dock, thus making greater use of the two tips recently erected on North Bank in the Old Dock. By July, steamers of 3,000 ton burden would be able to take advantage of

the facilities of the dock, although the largest vessels could not be dealt with until the south breakwater extension was completed. The dredger was now at work in the channel. The delivery of hydraulic machinery and tips had been delayed by a recent engineers' strike. Consequently, the engineers had arranged to work the lock gates by temporary appliances, but no delay was anticipated in the delivery of the remaining coal tips. The north pier was practically completed, but progress with the south breakwater extension was not so satisfactory, although the New Dock could be used before they were completed. Pearson's had assured the Board that progress would be advanced as fast as possible. Negotiations had been completed for a large patent fuel works to be erected at the docks, and were progressing for the erection of a large iron and steel works.[17]

The directors at their meeting the same day recognised that Pearson's could not complete the dock by the contract date and resolved that penalties, which were set in the contract at £200 per week, would be enforced from that date. This decision was made public in the report for the half year to 30th June 1898,[18] which also noted that the non-completion of the New Dock had resulted in a considerable loss of traffic to both the railway and dock. Dredging operations were also delayed. Somewhat surprisingly the issue of penalties was seemingly not mentioned at the shareholder's meeting held on 17th August. However, the proprietors were informed

A view from the seaward side showing the lock and gates approaching completion. It is not known what the stationary engine in the open wagon powered; possibly a pump.   *WGAS*

The massively constructed outer lock gates nearing completion, circa 1898. These gates were 37 feet high, the tidal range being about 25 feet, and were made of iron.
WGAS

that the New Dock had been filled with water, and the lock and gates were now workable. The dock would be complete as soon as the dam separating it from the river was removed. The inner dam separating the Old Dock from the new was being cut through, and by September vessels of 3,000 tons burden would be able to get through to the four new tips erected there. The north pier was again stated to be practically completed and progress on the south breakwater extension was much more satisfactory than hitherto.[19] In fact, the new lock was used by commercial shipping for the first time on the afternoon tide of 22nd August 1898.[20]

At their meeting on 19th October 1898 the directors resolved to send a deputation to meet Sir Weetman Pearson with authority to accept £5,000 for late completion of the railway. If this was agreed, the company would extend the date for completion of the dock to 1st September 1899. This move initiated a dispute with Pearson's which was not finally settled until January 1901.[21] On 15th November 1898 Charles Cheston, the company's solicitor, wrote to Knott, the

secretary, stating that Pearson's were astonished that the question of penalties had been raised, and claimed *force majeure*. The amount of excavation done was 40 per cent greater than the drawings showed, entitling them to nine months' extension of time, and waiting for land delayed matters by seven months. The directors noted this on 16th November and asked for a meeting with Sir Weetman as soon as possible; they also replied to Cheston that they did not admit to any extension of time, that the first of Pearson's claims was the contractor's lookout and the second was not true. The company also obtained the opinion of J D Fitzgerald, QC, in its favour that as the entrance channel had never been completed throughout, the period of maintenance had not yet begun, and that the silting encountered was not "fair wear and tear" but natural.

ARBITRATION

Sir Weetman Pearson appeared before the Board on 21st December 1898 and offered to continue dredging the channel to full width and

The completed inner lock gates, circa 1898 viewed from inside the chamber. These gates were 9 feet 6 inches shorter than the outer ones and were constructed of greenheart timber. The lie-by which increased the capacity of the lock is on the left. Also visible are the four sluices by which the lock was filled. The lock was emptied via four similar sluices at the outer gates.   *WGAS*

depth, following Meik's instructions, and to continue construction of the south breakwater extension as fast as possible, provided all claims for penalties were waived. The directors could not agree to this and, as Pearson's refused to continue dredging without prejudice and to delay arbitration until after the completion of the contract, at their meeting on 4th January 1899 they resolved to seek immediate arbitration. The contractors were to be given instructions to proceed as per contract, and a dredger and two barges were to be hired from Neath Harbour Commissioners at a cost of £80 per week to dredge the river and Old Dock, the costs being deducted from Pearson's guarantee fund. Charles Meik, Patrick Meik's brother and co-partner, was appointed engineer of the company for the purposes of the contract in place of James Adair McConnochie who had died in 1895.

As well as dredging, it was intended that the depth of the entrance channel would be maintained by the scouring effect of the ebb and flow of the tide and the outflow of the River Avon. Preliminary steps to direct the flow of the river had already been taken by the construction of a training wall which extended downstream for about half a mile on the right bank, commencing at the R&SBR bridge. This wall was built as a timber cribwork structure by Messrs David & Piper whose combined tenders totalled £3,500.[22] This firm

occupied premises on the opposite side of the river with a siding connection to the line leading to No. 7 tip.[23] The land on which the wall was built was claimed by Arthur Pendarves Vivian, and the dispute over this land eventually reached the Court of Appeal. The courts found in favour of the docks on both occasions; in the settlement that followed, the company's boundary was set 100 feet back from, and parallel to, the slag wall, and it gained access to the R&SBR and Aberavon Gas Works, both north of the river. A tripartite agreement to this effect between Sir Arthur Vivian, Miss Talbot and the PTR&D was sealed at the Board meeting on 17th June 1903.[24]

On 16th January 1899, Sir Weetman Pearson contended in a letter to the company's solicitor that the PTR&D should have extended this training wall further along the right bank of the river to increase the effect of its flow. The scouring so produced would have reduced the amount of dredging required. The additional cost of removing silt was about £33,000.[25] He also modified his earlier proposal and suggested that the company should pay for the additional dredging in the channel required, for which his company would keep two dredgers at work; penalties on the dock section up to December 1898 were to be adjudicated at the completion of the contract, and no penalties to be alleged on the dock section after 1st January 1899

The south breakwater extension under construction, showing the staging which linked the original with the new portion, circa 1896. This view was taken shortly after the decision was made to alter the method of construction, made necessary by the foundations having to be set in sand rather than the clay expected.   *NLW*

In this view the change in method of construction of the south breakwater from horizontal to sloping concrete blocks is apparent.   *NLW*

Construction of the north pier circa 1897. Note the open timber construction. Pearson's No. 33 *Carrington*, Manning Wardle No. 1081 of 1888, was apparently acquired solely for Pearson's PTR&D contracts, having previously been used at the R&SBR's River Neath bridge construction and subsequently on the GCR's London extension at High Wycombe, both by other contractors.   *Courtesy Arthur Rees*

nor claimed from the railway section; all retention money was to be paid except £20,000. This new offer was not accepted and at their meeting on 18th January the directors resolved to go to arbitration. However, at their next meeting on 15th February, they did come up with a counter suggestion to be put to Pearson's by Cheston, that if Pearson's would give up part of their contract for dredging, allowing the company £30,000 in consideration thereof, all penalties would be waived.

Some aspects of the dispute were mentioned in the report for the half-year to 31st December 1898. The dock works were still not complete as the south breakwater extension had not been carried out to its full length, nor the channel dredged to its full depth and width. However, the docks were judged by the directors to justify the purpose for which they had been designed.[26] At the half-yearly meeting on 15th February 1899 the shareholders heard that once the north side of the New Dock was complete it would be able to deal with 15,000 tons of coal per day. Port Talbot was now on the list of ports at which the Admiralty would accept shipments of coal. They were also told that the contractors were under penalties of £200 per week, and this would no doubt be a matter of arbitration eventually.[27]

At a hearing held on 1st March 1899, Sir Douglas Fox, the President of the Institution of Civil Engineers, made an interim arbitration award that Pearson's were to dredge and complete the

channel as per the contract and the company was to extend the slag wall as quickly as possible. All other issues between the parties were to stand over until works had been completed.[28] At their meeting on 15th March 1899 the directors accepted T W Davies' tender of £10,074 for the construction of this extension. The plan was almost immediately amended to make use of timber piling so as to reduce the amount of slag required[29] and a revised tender of £9,104 14s 6d was accepted. The R&SBR directors agreed at their meeting on 8th April to an urgent request for a siding to be put in at Aberavon for this contractor.[30] The siding was taken off the Down loop near Aberavon Seaside station. The slag wall, which now projected into the sea beyond the high water mark, was reported to have been completed at the Board meeting held on 24th January 1900. Pearson's original contention concerning this wall seemed to be confirmed in a letter the dock company's secretary wrote to Cheston on 2nd March noting that although the dredgers were doing good work, it appeared that as fast as the sand was taken away it filled up again.

The *status quo* of Pearson's contract was confirmed at the Board meeting on 19th April 1899 when the engineers reported that the dock, lock and associated work had been completed by 30th September 1898, whereas dredging, dolphins, jetties and all works seaward of lock masonry were not yet finished. The Board's May meeting considered Pearson's application to have released one half

According to the original caption for this view, which appeared in a Pearson's publicity brochure, this shows the Port Talbot New Dock ready for letting in water. The old lock is just visible on the right, before the ground was cut through to the Old Dock and the old entrance channel was blocked off. The new lock appears to be almost complete, as are the jetties on the left for what became Nos 1–3 tips. The jetties in the centre of the view, and the land they stood on, were removed when the New Dock was modified in 1908.

Author's collection

of the portion of the guarantee fund applicable to the completed work (£7,660), but this was not agreed to. Nevertheless Pearson's felt they were entitled to completion of payment for satisfactory work and reapplied for the immediate release of £12,500 plus a further £12,500 on 30th September 1899. The directors on 16th August agreed this should be paid, provided an undertaking was given to proceed with the protection of the south breakwater apron. £10,000 was to be paid as Lancashire Derbyshire & East Coast Railway 5% preference shares and the remainder as PTR&D 4% preference shares.

Col Wright, the deputy chairman, informed the half-yearly meeting held on 16th August 1899 that although there was general disappointment that the works contracted for, *viz.* the south breakwater extension and the entrance channel, were not finished, he believed they would be completed by the end of September or October. This prediction was to prove sadly optimistic. More encouragingly, the Crown Preserved fuel works expected to begin operating in May or June next year, with all the required coal coming over the company's lines and the product being exported at its dock.[31]

The arbitration hearing took place in November and December 1899, as recounted below, while work continued on the entrance channel and south breakwater extension. Pearson's were still employing 200 men under their manager J Davies in November 1899.[32] By then the contractor was no longer using the dredger *Bollin* and its owners, the Manchester Ship Canal Co., offered it for sale. Well aware that the company would need to continually

dredge the dock and entrance channel after Pearson's had finished, the directors agreed the purchase in November 1899.

Pearson's were evidently having trouble with the dredging and on 3rd February 1900 the directors agreed to their request that the PTR&D should finish the work as per the contract, provided they offered 2s 2d per cubic yard. Later that month the engineers reported that 3,113 of the remaining 7,300 cubic yards of the dredging was to be done by the company at that price, and if the remainder was not dredged by Pearson's by the end of April the cost would be deducted from their retention money. They also reported that at long last the basic structure of the south breakwater extension had been completed and that Pearson's had consented to maintain it as from 1st February.

Pearson's were requested to keep their other dredger, *Britannic*, at Port Talbot whilst the directors made arrangements to hire hopper barges from the Newport Harbour Commissioners. It was agreed that *Britannic* would work for 1s 3d per cubic yard, although Pearson's stipulated it might stop work and be removed at any time. One of the directors, Watson, advised against starting dredging until after the equinoctial gales towards the end of March, but the harbour master insisted it was commenced straight away as sand was falling into the channel very quickly from the north side. The directors were now very keen to get the dredging finished, and at their meeting on 18th April 1900 resolved to ask the solicitor to advise whether the company could hand over to any contractor the remaining dredging and other work to be done in the dock and charge Pearson's; if not, it would do the dredging for £500 cash to be paid by Pearson's.

Meanwhile, the report for the half-year ending 31st December 1899 had noted that the works in connection with the dock were sufficiently completed for traffic purposes, although there were several important items in connection with Messrs Pearson's contract that were still unfinished. The shareholders were told on 21st February 1900 that the most important of these was the entrance channel which was still not dredged to the full contract depth. At the time, ships with 27-foot draught could enter at ordinary spring tides, and 22-foot at ordinary neaps.

The delays of the contractors resulted in an arbitration before Sir Douglas Fox as to the question of penalties.[33] The full arbitration hearing took place over six days in November and December 1899. Sir Robert Reid QC led for the Port Talbot Docks company with J Fletcher Moulton QC representing Pearson's.[34] The differences between the companies became clear in letters submitted to the arbitrator prior to the hearing.

Pearson's letter listed the points upon which a decision was required as:

1. Compensation for the extra dredging of the siltation caused by an inadequate slag wall, by the moved position of the north pier, by problems arising from other contractors (a reference to the graving dock construction) and by being required to dredge the entrance channel immediately the New Dock was ready rather than waiting until the other works were finished; total of 639,962 cubic yards to 28th September 1899.

2. Compensation for the loss of benefit of the effects of scour if the slag wall had been built as planned.

3. An extension of time due to the foregoing and due to a change in the design of the south breakwater extension referred to earlier. Delays were also caused by deeper foundations being required than shown on the drawings, by the effects of an engineers' strike on other contractors and by bad weather.

4. Maintenance of the channel.
5. Maintenance of the north pier and the south breakwaters.
6. Amounts payable for extra work.

On the other hand, Messrs Cheston & Son, writing on behalf of the PTR&D, contended that the main questions to be arbitrated on were the question of maintenance and the non-completion of the channel. It was understood that Pearson's contended that the period of maintenance of the channel had expired because of its use by the company, but this was allowed by the contract and as the channel had not yet been finished, the period of maintenance could not have commenced. The company also contended that Pearson's position regarding the slag was unfounded since the contract made no mention of such a wall. As regards extensions of time, these were to be referred to the engineers, but no such applications had been made. The object of the company in entering into the contract in its existing form was to protect itself from the type of claims now put forward.

The only witnesses examined were Patrick Meik for the PTR&D and J H Davies for Pearson's, he having been appointed resident engineer on 17th August 1896 and agent in June 1898. The arguments mainly concerned the interpretation of the contract, the facts not being in dispute.

Sir Douglas Fox's award, dated 22nd February 1900, was against the PTR&D on every point.[35] He found that the channel had been dredged as per contract and that the period of maintenance had ended on 30th September 1899. A total of 492,952 cubic yards of additional dredging had been performed by Pearson's for which the company was liable to pay £33,943. A solicitor representing Pearson's swore the award before the Queen's Bench Division of the High Court on 12th March 1900 in order to legalise it. The award was submitted to the company's counsel for advice, and on 21st March the directors noted that a submission had been made

The River Avon flowed into the Bristol Channel between the north breakwater, nearing completion, and the south breakwater, still only partly constructed. Siltation hereabouts was a constant problem, which a training wall constructed along the right of the channel only partly solved. *NLW*

THE DOCKS, PORT TALBOT

Port Talbot, le 21 décembre 1903.
En attendant de tes bonnes nouvelles à Iquique,
Ton bien-aimé qui pense constamment à toi Louis

An early view of the new dock entrance taken at low tide showing the dolphins erected to guide vessels towards the lock gates. Postcard, postally used 21st December 1903.

Author's collection

to the High Court to have it either set aside or restated in the form of a special case. In the meantime, Pearson's had estimated that in addition to the £33,943 owing as at 30th September 1899 further dredging carried out to 21st February 1900 brought the total to £45,359, this seemingly being the date on which the contractor ceased work at Port Talbot.

It was decided to appeal the arbitrator's award and Hosgood was instructed to keep careful records of all dredging done. The appeal was heard on 25th May, Cheston reporting that the Court was clearly in the dock company's favour.[36] Cheston had informed the company that Pearson's were open to a reasonable settlement and in June the directors authorised him to take whatever action he considered best. Negotiations ensued but were interrupted in November 1900 when the directors learned of an agreement between Sir Weetman Pearson and Miss Talbot to purchase from her 10,000 ordinary shares if called upon to do so, and that he could not entertain Col Wright's suggestions unless he was relieved of his obligation under the agreement.[37]

Cheston wrote to Col Wright in December 1900 suggesting that although £64,344 was the total amount claimed by Pearson's to 21st February 1900, agreed allowances £5,080, penalties for late completion of contracts £19,600, a reduction by the High Court for dredging £7,378 and unsubstantiated claims by Pearson's £11,585 could all be deducted, leaving a balance of £20,701.[38] The Board of Directors agreed at its meeting on 10th December to offer Messrs Pearson £20,000 to include all matters mentioned in the letter, each party paying its own costs. Sir Weetman had hoped for £25,000,

but on 16th January 1901 the inevitable compromise of £22,500 was agreed. Sir Weetman demanded payment within ten days, but that was an impossible deadline for the company and a date of 8th February was agreed. A draft agreement with Pearson's was approved at the Board meeting held on 23rd January, and signed and sealed on 24th January.[39] Other than the settlement amount, the agreement provided for the immediate release of the Guarantee Fund of 2,000 4% fully paid PTR&D Preference Shares and £783 3s 2d cash, the payment of £550 for work done by Pearson's for Hosgood, for each side to pay its own costs arising from the dispute, and prohibited any further claims of one side on the other. The £22,500 was paid out of a loan to the company from Miss Talbot.[40] The shareholders were informed at the half-yearly meeting held on 27th February 1901 that the differences which had existed between the company and Pearson's had been settled, concessions having been made by both sides.[41]

COMPLETION

By mid-1899 the impression had been gained that the dock works were approaching completion. Mappin & Webb made enquiries regarding a presentation casket and G N Downall & Bros of Newport offered to provide luncheon.[42] The directors first considered the formal opening of the New Dock in February 1900, and the chairman, Lord Dunraven, undertook to try and arrange for the Prince of Wales to open the dock the following May. In this he was unsuccessful and Miss Talbot was asked to perform the task.[43] The directors at their April 1900 meeting deferred the

ABOVE: The dredger *Bollin* was hired by Messrs Pearson from the Manchester Ship Canal Co. to dredge the newly flooded dock. It is seen here being coaled from a jetty at the eastern end of Talbot Wharf on 18th August 1898. Immediately behind on North Bank is No. 5 tip of 1895. To the right is Messrs Jenkins' sawmill on Llewellyn's Quay and to the left the GWR's Port Talbot station above the Float. The *Bollin* was sold to the Port Talbot Dock Co. in November 1899   *WGAS*

BELOW: *Bollin* moored in the New Dock on 11th October 1898. The newly-built Docks Hotel is to the right with the R&SBR's Docks station just beyond. Wharf Row is to the left of centre with the approaches to No. 7 tip and jetty under construction on the far left.   *WGAS*

A panorama formed from a series of five overlapping photographs taken on 10th October 1898 from the top of No. 1 tip. Not all the dredging had been completed by this date, particularly the removal of the spit running from the left of the view, the former left bank of the old channel. From the left can be made out: (*above*) the graving dock under construction with the River Avon visible just behind, the accumulator for No. 7 tip nearby, the R&SBR Docks station, the new Docks Hotel, the accumulator on North Bank, (*below*) the moored dredger *Bollin*, the old lock, No. 6 tip, the Island (the staging on the end of which would shortly be removed), No. 5 tip, the hydraulic power house built for the New Dock, No. 2 tip behind which is No. 3, and the base for Messrs Pearson's operations. Very little railway development had yet taken place on the south side of the New Dock to the right of this panorama.
WGAS

The new lock full of water at the dock level, nominally 3 feet 6 inches above the highest Spring tide, and showing on the left the lie-by which doubled its capacity.
Author's collection

opening for three months and in the event the enlarged docks were never formally opened.

Hosgood reported in June 1900 that Pearson's had done no further dredging inside the dock and that the company would do the work and deduct the cost from the Guarantee Fund. The company had taken over the channel dredging, although the work done by its new dredger, the *Bollin*, was proving to be very unsatisfactory. The shareholders were informed at the half-yearly meeting held on 22nd August 1900 that the dock works were still incomplete, the

principal tasks outstanding being capping the new south breakwater extension, which Pearson's were finishing, and dredging the channel. All should be finished within the next two months.[44] The directors were informed by the engineer at their meeting on 17th October 1900 that everything in Pearson's contract would be finished by the end of that month.

Pearson's had earlier been instructed to complete their contract regarding filling in the gap between the old and new south breakwaters. This instruction had been revoked in September 1900

The trackwork associated with Nos 1–3 tips nearing completion in November 1898. The empty road from No. 1 tip comes under the left-hand bridge, that from No. 2 tip under the right-hand bridge, whilst that from No. 3 tip off to the right joined just behind the photographer. Loaded wagons were propelled from No. 3 grid onto the elevated road and gravitated down to the tips, those for No. 1 tip branching off between the two bridges. The sandy nature of the ground hereabouts is very apparent.
WGAS

A view across the River Avon downstream of the Newbridge Road bridge circa 1905 showing the approach lines to No. 7 tip. In the foreground is the temporary railway laid along the top of the training wall when it was being extended. Postcard, postally used 28th April 1910.   *Author's collection*

and the dock company undertook to do this work itself. It was not until September 1901 that Hosgood, the resident engineer, reported that this work was underway,[45] the gap being fully closed by March 1902.[46] The period of Pearson's maintenance of the breakwaters expired on 1st February 1901.[47] In June 1903, Hosgood reported that the original part of the south breakwater required repair.[48] The following month the directors accepted Hosgood's estimate of £1,500 for the work to be done by the company, this being much lower than the tenders received. The work was reported to be completed in November 1904.[49]

PROTECTION OF THE LOCK FROM DAMAGE

The Port Talbot company had entered into an agreement with Messrs Evan-Thomas and Bushby and the Sandhills Boring Co. on 3rd April 1895 to purchase 50 acres of foreshore in the Parish of Aberavon and to regulate the working of minerals under the company's property. The two gentlemen were lords of the Borough of Afon and the Manor of Afon Wallia, and Evan-Thomas was also a director of North's Navigation Collieries. In August 1902 they issued a writ against the company for non-fulfilment of the agreement. The matter was allowed to lie until October 1906 when Col Wright and Mr Byass met Evan-Thomas to arrange a settlement, when it was agreed that: the PTR&D would not purchase the foreshore but only a perpetual easement for North Pier, the company would have reserved for it 15 acres of coal under the existing and any proposed new locks, the company would give up 2.4 acres previously reserved under the old lock, the company would pay £3,250 in full settlement, and the agreement of 3rd April 1895 would hold good except as now varied. A principal concern was that any mining activity under the dock should not result in

damage to the lock above. The revised agreement was signed and sealed on 15th January 1908.

FURTHER EXTENSION OF TRAINING WALL

Siltation of the entrance channel to the dock was a continuing problem and the further extension of the training wall to combat this situation was first discussed at the Board meeting on 25th July 1900. Hosgood reported in October 1900 that the permanent way on the existing wall was in order and ready for any extension work.[50]

Matters came to head in January 1901 when Hosgood and Capt. Jones, the harbour master, reported heavy siltation in the channel following a recent severe gale.[51] They observed that the silt appeared to come from the seabed between the north pier and the training wall, and suggested the extension of the wall towards the end of the north pier without delay. Hosgood estimated that the proposed extension of 580 yards would require 45,000 tons of slag.

On Meik's recommendation the new wall was built straight and parallel to the entrance channel, except at its terminus where it curved gently towards the end of the north pier. It was not a high wall and would not have been visible at all states of the tide – being 8 feet above the seabed at the inner end and 5 feet at the far end – measuring 15 feet wide at the top with the sides sloping at about 20 degrees.[52] The building material was obtained from the copper slag tips and the Express Steel Works, both at Cwmavon.[53] The preferred route from Cwmavon to the training wall was via the R&SBR and the siding put in for T W Davies' contract, for which journey the Rhondda Co. proposed to charge 3d per ton.[54] Hosgood reported in March 1901 that he had commenced transporting slag, but had been unable to use the company's end-tipping wagons as the R&SBR had objected to their use. To get round the objection,

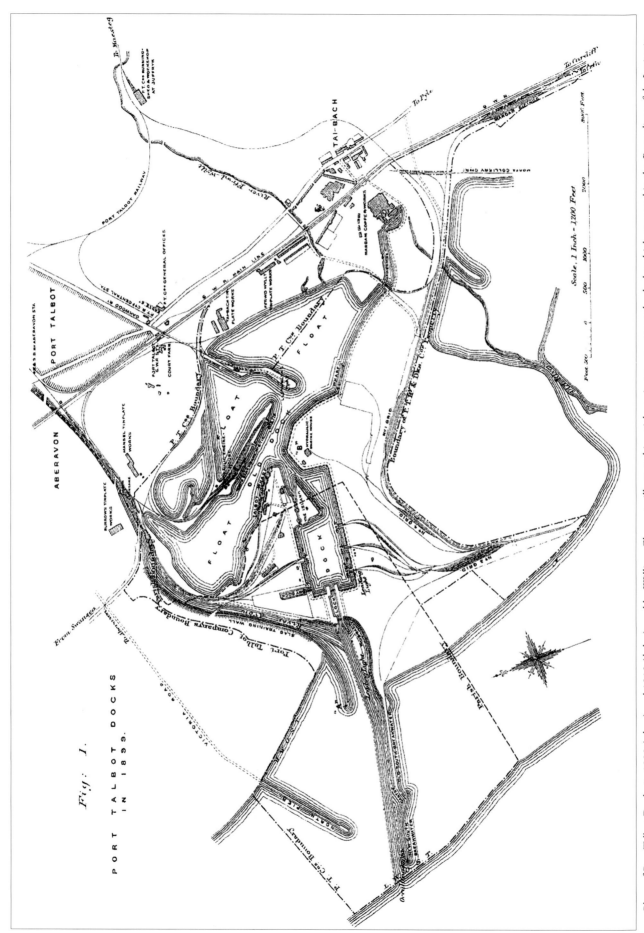

Plans of Port Talbot Docks in 1899 (*above*) and 1912 (*below*) used by William Cleaver to illustrate his article on improvements at the docks which appeared in the *Proceedings of the Institution of Civil Engineers, Vol. 191, 1912–1913*. Many changes are apparent by 1912, including removal of The Island and the old hydraulic power house site, the construction of Nos 4 and 8 tips and No. 9 conveyor, a new power house and Steelworks Wharf, and the provision of additional grids. Also marked is the position of the Port Talbot Co.'s boundary which was extended as a result of the 1910 agreement with Miss Talbot.

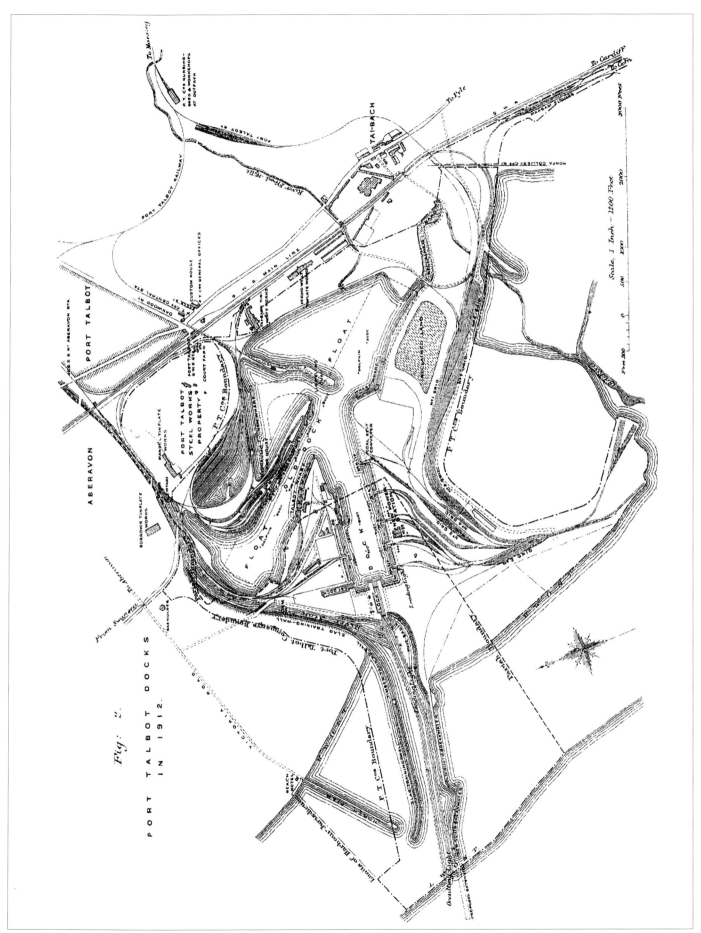

ABOVE: The approach to Port Talbot Docks was protected by two breakwaters. The old south breakwater nearer the camera was strengthened by Pearson's and connected by the open crib-work to a new extension off to the left. The new north breakwater was used as a public pier. The slag training wall which gave so much trouble was built along the right bank of the mouth of the River Avon and extended out to sea towards the end of the north pier, under water to a greater or lesser degree depending on the state of the tide. Postcard, postally used 31st October 1934. *Author's collection*

ABOVE: No. 6 tip on North Bank, August 1898. The fairly light construction of this tip erected in 1895 compares with the massive No. 8 tip of 1910–11 situated 250 yards along North Bank. *WGAS*

RIGHT: Storage sidings at the northern end of North Bank viewed from the top of No. 8 tip, circa 1912. The five loops were for loads for discharging at this tip, with the empties returning via the high level roads in the middle of the view, North's Navigation's wagons in this case. The next six roads were dead-end storage sidings, the first three of which are holding wagons belonging to Duffryn Rhondda Colliery near Cymmer which was served by the R&SBR.

From PTR&D Co. Handbook of Rates 1913, Author's collection

Hosgood planned to work via Ynysdavid sidings and the SWMJnR, presumably gaining access to the site over the bridge put in for Topham, Jones & Railton's graving dock contract. Approximately 22,000 tons had been tipped by the end of June.[55] Work was halted briefly in August 1901 due to a financial crisis, but by October the authorised length of 590 yards had been reached[56] and the desired height was attained the following month, 42,000 tons having been tipped.[57] Further remedial work continued until September 1903.[58]

OLD DOCK

While Pearson's were constructing the new lock and dock, the Port Talbot company concerned itself with improving the facilities of the existing dock, which remained open throughout.

NORTH BANK

As recounted earlier,[59] improvements to North Bank were already underway when the PTR&D Company was incorporated. A new tip at the eastern end of North Bank (which became known as No. 5) and a hydraulic engine house had been constructed during 1894. In June 1895 tenders were sought for a jetty for a further new tip, No. 6, and contracts for this and a general goods wharf were entered into immediately.[60] In July, two new hydraulic cranes were ordered to replace the existing cranes, which were moved to Talbot Wharf. All the new machinery was supplied by Sir W G Armstrong & Co.[61] At the time of the opening of the railway for mineral traffic it was reported that these tips could discharge about 1,200 tons in 24 hours.[62] North Bank saw relatively little development until tip No. 8 was constructed towards its western end in 1910–11.[63]

LLEWELLYN'S QUAY

Llewellyn's Quay had reverted to Miss Talbot when Messrs Byass & Co. gave up their lease of the Oakwood Railway.[64] The PTR&D leased the quay from Miss Talbot in January 1896, and sub-let it to Messrs D Jenkins & Sons, Port Talbot, for £200 per annum the following April. The directors attempted to purchase the shallow water east of Llewellyn's Quay from Miss Talbot in August 1901 with the intention of filling it in so as to provide a potential industrial site, but were rebuffed. Other than this, the quay saw little industrial use, but its proximity to the south side of the dock led Edward Lowther, the general manager, in October 1905 to investigate the possibility of a floating bridge to connect the two. A craft lying at Southampton was available, but in March 1906 was found to be unsuitable for the purpose. The dock around Llewellyn's Quay was deepened in 1911 so that sailing ships could go alongside and discharge their ballast there.

MARGAM COPPER WORKS WHARF

Messrs Vivian & Sons had long enjoyed free wharfage rights on the cut which had been constructed to their premises when the dock was first created.[65] In November 1896 Messrs Vivian refused to negotiate over the surrender of these rights, which prompted a more forceful approach from Knox, acting as both Miss Talbot's agent and the PTR&D's secretary.[66] Vivian's were reminded that the current agreement was for the Copper Works Wharf only, with no rights to load vessels with coal at the tips, the leases for the land

over which the connecting tramroads ran having expired. The value of the exemptions over the period 1867–96 totalled nearly £11,000, and Miss Talbot desired to settle on that basis. In the event she purchased the rights in November 1897 for £14,000, generous compensation for the loss of the wharfage rights. Messrs Vivian were also informed that they would have to construct a connection to the Oakwood Railway and that in future the PTR&D would levy wharfage on all their traffic other than at the Copper Works Wharf, but by then the Copper Works were being run down.[67] The site remained unused until 1918 when the construction of Margam Steelworks commenced.

TALBOT WHARF

As already noted, Messrs Wright, Butler & Co. owned the wharf in the Old Dock which had been established by the English Copper Co.[68] The wharf passed briefly to Miss Talbot in January 1895, but on 25th March the PTR&D agreed to purchase it from her for £30,000 – a transaction concluded in July 1896 – and resolved to rename it Talbot Wharf.

Pearson's tendered £6,906 to renew the wharf,[69] but with extras a revised figure of £7,400 was accepted on 18th June 1895, becoming their Contract C. The contract required completion within four months of acceptance of the tender and included the laying of 370 yards of rails supplied by the PTR&D. The R&SBR claimed ownership of some land towards the eastern end of Talbot Wharf as a result of its acquisition of the Cwmavon Railway[70] and also claimed some rights over the wharf there under a deed of conveyance with Mr Talbot made on 22nd June 1885. The Port Talbot directors resolved on 11th December 1895 that a telegraph pole belonging to the R&SBR situated on their land was to be moved onto its owner's land. The R&SBR's property on Talbot Wharf was to be fenced off and piles obstructing the waterway removed. On 21st December the R&SBR obtained an injunction restraining the PTR&D from removing posts and piles or dumping waste on the land it claimed. At the renewal hearing on 11th January 1896 the PTR&D's counsel protested that the injunction prevented the defendants from constructing their dock, and the order was modified to restrain the company from removing any posts or piles in the disputed land.[71] At a further hearing on 24th January, the GWR's engineer was appointed the sole arbitrator between the parties.[72] This was the first of several relatively minor disputes that arose between the two companies in the dock area. The R&SBR obtained a further injunction against the PTR&D in March 1896, this time concerning repairs to their part of Talbot Wharf, but nevertheless, by the time of the half-yearly meeting held on 19th August 1896, most of it had been entirely reconstructed and was available to steamers of large tonnage.[73]

The first of several joint meetings of the Port Talbot and Rhondda companies' directors was held on 2nd December 1896. The latter's agenda, agreed at a Board meeting the previous day, included land at Port Talbot Docks station, frontage at Port Talbot Dock, access to Vivian & Son's, David's and other works, the injunction against PTR&D regarding trespass on R&SBR land to gain access to the wharf, prevention of the PTR&D from extending their wharf to the detriment of the Rhondda wharf, and the right of way from Aberavon to Port Talbot Dock alongside the railway.[74] Col Wright and Messrs Watson and Knox represented the PTR&D, while Sir

ABOVE: A load of what looks like steel shuttering spread over seven GWR bogie bolster wagons at the western end of Talbot Wharf at the time of the first extension, circa 1905. The number of the nearest wagon is 70822, a Macaw B to Diagram J11 of 1904. The tripod in the background is standing in the scrap yard of the Port Talbot Iron & Steel Co. *Author's collection*

LEFT: Pit props were a major import at Port Talbot and are seen here being unloaded at the eastern end of Talbot Wharf, circa 1912.
From Port Talbot and its Progress, *PTR&D Co. 1919, Author's collection*

J J Jenkins and Messrs Williams and Lambert Bath represented the R&SBR.[75]

After a lengthy discussion it was agreed that the two actions against the PTR&D should be withdrawn for the time being and that key proposals from each side should be further considered. The PTR&D desired to purchase the land with the frontage at the Port Talbot Docks for £3,000 and that the two actions should be settled, the PTR&D to pay the costs of the first action and each paying their own costs in the second action. The R&SBR, on the other hand, sought concessions over the implementation of the PTR&D's SWMJnR Act which had recently gained the Royal Assent.[76] Although further correspondence ensued, nothing was immediately resolved.

The disputes over access and ownership impeded further development of the Talbot Wharf area, although the wharf itself was reported to be complete and fully equipped at the half-yearly meeting held on 16th February 1898.[77] It was not until June 1898 that Mr Justice Sterling delivered his judgment in the first action against the PTR&D. He found in favour of the R&SBR on all points, but expressed the opinion that the leasehold of the wharf had not passed to it. The R&SBR decided not to challenge this decision unless the PTR&D appealed.[78] The second action was discontinued in December 1899 on the advice of counsel.[79]

On 4th November 1898, Col Wright met the chairman of the R&SBR who, not surprisingly, learned that the PTR&D were still anxious to acquire the 66 feet of frontage at the end of the Talbot Wharf. It was suggested that an exchange might be effected if the R&SBR were offered a frontage and tip in the New Dock.[80] This idea would have been an anathema to the Port Talbot directors, but nevertheless another meeting with the R&SBR was arranged for mid November. This time the Port Talbot directors set the agenda, which included land at Talbot Wharf, joint lines between Mansel Junction and Talbot Wharf, and land for sidings. The directors noted at their December meeting that negotiations were to continue on the basis of £3,000 for the land required at the wharf, the R&SBR paying half the cost of the sidings.

This stalemate continued for almost another year. A typical situation arose in May 1899 when the R&SBR set the easement for some pipes under the line to their Docks station at £4 10s 0d per annum, but offered to reduce it to £2 2s 0d if the PTR&D would accept the same figure as rent for the land occupied there. The Port Talbot directors decided at their meeting on 17th May to pay the amount first asked for, as the rent of the land on which part of the Docks station was situated could not be reduced from £25 per annum, a figure which in January 1898 had caused the Rhondda directors to remark that it would be better to close the

Unloading pit props at the eastern end of Talbot Wharf, April 1927. The railway works here were completed in January 1906. The view includes a rare glimpse of an unidentified ex-PTR 0-6-0ST working in the docks.　　　　*NM&GW*

The eastern end of Talbot Wharf looking west. April 1927.　　　*NM&GW*

station than pay. The PTR&D reiterated its offer of £3,000 for the land at the docks in June 1899. It is not clear exactly what followed, but the following month, and again in August, the company's newly appointed resident engineer, Hosgood, reported that the disused portions of Talbot Wharf, including the east and west ends, were to be repaired so as to hold steam cranes. These did not materialise but, in December 1899, four new hydraulic cranes were reported to be in use and the extension of the sidings at Talbot Wharf was about to begin.[81]

A further joint meeting of the two boards was held on 30th November 1899, followed by another on 9th February 1900. Although the details are unclear, on 21st March 1900 the Port Talbot directors agreed the minutes of the meetings of the officials who conducting the detailed discussions. These included the exchange of the land on which part of the Docks station was built for some land near the wharf and the waiving of the back rent due to the PTR&D. One topic left for future discussion was access for the R&SBR's engines to the south side of the dock, as allowed for

The trackwork on Talbot Wharf extension, which was finished in September 1918, consisted of three parallel sidings.

ABOVE: The SS *Haugland* is discharging iron ore. June 1923.
BR/OPC

LEFT: The SS *Evandros* at Talbot Wharf Extension. The tracks in the foreground are shunting loops for Talbot Wharf off to the right. May 1928. NM&GW

FACING PAGE: The SS *Evandros* is discharging iron ore. May 1928.
NM&GW

in the 1894 Act. One result of the improving relationship between the two companies was that in November 1900 the R&SBR agreed without prejudice to the removal of the contentious piles at the end of Talbot Wharf to allow safe navigation.

Hitherto the cranes installed on North Bank and Talbot Wharf had a maximum lift of 2 tons, adequate for the goods handling practices of the time. However, some items were heavier than this and in August 1900 the directors instructed Hosgood to enquire as to the price of a secondhand 12-ton crane for lifting heavy goods. In November 1900 he reported that an ex-Barry Railway 12-ton hand-crane had been reconditioned by Andrews & Baby of Cardiff and was offered at £250 delivered to Port Talbot.[82] This offer was accepted and the crane was installed on the north side of the New Dock opposite No. 3 tip and next to the old lock gates. A railway connection was provided via the Talbot Wharf lines.

Talbot Wharf was destined to become the import wharf and, in an attempt to increase its usefulness, in March 1902 Lowther undertook to consider unloading vessels by means of crane barges placed between the dock slope and ship's sides. It is not known whether this procedure was employed, but in December 1904 the directors authorised the extension of Talbot Wharf by about 200 feet at its western end to give a new length of 700 feet, and accepted the tender of Messrs Tannett Walker & Co. for one luffing crane of 2 to 4 tons capacity and three 2-ton fixed-radius cranes for erection there. There was a slight delay while the relative merits of timber and ferro-concrete construction were considered.

The PTR&D was one of the first to use ferro-concrete for this type of work,[83] it having been introduced into South Wales by the French engineer Louis Gustave Mouchel (1852–1908) who lived in Briton Ferry.[84] Its introduction at Port Talbot followed an incident in which the ignition of a floating film of oil resulted in a serious fire which threatened nearby timber jetties. In March 1905 the tender of Messrs Topham, Jones & Railton utilising ferro-concrete was accepted, it being combined with other new works in the docks. The contractors' work was reported to be finished in December 1905, together with erection of the cranes – bringing the total on the wharf to eight – and the installation of two hydraulic capstans.[85] The extension was ready for use in January 1906 after new railway connections had been laid in.[86]

In August 1906 the engineer reported that the old warehouses on Talbot Wharf were in a bad state of repair, with the recommendation they should be demolished and replaced with a proper corrugated iron warehouse.[87] This course of action was accepted, but the following month a revised scheme of moving a front wall backwards 5 feet and reroofing was approved.[88] Nothing was done for over a year until it was reported that the adjacent Rio Tinto warehouse was being dismantled and that some of the liberated material would be used to rebuild the company's warehouse.[89] The permanent way was rearranged once more and the warehouse work was reported to have been completed by June 1908.[90]

TALBOT WHARF SECOND EXTENSION

Further development of Talbot Wharf was first considered in November 1908 when the general manager proposed a 400-foot westward extension at an estimated cost of £23,000. The company's financial situation at the time did not favour such expenditure, but in June 1910 a more modest 100-foot eastward extension was approved. The tender of Messrs Perry & Co. of £1,950 to construct this extension in ferro-concrete was accepted in September 1910.[91] Although initially good progress was made, the engineer reported in May and again in November 1911 that Messrs Perry were experiencing such severe problems with the piling that the work had stopped. The solution was to use ferro-concrete cylinders set in the dock floor and tied back to the wharf embankment. Work stopped again in April 1912, but after threats of enforcing the contract by legal action the underwater work was resumed and completed the following June.[92] The extension was ready for use in October 1912. Messrs Perry later claimed £3,857 for the extra work they had undertaken, but the directors resolved to settle for not more than £2,000.

TALBOT WHARF THIRD EXTENSION

By November 1912 the westward extension of Talbot Wharf could be put off no longer, and the directors authorised a 500-foot addition in that direction for import traffic, with siding accommodation for 370 wagons, at an estimated cost of £27,000 inclusive of dredging. The new extension was increased to 685 feet in January 1913 when the tender of £8,723 submitted by Messrs J B Cooper & Co. of Bristol was accepted. The tender of Messrs Tannett Walker & Co. of £3,376 for movable hydraulic cranes – three 2-ton fixed-radius and one 2/6-ton luffing – was accepted in February 1913, but this firm went into receivership in the April and the contract was passed to the East Ferry Road Engineering Works Co. Ltd in May

Port Talbot Docks, May 1920. The lines of coal wagons awaiting shipment clearly define the sidings associated with Nos 1–4 tips, Nos 9 and 10 conveyors and, on the right, No. 8 grid. *Aerofilms*

1913. The concrete portion of the wharf was not finished until May 1915,[93] progress having been impeded by the shortage of labour and materials occasioned by the war effort.[94] As with the new Steelworks Wharf, one of the PTR&D's Sharp, Stewart 0-8-2 tank engines was used to test the deflection of the reinforced concrete beams on the Talbot Wharf extension on 3rd September 1915.[95] Construction of the extension was eventually completed in December 1917 and one road was laid in for temporary use as a pitwood siding.[96] Two more sidings were laid in and ready for use in September 1918.[97] Large amounts of pitwood were imported through Port Talbot Docks and 16,000 tons of what was described as Government pitwood were stocked there by October 1917. The specification for a steam crane for stacking this pitwood was approved in July 1918 and two months later the Government supplied a suitable crane, the PTR&D having the option of taking over the crane at market value when the Government had finished with it. This 5-ton crane had been built by Messrs J H Wilson & Co. in 1916 and was purchased by the PTR&D in September 1920 for £1,800.

CUSTOMS PORT

It was highly desirable that Port Talbot should be declared a customs port, the company receiving much encouragement from shippers to seek this status as it would greatly expedite trade.[98] The first application in 1900 was declined on the grounds that the trade of the port was insufficient. The application was renewed annually and in October 1903 the directors was informed that the Lords of the Treasury had approved Port Talbot as a customs port, as from 1st January 1904. A new customs house was erected at the rear of the company's general offices by J Davies & Sons for £1,325, the tenancy commencing February 1905. An old grain warehouse near the old lock[99] was converted to a bonded warehouse and leased to the Board of Customs for that purpose. In March 1904 the Board of Customs approved the use of Talbot Wharf for the landing of all goods except tobacco and saccharine, provided a weighing machine was provided in the warehouse. A sufferance bond of £1,000 was given in respect of unrestricted access for the collection of customs dues on Talbot Wharf. Similar bonds were also given for North Bank, Crown Preserved Wharf and the Rio Tinto Wharf.[100]

FURTHER LAND AT THE DOCKS

The Port Talbot directors first identified the need for additional land at the docks in January 1906. Approximately 85 acres, some of which were under shallow water, were required for further tips to cope with growing coal shipments. According to a letter to Geoffrey Lipscomb, Miss Talbot's agent, in March 1906, the coal was anticipated from new sinkings at Duffryn Rhondda Colliery in the Avon Valley, a new shaft sunk by North's Navigation Collieries at Caerau, developments at Cymmer, Glyncorrwg and Whitworth, and from the GWR's proposed Brynamman line.[101] No reply was forthcoming until January 1909 when the directors were informed that land for tips and sidings would be provided *gratis* with a ½d per ton toll on all traffic, as hitherto. Land for other purposes would be considered on merits, the PTR&D having first refusal. This produced a sharp response from Mr Watson, one of the directors, who pointed out that he was invited to join the Board by Knox, Miss Talbot's previous agent, on the promise that she would provide all

the land required for docks purposes, and that the proposed terms were not *gratis* as they amounted to a very generous rental. The matter then passed to solicitors to prepare the necessary documents. In June 1910 the directors were made aware of a letter from Messrs May, How & Chilvers, Miss Talbot's solicitors, expressing her concerns on how the land was to be transferred, and the secrecy desired by the GWR; she had intended to be an intermediary between the PTR&D and the GWR, receiving from the latter and paying to the former a very considerable sum of money; the GWR had refused to execute any legal deed and it was then arranged that Col Wright would be the intermediary, Miss Talbot's role being limited to providing the land. The letter concluded by stating that as far as her estate was concerned the port would become part of the GWR system and the PTR&D could expect no further favours. This letter in fact referred to an informal agreement made by Viscount Churchill, the chairman of the GWR, and James Inglis, the general manager, with Col Wright and Edward Lowther to the effect that the GWR undertook to guarantee interest at the rate of 6 per cent on the PTR&D's dock capital once it had gained possession of certain land belonging to Miss Talbot.[102] This offer was not discussed by the GWR directors, which would account for the secrecy referred to.

The agreements in question provided for Miss Talbot to lease an additional 117.13 acres in the dock area to the PTR&D and to convey these lands to the company if, within twenty-one years, capital works estimated to cost £400,000 were executed there. These included a new lock and entrance channel, new tips, railways, storage sidings and wharves. For its part, the PTR&D undertook to pay a perpetual rent charge of ½d per ton on all coal, minerals and merchandise shipped or discharged at the docks, and to pay £300 annually in lieu of interest upon the capital expended by Miss Talbot on the Oakwood & South Side Railway (O&SSR),[103] which was to be included in the conveyance. Miss Talbot's solicitors were assured that the transaction was to the advantage of the PTR&D's shareholders, that Miss Talbot had fully performed the part of the transaction incumbent upon the Margam Estate and herself, and that she would not be expected to make good any deficiencies consequent upon the carrying out of the policy adopted by the Board. The agreements were sealed on 5th October 1910.

Miss Talbot died in September 1918 aged 78[104] and her estates were administered by her trustees, Thomas Mansel Franklen, Lt Col Venables Llewellyn and Brig. Gen. A D Miller.[105] The required amount of capital expenditure was reached in 1921 and the land, together with small areas substituted or exchanged, was transferred to the PTR&D under a conveyance dated 10th January 1922. The PTR&D thus became the owner of all the land in the dock area not occupied by the late Miss Talbot's tenants, and of the O&SSR connecting the Old Dock and the New Dock. Also included were the twenty-five houses in Dock Street not far from No. 1 tip and Messrs D Jenkins & Sons' sawmills on Llewellyn Quay.

1914 ACT NEW LOCK AND EXTENSION OF BREAKWATERS

The approach to the lock was always under threat from shifting sand and the depth of the entrance channel had to be maintained by dredging and sluicing. The north and south breakwaters and the training wall protected the channel and helped

Port Talbot Docks, 10th May 1920. No. 4 tip and Nos 9 and 10 conveyors are on the near side of the dock, the extent of the latter shows up well. A PTR&D tug is moored in the old lock. The Docks Hotel is on the far left centre, with the R&SBR Docks station behind. The protruding Talbot Wharf Extension is prominent with the original wharf to its right. Further to the right is the massive No. 8 tip, the short North Bank Wharf and No. 6 tip. The R&SBR Seaside station can be made out in the left background, with the line heading towards Briton Ferry in the far distance. *Aerofilms*

Port Talbot Steelworks, with Mansel Tinplate Works to the left, the GWR main line behind and Nos 11 and 12 grids in front, 10th May 1921. Steelworks Wharf is to the lower right, connected to the railway leading round to Burrows Junction off to the left. The lines at the bottom right lead to Nos 5 and 6 tips on North Bank. *Aerofilms*

to maintain its integrity, and in January 1912 the directors called for plans to extend the breakwaters to make them more effective. William Grierson, the GWR's engineer, recommended that the PTR&D should approach the eminent dock and harbour engineer Sir William Matthews (1844–1922), who in turn desired Charles Meik to be involved. These two gentleman recommended in June 1912 that both breakwaters should be extended by about 1,000 feet and the training wall raised, but nothing further was done at this time. In view of the continued increase of traffic at the docks and with the new Margam Steelworks in prospect,[106] in January 1913 the directors further decided that a new lock was required. This lock, 750 feet long by 80 feet wide, was proposed to be constructed alongside and to the south of the existing lock and set at such an angle as to give a straight run to the end of the south breakwater. News of this scheme reached the Board of Trade which enquired as to under what Parliamentary powers the company proposed to extend the south breakwater and construct a new lock. This seemed to come as something of a surprise to the directors, who nevertheless in May 1913 called for work to go on pending any necessary powers being obtained. Matthews and Meik were asked to undertake responsibility for the works at 4 per cent commission. The initial estimate amounted to £459,627, made up as follows:

1,000-foot extension south breakwater	£120,530
new lock, 875 × 90 feet	£321,097
fees	£ 18,000

To which the engineers added a further £30,500 for a new suction hopper dredger, a centrifugal pump for maintaining the dock water level, and for deepening the channel. A scheme of this magnitude inevitably required an Act of Parliament and the Notice for a Bill for the 1914 Session of Parliament appeared in the 27th November 1913 issue of the *London Gazette*. By then the intended works had changed again and now included extending both breakwaters as well as constructing a new lock. Powers were also sought to exchange land with the R&SBR and to make more effective provisions for the prevention and punishment of trespass. The length of the extensions had been increased substantially and so had the cost. The Parliamentary Estimate amounted to £596,167:[107]

Work No. 1	600-yard westerly extension of the south breakwater	£230,224
Work No. 2	330-yard westerly extension of the north breakwater	£ 44,846
Work No. 3	A 350 yard long entrance lock	£321,097

A view of the lock, graving dock and No. 7 tip at what looks like high tide, taken in the 1920s.   *Author's collection*

This lock commenced at the west end of the existing dock and lay parallel to, and to the south of, the existing lock. It was planned with three pairs of gates, the inner two pairs approximately in line with the existing gates.

The directors were keen to start work on the south breakwater but, fearful of being made hostages to fortune, held back from letting the contract until after 27th February 1914, the last day for notices of objection to the Bill. None were forthcoming and the Bill passed through both Houses of Parliament with only minor amendments, the principal one being the deletion of the clause regarding the exchange of land with the R&SBR.[108] The resulting Act received the Royal Assent on 31st July 1914.[109]

Some preliminary work had already been done. The probable contractors for the lock, Messrs Topham, Jones & Railton, had been given a small contract in January 1914 to sink a trial shaft on its site and had reached a depth of 50 feet by April. The seabed site for the south breakwater extension was purchased from the Crown in February 1914 for £60 5s. But time had run out. War with Germany was declared on 4th August 1914 and on 17th September the directors took the inevitable step of deferring indefinitely the invitation of tenders for constructing these new works. Meik enquired in January 1919 about re-entering into contracts, but nothing could be done at the time due to government restrictions. Meik then claimed £3,000 for fees and out-of-pocket expenses, and in February 1921 settled for £4,500 which included the detailed plans he had prepared.

PROPOSED PUMPING PLANT

The dock level was maintained by the River Ffrwdwyllt, which flowed directly in, and by water diverted from the River Avon via a feeder channel near the Mansel Tinplate Works where the flow was held back by a weir. At times of severe drought both these sources were likely to fail, a situation which could also affect the supply of fresh water for hydraulic pumping purposes. Dock water had to be used for this purpose in September 1919.[110] The company's suction dredger *Nereus* was used to pump water from the lock to the dock in the summer of 1918[111] and in August 1921 the Port Talbot Graving Dock Co. was paid £257 for pumping water for eight tides because of a drought. Plans for a pumping plant to improve locking, docking and sluicing were prepared in March 1920,[112] for which the tender of Messrs Gwynnes Ltd (£42,180) was the lowest.[113] Subsequently this company quoted £11,930 for a single 60-inch pump and £13,450 for two 42-inch pumps, the latter being preferred to allow for breakdowns.[114] Consideration of the tenders was postponed, however in January 1922 there was a breach in the north breakwater which resulted in increased siltation in the entrance channel; this would normally have been cleared by sluicing with dock water, and re-emphasised the need for a sufficient water level to be maintained. The directors resolved to lay before the GWR their engineer's plan for a pumping plant with a recommendation for adoption, but nothing was done in this regard.

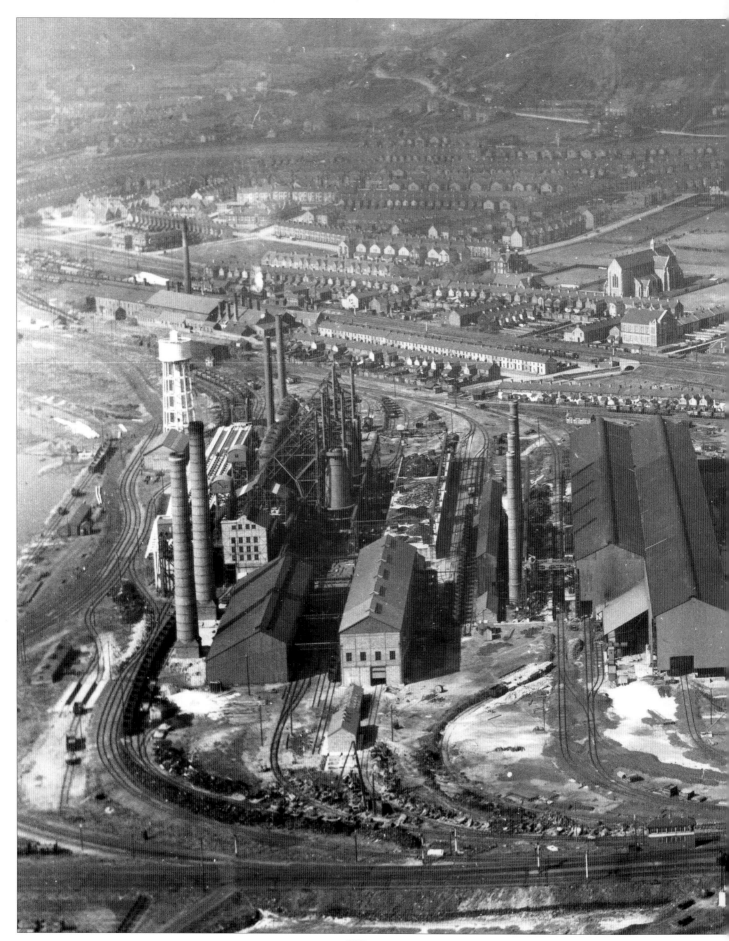

Margam Steelworks, with a Cardiff-bound express on the GWR main line behind, 10th May 1921. Prominent in front of the steelworks is the 1915 signal box for Copper Works Junction which had been remodelled in conjunction with the construction of the new West Curve to the GWR main line. The Dock Branch from Duffryn Junction can be discerned on the falling gradient to the right of the view. The end of No. 6 grid is visible at the bottom left. At this date no ore unloading facilities had been erected on Margam Wharf, nor had the kink in the O&SSR through this area been removed. Iron ore was imported at Steelworks Wharf or brought in by rail from Oxfordshire. *Aerofilms*

NOTES

1. TNA: PRO RAIL 1057/1531.
2. *The Times*, 3 August 1896.
3. JA Spender, *Weetman Pearson, First Viscount Cowdray, 1856–1927* (Cassell & Co. 1930).
4. Listed in *Slater's Directory of South Wales, 1859*.
5. TNA: PRO BT 31/6176/43743.
6. TNA: PRO RAIL 574/75.
7. TNA: PRO RAIL 1057/1059.
8. TNA: PRO RAIL 1057/1530/6.
9. *Railway Times*, 20 August 1898.
10. TNA: PRO RAIL 1057/1529/31.
11. TNA: PRO RAIL 1057/2619.
12. SML PEA 4/2.
13. SML PEA 4/3.
14. *Railway News*, 20 February 1897.
15. *Railway Times*, 7 August 1897.
16. TNA: PRO RAIL 1057/1531.
17. *Railway News*, 19 February 1898; see also Chapter 14.
18. *Railway Times*, 6 August 1898.
19. *Railway Times*, 20 August 1898.
20. Arthur Rees, 'The Port Talbot Railway & Docks Company', *South West Wales Industrial Archaeology Society Bulletin*, No. 42 (1986).
21. TNA: PRO RAIL 1057/1531.
22. TNA: PRO RAIL 1057/1530/6.
23. TNA: PRO RAIL 574/74.
24. TNA: PRO RAIL 1057/2472.
25. TNA: PRO RAIL 1057/1531.
26. *Railway Times*, 4 February 1899.
27. *Railway News*, 18 February 1899.
28. TNA: PRO RAIL 1057/1531.
29. TNA: PRO RAIL 1057/2555.
30. TNA: PRO RAIL 581/5.
31. *Railway Times*, 19 August 1899.
32. Spender, *Weetman Pearson*, pp. 140–41.
33. *Railway Times*, 24 February 1900.
34. TNA: PRO RAIL 1057/1531.
35. SML PEA 4/8.
36. TNA: PRO RAIL 1057/1531.
37. See Chapter 17.
38. TNA: PRO RAIL 1057/1531.
39. TNA: PRO RAIL 574/76.
40. See Chapter 17.
41. *Railway News*, 2 March 1901.
42. TNA: PRO RAIL 1057/2574.
43. John Vivian Hughes, 'Emily Charlotte Talbot (1840–1918)', *Trans. Port Talbot Historical Society*, II/3 (1974), p. 91.
44. *Railway Times*, 25 August 1900.
45. TNA: PRO RAIL 1057/1529/54.
46. TNA: PRO RAIL 1057/1528/65.
47. TNA: PRO RAIL 1057/1531.
48. TNA: PRO RAIL 1057/1529/71.
49. TNA: PRO RAIL 1057/1529/80.
50. TNA: PRO RAIL 1057/1529/43.
51. TNA: PRO RAIL 1057/1529/46.
52. Cleaver, 'Alterations and Improvements', pp. 104–5.
53. TNA: PRO RAIL 1057/1529/48.
54. TNA: PRO RAIL 581/13.
55. TNA: PRO RAIL 1057/1529/52.
56. TNA: PRO RAIL 1057/1529/55.
57. TNA: PRO RAIL 1057/1529/56.
58. TNA: PRO RAIL 1057/1528/73.
59. See Volume 1, Chapter 2.
60. *Railway Times*, 20 July 1895.
61. TNA: PRO RAIL 1057/1530/6.
62. *Railway News*, 4 September 1897.
63. See Chapter 12.
64. See Volume 1, Chapter 1.
65. See Volume 1, Chapter 2.
66. TNA: PRO RAIL 1057/2528.
67. Martin Phillips, *The Copper Industry in the Port Talbot District* (Guardian Press 1935), pp. 35–6.
68. See Volume 1, Chapter 2.
69. SML PEA 4/6.
70. See Volume 1, Chapter 1.
71. *Railway Times*, 18 January 1896.
72. *Railway Times*, 1 February 1896.
73. *Railway Times*, 22 August 1896.
74. TNA: PRO RAIL 581/4.
75. TNA: PRO RAIL 581/10.
76. See Volume 1, Chapter 5.
77. *Railway Times*, 19 February 1898.
78. TNA: PRO RAIL 581/12.
79. TNA: PRO RAIL 581/5.
80. TNA: PRO RAIL 581/12.
81. TNA: PRO RAIL 1057/1529/34.
82. TNA: PRO RAIL 1057/1529/44.
83. Cleaver, 'Alterations and Improvements', pp. 110–11.
84. Malcolm J Hill, 'L G Mouchel', unpublished manuscript.
85. TNA: PRO RAIL 1057/1528/94.
86. TNA: PRO RAIL 1057/1528/95.
87. TNA: PRO RAIL 1057/1528/102.
88. TNA: PRO RAIL 1057/1528/103.
89. TNA: PRO RAIL 1057/1528/118.
90. TNA: PRO RAIL 1057/1528/124.
91. TNA: PRO RAIL 1057/2616.
92. TNA: PRO RAIL 1057/1528/165.
93. TNA: PRO RAIL 1057/1528/194.
94. TNA: PRO RAIL 1057/1528/193.
95. TNA: PRO RAIL 1057/1528/197.
96. TNA: PRO RAIL 1057/1528/221.
97. TNA: PRO RAIL 1057/1528/229.
98. TNA: PRO RAIL 1057/2620.
99. TNA: PRO RAIL 1057/2653.
100. TNA: PRO RAIL 574/102.
101. TNA: PRO RAIL 1057/2473.
102. TNA: PRO RAIL 253/757; RAIL 1057/2952.
103. See Chapter 13.
104. Hughes, 'Emily Charlotte Talbot', p. 94; *Railway News*, 28 September 1918.
105. TNA: PRO RAIL 253/757.
106. See Chapter 14.
107. PA HL/PO/PB/3/plan1914/P3.
108. TNA: PRO MT 10/1706.
109. 4 & 5 Geo. 5 c.xcix.
110. TNA: PRO RAIL 1057/1528/236.
111. TNA: PRO RAIL 1057/1528/228.
112. TNA: PRO RAIL 1057/1528/240.
113. TNA: PRO RAIL 1057/1528/243.
114. TNA: PRO RAIL 1057/1528/245.

13

Dock Facilities

RAILWAYS: OLD DOCK

Prior to 1894 the railways in the dock area were rather sparse. A branch ran from Old Dock Junction on the GWR South Wales main line to the North Bank area,[1] the Oakwood Railway on Llewellyn's Quay was moribund,[2] while the R&SBR had rebuilt the Cwmavon Railway into the Talbot Wharf area and opened its rather basic Docks station near the old lock in 1891. The rails to the English Copper Co.'s wharves were derelict. J David, the R&SBR's traffic manager, informed a House of Lords Select Committee in May 1896 that his company's lines at Port Talbot Dock consisted of one siding, an extension of the main line, and a run round loop. All traffic, which was shipment only, was handled on the PTR&D's lines by the Port Talbot company, the Rhondda company having no staithes or tips of its own.[3] In August 1895 the directors asked for plans to be prepared and tenders sought for a railway between Talbot Wharf and North Bank. The proposed line did not directly

achieve this, but instead left the existing Dock Branch from Old Dock Junction with the GWR near to where it crossed the Oakwood Railway, it then passed through the land occupied by the Mansel Tinplate Works under an agreement with Messrs R B Byass & Co., skirted round the north-west end of the Old Dock and ran parallel to the R&SBR to reach Talbot Wharf. North Bank was reached by a connection to the branch off the former Cwmavon Railway which led there. The contractor for the scheme, which included sidings for the new No. 6 tip being erected on North Bank, was T W Davies who tendered £10,157. The works included siding connections to the Taibach Tinplate Works and the Ffrwdwyllt Tinplate Works (which were adjacent to Old Dock Junction) to permit direct rail access to the docks, and also a line constructed at Miss Talbot's expense connecting the two works.[4] A loop was added to the connection to the Taibach works in November 1896. The roads to Nos 5 and 6 tips on North Bank were raised in 1900 so that wagons could gravitate to the turntables, thereby saving locomotive power. Much later, in

Looking across North Bank towards Port Talbot circa 1904. The GWR station, although not clearly visible, is in the centre of the view. The North's Navigation Collieries wagons in the foreground are on the sidings serving North Bank Wharf off to the left. Those belonging to Cory Brothers in the next row are for No. 6 tip off to the right. The distant row of wagons marks the line of the Old Dock Branch, later the site of the Steelworks Wharf. The defunct works of the Port Talbot Iron & Steel Co. are in the left background. *Author's collection*

315

1916, a siding connection was put in on the line to Talbot Wharf to give access to the Gloucester Railway Carriage & Wagon Co.'s new wagon repair works on a site south of Mansel Tinplate Works.[5] These works became part of the Wagon Repairs Ltd empire in 1925.

For several years little was done to improve the railways on North Bank, but during 1906 a loop was brought into use near the connections to the roads leading to Nos 5 and 6 tips to facilitate their working.[6] A portion of line leading to North Bank was doubled in 1907 so that the Port Talbot Steel Co. could do its shunting without fouling the main line.[7] Also in 1907 construction was started of what was known as Old Dock grid on land towards the inner end of North Bank.[8] The five loop sidings were completed in January 1908,[9] and were intended to serve the forthcoming No. 8 tip. Tip No. 5 on North Bank was the oldest in the dock and by 1908 the permanent way had deteriorated to such an extent as to require immediate renewal.[10] New jetty framing and turntables with revised full and empty roads for Nos 5 and 6 tips were provided in 1916/17.[11] The curves on North Bank were eased in 1912 so that GWR Macaw B rail wagons could use the short wharf there.[12]

OAKWOOD & SOUTH SIDE RAILWAY

A railway connecting the north and south sides of the dock would be a necessity at some time in the future and powers for such a line were included in the 1894 Act. In August 1896 Meik, the engineer, proposed a line through Messrs Vivian's Margam works[13] which would connect them with Talbot Wharf and North Bank and give a connection between both sides of the dock without the need to go all the way round by Duffryn Yard and over the R&SBR or the Oakwood Railway. The cost, excluding land, was estimated to be £11,000.[14] This idea was considered at the Board meeting on 19th August 1896, but was deferred indefinitely, the New Dock being nowhere near completed.

The moribund Oakwood Railway would be part of such a scheme and in April 1897 the directors agreed to Miss Talbot relaying this line, provided the PTR&D had exclusive benefit of traffic over it. However, Mr T M Franklen, Miss Talbot's advisor, could not agree to this proposal, possibly because the dispute with the GWR over the use of Oakwood Crossing had not, at the time, been resolved. Consequently, at their meeting on 15th June 1897, the directors decided to provide their own line as a substitute.

The scheme was revived in February 1899 when the directors called for plans to be prepared for a railway around the dock. On 15th March the tender of Messrs J Clarke of £4,429 for a railway from a crossing and junction with the Oakwood Railway to Copper Works signal box was accepted. The line was to be signalled and worked from the existing box which was to be moved to a suitable position. By the following month this new line, which was just under one mile in length, had acquired the somewhat grandiose title of the Oakwood & South Side Railway (O&SSR). The directors noted at their meeting on 19th April that Miss Talbot would pay for the construction of the railway where it crossed her property, the PTR&D paying her interest on the capital expended at the same rate as paid on its ordinary shares. The plan was modified slightly in that the line was to be carried over the cut to Margam Copper Works[15] by a movable bridge rather than the embankment originally intended. Miss Talbot offered to pay not more than £3,000 for the bridge and agreed to surrender all rights of dock and wharfage dues.

The route of line was altered slightly to avoid the need to move Copper Works Junction signal box. Although good progress was made with the construction of the line, the contract was delayed by problems with the bridge.

The engineer reported at the Board meeting on 24th January 1900 that the O&SSR was open and in use. However, due to what must have been an oversight, the bridge had not been designed to take the heaviest locomotives then in service, the 0-6-2 tank engines that had been ordered in 1896.[16] Meik was instructed to prepare a plan for replacing the bridge with one able to take this class and at the February meeting he proposed three schemes:

1. Additional piles under both ends, cost £150.
2. Replacing the existing girders with stronger ones of the same span, 43 feet, cost £300.
3. Replacing the present bridge with a hydraulic swing bridge, cost £4,000.

The second option was decided on, the matter having become urgent. The company's secretary noted in March 1900 that traffic was extremely disorganised because only small engines could run over the existing bridge.[17] There was some delay in delivering the new girders, but in June 1900 the tender of the contractors for the O&SSR to erect the bridge for £355 was accepted. In April 1901 the new bridge was reported to be in position and was capable of carrying all the company's engines except the American 0-8-2 type which had been ordered in 1899.[18] This situation was rectified by placing piles under the bridge, on the understanding that they could be withdrawn at Miss Talbot's request so as to maintain the agreed 45 feet wide passage. The strengthening was completed by June 1901,[19] but had to be further increased in 1903 to permit the even heavier Sharp, Stewart locomotives to pass over.

The PTR&D was granted a perpetual easement over the O&SSR, the wayleave agreement being signed and sealed at the Board meeting held on 21st March 1900. The cost of constructing this line and the bridge, together with some ancillary works on the Oakwood Railway and Llewellyn's Quay, amounted to just over £6,417.[20] The wayleaves, at 2d or 5d per ton depending on the class of goods, were to be applied to:

1. Maintaining Miss Talbot's railways and all signals and junctions, and making any improvements and additions.
2. Paying £175 to Miss Talbot each six months during which the company would benefit from copper ore traffic from the docks to Rio Tinto Co.
3. Paying interest on the sum of £6,417 to Miss Talbot at the same rate as the dividend paid on the ordinary shares of the company.
4. Repaying Miss Talbot the money spent by her in attracting traffic to the docks or railways.
5. Repaying excess charges to Miss Talbot or her tenants.[21]

Although the O&SSR saw an increasing amount of traffic over the years, it was not until April 1914 that work commenced on doubling the single line.[22] The work was finished in March 1915,[23] as the same time as extensive reworking of the Copper Works Junction area was completed.

PTR No. 27 at Burrows Junction. Behind the engine can be seen the signalling platform erected in 1913 to enable shunters to more effectively control PTR and R&SBR trains in the vicinity. Also visible is the water crane provided there to replenish engines shunting North Bank and Talbot Wharf in the Old Dock and so obviate a lengthy trip to Duffryn Yard. *Author's collection*

BURROWS JUNCTION EXCHANGE SIDINGS

The PTR and R&SBR engineers produced plans for sidings for exchanging traffic between the two railways; these were approved by the Port Talbot directors on 16th May 1900, adding that Hosgood would carry out the work. The R&SBR, however, delayed matters[24] and on 19th June Mr Watson reported to the PTR&D Board that the Rhonda directors had amended the tentative agreement by adding that the running powers for the PTR would be five years initially, and that the perpetual easement over the their land for junctions between the PTR and the sidings would be £5 per annum. In addition, these junctions were not to be used by the PTR for access to the north side of the New Dock by traffic for which there was competition between the companies – except that traffic to and from places served by the PTR should not be considered as competitive. The directors approved these changes and ordered a draft agreement to be prepared.

Work started straight away and Hosgood reported in October 1900 that the ground for the exchange sidings, which was situated near Burrows Junction between the respective running lines to Talbot Wharf and the Docks station, had been prepared and was ready for the permanent way. The PTR&D agreed to purchase the necessary land from the R&SBR for £1,500, this amount being set against the agreed price for the sale of two locomotives to the latter.[25] The plans for the sidings were amended several times and it was not until May 1902 that a draft agreement was ready for

consideration by a committee of R&SBR directors, the only point outstanding being access to the Docks station.[26] The agreement was signed and sealed on 18th June 1902. The Port Talbot directors stipulated that no new materials were to be used for the sidings, and that the particulars were to be approved by the Board.

Although most of the work was beyond the remit of the Board of Trade, the R&SBR sought the Board's approval in June 1902 to put in two connections on its Dock Branch.[27] One was for a dead-end siding to be worked from Burrows Junction signal box. The other, much more important from the PTR&D's point of view, was for a crossover from its Talbot Wharf line to the R&SBR's Docks station line. It was situated adjacent to the existing siding connection on the R&SBR to No. 7 tip and the graving dock. The new crossover, which was worked from the existing graving dock ground frame, allowed access to and from the western end of the exchange sidings and gave the PTR a far more convenient route to this tip. Hitherto the tip had been reached via Aberavon and running powers over the R&SBR, and this may account for Hosgood's comment in May 1901 that this tip had not seen much use.[28] Both companies could enter the exchange sidings at the eastern end. In addition, the PTR's running line was moved so that it skirted round the exchange sidings on the south-east side. Hosgood reported in August 1902 that the work had started[29] and that completion was expected by the end of December,[30] although inspection did not take place until August 1903. A modified agreement for the exchange of land, the

Looking north along Margam Wharf, September 1926. The O&SSR is seen on its 1918 realignment, curving round to Copper Works Junction off to the right. This curve was removed in 1948 and replaced by a double-line connection to No. 1 grid off to the left. Margam Steelworks' two blast furnaces are visible on the right.

NM&GW

Mansel Tinplate Works is in the centre of this view circa 1930, with Port Talbot Steelworks to the right. The GWR main line runs from left to right behind the steelworks and crosses the R&SBR on the level just above the tinplate works. The R&SBR follows the River Avon down the view and turns towards Briton Ferry, crossing the river at the bottom left-hand corner. Just to the right is the culvert carrying the dock feeder under the tracks to enter the Old Dock off the bottom of the view. Above the culvert is Burrows Junction signal box which controlled movements into the Talbot Wharf area of the docks. The trackbed of the former direct connection from the R&SBR to North Bank can be seen, with the works of Wagon Repairs Ltd to its right. *Author's collection*

construction of sidings and the working arrangements was sealed on 25th March 1903 and scheduled to the PTR&D's 1903 Act.[31] In September 1903 the PTR&D paid the R&SBR a total of £1,983 for the land and expenses associated with the sidings. Additional loops for the exchange of traffic were provided in 1905, so that there was now a total of six, with four of them laid on land conveyed to the R&SBR.[32] The bridge over the dock feeder channel at Burrows Junction was strengthened in 1906 to enable the company's largest engines to cross.[33]

The question of providing additional exchange siding accommodation at Burrows Junction was first raised with the R&SBR in February 1907. It was not until July 1910, however, that a plan was produced showing a running road and a nest of sidings with a capacity of about 940 wagons to be situated between the Mansel Tinplate works and the North Bank railway. Apart from the division of cost, this scheme was agreed by both companies, but as it concerned the R&SBR the approval of the GWR was required. Although the plan was approved by its officers on 28th April 1911,[34] sanction by the GW/R&SB Consultation Committee of Directors was not forthcoming and the proposal in this form foundered. Nevertheless, the PTR laid in two large storage grids on the proposed site. These sidings were arranged in groups of eight, known as Nos 11 and 12 grids, and had a total capacity of 930 wagons. Direct access was possible from the O&SSR and from the GWR at Old Dock Junction, but not from the R&SBR. Work started in February 1912,[35] and both grids were brought into use in November that year.[36] A signalling platform was provided at Burrows Junction in 1913 so as to properly signal drivers of R&SBR and PTR trains when propelling towards the junction, the cost being divided equally between the two companies. The alignment of the existing sidings was improved in November 1914 so that PTR and R&SBR heavy engines could run on all roads.[37] At the same time the bridge over the dock feeder was rebuilt and the adjacent junction relaid. The directors recognised in December 1914 that the new works at Aberavon authorised by the GWR's 1914 Act[38] meant that the contemplated sidings at Burrows Junction would have to be revised; they suggested that the R&SBR should site theirs west of the bridge over the River Avon, with the PTR's

sidings on the east. Nothing could be done in this regard during the First World War and it was not until May 1920 that a plan – made in February 1915 – was approved by the three companies involved. The economic conditions of the time and the prospect of the grouping meant that it was not pursued.

RAILWAYS: NEW DOCK

The railway from Duffryn Junction to Copper Works Junction, where a connection was made with the line from Margam Junction, was conceived as a single line and for most of its length remained so throughout its existence. The railway from Copper Works Junction to the end of Railway No. 1 authorised by the 1894 Act, a distance of about three-quarters of a mile, was planned from the outset as a double line.

The dock railways serving the tips on the south side of the New Dock commenced at the termination of Railway No. 1. In the first phase of the dock development two sets of storage loops, grids Nos 1 and 4,[39] each initially having four roads, were constructed to the north of the main line. In December 1897 the directors sanctioned a further set of storage loops, grid No. 3, on the approach to the three new tips, Nos 1, 2 and 3. The lines leading to these tips were arranged so that loaded wagons were led by gravity down a gradient of about 1 in 100 to the weighbridges and turntables; when empty they returned over separate weighbridges down gradients of between 1 in 53 and 1 in 200 to a low-level line before being removed by locomotives.[40] The gravity system was evidently inadequate for the purpose and in June 1900 – on the recommendation of Lowther, the new traffic manager – the tip roads on the south side of the dock were raised to allow wagons to run the whole length of the sidings,[41] a task which took three months to complete.[42]

The low-level roads from Nos 1–3 tips were seriously flooded in December 1906[43] and over 11 million gallons of water had to be pumped out.[44] The south side dock drains were relaid by Barnes, Chaplin & Co. at a cost of £1,990, the work being completed in February 1908.[45]

Grid No. 1, which was mainly intended for empty wagons, was found to be too short by December 1899, and by June 1900 an

The New Dock grids, May 1928. The wagons in the foreground are loads for No. 10 conveyor. Behind is the ramp for No. 11 conveyor, loads for which can be seen behind the water tank conveniently placed for replenishing dock engines. Empties from this tip returned at a lower level to join No. 1 grid seen in the middle distance to the left of the four running lines. No. 5 grid, GWR numbering, is the nearest beyond the running lines, with Nos 6 and 7 in the distance. Interestingly, all the identifiable wagons belong to anthracite producers operating in the coalfield to the north and west of Swansea. The background of this view is now occupied by the Abbey Steelworks.

NM&GW

extension was in hand, a task completed by the following November. A loop round this grid was completed in September 1905.[46]

The position of the new No. 7 tip was somewhat anomalous. Although situated in the New Dock, it was reached by a siding connection off the R&SBR near the Docks station. Despite this being a passenger carrying line, there is no record of the connection being inspected and it may have already been in existence when the line was inspected and sanctioned by the Board of Trade in August 1891.[47] Little extra siding provision was made in this part of the dock, No. 7 tip being limited to an additional line of rails laid down in 1904 to facilitate the efficient mixing of coal. A 10,000-gallon, later increased to 17,250 gallons, water tank for engines was erected near the western end of No. 1 grid.

In July 1898 Probert, the general manger, noted that there was no provision for signalling beyond Copper Works Junction, and that it was proposed to work the line to the end of Railway No. 1 and the dock railways beyond by hand-points.[48] He considered it essential to have a signal box at the neck of No. 4 grid and another at the junction between Nos 3 and 4 grids, this arrangement being cheaper than employing pointsmen. Meik suggested that before proceeding with this idea a visit should be made to the North-East of England to see how traffic was worked there. It is not known whether this visit took place, but the directors decided in October 1898 – when the New Dock opened on a restricted basis – that grids 3 and 4 were to be worked without signals experimentally for six months. Furthermore, on no account was the GWR to be given a hint that the PTR&D wished to relieve them from bringing traffic by their own engines right up to the tips in question. By this time there were already about 15 miles of railways and sidings around the new and old docks.[49]

Grids Nos 1, 3 and 4 sufficed until December 1904, when the directors decided that No. 2 grid was to be laid down at an estimated cost of £4,500. This set of eight long sidings was positioned between No. 4 grid and the planned approach roads to the recently authorised tip No. 4, and was completed and in use by October 1905.[50] Also in December 1904 the directors authorised the construction of sidings at the seaward end of the grids so that shunting could be carried out clear of the running lines.

GRIDS POST 1907

One consequence of the 1908 running powers agreement with the GWR was increased coal traffic to the south side of the docks destined for shipment at tips 1–4. Although a tentative plan for an additional shunting grid was produced in January 1908, nothing was done until the following November when the general manager pointed out the proportionately small amount of siding accommodation provided by the GWR at Port Talbot compared to Swansea. Lowther was instructed to attempt induce the GWR to increase its storage capacity between Margam Junction and the New Dock, the PTR&D being prepared to provide the necessary land and to put in one grid near the commencement of Railway No. 1 at the south end of the dock. This request was repeated in April 1909, but it was not until November 1910 that the matter was formally considered by the Consultation Committee.[51] In the meantime, on 9th August 1910 the GW/PT Officers' Conference had decided on the provision of additional sidings and other works at the docks as part of a number of improvements designed to

alleviate the considerable delays that had arisen in working traffic between Port Talbot and Tondu. The initial estimate for this scheme, which provided for storage of almost 2,200 wagons, amounted to £58,384, made up as follows:

New Military Road, replacement for existing*	£ 7,000
Additional double line between Copper Works Junction and dock head	£ 8,500
Doubling a short portion of Duffryn line	£ 800
No. 6 reception sidings for loaded wagons (720 wagons)	£14,070
No. 7 reception sidings for loaded wagons (480 wagons)	£11,108
No. 8 reception sidings for loaded wagons (480 wagons)	£ 9,256
Sorting sidings for empty wagons (500 wagons)	£ 6,500
New signal cabin Copper Works Junction	£ 750
Huts, telephone, lighting	£ 400
* a road which ran alongside the southern perimeter of the docks and served Dock Street cottages on Morfa Newydd (see below).	

The Consultation Committee approved this scheme, the cost being apportioned 25 per cent to the GWR, 25 per cent to the PTR&D railway undertaking, and 50 per cent to the PTR&D docks undertaking. Some saving was effected by using secondhand GWR rails in lieu of new for the sidings. These works were timely as by January 1911 the directors of the PTR&D were seriously considering the erection of the first of what turned out to be three belt conveyors for coal shipments.

The empty wagon grid, No. 5, on Morfa Newydd at the southern end of the Dock Branch, consisting of two groups each of seven sidings, was commenced in February 1911[52] and brought fully into use in June 1912.[53] Of the reception sidings, the twelve roads of No. 7 grid were constructed first and were ready for traffic in February 1912.[54] Construction of No. 8 grid commenced in July 1912[55] and was completed in February 1913.[56] This grid was atypical in that the eight sidings were bisected by a through road running off the ladder of No. 7 grid. Work started on the twelve sidings of the largest grid, No. 6 at the Copper Works Junction end of the dock railway, in December 1913[57] and was completed in September 1914.[58] Interspersed with all this siding construction was the quadrupling of the one mile long Dock Branch from Copper Works Junction to its terminus. This work was well in hand by December 1911[59] – one additional line being ready in February 1912[60] and the second the following July.[61]

Further work in the New Dock at this time included altering the approaches to No. 3 grid[62] and providing new junctions for the extended Crown Preserved Fuel Works[63] which were brought into use in September 1913.[64]

DOCK MACHINERY

HYDRAULIC PLANT

The hydraulic engine house on North Bank was of insufficient capacity and in the wrong place to provide power for the New Dock. In April 1896 Meik submitted to the directors a plan for a new power plant consisting of two pairs of pumping engines and two Lancashire boilers; these were to work the four new tips, two 5-ton capstans and the lock gate machinery associated with the New Dock.[65] In August 1896 the engineer presented tenders for the necessary work broken down into four categories: engines, boilers, hoists and capstans, and pipework. A total of twelve engineering companies submitted tenders, although only two, Sir W G Armstrong & Co. and the Hydraulic Engineering Co., were prepared to undertake all the work.[66] Meik emphasised that as the work was interdependent it should be placed in as few hands as possible. The directors accepted Messrs Armstrong's tender at a combined price of £22,000, later increased to £23,000, the work to be completed by February 1898.[67] The hydraulic engine house was to be erected on spare ground to the east of the New Dock. Initially work was carried out in the open, but in March 1897 Messrs W H Allen & Co.'s tender of £2,429 for construction of the engine house was accepted. Armstrong's contract was another that overran, the PTR&D not taking over the machinery until 1st November 1898, although No. 1 tip was not reported to be ready until 15th February 1899. Tips Nos 1–3 were constructed on the south side of the New Dock, and No. 7 on the north side.

In January 1901 Hosgood, the resident engineer, raised the question of increasing the hydraulic pumping plant at the New Dock as the existing pumps were occasionally overwhelmed.[68] Since installation they had been required to meet the additional demands of four 2-ton hydraulic cranes on Talbot Wharf, two more 5-ton capstans, three 1-ton capstans and the graving dock sluices, and to provide steam for the dock electric light installation. The existing plant could not cope with increased traffic that was hoped for, or with a serious breakdown. Hosgood requested instructions to invite tenders for an additional pair of engines and one boiler. A delay of nine to twelve months was expected owing engineering firms having full order books. This matter was considered by the directors on 23rd

January, but action was deferred until the output of the existing plant had been ascertained. It transpired that the real shortcoming was in boiler capacity. At their meeting in February 1901 the Board resolved that tenders for one additional boiler should be sought. The following month they accepted the tender of J Thompson of Wolverhampton for £350 including all accessories. The new boiler was in use by 12th October 1901 and considerably reduced the demands on the existing installation.[69] The directors also decided to ascertain that sufficient water was available from the Cwm Brombil reservoir for hydraulic purposes if required, and to connect the hydraulic mains of North Bank with those of the New Dock.

By May 1904 the hydraulic plant was again working to capacity.[70] The following month the directors accepted the tender of Messrs Tannett Walker & Co. for an engine of double the capacity. Although the new engine was delivered in December 1904, it was a full year before it was reported to be running satisfactorily.[71] In March 1906 Albert Hertz, the mechanical engineer, suggested that it was desirable to erect a new hydraulic accumulator between Nos 2 and 3 tips to provide additional power storage for new cranes, capstans and tips.[72] Armstrong, Whitworth's tender, although higher than Tannett Walker's, was accepted as their parts were interchangeable with existing plant, and the new accumulator was in use by January 1907.[73]

New Hydraulic Power House

The general manager reported to the Board in November 1908 that once again the existing hydraulic plant was being worked to its limit; additional plant was therefor required to cope with the forthcoming No. 8 tip and any increase in traffic. The following March the directors were informed that the existing South Side hydraulic house was inconveniently situated for any extension of the hydraulic and electric plant, and a site near Nos 2 and 3 tips was suggested. There was a not inconsiderable expense element to this

RIGHT: The new electrical power house, showing its rather utilitarian construction, erected near Copper Works Junction in 1914.
From Port Talbot and its Progress, *PTR&D Co. 1919, Author's collection*

LEFT: The new hydraulic power house erected between No. 2 tip (off to the right) and No. 3 tip (behind the photographer) during 1910–11. The new accumulator is prominent in front of the engine house.
From Port Talbot and its Progress, *PTR&D Co. 1919, Author's collection*

move. Extending the existing building was estimated to cost £4,349, whereas a new engine house amounted to an estimated £8,387, both figures excluding new plant. Nevertheless, the directors at their June 1909 meeting decided on a new building to house the existing and any new hydraulic and electric plant.

The original engine house was a substantial brick-built structure. In the interests of economy the new building consisted of a light steel roof covered with matchboard and felt resting on rolled steel stanchions.[74] The walls between the stanchions consisted of hollow concrete blocks. The structural steelwork was supplied and erected by Messrs Walker Bros of Walsall for £840,[75] the rest of the building being constructed by the PTR&D's Engineering Department. The new hydraulic engine, specified as being capable of delivering 900 gallons per minute at 750 psi, was made by Messrs Tannett Walker & Co. at a tender price of £5,155[76] and delivered in May 1910.[77] Four of the original Lancashire boilers were moved to the new power house. The tender of Messrs J Thomson for the supply of three additional boilers – 30 feet long by 8 feet 6 inches diameter and working at 120 psi – for £461 each was accepted in September 1909, but for an unstated reason was replaced the following month with a contract with Messrs E Danks & Co. for three boilers at £390 each. All this plant was set in place and connected up by the PTR&D's Engineering Department. A conventional natural draught chimney would have required substantial foundations, so to avoid this expense the new power house was equipped with an induced draught plant supplied and installed by the Sturtevant Engineering Co. for £540. To complete the new power station, the tender of Messrs Tannett Walker & Co. of £1,040 for an additional hydraulic accumulator was accepted in November 1909. It took some time to get the new hydraulic engine working satisfactorily and it was not working regularly until 1st November 1911.[78]

Removal of the original hydraulic engines from the old to the new power house was also done by the company's men, starting in July 1911. All the machinery had been moved by June 1912,[79] and after overhaul was placed back in service. Four old boilers were also moved[80] and all the old engines were working again by December 1912.[81] The carpenters, electricians and blacksmiths, all concerned with maintaining the docks machinery and equipment, moved in November 1911. The old engine house and accumulator tower were demolished by blasting[82] and some 5,000 tons of brickwork and concrete removed, the task being completed by June 1912.[83]

The existing electric plant in the South Side power house had been installed to provide lighting for the dock area. The lighting had been gradually extended over the years and in January 1909 the tender of Messrs Crompton & Co. of £1,050 for additional generating plant was accepted. This was installed in the new power house and provided all electric light as from 21st July 1911.[84] The old electric engines and dynamos were sent away for overhaul[85] and were re-erected in the new engine house by January 1912.[86] Condensing plant was installed on all the electric engines in order to effect a 20 per cent economy in working.[87]

Plans to connect the hydraulic mains on North Bank to those in the New Dock were first considered by the directors in April 1905. The subject was raised again in March and May 1906 when a scheme to lay new mains across the dock and close the North Bank engine house was proposed. The estimated cost of £1,215 was calculated to save £220 per annum in wages alone. Again, nothing

was done, but in May 1907 Hertz proposed an alternative scheme, taking the connections round the west end of the Old Dock.[88] Although more expensive than the direct route, this plan was much safer and more reliable, and was approved by the directors in June 1907, to be carried out as and when necessary. The work was done piecemeal; relaying the hydraulic mains on North Bank commenced in June 1908[89] and was completed there and on Talbot Wharf in October 1908.[90] The mains were carried round the end of the Old Dock on a piled timber trestle which was finished in November 1909.[91] This 1,500-yard stretch was brought into use on 28th May 1910 enabling the North Bank tips and cranes to be worked from the South Side hydraulic house.[92] This was timely, as the North Bank hydraulic engine had just broken down after sixteen years of continuous service. The North Bank engine was overhauled and put back into use on 30th June and worked well in conjunction with the new South Side engine.[93] The circuit was completed by a submerged hydraulic main between North Bank and Talbot Wharf which was brought into use on 15th June 1910.[94] Although this section was damaged in July 1911, plans to replace it with an extension right round the east end of the dock were not pursued. In conjunction with this work, an additional hydraulic accumulator, again supplied by Messrs Armstrong, Whitworth, was erected on North Bank and was brought into use in September 1908.[95]

OLD POWER STATION SITE

The decision to erect the new hydraulic engine house on the South Side of the New Dock and to move the existing plant there liberated a useful area of land on which additional tips could be constructed. The directors resolved in March 1911 to have most of the protruding land on which the old engine house used to stand dredged away so as form a straight dockside, consequently substantially widening the channel between the Old Dock and New Docks east of the old lock. The tender of £16,435 18s 3d submitted by Messrs Perry & Co.[96] was accepted on 17th May 1911. This was a significant project and the contract allowed thirty-six weeks for completion. Messrs Perry employed a Lübecker land dredger for this job,[97] which started operation in November 1911, eventually working twenty-four hours a day.[98] The spoil was taken a short distance by rail and deposited on muddy ground above the high water mark to the east of the Crown Preserved Coal Co.'s works to create more usable land. Messrs Perry seriously underestimated the time required for this task, the work with the land dredger not being completed until March 1913, an overrun of one year.[99] The Lübecker machine was unable to remove all the silt, and this work was done by the PTR&D's dredger *Bollin* at Messrs Perry's expense, they being charged £661 17s 6d to remove 17,650 cubic yards.[100] Conveyors Nos 9 and 10 were erected on this newly created dockside.

ADDITIONAL TIPS

NO. 4 TIP

By the end of 1903 it was becoming apparent that increasing trade warranted the erection of a further tip in the New Dock, although the suggestion of Sir Alfred Jones, chairman of Elder, Dempster,[101] that a movable tip should be provided was rejected on the grounds of cost. In October 1904, the directors approved the provision of

Tips Nos 1–4, with No. 9 conveyor visible beyond. Note the reinforced concrete jetty supporting the newly replaced No. 1 tip. The buildings on the right are part of the hydraulic power station. April 1927.
NM&GW

No. 4 tip, with a Cory Brothers wagon waiting to be discharged, circa 1925.   *NM&GW*

a new tip, No. 4, to be situated to the east of No. 3. The tender of Messrs J Abbot & Co. for a 30-ton high level tip was accepted in January 1905. The jetty for the tip – which was built by Messrs Topham, Jones & Railton as part of their contract which included the Talbot Wharf extension and a new wharf for Rio Tinto – was completed by May 1906,[102] but the new tip, which included a 30-ton weighbridge, was not in use until March 1907.[103] Although not a designated grid, a more comprehensive set of roads for full wagons was provided for No. 4 tip than had been laid down for the adjacent earlier tips Nos 1–3.

No. 8 Tip
Increasing congestion in the New Dock led the directors in January 1907 to approve a scheme for a new tip, No. 8, to be erected on North Bank on a site beyond the existing wharf, at an estimated cost including sidings of £20,000. The tender of Messrs Tannett Walker & Co. of £6,570 for a 32-ton, 60-foot, chain-lift tip was accepted in June 1907 – seven months from the date of the order being allowed for erection.[104] At the same meeting the directors resolved to seek tenders for a ferro-concrete jetty for the new tip, but this was deferred when it was realised that extensive dredging would be necessary to allow modern vessels to reach the proposed location. In October 1907 the tender of the London & Tilbury Dredging Co. for the sum of £11,750 if material was taken out to sea, or £13,235 if deposited on land where required, was accepted. The contract had two elements: dredging a sufficient channel for most of the length of the Old Dock and removing "The Island", a triangular piece of land adjacent to the original lock that remained when the New Dock was cut through to the old in 1897. Preliminary widening of the waterway hereabouts had been completed in August 1905.[105] The new work could not begin until March 1908

because of the winter weather, and was then put off for a further three months. In the meantime exports had declined, the finances of the PTR&D had deteriorated and the directors were inclined to delay the erection of the tip and the dredging for a further twelve months. However, numerous complaints from ship owners as to impediments to navigation and the lack of accommodation within the dock compelled the directors, in November 1908, to agree to complete the work without delay. A revised, less expensive contract was agreed with the London & Tilbury Dredging Co. for removal of 250,000 cubic yards at prices of £8,281 and £9,251 for the two disposal routes respectively.[106] The dredging company started work on 1st January 1909 and was allowed to hire the dredger *Bollin*, provided the PTR&D had priority of use.[107] The work was reported to be completed by November 1909.[108] There was a cost overrun on this contract, for which the dredging company accepted a liability of £719 in settlement of the £1,163 claimed; this was due to the gravelly nature of the dock bottom hereabouts – a problem that was also to be encountered in later dredging operations.

The tender for the construction in ferro-concrete of No. 8 tip jetty and gantry was awarded in May 1909 to G Palmer of Neath for the sum of £3,400.[109] Progress was painfully slow; the jetty was not finished until May 1910[110] and the erection of the new tip could not commence until then, despite its components having been delivered one year previously. No. 8 tip was reported to be in use in April 1911[111] and the adjacent six storage sidings, which complemented the nearby Old Dock grid, were ready the following month.[112]

Nos 9, 10 and 11 Belt Conveyors
In November 1908, Elder, Dempster reiterated their suggestion that movable tips should be provided at Port Talbot. A decision was deferred pending the completion of more pressing requirements.

ABOVE: Loading the SS *Maplewood* at No. 8 tip on North Bank. This tip went into use in April 1910. At least three GWR 20-ton coal wagons assigned to North's Navigation Collieries are visible. A Graigola Merthyr wagon is on the hoist. The photographer is standing by the short North Bank Wharf. May 1928. *NM&GW*

BELOW: The Lübecker land dredger used by Messrs Perry to remove part of the old power station site in 1911/12 to create a new dockside on which Nos 9 and 10 conveyors were erected. A similar machine was used on Llewellyn's Quay in 1913. Postcard, postally used 19th July 1912. *Author's collection*

ABOVE: The massively-constructed No. 8 tip which was erected on North Bank and put into use in April 1911. At the time the 32-ton capacity of this tip was the highest in the dock.

From Port Talbot and its Progress, *PTR&D Co. 1919,*
Author's collection

In March 1909 the general manager submitted to the Board photographs and plans of coal conveyors then being adopted by the North Eastern Railway at Hull.[113] As an ex-NER manager, Lowther had evidently kept himself informed of developments being pursued by his old employers, and was encouraged by his present directors to keep this method of shipment under observation. Eighteen months later they called for plans to be prepared for an additional high-level tip to be positioned to the east of No. 4 tip. As a preliminary, in November 1910 Lowther visited Hull to observe coal shipment by conveyor; suitably encouraged by his report, Col Wright and Mr Watson were nominated by the Board in January 1911 to visit Hull and West Hartlepool to do likewise. They returned favourably impressed and convinced that the system could be adopted with advantage at Port Talbot. Messrs Spencer & Co. of Melksham attended the Board meeting held on 15th March 1911, explained the method of erecting and working conveyor belts, and were asked to tender for the construction of one such conveyor at Port Talbot, the first in South Wales. The tender price was £6,579 plus £1,000 for the foundations, to be completed by 31st December 1912. This turned out to be extremely optimistic: although the conveyor was ready for delivery in July 1912, the tender for the construction of the associated jetty submitted by Messrs Watt Bros of Cardiff was not accepted until September 1912. Further delay was caused by the need to dredge away part of the site of the old hydraulic engine house, work not sufficiently far advanced until March 1913. Messrs Watt started work that month,[114] followed by Messrs Spencer & Co. in June.[115]

Sidings for the new No. 9 conveyor – holding 270 full wagons and 108 empties, costing £8,982 – were approved in March 1913. The sidings were unusual in that they were reached via a kickback layout. Laid on the site of the old No. 4 storage grid,[116] they were completed in October 1913.[117] Despite the conveyor being expected to be ready for use by the end of 1913, the contract was not completed until April 1915, further delay no doubt brought about by the outbreak of the First World War.

BELOW: No. 9 conveyor, April 1927   NM&GW

Wagon tippler for No. 9 conveyor, showing the substantial hydraulic ram required. April 1926.
Author's collection

No. 10 moveable conveyor after it had been converted to a static type capable of handling 20-ton wagons in 1925. The jetty and foundations of the original gantry can be seen clearly in this photograph of May 1928.
NM&GW

ABOVE: The loading gantry of No. 10 moveable conveyor on the left, followed by No. 9 conveyor and tips Nos 4, 3, 2 and 1 near the entrance lock. June 1923.   *BR/OPC*

RIGHT: The gantry and loading tower of No. 10 movable conveyor. The rather delicate nature of the whole appliance is apparent. The Rio Tinto works can be glimpsed to the right of the view, circa 1915.
   From Port Talbot and its Progress, *PTR&D Co. 1919, Author's collection*

BELOW: Nos 10 (idle) and 9 conveyors and Nos 4 and 3 tips on the South Side of the New Dock, circa 1915.
   From Port Talbot and its Progress, *PTR&D Co. 1919, Author's collection*

A view looking down the length of the New Dock with No. 10 moveable conveyor in front and No. 9 conveyor behind. *Author's collection*

In September 1911 the directors noted that during the past year all the high level tips, Nos 1–8, were fully occupied and that on average one ship per day had to wait for a berth. They resolved that Messrs Spencer & Co. be asked to quote for an additional conveyor belt, but the next month deferred that action until the results of using the conveyor then being built were know. By December 1912 the pressure on the export of coal at Port Talbot had reached the point where additional coal shipment facilities were required and, despite No. 9 not yet being in use, the directors decided to invite tenders for two more conveyors. At their January 1913 meeting they accepted the tender of Messrs Frazer & Chalmers for one fixed, No. 11, and one movable conveyor belt, No. 10, for £3,500 and £8,211 respectively, with delivery at the end of May 1913. No. 11 was planned to be sited to the east of the Crown Preserved Coal Co.'s works, whilst No. 10 was constructed adjacent to No. 9 conveyor. The contract for the jetties was awarded to Messrs J B Cooper & Co. of Bristol; that for No. 11 conveyor was priced at £1,003 and that for the much longer No. 10 jetty amounted to £4,900. The advantage of the movable conveyor was that ships could be loaded throughout their length without the need to warp the vessel so that its hatches were under a fixed discharge point, thereby saving much time.

Again there were delays, Messrs Frazer & Chalmers not starting to erect these conveyors until April 1914.[118] The jetties for Nos 11 and 10 conveyors were completed in July and November 1914 respectively.[119] In spite of its greater complexity, No. 10 conveyor was completed first and test run in February 1915, but was not working satisfactorily until October 1915. No. 11 conveyor was put into use in May 1915.[120] No 10 conveyor was served by four sidings with a capacity of 355 loaded wagons and two holding 120 empties; No. 11 was provided with three sidings holding 300 loaded wagons with empties being collected on two sidings connected directly to No. 1 grid.

All three belt conveyors were driven by electric motors whose combined power requirements were far in excess of what was available from the existing electric plant. In March 1913 the directors accepted the tender of £3,522 submitted by Messrs Browett, Lindley & Co. for two 350 kW generator sets, each consisting of a Browett compound steam engine driving a dynamo supplied by the Lancashire Co. Steam was supplied by two high-pressure boilers obtained from the Yorkshire Boiler Co. At first it was intended to extend the existing power house, but in May 1913 it was decided that a new electrical power house should be erected near Copper Works Junction, and Messrs Walker Bros, who had constructed the frame of the new hydraulic power house, were awarded the contract. The building was finished in April 1914,[121] but the engines were not running under a test load until November 1914.[122] The new electrical power station did not go into use until 20th February 1915.[123] All the PTR&D's superseded generating plant was sold to the Government in 1918 for £2,400.

Roberts, the mechanical engineer, reported in May 1919 that the dock then had eight tips, three conveyors and twenty hydraulic cranes, some of which where twenty-four years old and would require substantial overhaul.[124] Apart from repairs to some of the jetties, nothing was done at the time and the problem passed to the GWR at the grouping.

ABOVE: A postcard produced for the GWR showing Nos 9 and 10 conveyors, the latter by this date converted to a fixed machine.

Author's collection

ABOVE: Wagon tipping, No. 11 conveyor. Wagons dropped by gravity from the loaded sidings on the left and were worked away also by gravity to the empties sidings on the right. Note the turntable on the left to enable the rotation of wagons that arrived at the tip with the end door facing the wrong way.

From Port Talbot and its Progress, *PTR&D Co. 1919,*
Author's collection

LEFT: No. 11 conveyor, looking towards the site of the future Margam Wharf, circa 1915.

From Port Talbot and its Progress, *PTR&D Co. 1919,*
Author's collection

There were originally three roads for loaded wagons on the approach ramp for No. 11 conveyor. This appliance was dismantled in 1937 and only one disused siding remained when this view was taken on 16th October 1947. The empty roads for this conveyor were connected to No. 1 grid at a point directly behind the brick-built cabin. Alongside the grid are the Up Slow and Up Fast lines, with the corresponding Down lines further to the right. The loaded wagons appear to be carrying limestone. Partly hidden by the ramp are the former Crown Preserved Works, now occupied by Steel Ceilings Ltd. At this date Margam Steelworks had two blast furnaces and two ore unloaders, all visible in the background. *Author's collection*

WATER SUPPLY

Apart from the immediate Port Talbot area, the water needed for locomotive use was obtained from local sources, usually springs. One water crane was provided at each of Bryn, Maesteg and Pontyrhyll as part of Pearson's contract.[125] The engineer requested one more at each of these three places and also one at Central station and in the dock area. Only those at Central and Bryn were agreed to, leading to a problem in the dock area. Probert reported in December 1898 that engines had to run from the grids to Duffryn Yard to get water, the round trip taking about one hour.[126] A temporary supply had been obtained by tapping into Messrs Vivian's supply near Margam East signal box, but a water supply for engines at No. 3 grid was essential. In due course an 11,250 gallon tank was erected there with the water crane situated between the Down Fast and Down Slow lines.

The situation in the dock area was totally different. Knott estimated in June 1899 that the company required 120,000 gallons a day for its own purposes, which excluded the needs of the works being established in the dock area and the provisioning of ships. These needs dictated a reliable, large-scale supply. Prior to the development of the New Dock at Port Talbot, Margam Urban District Council (UDC) possessed two small reservoirs in the Duffryn Valley with a total capacity of 310,000 gallons.[127] The PTR&D had a connection to the water main where it ran under the road behind Duffryn Yard, but needed an alternative in case of failure. This issue was first addressed by Meik in August 1896 when he recommended the sinking of a well at Duffryn Yard, erecting large tanks there and at Duffryn Junction, with a small tank in the dock area for the dock locomotives, all for an estimated cost of £3,600. This scheme was on too small a scale to be of great benefit and was not pursued. In 1897 the Margam Estate became involved, probably at the instigation of Margam UDC. On 11th May, Messrs John Taylor, Sons & Santo Co., Civil Engineers, submitted to Knox, Miss Talbot's agent, a proposal for a 4.5 million gallon reservoir to be constructed in Cwm Brombil or Cwm Wernderi for a total of £3,300, including two and a half miles of mains pipes.[128] This scheme was discussed at the Board meeting on 19th May, when it was noted that Margam UDC could offer water from Cwm Wernderi at 3d per 1,000 gallons, with a minimum charge of £150 per annum. The directors agreed to this, but also resolved that plans should be made for an alternative in Cwm Brombil.

In November 1897 the Port Talbot Co. made a connection near Duffryn Yard to Margam UDC's main which had been extended towards the docks. Case, the resident engineer, pointed out that this water was for use at the engine shed and Central station only.[129] This brought an objection from Meik, who required water at the dock and also three day's notice of the supply being shut off; it was pointed out by Margam UDC's engineer that this arrangement was only to cover water supply until the new scheme was in operation.

The lease to Margam UDC of the land for a reservoir in Cwm Wernderi was signed by Miss Talbot on 10th January 1898.[130] One of the conditions stipulated that the council was to supply the PTR&D with all the water needed for its undertaking from its existing Cwm Gwyneu reservoir, which the new reservoir was to feed by pipeline. It is not clear when work started, but it was not until

October 1898 that the directors approved a plan for a siding to be put in at Tynyffram for Barnes, Chaplin & Co., the contractors for the reservoir. This siding was provisionally sanctioned by the Board of Trade provided all trains had an engine at the lower end.[131] Two months later the Board of Trade approved the use of a temporary platform put in on the main line near the siding for the use of workmen, the men arriving on the 5.55 a.m. train from Port Talbot and returning by the train due at 6.20 p.m. – the proviso being that the platform would not be open to the public or appear in any timetable. Although the railway works were reported as finished by 15th November,[132] they were not inspected until May 1899.[133] In April 1899 the directors agreed to run an engine from the Morfa Railway to Tynyffram Siding with clay for reservoir construction at 1s 0d per ton in the contractor's wagons.

Until its new reservoir was completed Margam UDC did not have the capacity to supply the company with all its needs, and it had to be content to take the free water for locomotives. Of particular concern was the 30,000 gallons per day the PTR&D had undertaken to supply to the Crown Preserved Coal Co., whose works were then under construction. To address this situation the directors decided at their meeting on 19th April 1899 to make a new reservoir in Cwm Brombil. The Board heard at the meeting on 21st June that Miss Talbot would construct this reservoir provided the company took a minimum of 15,000 gallons per day at 4½d per 1,000 gallons plus 60,000 gallons at 3d. These conditions were accepted, provided Miss Talbot undertook not to allow minerals to be worked under or around the reservoir so as to guarantee its long-term future. Knox explained in a letter to Knott dated 3rd July that Miss Talbot was advised not to allow the PTR&D to make the reservoir itself as the watershed in Cwm Brombil was the only water on the estate convenient for Port Talbot, and she should retain control over it. There would be no time limit in the agreement with the company. Miss Talbot's expenditure was estimated to be £7,500. The resulting agreement was approved in September 1899, but not signed until 21st August 1900. The engineer reported in August 1900 that the Cwm Brombil water would be piped to supply ships, works, and so on. Every use would be made of Margam UDC's supply for the hydraulic engine house and the dock locomotives. The two sources of supply were to be connected, but isolated from each other by valves, so that either could be used if necessary, the estimated cost of this work being £650. Cwm Brombil reservoir, also built by Barnes, Chaplin & Co., was reported to be completed and supplying water in January 1901,[134] although it was not declared watertight until March 1905 when the PTR&D was permitted to take water from below it rather than the stream above as hitherto. It had a capacity of about 17,500 gallons from which the company initially drew about 12,000 gallons per day.[135] The water main terminated on Talbot Wharf and in March 1903 was extended under water to North Bank to supply Messrs Burt, Boulton & Haywood's creosoting works there.[136] Hitherto their supply had occasionally been turned off without notice by Margam UDC.[137]

Duffryn Yard also suffered from occasional interruption of supply, which inevitably led to operational difficulties. This led to a dispute in 1903 with Margam UDC over water supply from the two Duffryn Valley reservoirs.[138] The situation was complicated by the fact that the PTR&D had rights only to water from Cwm Gwyneu reservoir but not from the much larger one in Cwm Wernderi. Hosgood calculated that the company had an absolute minimum daily requirement of 190,500 gallons water, a figure which included 88,000 gallons for twenty-two engines and 45,000 gallons for three boiler washouts. It was eventually agreed in April 1904 that Margam UDC would supply 190,500 gallons per day for ten months of a year, and any excess over that amount at 3½d per 1,000 gallons The total was limited to 100,000 gallons per day in the dry months of June and July, for which an incremental scale of payments was agreed. An agreement with Margam UDC for the supply of water was dated 13th March 1905 and signed and sealed in April 1905.

This was soon found to be insufficient, and in September 1905 Margam UDC's offer of water from its Cwm Wernderi reservoir at 3½d per 1,000 gallons was accepted. The March 1905 agreement expired on 31st December 1908. After prolonged negotiations another agreement was signed whereby the Council would supply for five years from 1st January 1910 – a maximum of 151,090 gallons of water per day for the company's engines and boilers at 3½d per 1,000 gallons, with a minimum payment of £400 per annum.[139] This agreement was renewed periodically until December 1918 when it was agreed that the rate would be 4d per 1,000 gallons, with a minimum payment of £600 per annum. Separate agreements dealt with the supply of water to the works at the docks.

ROAD ACCESS TO NEW DOCK

NORTH SIDE

Adequate road access to Port Talbot Docks was an obvious necessity. As early as January 1896 the directors had requested the R&SBR to put in order the road that ran from Aberavon alongside its railway to the north side of the dock. This road had its limitations as it crossed several railway tracks, particularly those leading to the Mansel Tinplate Works,[140] which were frequently blocked. This issue also concerned the local authority and, in March 1897, Aberavon Corporation produced a plan for a bridge over the River Avon opposite the tinplate works to replace an old bridge which had been washed away.[141] Patrick Meik, the PTR&D's engineer, proposed an alternative plan for a combined road and rail bridge about 660 yards downstream as part of the contemplated scheme for a railway north of the river. The Corporation objected to this on safety grounds and there matters rested for over a year.

Aberavon Corporation produced a new plan in September 1898 for a road which avoided level crossings over the R&SBR and crossed the river just below the temporary bridge erected by Topham, Jones & Railton in association with their graving dock contract.[142] The Port Talbot directors had resolved in September 1898 that they could not entertain this plan unless the R&SBR agreed to keep the present road open, but were informed by their solicitor one month later that the Corporation was applying for a Provisional Order with compulsory powers for a new road. The directors then changed their tune and agreed to the site, provided the bridge was made wide enough to take a single or double pair of rails. Meik estimated the cost of the bridge to be £3,614, or £6,380 if widened to take one line of rails. The additional cost was not likely to be recovered and in January 1899 the directors paid Topham, Jones & Railton £250 for their temporary bridge to provide an alternative rail crossing. The House of Commons Committee duly passed the preamble to the Local Government Board's Provisional Orders Confirmation (No. 6) Bill despite evidence that the southern part of the road in the dock area was a private one.[143] A clause for the protection of the PTR&D was inserted, stipulating that the bridge was to be built alongside the temporary bridge with matching spans, that the company could lay line of rails over the new road (Newbridge Road) in line with those leading to the temporary bridge so as to enable the Sandhills traffic[144] to be brought to the docks, as required by an agreement made in April 1895, and that the cost of any works done by the company towards the new bridge would be repaid by the Corporation. The Aberavon Order 1899 was appended as a Schedule to the ensuing Act which received the Royal Assent on 1st August 1899.[145] In September 1900 the PTR&D belatedly realised that the new bridge would prevent seaborne access to the contemplated wharves upstream of it, having no powers to require it to be a swing bridge. The directors decided not to press for compensation for loss of use of the river bank provided the Corporation granted an easement across the new road for the railway along the training wall, which was agreed to in February 1902.

The directors considered a draft tripartite agreement between the Mayor & Burgesses of Aberavon, the PTR&D and Miss Talbot concerning the new road and bridge on 21st January 1903, although it was not sealed until 16th September. Among its provisions the Corporation agreed to cooperate with the company in preventing attempts to close the existing road to the docks along the left bank of the river, and the land required for the road and bridge would be sold at £500 per acre. The conveyance reserved the company's existing level crossings, and the Corporation agreed to indemnify the company regarding the liability to the public using the road to reach the new Docks Hotel. The new bridge was opened on 29th October 1903.

Meanwhile, the R&SBR was asked to improve the road alongside its tracks as it continued to deteriorate.[146] The R&SBR disputed its obligations, but counsel's opinion was not favourable to its case and an accommodation was agreed with the PTR&D. This road had been extended to the graving dock in 1899.

Periodic dredging of the lower River Avon gradually undermined the foundations of the new bridge and in May 1908 work started on the construction of a reinforced concrete dam a short distance downstream of it.[147] The objective was to induce siltation upstream of the dam and so protect the piers, which was rapidly achieved.[148]

SOUTH SIDE

Road access to the south side of the docks was made more difficult by the presence of the GWR main line. Meik opined in September 1898 that the GWR was likely to refuse to allow road traffic to the dock to use the level crossing at Taibach.[149] Two schemes from Taibach were proposed by Meik in July 1899: a direct route which used an existing bridge under the GWR but necessitated a new bridge under the Morfa Railway, and a route from West End, Taibach, alongside the River Ffrwdwyllt and making use of the O&SSR bridge over the cut to Margam Copper Works.[150] The latter was selected and was at first proposed to be a public road, but differences with Margam UDC over uncontrolled access resulted in the directors agreeing in March 1900 that this road would be made by the PTR&D. It had earlier been decided that the road would be extended along the edge of the dock to give access to ships lying there. Miss Talbot granted the company an easement across her property from Taibach to Oakwood Bridge over Float on the same terms as were offered to Margam UDC – in return for a level crossing from there over the dock railways to the so-called Military Road which ran along the southern edge of the company's property – which the directors agreed to in July 1900. The road was completed in October 1900, but Hosgood suspended work on making the bridge suitable for vehicles in June 1901 as he considered that horses or carts could be trapped on it, and suggested using the old bridge instead.[151] Mr Franklen, Miss Talbot's advisor, objected to this, and work was resumed, being completed in November 1901.[152] The GWR tried this route but found it dangerous and declined to use it any more. Hosgood asked the directors to reconsider using the old bridge and this time they agreed to reinstate this bridge for cart traffic, the work commencing in March 1902.[153] The construction

The Aberavon Corporation bridge carrying Newbridge Road over the River Avon which was opened in 1903. Beneath the spans can be seen the supports for the bridge built by Topham, Jones & Railton in 1897 in order to transport spoil from the graving dock site to the watery area seen centre left. *Author's collection*

This view, taken on 30th April 1946, shows the Military Road where it crossed the main lines to the docks near Copper Works Junction off to the right. Following its diversion as a consequence of the construction of Margam Steelworks, this sole road access to the South Side of the docks approached the crossing alongside the O&SSR, passing under the ore unloaders on Margam Wharf, visible back left. The twelve sidings comprising No. 6 grid (No. 7 in the GWR scheme) are on the left. *Author's collection*

of Margam Steelworks caused this road to be diverted in 1917 from where it passed along Margam Wharf.

In December 1900 local traders petitioned the PTR&D to provide more direct access to the dock from Llewellyn's Quay.[154] The suggested route was not practical but Miss Talbot did agree to improve the existing road, it having got into a bad state.[155] The directors eventually agreed to a ferry service around the docks in

February 1903. The Military Road led to firing ranges on Morfa Newydd and in February 1909 Margam UDC enquired as to whether the PTR&D would extend it so as to provide access to the beach. This was denied on safety grounds, as was a further request two months later to hand over the road to the Council for adoption as a public highway, subject to the rights of Miss Talbot, her tenants and the War Office.[156]

Notes

1. See Volume 1, Chapter 2.
2. See Volume 1, Chapter 1.
3. TNA: PRO RAIL 1066/2506.
4. TNA: PRO RAIL 1057/2548.
5. TNA: PRO RAIL 1057/1528/206.
6. TNA: PRO RAIL 1057/1528/99, 100.
7. TNA: PRO RAIL 1057/1528/118.
8. TNA: PRO RAIL 1057/1528/109.
9. TNA: PRO RAIL 1057/1528/119.
10. TNA: PRO RAIL 1057/1528/124, 134.
11. TNA: PRO RAIL 1057/1528/204, 215.
12. TNA: PRO RAIL 1057/1528/162.
13. See Volume 1, Chapter 1.
14. TNA: PRO RAIL 1057/1529/7.
15. See Volume 1, Chapter 2.
16. See Volume 1, Chapter 9.
17. TNA: PRO RAIL 1057/2647.
18. TNA: PRO RAIL 1057/1529/49.
19. TNA: PRO RAIL 1057/1529/51.
20. TNA: PRO RAIL 1057/2647.
21. TNA: PRO RAIL 1057/2564.
22. TNA: PRO RAIL 1057/1528/182.
23. TNA: PRO RAIL 1057/1528/191.
24. TNA: PRO RAIL 581/12.
25. See Volume 1, Chapter 9.
26. TNA: PRO RAIL 581/13.
27. TNA: PRO MT 6/1197/1.
28. TNA: PRO RAIL 1057/1529/50.
29. TNA: PRO RAIL 1057/1529/58.
30. TNA: PRO RAIL 1057/1529/59.

31. See Chapter 17.
32. TNA: PRO RAIL 1057/1528/86.
33. TNA: PRO RAIL 1057/1528/99.
34. TNA: PRO RAIL 242/3.
35. TNA: PRO RAIL 1057/1528/162.
36. TNA: PRO RAIL 1057/1528/169.
37. TNA: PRO RAIL 1057/1528/188.
38. See Chapter 11.
39. Some grids were renumbered by GWR, see Chapter 20.
40. Albert Havelock Case, *Port Talbot Railways and Docks, General Information, etc. taken from a Paper read on the Occasion of the Visit of the Members of the Institution of Marine Engineers, September 1898*, p. 15.
41. TNA: PRO RAIL 1057/1528/57.
42. TNA: PRO RAIL 1057/1529/42.
43. TNA: PRO RAIL 1057/1528/106.
44. TNA: PRO RAIL 1057/1528/107.
45. TNA: PRO RAIL 1057/1528/120.
46. TNA: PRO RAIL 1057/1528/91.
47. TNA: PRO MT 6/554/7.
48. TNA: PRO RAIL 1057/1528/22.
49. Case, *Port Talbot Railways and Docks, General Information*, p. 15.
50. TNA: PRO RAIL 1057/1528/92.
51. TNA: PRO RAIL 242/1.
52. TNA: PRO RAIL 1057/1528/150.
53. TNA: PRO RAIL 1057/1528/165.
54. TNA: PRO RAIL 1057/1528/162.
55. TNA: PRO RAIL 1057/1528/166.
56. TNA: PRO RAIL 1057/1528/172.
57. TNA: PRO RAIL 1057/1528/181.
58. TNA: PRO RAIL 1057/1528/186.
59. TNA: PRO RAIL 1057/1528/160.
60. TNA: PRO RAIL 1057/1528/162.
61. TNA: PRO RAIL 1057/1528/166.
62. TNA: PRO RAIL 1057/1528/173.
63. See Chapter 14.
64. TNA: PRO RAIL 1057/1528/178.
65. TNA: PRO RAIL 1057/1529/45.
66. TNA: PRO RAIL 1057/1529/4.
67. TNA: PRO RAIL 1057/1530/6.
68. TNA: PRO RAIL 1057/1529/45.
69. TNA: PRO RAIL 1057/1529/55.
70. TNA: PRO RAIL 1057/1528/77.
71. TNA: PRO RAIL 1057/1528/94.
72. TNA: PRO RAIL 1057/1528/97.
73. TNA: PRO RAIL 1057/1528/107.
74. Cleaver, 'Alterations and Improvements', pp. 113–14.
75. TNA: PRO RAIL 574/101.
76. WGAS D/D PRO/BRB/325.
77. TNA: PRO RAIL 1057/1528/142.
78. TNA: PRO RAIL 1057/1528/159.
79. TNA: PRO RAIL 1057/1528/165.
80. TNA: PRO RAIL 1057/1528/166.
81. TNA: PRO RAIL 1057/1528/170.
82. Cleaver, 'Alterations and Improvements', pp. 118–20.
83. TNA: PRO RAIL 1057/1528/165.
84. TNA: PRO RAIL 1057/1528/156.
85. TNA: PRO RAIL 1057/1528/158.
86. TNA: PRO RAIL 1057/1528/161.
87. TNA: PRO RAIL 1057/1528/164.
88. TNA: PRO RAIL 1057/1528/109.
89. TNA: PRO RAIL 1057/1528/124.
90. TNA: PRO RAIL 1057/1528/127.
91. TNA: PRO RAIL 1057/1528/136.
92. TNA: PRO RAIL 1057/1528/143.
93. TNA: PRO RAIL 1057/1528/144.
94. TNA: PRO RAIL 1057/1528/144.
95. TNA: PRO RAIL 1057/1528/126.
96. WGAS D/D PRO/BRB/330.
97. K Haddock, *Giant Earthmovers: An Illustrated History*, MBI Publishing Co., 1998.
98. TNA: PRO RAIL 1057/1528/159.
99. TNA: PRO RAIL 1057/1528/173.
100. TNA: PRO RAIL 1057/1528/174.
101. See Chapter 21.
102. TNA: PRO RAIL 1057/1528/99.
103. TNA: PRO RAIL 1057/1528/109.
104. WGAS D/D PRO/BRB/315.
104. TNA: PRO RAIL 1057/1528/91.
106. WGAS D/D PRO/BRB/321.
107. WGAS D/D PRO/BRB/320, 322.
108. TNA: PRO RAIL 1057/1528/136.
109. WGAS D/D PRO/BRB/324.
110. TNA: PRO RAIL 1057/1528/142.
111. TNA: PRO RAIL 1057/1528/152.
112. TNA: PRO RAIL 1057/1528/153.
113. Terry Powell, *Staith to Conveyor: An Illustrated History of Coal Shipping Machinery*, Chilton Ironworks, 2000.
114. TNA: PRO RAIL 1057/1528/173.
115. TNA: PRO RAIL 1057/1528/176.
116. TNA: PRO RAIL 1057/1528/173.
117. TNA: PRO RAIL 1057/1528/179.
118. TNA: PRO RAIL 1057/1528/182.
119. TNA: PRO RAIL 1057/1528/185, 188.
120. TNA: PRO RAIL 1057/1528/194.
121. TNA: PRO RAIL 1057/1528/182.
122. TNA: PRO RAIL 1057/1528/188.
123. TNA: PRO RAIL 1057/1528/192.
124. TNA: PRO RAIL 1057/1528/235.
125. TNA: PRO RAIL 1057/1529/22.
126. TNA: PRO RAIL 1057/1528/31.
127. OS 6in Glamorgan Sheet 25, 1st revision 1896–97, marked up by H Rofe & Son, Civil Engineers, authors collection.
128. TNA: PRO RAIL 1057/2532.
129. TNA: PRO RAIL 1057/2649.
130. TNA: PRO RAIL 1057/2649.
131. TNA: PRO MT 6/880/2.
132. TNA: PRO RAIL 1057/1528/27.
133. TNA: PRO MT 29/61 p. 130.
134. TNA: PRO RAIL 1057/1529/45; Harold D Botwell and Geoffrey Hill, *Reservoir Builders of South Wales*, Industrial Locomotive Society 2006, p. 118.
135. TNA: PRO RAIL 1057/1529/47.
136. TNA: PRO RAIL 1057/1528/70, 71.
137. TNA: PRO RAIL 1057/2650, RAIL 1057/1529/59.
138. TNA: PRO RAIL 1057/2650.
139. TNA: PRO RAIL 1057/2651.
140. See Volume 1, Chapter 1.
141. TNA: PRO RAIL 1057/2623.
142. See Chapter 14.
143. TNA: PRO RAIL 1068/1.
144. Chapter 14.
145. 62 & 62 Vict. c.cxlvi.
146. TNA: PRO RAIL 1057/2652.
147. TNA: PRO RAIL 1057/1528/123.
148. Cleaver, 'Alterations and Improvements', pp. 107–108.
149. TNA: PRO RAIL 1057/1529/26.
150. TNA: PRO RAIL 1057/2567.
151. TNA: PRO RAIL 1057/1529/51.
152. TNA: PRO RAIL 1057/1529/56.
153. TNA: PRO RAIL 1057/1528/65.
154. TNA: PRO RAIL 1057/2582.
155. TNA: PRO RAIL 1057/2572.
156. TNA: PRO RAIL 1057/2488.

14

Dockside Industries

IT WAS IN THE interests of the PTR&D to attract large-scale industries to Port Talbot, both for the rental income that would be generated and for the maritime and railway traffic that would ensue. To this end the company constructed wharves and siding connections and provided mains water and other services to meet its tenants' needs. Not surprisingly these tenants were mostly at the heavier end of the industrial spectrum.

PORT TALBOT GRAVING DOCK & SHIPBUILDING CO. LTD

The first application for land for a dry dock was made in April 1895 by Mr Watson, one of the PTR&D's directors who, as well as his coal mining interests, had an involvement with shipbuilding at Newport. Although approved, the proposal came to nothing. In August 1896 Mr M Mordey, an associate of Mr Watson, applied for a site in the New Dock area to construct a graving dock and was offered 6 acres at £250 per year for five years, and £500 per

year thereafter. This was not taken up, but in April 1897 a site near the new lock was decided on, the terms now being a peppercorn rent for eighteen months, thereafter £250 per year for five years, then £400 per year, with a monopoly for ten years. Progress was held up until the Port Talbot Graving Dock and Shipbuilding Co. Ltd was formed in July 1897.[1] The monopoly was queried at the PTR&D's half-yearly meeting held on 18th August 1897.[2] Col Wright rather blandly informed the shareholders that the policy was dictated by circumstances and justified by the increased rent received.

The Graving Dock Co. was closely associated with the Port Talbot Syndicate Ltd, which was formed at the same time and shared some of its directors.[3] Its Memorandum of Association stated that its particular activity related to "all such other things as are incidental or conducive to the improvement and development of Port Talbot, the County of Glamorgan, and the districts adjacent thereto." The Syndicate appeares to have functioned as what later became termed

The graving dock under construction looking northwards, circa 1898. The photographer is standing where the entrance caisson was later erected.
Courtesy Arthur Rees

ABOVE: A second view of the graving dock under construction, this time looking south across the entrance to the docks.
Courtesy Arthur Rees

LEFT: An interior view of the Port Talbot Graving Dock Co.'s dry dock looking towards the entrance caisson at the southern end, circa 1912. This dock, which could accommodate two large vessels, could be pumped dry in one and a half hours, and vessels visiting for repairs could do so without incurring harbour dues. *From* Port Talbot and its Progress, *PTR&D Co. 1919, Author's collection*

a holding company, although its only interest, at least in the Port Talbot area, was the graving dock. It was wound up voluntarily in May 1900.[4] The contract for the construction of the graving dock was awarded to Messrs Topham, Jones & Railton in October 1897,[5] who at the time were building the OVER and SWMJnR.[6] Spoil from the graving dock excavation was dumped, with the agreement of the landowner Mr A P Vivian, behind the upper training wall on the right bank of the River Avon.[7] This muddy area was covered at high water and was known as the "sinking pool". The temporary wooden bridge over the river built by the contractors to gain access

to the dumping ground was sold to the PTR&D in January 1899 for £250. It was used for access to the training wall and condemned in May 1908 after plans by the Sandhills Boring Co. to open up a mine on Aberavon Burrows had been abandoned.[8] The engineer reported in June 1899 that the dry dock was almost completed and that water had been admitted.[9] The finished dry dock had dimensions of 422 by 110 feet. The 60-foot wide entrance was closed by a caisson which the Port Talbot Co. directors agreed in January 1898 could be substituted for the gates originally proposed. It was served by a siding connection off the line leading to No. 7 tip.

LEFT: The SS *Aidan* loading patent fuel at the Crown Preserved Coal Co.'s wharf circa 1918. The briquettes were transported from the works by what looks like standard gauge trolleys moved by a haulage wire system.

From Port Talbot and its Progress, *PTR&D Co. 1919, Author's collection*

RIGHT: A heavily retouched view of the Crown Preserved Coal Co.'s Port Talbot works looking north-east, circa 1912. Rows of briquettes stacked on trolleys are visible to the left of the works.

From Port Talbot and its Progress, *PTR&D Co. 1919, Author's collection*

The directors were concerned that they would be left with a partly-built graving dock and to avoid this eventuality stipulated that one of the conditions for the lease of the site, which was executed in August 1898, would be that all the company's capital was to be expended on the dry dock.[10] Furthermore, Col Wright was named as a trustee for the debenture holders, the other being Mordey. The Graving Dock Co.'s financial position was initially insecure, so much so that the PTR&D offered to forego half the £500 per annum rent for five years if it raised £15,000. The Graving Dock, which engaged in ship repairs and small-scale shipbuilding, including some for Port Talbot Docks,[11] ceased business in 1971, by which time it was owned by the Prince of Wales Dry Dock Co. (Swansea) Ltd.

CROWN PRESERVED COAL CO.

The concept of compressing small coal (defined as coal which passes through a 1⅛-inch mesh) with some sort of a binding agent originated in the late sixteenth century.[12] One of the first works for the manufacture of such briquettes in South Wales appears to be that of Bell's Patent Fuel Co. which had been set up on an unidentified site at Port Talbot by 1848.[13] This apparently short-lived business was listed in local trade directories for 1849, 1850 and 1852.

A second works was established in 1851 when Mr T H Wood of Briton Ferry set up an experimental patent fuel works on the site of the later graving dock at Port Talbot.[14] Increased demand for the product of this works led to the formation of the Crown Preserved Coal & Coke Co. Ltd by 1856, and to the construction of a new works at Maindy, north of Cardiff and adjacent to the Taff Vale Railway. This business was acquired by the newly formed Crown Preserved Coal Co. Ltd in 1860.[15] Financial difficulties resulted in the company going into voluntary liquidation in 1878; it was eventually acquired by Samuel Butler who reincorporated the Crown Preserved Coal Co. Ltd in 1890.[16] Further expansion resulted in the erection of a large works at Roath Dock, Cardiff.

In February 1898 the PTR&D entered into a provisional arrangement with Samuel Butler for a site of a patent fuel works at Port Talbot, the intention being to close the original works at Maindy. The rent was set at £500 per year, reducing to £400 per year if more than 6,000 tons of fuel were shipped annually. The engineer estimated that the cost to the PTR&D of constructing a 300-foot wharf, dredging the dock at the site and providing a railway connection to be £13,010, with a further £5,200 attributable

Loading briquettes, Crown Wharf, April 1927. *NM&GW*

to Crown Persevered Coal for levelling the site and providing the internal railways. PTR&D's portion was soon revised to include an extended wharf 350 feet long and the internal earthworks, bringing the total to £17,000; the estimated cost attributable to Crown Preserved Coal for the internal railways was reduced to £2,285. Meik pointed out in March 1898 that the selected site prevented the erection of one of the planned coal tips while the works were in operation – but the sidings had been arranged so as to serve this tip if the works were abandoned.[17] Negotiations proceeded fairly slowly, but in September 1898 the directors resolved that the PTR&D would construct the wharf and associated works for not more than £20,000. In December 1898, Mr T M Franklen, on behalf of Miss Talbot, agreed to the necessary expenditure. An agreement with the Crown Preserved Coal Co. was confirmed at the Board meeting on 22nd January 1899, but it was not until the following May that Messrs Ridley& Sons' tender of £11,752 17s 0d for the construction of the wharf was accepted. The wharf, which became known as Crown Wharf, was completed in October 1900 and the dredging in December that year. The construction of the plant approached completion in November 1900 and the PTR&D was informed that sales had been made for shipment in December. The ninety-year lease on the site was signed on 23rd January 1901, backdated to 20th June 1898.

In 1902 the docks initiated a claim for outstanding debts against the Crown Preserved Coal Co., which counter-claimed that the rates being charged were too high. The PTR&D lost this action but decided not to appeal as the fuel company planned to double the size of its works. The Crown Preserved Coal Co. subsequently leased a further ¼ acre in November 1903 to give them sufficient land on which to construct a coal washery, the plans for which were approved in March 1904.

In August 1908 the Crown Preserved Coal Co. announced plans to increase the size of its plant so as to double its output to a maximum of 1,000 tons per day, provided its wharf was extended by 100 feet, the whole of length was dredged to the dock depth of 27 feet 6 inches and there was an ample supply of fresh water. Although the last two conditions were soon satisfied by the PTR&D and Margam UDC, work to extend the plant did not begin until 1912. The siding accommodation for the works was already too small, although a connection for an additional low-level empty wagon siding was agreed in 1910.[18] The PTR&D agreed to lease an additional 3 acres to the Crown Preserved Coal Co. in February 1912, provided an undertaking was given to provide storage for 300 wagons on this land. The wharf extension, in ferro-concrete, was eventually approved in January 1913 and the work was awarded to Messrs J B Copper & Co. of Bristol for £1,446 as part of their contract for new wharves and jetties. The approaches to the two new high-level full wagon sidings and the three new empties sidings were laid in by the PTR&D, the former leading off No. 4 grid and the latter directly off the main line. The wharf extension was reported to be finished in July 1914[19] and the enlarged fuel works were completed the following October.[20] The Crown Preserved Coal Co. went into voluntary liquidation in February 1920 so as to effect a financial reconstruction.[21] At the new company's request, the old leases were consolidated and a new lease was sealed in December 1920.[22] A new siding agreement was made in March 1921.

PHOENIX PATENT FUEL LTD

The demand for briquettes as a convenient and durable form of smokeless fuel greatly increased in the early years of the twentieth century, and the PTR&D received a number of applications for sites at the docks for fuel works. Most of these did not progress very far, leading the directors to demand in a number of cases a deposit and proof of financial standing before proceeding with negotiations. The nine businesses whose interest waned were Mr W Westlake of Swansea (1899), Nelson Smokeless Briquettes Ltd and the Orient Patent Fuel Co. (both 1908), Messrs D Davis & Sons of Ferndale and the Ovex Fuel Co. of London (both 1911), the Vulcan Coke & Patent Fuel Co. (1912), Messrs Pyman, Watson & Co. (1915), Lord Rhondda (1916) and the Société Français Anglo de Briquette Co. (1918).

The first successful application was that of the Atlas Coke & Patent Fuel Co. Ltd, formed in April 1914,[23] with which an agreement for a site at the eastern end of the dock was signed in September 1914. However, the outbreak of war prevented anything being done and Atlas failed to assure the directors that it would proceed once hostilities had ended. In December 1917 the PTR&D received an application from the Phoenix Patent Fuel Ltd for land for a works. This company had been formed in December 1912[24] and established a patent fuel works at King's Dock, Swansea, having acquired from the Cory estate the rights to work the process invented by the Cory brothers.[25] Negotiations were deferred until June 1918, when Phoenix was offered the site

previously granted to Atlas, which agreed to give up its rights and surrendered its lease in April 1919. Phoenix paid £1,500 for the rights, although £500 was allowed by a rebate on the rent. The terms of a new sixty-year lease – under which Phoenix was to construct its own wharf but also had permission to ship at the adjacent No. 11 belt conveyor any washed small coal it made at 50 per cent of the PTR&Ds rate, and to guarantee the shipment of 300,000 tons of patent fuel and 150,000 tons of washed coal per annum – were accepted in February 1919. Construction of the storage sidings and connections, which were estimated to cost £7,100, started in March 1920[26] and dredging the channel to the new wharf commenced in August 1921.[27]

The final application for a site came in January 1919, from Messrs D R Llewellyn, Merrett & Price Ltd on behalf of the Graigola Merthyr Co. Ltd. Negotiations proceeded for an area south-east of Llewellyn's Quay on similar terms to those offered to Phoenix. These were broken off in January 1920 after it was revealed that Graigola had taken a substantial interest in the new works of the Phoenix Co. This involvement presaged the acquisition of the Phoenix Works by Gueret, Llewellyn & Merret Ltd in 1927, the Phoenix Co. having gone into voluntary liquidation in May 1924.

In 1929 there was a wholesale reorganisation of the briquette and patent fuel industry in South Wales. Eight large companies, including the Crown Preserved Coal Co. Ltd and part of Gueret, Llewellyn & Merrett Ltd, were amalgamated into a new company, British Briquettes Ltd, with a capital of £2m.[28] By June 1938 virtually all the shares had passed to Powell Duffryn Associated Collieries Ltd. The Crown Preserved Works were dismantled at about this time and replaced on part of the site by South Wales Metal Refiners (1941) Ltd. With nationalisation of the coal industry in 1945 the Phoenix Works became a Ministry of Fuel and Power Briquetting Plant, which closed in 1966.

RIO TINTO

Technical developments in smelting had made it more economical to produce crude copper alongside the mines using the Bessemer process; consequently, by June 1903 Rio Tinto's

A post-Second World War view of briquettes leaving the former Phoenix Works, by then a Ministry of Fuel and Power briquetting plant, and being taken round to join the Dock Branch behind the photographer. Note that by this date the third blast furnace at Margam Steelworks had been erected.   *Author's collection*

Cwmavon labour force[29] had been reduced to 150 refinery workers.[30] On 14th March 1904, Mr Macleod, the Rio Tinto company secretary, wrote to the PTR&D pointing out that his company now did all its smelting in Spain and merely brought copper to Wales for melting down and casting.[31] The large works at Cwmavon were now not needed and were to be replaced by a few furnaces close to deep water. He understood there were sites in the dock which might be suitable and asked for the matter to be discussed with George Deer, the manager at Cwmavon. The Board react with unusual alacrity and interviewed Deer on 16th March, when he was offered a 5-acre site with a deep water frontage between the South Side hydraulic engine house and the Crown Preserved Coal Co.'s works. Rio Tinto proposed to do most of the work themselves. From the PTR&D's point of view, its turnover would be about the same but it would be spared the need to pay Miss Talbot £350 per annum as a consequence of benefitting from the ore traffic to Cwmavon. Furthermore, Talbot Wharf would be relieved of this traffic,

enabling it to be developed as a general import wharf. An agreement whereby Rio Tinto leased the offered 5-acre site at £55 per acre per year was sealed on 15th June. Provision of the necessary supports for the transporter crane required careful planning, and in October 1904 it was agreed that Rio Tinto would lease an additional 5 acres and pay the PTR&D £1,500 towards an open crib-work wharf, 300 feet long, the face of which was to be 80 feet from the sloping dock side to minimise the dredging necessary. The old lease was cancelled and a new lease for the combined sites was sealed on 15th February 1905. Tenders for the construction of the wharf in timber or ferro-concrete were sought in February 1905. The PTR&D directors were inclined to accept Topham, Jones & Railton's quotation for a wharf built to Mouchel's design in ferro-concrete[32] as this was the cheaper method, but this was rejected by Rio Tinto's engineer as being too weak. Consequently, Topham, Jones & Railton's tender to build the Rio Tinto wharf in timber for £3,860 was accepted in March 1905 and combined with their contract to construct

LEFT: The SS *Don Hugo* unloading copper concentrate at Rio Tinto's wharf by means of Temperley Transporters. The *Don Hugo*, of 2,244 gross registered tons, was built for Rio Tinto in 1899, sold in 1915, and wrecked in 1916.
Author's collection

BELOW: Rio Tinto wharf circa January 1909. Again showing the Temperley Transporters for unloading copper concentrate. *Author's collection*

LEFT: Rio Tinto Wharf, circa 1917, showing the open crib-work staging and crude copper discharging cranes in their raised position.
From Port Talbot and its Progress, *PTR&D Co. 1919, Author's collection*

the Talbot Wharf extension and No. 4 tip jetty in ferro-concrete. The wharf was reported to be ready in October 1905.[33] Rio Tinto completed their move from Cwmavon and commenced operations at Port Talbot in September 1906.[34] The works were connected to the long siding off the dock running lines previously laid in for the Crown Preserved Coal Co.[35]

Rio Tinto was a growing multinational company and the Port Talbot works were only a small part of its operations. By 1913 the PTR&D directors, concerned that the small amount of work apparently being carried out there was generating only a nominal amount of traffic, resolved to request their tenant to surrender as much of its leased land as possible. No land was surrendered, and consequently in July 1917 the PTR&D directors declined to authorise a 100-foot extension to Rio Tinto's wharf. In fact about 1,000 tons of refined copper were being produced per month and the works did not close until 1937.

PORT TALBOT IRON & STEEL CO.

In August 1900 the first seeds were sown for what was to become Port Talbot's dominant industry.[36] William Gilbertson[37] had left Cwmavon in 1861 and established himself as a major manufacturer of tinplate based at Pontardawe in the Swansea valley.[38] Gilbertson died in 1882 and control of the business passed to his third son, Arthur, who embarked on a programme of industrial expansion. The family business was registered as a limited company in 1885 with nominal capital of £35,000.[39] Two Siemens open-hearth steel furnaces were built at the Pontardawe works in 1890 to provide an improved base material for the production of tinplate.

In 1900, Arthur Gilbertson sought to expand his steelmaking capacity by constructing a new works at Port Talbot, influenced no doubt by the much improved facilities there. The Port Talbot Iron & Steel Co. Ltd was registered in August 1900 with a nominal capital of £10,000.[40] All 200 shares had been taken up within one month, the majority by Arthur Gilbertson and his family, although fifty-eight were held by Cheston, Miss Talbot's solicitor and presumed nominee. By January 1901 Mr T M Franklen, Miss Talbot's cousin and business advisor, was one of the directors. The nominal capital was increased to £40,000 in February 1902 by the issue of 300 6% Preference Shares of £100 each, Mr Franklen holding 130, also presumably as Miss Talbot's nominee, and the remainder being distributed amongst the Gilbertson family.

It was originally planned to erect steelworks in the south-east corner of the dock area near Margam Copper Works, but the ground proved unsuitable and a 20-acre site close to Mansel Tinplate Works was selected instead.[41] The PTR&D expected to benefit from the rail traffic associated with the works and from handling exports and imports, mainly pig iron, at the docks, but of more immediate concern was the disposal of slag and other waste. Mr Knox, writing on behalf of Miss Talbot and the Steel Co., requested permission to use the O&SSR and Oakwood Bridge,[42] and to make a new railway from there under Railway No. 1 to reach a tipping place in the old harbour south of the PTR's main line to the docks. Gilbertson also asked what the PTR&D would charge for the supply of iron wagons for the removal of hot slag, and for wooden wagons for the removal of ashes and cold slag. Lowther pointed out that they would have to expend at least £600 on iron wagons and keep an

engine on standby, whereas the Steel Co. could do the work for themselves at far less cost. Consequently, the directors agreed in September 1900 to haul ashes, rubbish and hot slag in the Steel Co.'s wagons, that the PTR&D's wagons could be used for cold slag only, and that the Steel Co. could use the O&SSR provided its own traffic had precedence. The following month they agreed to put in the necessary rail connections to the new works, the expense being recovered by an extra rate on all traffic.

Mr Watson, one of the directors, expressed concern that the proposed agreement with Miss Talbot could make the O&SSR competitive with the PTR. However, the solicitor pointed out the agreement was for the carriage of slag only and that the proposed extension of the O&SSR was in the nature of an accommodation work to provide access to Miss Talbot's land on the south side of the docks which otherwise was cut off, and a proviso to this effect was added to the agreement. The directors resolved in December 1900 that the agreement would only be signed when applied for on behalf of Miss Talbot. The following March they agreed to the water level in the dock being lowered to aid construction work provided there was no inconvenience to the docks. The Steel Co. had its own locomotives and in October 1901 was given permission to run them over the dock railways from near Mansel Tinplate Works to the junction with the Oakwood Railway near Port Talbot GWR station. The proposed extension of the O&SSR was never built.

The new works were designed to produce 700 tons of steel per week by the untried Pourcell process. A catalogue of technical, labour and financial problems, and the refusal of Miss Talbot to further increase her already substantial investment, led to a costly failure and work was suspended in February 1903. Mr Lipscomb, Miss Talbot's agent, was appointed liquidator in March 1903[43] and the company was formally wound up twelve months later.[44] Thereafter, Gilbertson's energies were concentrated on developing the Pontardawe works.

PORT TALBOT STEEL CO.

The Port Talbot Iron & Steel Co.'s works remained idle until December 1905 when they were taken over by Messrs Baldwins Ltd, with Col Wright personally holding the lease of the works from W Gilbertson & Co. Ltd. Baldwins was formed in 1902 by the amalgamation of a number of large undertakings, including Wright, Butler & Co., Alfred Baldwin & Co. Ltd and Bryn Navigation Colliery Co. Ltd.[45] Wright, Butler & Co. Ltd had been registered in December 1887 with a capital of £350,000, and by agreements dated 21st December 1887 and 26th June 1888 purchased the steelmaking and colliery business of Wright, Butler & Co. which had been formed in 1882.[46] In January 1906 the PTR&D directors agreed to Baldwins' request that the agreement with their predecessors for the carriage and deposit of slag, ashes, etc. might to be applied to them.

A new company, the Port Talbot Steel Co. Ltd, was registered in August 1906 with a nominal capital of £100,000, having the principal objects of acquiring certain works, lands, and so on belonging to Miss Talbot at Port Talbot and carrying on business as iron, steel and coal proprietors, and of putting into effect an agreement with Baldwins Ltd to take over the Port Talbot Steelworks. The shares were held equally by Baldwins Ltd and the

Port Talbot Steelworks, with Mansel Tinplate Works to the left, the GWR main line behind and Nos 10, 11 and 12 grids in front. Steelworks Wharf is to the right, connected to the railway leading round to Burrows Junction off to the left.
Author's collection

Gloucester Railway Carriage & Wagon Co. Ltd. Col Wright was appointed chairman and William Charles Wright, his son, became managing director. The old plant was immediately remodelled and the furnaces rebuilt for the conventional open hearth processes, the first steel being rolled in January 1907. Baldwins acquired all the shares in 1915, although the Port Talbot Steel Co. Ltd was not formally wound up and absorbed into Baldwins until 1930.[47]

The Steel Co. first asked the PTR&D to construct a wharf for its use in August 1908, it being willing to pay a reasonable rate of interest on the capital expended. In December 1908 the directors considered a plan submitted by the general manager for a 500-foot wharf on the north side of the Float adjoining the North Bank railway for use by both companies; the estimated cost was £12,500 for the wharf, sidings and cranes, and £9,500 for dredging. Lowther proposed that the company should construct this wharf and provide crane power at 1s 1d per ton on all imports and exports, plus 1½d per ton as interest on part of capital cost. The following January the PTR&D considered it was better if they did the haulage and the Steel Co. paid the usual charges, provided the PTR&D was not to be responsible for providing wagons or for the loading of manufactured iron or steel of abnormal size into ships. It seems that nothing further was done at this time, as in September 1909 the Steel Co. complained about the lack of loading and discharging facilities. Lowther's plan was resurrected and tenders sought. The dredging costs had been seriously underestimated, the London & Tilbury Dredging Co. quoting £18,881 7s 9d and Messrs K E Kalis & Co. £18,400 for removing 292,357 cubic yards. These figures raised the total capital outlay to about £32,000 and prompted Lowther to recommend in April 1910 a cheaper scheme of extending North Bank import wharf by 185 feet, increased in June 1910 to 350 feet, at a cost, including four cranes, of £12,000.

Again nothing was done, and matters remained in abeyance until March 1912 when it was reported to the directors that a scheme was under consideration for the erection of significant additional steelmaking plant at the Port Talbot Steel Co. The directors resolved that should this extension go ahead, the necessary expenditure on a new Steelworks Wharf alongside the North Bank railway, estimated to total £40,000, was to be agreed to, the wharf remaining the property of the PTR&D who could make use of it in common with the Steel Co. It took a little while to finalise the dredging contract, the joint tender of Messrs K E Kalis & Co. and Messrs Topham, Jones & Railton for £20,600 being accepted in September 1912. Also that month, the tender of Messrs Watt Bros of Cardiff for the construction of the wharf for £11,000 was accepted; this contract included the construction of the jetty for No. 9 conveyor,[48] which took priority. Soon after starting work Messrs Kalis asked to be released from the contract as they were unable to pump ashore the large amounts of gravel found. Topham, Jones & Railton were prepared to continue, provided they could retain for their own use all gravel deposited higher than one foot above dock water level and they could hire the PTR&D's dredging plant to assist in the task. These terms were accepted in January 1913 and Topham, Jones & Railton erected a Lübecker land dredger[49] on Llewellyn's Quay to lift the gravel previously dredged by Messrs Kalis and deposit it on shore by rail.[50] This operation was completed November 1913[51] and enabled a considerable portion of shallow water to the south-east of the quay to be reclaimed.[52]

Messrs Tannett Walker & Co. were awarded the contract for four 2-ton and one 5/15-ton cranes for the wharf, but this firm went into liquidation in April 1913 and the order was passed to the East Ferry Road Engineering Works Co. Ltd. The sidings for the new steelworks were completed in October 1913,[53] but the wharf was not finished until October 1914,[54] the sidings and cranes on it being brought into use in March 1915.[55] All previous siding agreements with the Port Talbot Steel Co. were cancelled and a new agreement was sealed on 20th January 1915. One of the PTR&D's Sharp, Stewart 0-8-2 tank engines was used to test the deflection of the reinforced concrete beams on the wharf on 11th August 1915.[56] The GWR supplied special wagons for conveying steel plate between Port Talbot Steelworks and the docks at a hire charge of 6d per ton.

Towards the end of the First World War, iron ore was imported through Port Talbot, presumably for transport further afield as there were no blast furnaces there at that time. The directors noted in June 1917 that the Priestman grab system was to be employed provided the Government advanced the necessary funds for the purchase of one grab adaptable to the existing 2-ton hydraulic cranes on the Steelworks Wharf. Roberts, the mechanical engineer, reported in

The general offices of the Port Talbot Steel Co. Ltd circa 1917, although by this time this company had been acquired by Messrs Baldwins Ltd and the offices also served the nearby Margam Steelworks.
From Port Talbot and its Progress, *PTR&D Co. 1919, Author's collection*

December 1917 that the grab was working well and by September 1918 the Government had provided three more. The total cost was £870, and in March 1922 the Government accepted £450 for them. This system apparently sufficed until 1927 when two transporter unloaders were erected on Margam Wharf as part of the modest investment programme at the steelworks there.

MARGAM STEELWORKS

On 18th December 1912 Col Wright outlined to the Board of the PTR&D the negotiations that were in progress with Messrs Baldwins Ltd for a site at the east end of the docks for a proposed major new blast furnaces and steelworks. Col Wright was granted an option on behalf of Baldwins for a 10-acre site with an 800-foot wharf at £40 per acre per annum. The following month the option was increased to 25 acres. Planning the new works took some time and it was not until October 1914 that they were sufficiently far advanced that further details could be negotiated. By then a further 8 acres were required and these were leased at £60 per acre for a term of 99 years. The railway companies had been under Government control since 4th August 1914 immediately following the outbreak of the First World War, and the Board of Trade had in May 1915 stopped all but absolutely essential capital expenditure and required companies to obtain its approval if they needed to raise loans or new capital. Steel was of course essential for the war effort, and in May 1915 the Treasury was asked to sanction the

SS *Clyne Rock* loading pipes from GWR bogie bolster wagons on Steelworks Wharf, June 1923.　　*BR/OPC*

RIGHT: Steelworks Wharf, photographed from the top of No. 8 tip, circa 1915. The sidings on North Bank with loaded wagons for No. 5 tip run across the lower right-hand corner. The defunct Margam Copper Works are visible in the background across the Float with Llewellyn's Quay just in front. The steelworks this wharf was constructed to serve are off the view to the left.

From Port Talbot and its Progress, *PTR&D Co. 1919, Author's collection*

Unloading pitwood at Steelworks Wharf, looking west, with North Bank in the background. The reinforced concrete construction of the wharf is clearly seen. May 1928.   *NM&GW*

works and provide the necessary funds.[57] The PTR&D's engineer submitted the following estimate:

Dredging	£13,500
600-foot wharf	£15,000
Reclamation of land	£ 2,500
Diversion of the O&SSR	£ 550
Diversion of Military Road	£ 200
Dolphins, moorings, etc.	£ 500
Earthworks for new railways	£ 900
Laying rails	£ 3,600
Total	£36,750

At their meeting in June 1916 the directors were informed that the Treasury was prepared to advance to the company the sum required to construct the wharf and railways, and for the dredging necessary, free of interest during the period of Government control of the railways. The PTR&D was able to do the dredging and alter the railways itself, but the construction of the wharf required an outside contractor. The Treasury preferred this to be done as a fixed price contract, but Messrs Topham, Jones & Railton, who had been awarded the contract for building the new steelworks, had intimated that this was not possible although they could start immediately on cost plus 5 per cent basis. Baldwins then decided that the wharf should be placed at the eastern end of the Old Dock rather than where originally intended, at right angles to the end of Llewellyn's Quay. Baldwins were allowed to retain the original site of about 4¾ acres and were granted first refusal on four acres adjacent. Detailed

plans and specifications of the wharf were prepared and sent out for tenders in October 1916.[58] Col Wright was empowered by the Board to deal fully with the tenders, and although that of £28,000 submitted by Messrs Holloway Bros was preferred, it was subject to them being able to get men and materials. Instead, Messrs Topham, Jones & Railton, already engaged on the blast furnace site, were given the work in February 1917 on a cost plus 5 per cent basis, the total not to exceed Messrs Holloway's tender price.

In February 1917 the directors agreed to an application from Topham, Jones & Railton for a siding connection at the English Celluloid Works camp;[59] this was for the conveyance by train of German prisoners of war to and from the new steel works site where they worked on its construction. Temporary platforms were rapidly erected at the Celluloid Works and at Copper Works Junction.[60] Topham, Jones & Railton at first objected to part of the indemnity which absolved the PTR&D from any liability where trains were hired to run over lines not authorised for passenger traffic – that is, from Duffryn Junction to Copper Works Junction – but as this was standard practice for workmen's trains, they eventually complied in June 1917.[61] The hire charge for one six-coach train each way was £4 per day.

Meanwhile, the PTR&D had made a start on its part of the project. A temporary siding was laid in to bring in spoil for building up the ground for the new wharf.[62] Dredging the channel towards the wharf was underway by November 1916,[63] as was the diversion of the O&SSR.[64] This line – which originally followed the water's edge round to the landward end of Llewellyn's Quay and had been doubled in 1915 – was moved so that it ran due north along the

LEFT: Blast furnaces and stoves being erected at Baldwins' Margam Steelworks, circa 1917, viewed from the landward side.
From Port Talbot and its Progress, *PTR&D Co. 1919, Author's collection*

BELOW: Margam Steelworks from the north circa 1923, with the O&SSR and Margam Wharf visible on the far right. The view pre-dates the erection of ore unloaders on Margam Wharf. *Courtesy Arthur Rees*

intended line of the new wharf. A temporary siding for delivering materials to Messrs Topham, Jones & Railton's yard was laid in at the rear of Taibach Tinplate Works during January 1917.[65] The PTR&D's 6-inch fresh water main was diverted away from the blast furnace site in March 1917.[66] Trial piles for the new wharf were driven by the contractors in July 1917.[67] However, as the war progressed and U-Boat activity increased, Baldwins changed their plans to obtaining most of their iron ore by rail from Oxfordshire rather than by sea from Spain, and new siding connections were put in for the purpose. The directors resolved in May 1917 that as

this arrangement took the place of the more profitable, to them, water-borne traffic, the original agreement with Baldwins would be reviewed. This development removed the immediate need for the new wharf and in December 1917 sanction was obtained from the Ministry of Munitions to postpone its construction. Up to this point the PTR&D had received a single payment of £5,000 towards the cost of this works.

Work on the diversion of the O&SSR resumed in February 1918, along with the diversion of, and a new bridge over, the River Ffrwdwyllt.[68] This work was finished in October 1918 with

Margam Steelworks in 1924 with No. 1 (on the right) and No. 2 blast furnaces prominent. In front of the stoves is the 620 feet long row of bunkers for the storage of raw materials. Loaded wagons were raised to the discharge level by an electric hoist at the right-hand end, moved into position by electric capstans, and empties lowered by a gravity drop at the left-hand end. *NMGW*

tracks roughly in place awaiting the completion of the wharf.[69] Two connections for the new works were laid in at Copper Works Junction in September 1918.[70] Plans for six reception sidings for ore from Banbury were approved in 1919; work on these, which were connected to the Dock Branch near Copper Works Junction and to the Morfa Railway at their other end, started in June 1920[71] and was finished circa October 1921.[72] Steel production at Margam Steelworks had commenced during 1918.[73] Almost immediately the need arose for a hot metal road to Baldwins' Port Talbot Steelworks about half a mile distant where the steel was rolled. A third line to connect the two sites was laid in in April 1919, parallel to the O&SSR which was slewed slightly in the vicinity of Taibach Tinplate Works to provide the necessary space.[74]

The directors were informed at their Board meeting in June 1919 that Baldwins were now asking for the construction of the new wharf. This request brought about contractual problems as the cost had increased by about 100 per cent due to the enforced delay, and made worse by the fact that the PTR&D could not issue any stocks or shares except at a serious discount owing to the depressed state of the markets. The directors were informed in September 1919 that the Treasury could not advance the further monies required. The banks were more amenable and in March 1920 the general manager provisionally arranged for the London, City & Midland Bank to advance £80,000–100,000 at 5% for five years. The directors resolved to accept this offer, but the following month the GWR recommended that the PTR&D should do the work, the GWR providing the necessary funds which would be added to the existing advance.[75] This proposal was, of course, accepted and construction of the wharf proceeded on that basis. A new lease with Messrs Baldwins of land for the wharf and for further sidings was sealed on 26th October 1921. The PTR&D was informed by the Treasury that interest on the funds already advanced, £20,094, would run from 14th February 1922. Following negotiations with the Treasury, the GWR repaid this sum interest free in March 1923.[76]

Early in 1923 Baldwins impressed upon the GWR the need to improve the facilities at Port Talbot as the restriction on tonnage prejudiced them in the export market. It was suggested that if the

GWR wished to avoid the outlay necessary to increase the capacity of the docks it would agree to Baldwins shipping at Swansea at the same rate as at Port Talbot. However, and the despite the limitations imposed by the existing lock, Sir Charles Wright, Baldwins' managing director, urged the GWR to complete the wharf.[77]

Preliminary work on the wharf had commenced in July 1920 when trial piles were driven,[78] whilst filling of the marshy land behind the line of the wharf was well in hand by December 1920.[79] A temporary siding was laid in January 1921 for the wharf construction and the hulk *Sonia*[80] was converted to a pile driving barge.[81] Piles were ordered from the GWR's concrete works at Taunton, 214 having been delivered by October 1921.[82] Despite all this preparatory work, Baldwins had not yet given the go-ahead to start construction due to the downturn in demand following the brief post-war boom. Although foundations had been laid for three blast furnaces only two were erected at this time, No. 1 being blown-in in February 1922 and No. 2 in April 1923. Likewise, little seems to have been done on the wharf until June 1923 when the GWR directors authorised the expenditure of £61,000.[83] A further expenditure of £4,163 was required in December 1926.[84] Associated with this work, the area of deep water in front of the wharf was extended by dredging at a cost of £11,000.[85] The third blast furnace was not built until 1941 to cope with the additional demand in the Second World War.

SMALL BUSINESSES

CREOSOTING WORKS
In December 1900 Messrs Burt, Boulton & Haywood applied for land on which to erect a creosoting works and were offered a site of just over one acre at the east end of North Bank behind No. 5 tip, the right to lay in a siding and authority to use the whole of the Float for storing timber rafts.[86] The seven-year lease was signed in August 1901, and because of its proximity to the GWR and R&SBR the company was granted a reduction in haulage rates to their junctions. This site experienced problems with water supply which were not resolved until March 1903.[87] The lease expired in

ABOVE: The blast furnaces at Margam Steelworks with the ore unloading gantries behind and what looks like a pile of scrap metal awaiting refining.

Author's collection

Margam Wharf, with the unloaders for Margam
Steelworks behind. April 1927.   *NM&GW*

November 1908 but the business was allowed to remain as a "tenant at will". Messrs Burt, Boulton & Haywood gave notice to terminate their tenancy of the site in December 1919.

Messrs Calder & Co. of Swansea applied for a site for a sleeper creosoting works in January 1921 and were offered the land on North Bank previously occupied by Messrs Burt, Boulton & Haywood. In October 1921, shortly after the lease been prepared, Messrs Calder applied for a fresh site and were then offered 4½ acres between North Bank and the Port Talbot Steelworks. Siding connections to the North Bank railway were agreed in February 1922.

MESSRS ROBINSON, DAVID & CO.
In November 1901 Robinson, David & Co. were offered a 2-acre site with a water frontage on the north side of the New Dock between the old lock and No. 7 tip for timber storage and a sawmill. The lease was signed in December 1901 and a railway connection, which trailed off the lines on Talbot Wharf, was laid in. Although they occupied the site, the lessees apparently did nothing for almost a year and in October 1902 the directors demanded the erection of plant greater than £3,000 in value or a satisfactory minimum guarantee of traffic. By November 1908 the lease had expired and the directors decided that it would be not renewed although the firm could remain as a "tenant at will".

MARGAM UDC GASWORKS
In anticipation of obtaining its 1911 Act,[88] Margam UDC in November 1910 enquired of the PTR&D its price for the designated site for a proposed gasworks which was to be erected on

surplus land between the GWR main line and the Morfa Railway near the PTR overbridge.[89] Industrial land in the dock area was valued at £500 per acre and £875 was agreed for the 1¾ acres, a condition of the conveyance being that no vehicular or pedestrian traffic was to cross the GWR or PTR from Lady Charlotte's Road, access being through Vivian's site to the north. A complication arose in that, being surplus land, it had first to be offered to Miss Talbot, from whom it had been acquired. She declined the offer, although she was a party to the conveyance which was completed in May 1914. By then the construction of Margam West Curve, which skirted the site to the south and east, was well under way.[90] A siding agreement for a connection to the West Curve was sealed on 18th August 1914, the siding being put into use in September 1915.[91] A further agreement for the maintenance of the gasworks siding by the PTR&D was signed in 1916.

PORT TALBOT COLLIERY
One development which would have had a profound effect on the shoreline at Port Talbot was a proposed colliery on Aberavon Burrows. The minerals under the foreshore were owned by Charles Evan-Thomas and Henry Jeffreys Bushby, the Lords of the Borough of Afon and the Manor of Afon Wallia. The Sandhills Boring Co. was formed in 1892 to sink trial shafts and work the coal.[92] T Forster Brown, later one of the PTR&D's engineers, and Edward Knox, Miss Talbot's agent, were two of the subscribers. The Port Talbot Colliery Co. was formed in 1899 to underlease 2,500 acres of the coal and sink a colliery thereon, Forster Brown and Knox again being subscribers.[93] Neither of these companies ever carried

Looking south along Margam Wharf with iron ore being unloaded from SS *Albatross*, April 1927. Note the covers protecting the tracks and anything passing from spilt ore.
NM&GW

ABOVE: A view of the outer end of North Bank with the row of Nos 5, 6 and 8 tips with Burt, Boulton & Haywood's creosoting works on the right.
Author's collection

BELOW: Another view of the outer end of North Bank, showing Burt, Boulton & Haywood's creosoting works with Nos 5 and 6 tips behind.
Author's collection

on any business and both were dissolved in 1902.[94] Meanwhile, the PTR&D had entered into an agreement in April 1895 with Messrs Evan-Thomas and Bushby and the Sandhills Co. to protect its dock property from the effects of mining.[95] As part of this agreement, there was a requirement on the PTR&D to provide a connection to transport the Sandhills colliery traffic to the docks. Evan-Thomas eventually began to make his own plans to work the minerals and in January 1907 wrote regarding the point to which it was proposed to bring a tramway from an intended pair of pits on

Aberavon Burrows to meet a railway to be built by the PTR&D, as stipulated in the agreements. This plan was objected to as it would have required a new bridge over the River Avon, but in August 1907 a route leading to the PTR&D's existing wooden bridge over the river was approved – this bridge had been constructed in 1897 by Topham, Jones & Railton in conjunction with their Graving Dock contract and subsequently purchased by the PTR&D. The resulting agreement with Bushby & Others was signed on 15th April 1908. Fortunately perhaps for Port Talbot, nothing further was done.

Notes

1. TNA: PRO BT 31/7518/53533.
2. *Railway News*, 21 August 1897.
3. TNA: PRO BT 31/7515/53511.
4. *The London Gazette*, 8 June 1900.
5. TNA: PRO BT 31/7518/53533.
6. See Volume 1, Chapter 5.
7. TNA: PRO RAIL 1057/2472.
8. TNA: PRO RAIL 1057/1528/136.
9. TNA: PRO RAIL 1057/1059; *Railway Times* 12 August 1899.
10. TNA: PRO RAIL 1057/2626.
11. See Chapter 15.
12. Philip R Björling, *Briquettes and Patent Fuel: Their Manufacture and Machinery Connected Therewith* (Rebman Ltd 1903), pp. 1–4.
13. Henry T de la Beche, 'First report on the Coals suited to the Steam Navy', *Memoirs of the Geological Survey of Great Britain*, Vol. 2 part 2, (1848), p. 606.
14. 'The Crown Preserved Coal Co. Ltd', in *The South Wales Coal Annual 1909–1910*, pp. 1–32.
15. TNA: PRO BT 31/496/1962.
16. TNA: PRO BT 31/15092/32160.
17. TNA: PRO RAIL 1057/2657.
18. TNA: PRO RAIL 1057/2630.
19. TNA: PRO RAIL 1057/1528/185.
20. TNA: PRO RAIL 1057/1528/187.
21. TNA: PRO BT 31/25619/164345.
22. TNA: PRO RAIL 1057/2633.
23. TNA: PRO BT 31/22208/135215.
24. TNA: PRO BT 31/21116/126076.
25. TNA: PRO BT 31/1988/8515.
26. TNA: PRO RAIL 1057/1528/240.
27. TNA: PRO RAIL 1057/1528/253.
28. TNA: PRO BT 31/33116/241691.
29. See Volume 1, Chapter 6.
30. Charles E Harvey, *The Rio Tinto Company: An Economic History of a Leading International Mining Concern 1873–1954* (Alison Hodge Publishers, 1981), p. 156.
31. TNA: PRO RAIL 1057/2617.
32. See Chapter 12.
33. TNA: PRO RAIL 1057/1528/92.
34. TNA: PRO RAIL 1057/1528/103.
35. TNA: PRO RAIL 1057/1528/82.
36. Stephen Parry, 'History of the Steel Industry in the Port Talbot Area 1900–1988' (unpublished PhD Thesis, University of Leeds 2011, http://etheses.whiterose.ac.uk/2591/1/parrystephen.pdf).
37. See Volume 1, Chapter 2.
38. PW Jackson (ed.), *The Letter-Books of W Gilbertson & Co. Ltd., Pontardawe, 1890–1929* (West Glamorgan Archive Service 2001).
39. TNA: PRO BT 31/31031/21848.
40. TNA: PRO BT 31/9058/67018.
41. TNA: PRO RAIL 1057/2471.
42. See Chapter 13.
43. *The London Gazette*, 17 March 1903.
44. *The London Gazette*, 28 March 1904.

45. TNA: PRO BT 31/36851/73336; *British Coal, Iron and Steel: A Brief Survey of the Productions of Baldwins Limited* (Burrow & Co., 1934)
46. TNA: PRO BT 31/4018/25588.
47. *The London Gazette* 14 February 1930.
48. See Chapter 13.
49. See Chapter 13.
50. TNA: PRO RAIL 1057/1528/172, 173.
51. TNA: PRO RAIL 1057/1528/180.
52. TNA: PRO RAIL 1057/1528/175.
53. TNA: PRO RAIL 1057/1528/179.
54. TNA: PRO RAIL 1057/1528/187.
55. TNA: PRO RAIL 1057/1528/192.
56. TNA: PRO RAIL 1057/1528/197.
57. TNA: PRO MUN 4/4207.
58. TNA: PRO RAIL 1057/1528/209.
59. See Chapter 21.
60. TNA: PRO RAIL 1057/1528/214.
61. TNA: PRO MT 6/2458/3, RAIL 574/54.
62. TNA: PRO RAIL 1057/1528/208.
63. TNA: PRO RAIL 1057/1528/210.
64. TNA: PRO RAIL 1057/1528/211.
65. TNA: PRO RAIL 574/53, 1057/1528/212.
66. TNA: PRO RAIL 1057/1528/214.
67. TNA: PRO RAIL 1057/1528/217.
68. TNA: PRO RAIL 1057/1528/223.
69. TNA: PRO RAIL 1057/1528/230.
70. TNA: PRO RAIL 1057/1528/229.
71. TNA: PRO RAIL 1057/1528/243.
72. TNA: PRO RAIL 1057/1528/254.
73. Robert Protheroe-Jones, *Welsh Steel* (National Museums and Galleries of Wales 1995), p. 35.
74. TNA: PRO RAIL 1057/1528/234.
75. See Chapter 17.
76. TNA: PRO RAIL 250/54, RAIL 1057/2952.
77. TNA: PRO RAIL 1057/2952.
78. TNA: PRO RAIL 1057/1528/244.
79. TNA: PRO RAIL 1057/1528/247.
80. See Chapter 15.
81. TNA: PRO RAIL 1057/1528/248, 249.
82. TNA: PRO RAIL 1057/1528/254.
83. TNA: PRO RAIL 250/54.
84. TNA: PRO RAIL 250/55.
85. TNA: PRO RAIL 250/179.
86. WGAS D/D PRO/BRB/307.
87. See Chapter 13.
88. *The London Gazette* 25 November 1910; 1 & 2 Geo. 5 c.cxv.
89. TNA: PRO RAIL 1057/2469.
90. See Chapter 11.
91. TNA: PRO RAIL 1057/1528/197.
92. TNA: PRO BT 31/5297/36207.
93. TNA: PRO BT 31/8620/62838.
94. *The London Gazette* 18 November 1902, 26 December 1902.
95. See Chapter 12.

15

Floating Plant

THE PTR&D ASSEMBLED A modest fleet of tugs, dredgers, barges and smaller craft for use in and around the docks. Initially these vessels were the responsibility of Hosgood, the locomotive superintendent. They then passed to his successor, Hertz, before being put in the charge of the mechanical engineer, Roberts, when he was appointed in 1908.

Tugs

The company acquired its first vessel in April 1895 when the steam tug *Margaret*, which had been owned by the old company, was handed over by Miss Talbot. This tug had been insured for £700, but became uninsurable later that year when it failed a boiler test. Meik was instructed to put the tug into a saleable condition and to report on the matter of a new replacement. A secondhand engine and boiler were purchased and the *Margaret* was put up for auction at the end of 1896, although the outcome is not recorded.

In March 1896 the directors accepted the tender of Messrs Mordey, Carney & Co. of Newport for a new tug, 122 tons gross, for £3,750. This new tug, named the *Emily Charlotte* after the company's principal shareholder, was in service in December 1896, crewed by five men. But not for long; the following February a serious fault was discovered in the boiler, the builders agreed to replace this and the tug was back in service in April 1897. A second new boiler was required in July 1903 and later that year the tender of Messrs Joseph T Eltingham & Co. of South Shields was accepted. The *Emily Charlotte* left Port Talbot on 25th April 1904 for South Shields, the voyage taking three and a half days of continuous steaming,[1] and returned in service in June 1904. Further repairs were required in 1910; while these were being carried out the steam tug *Conqueror* was hired from Swansea[2] until the *Emily Charlotte* was back in service in June 1911.[3]

In 1915 consideration was given to selling or leasing the *Emily Charlotte* to the towing contractors Messrs D Jenkins & Sons of Port Talbot and also to having the sole use of their tug *Harmony*, but

The PTR&D's tug *Emily Charlotte* with the dredger *Bollin* behind. The *Emily Charlotte* was a single screw tug of 60 registered horse power built by Mordey, Carney & Co. of Newport in 1896. Postcard, postally used 12th May 1910. *Author's collection*

Above: *Emily Charlotte* in Port Talbot Docks circa 1914. If the date is accurate, the tug appears to be in good condition having just returned to service after being sunk in the harbour in October 1913.   *Author's collection*

The Port Talbot Pilotage Board's cutter *Guide*, purchased secondhand in 1908. This vessel was converted into a tug in January 1913, although there is no sign of the usual fittings in this view, and was sold in March 1914.   *Courtesy Arthur Rees*

this idea was not pursued. This firm already held a license to operate within the dock limits if the PTR&D's tug was not available.

On two occasions the *Emily Charlotte* sank in the dock as a result of collisions with steamers. The first occurred on 10th October 1913 and the tug was not raised by the Port Talbot Graving Dock Co. until 21st March 1914[4] at a cost of £500. Repairs cost a further £1,845 and the tug was back in use on 21st May 1914.[5] The *Emily Charlotte* was badly holed on 22nd December 1919 and scuttled in shallow water after colliding with the SS *Nervona*.[6] The vessel was refloated on 23rd February 1920 and put in the graving dock for repairs.[7] The *Emily Charlotte* became part of the GWR fleet in 1922 and was broken up in 1949 having been sold to Britannia Steam Towage Ltd in 1933.[8]

One tug was not always sufficient to deal with the shipping in the docks. Following complaints from Messrs Bordes et Fils of Paris regarding delays to their vessels, the directors in September 1908 contemplated acquiring an additional, more powerful, tug. The general manager, Lowther, arranged for the Alexandra Towing Co. Ltd to experimentally station one at Port Talbot for three months, they being allowed to retain all outside towage and so much of the dock towage as the PTR&D was unable to undertake. This arrangement was not continued[9] and nothing more was done until October 1912 when the company's steam cutter, the *Guide*, was deemed suitable for conversion to a tug. The *Guide* had been purchased in May 1908 for £1,237 and the following month was hired, together with the sailing cutters *Minerva* and *Dorothy*, to the Port Talbot Pilotage Board. Pilots had been authorised by the PTR&D's 1894 Act and the Pilotage Board by the 1899 Act, and Bye-Laws and Regulations were approved by Parliament.[10] The *Guide* was offered for sale in January 1911, but found no takers and the conversion to a tug was made by the provision of a towing hook, the work being completed by January 1913.[11] The *Guide* was then put into commission as a tug for dredging work and the *Emily Charlotte* used for towing. The *Guide* was eventually sold in March 1914 for £1,635, an overall loss of £2,065, of which the GWR agreed to bear £1,100. A replacement of sorts was found in January 1916 when the pilot cutter *Briton* was authorised to assist in outside towages.

By 1920 the directors had concluded that the traffic in the docks warranted two tugs and resolved to purchase, subject to inspection, the *Gaviota* which was based at Hull. This tug arrived at Port Talbot in February 1920 and was registered as the *Sir John R Wright* the following September; however, this vessel was laid up in January 1921 due to a depression in trade, all necessary work being done by the *Emily Charlotte*.

DREDGERS

From the outset it was realised that extensive dredging would be necessary to open up, and in due course extend, the enclosed dock area and also to maintain the depth of the entrance channel. The PTR&D asked for tenders for a dredger as early as December 1895, and in March 1896 a dredging crane barge was ordered. Messrs Pearson made their own arrangements for creating the New Dock. In January 1899 a dredger and two barges were hired from the Neath Harbour Commissioners to dredge the river and float during the dispute with the contractor.[12] Pearson's had hired the dredger *Bollin* from the Manchester Ship Canal Co. and as it was no longer needed by either of them it was offered to the PTR&D for £9,000. A counter offer of £7,500 was rejected, but on 15th November 1899 a price of £8,500 was agreed. The *Bollin* had been built by Messrs Fleming & Ferguson Ltd of Paisley and erected on site in 1892 for excavating the Manchester Ship Canal. It was estimated that the *Bollin*, which was put in the charge of the locomotive engineer, could be put in working order and fitted with a sand pump in one to two weeks. In January 1900 two hopper barges to accompany the dredger were ordered from the Port Talbot Graving Dock Co. It evidently did not carry that much fresh water and in November 1902 the *Emily Charlotte* was fitted with a fresh water tank in its forepeak so that the *Bollin* could be supplied without going alongside a quay. The *Bollin* was fitted with a 20-inch suction pump to deal with the very fine sand found in the entrance channel.[13]

Dredging the sand and gravel in the dock and entrance channel, as well as accidental groundings, caused considerable wear and tear to the operating parts of the *Bollin* and frequent repairs, usually carried out in the graving dock, were necessary. On occasions replacements were hired from Swansea and Merseyside. The suction hopper barge *Tulip* was used for six weeks in 1906,[14] and *No. 5 Mersey* sand dredger was at Port Talbot for two months in 1909.[15] On occasion the reverse was done: in 1903 the PTR&D's Priestman steam grab dredger and a dumb hopper steel barge were hired to the Swansea Harbour Trust (SHT);[16] in September 1906 the *Bollin* was hired out for two months to Mr George Palmer of Neath to deepen the berth at Giants Grave, Briton Ferry, for Messrs T W Ward who planned to use this site for breaking up old warships.[17]

The tug *Emily Charlotte* engaged in one of her principal tasks, leading ships through the entrance channel towards the lock. This undated postcard view, taken from the south breakwater, shows the SS *Magellan* under tow. The French-owned *Magellan*, of 6,265 gross registered tons, was built in 1904, and torpedoed and sunk 1917.   *Author's collection*

Steam hopper barges *Hoptree* and *Hopgarden* tied up alongside Talbot Wharf. *Courtesy Arthur Rees*

The steam hopper barge *Hopgarden* passing No. 9 conveyor. Postcard, postally used 22nd August 1928, but photographed a few years earlier.
Author's collection

The purchase of a second dredger was first considered in March 1909. The twin screw suction hopper dredger *Thames*, built in 1904 and lying at Newport, was available for £7,500 and the directors resolved to hire this craft and to purchase it if found suitable. It transpired that this dredger could not hold the pumped sand, but nevertheless it was purchased for £6,800 and altered to be similar to the *No. 5 Mersey* sand dredger then at Port Talbot. The *Thames* was used to pump ashore from hopper barges gravel dredged from the dock bottom that was then used to reclaim low lying land.[18]

The PTR&D advertised its need of another self-propelled sand suction hopper dredger in August 1913.[19] In due course the *Nereus* was hired from Messrs R E V James Ltd in October 1913 for £50 per week.[20] This dredger proved satisfactory and in May 1914 the directors agreed to purchase it for £9,050,[21] reduced to £7,805 18s 9d net of the necessary repairs. The *Nereus* was built with two boilers, when these were in need of repair they were replaced in 1920–21 with a single, larger, boiler.[22] The *Nereus* was condemned in November 1925.[23]

BARGES

Barges were needed to accompany the dredgers and, towed by the *Emily Charlotte*, to take spoil to be dumped out at sea. The hopper barge *Jubilee* was bought in March 1896 and two more, ordered from the Port Talbot Graving Dock Co. in January 1900, were delivered in November that year. They were not needed all the time and were variously hired out to the SHT and the Cardiff Railway in 1903/4[24] and to Messrs Easton, Gibb & Son for their Alexandra Dock contract at Newport in 1905/6.[25]

The obvious drawback with these dumb barges was that they required a tug to move anywhere. In January 1914 the aforesaid Messrs R James offered the PTR&D two steam hopper barges of 350/400 tons gross. In response the docks offered two dumb barges in part exchange, for which Messrs James offered £1,750 each and asked for £3,750 each for the two steam barges. This bargain was accepted subject to inspection and was agreed in March 1914 for a net payment of £3,547.[26] These vessels became steam hopper barges Nos 1 and 2 and were named *Hoptree* and *Hopgarden* respectively, the names probably being the existing ones. Both were

commandeered by the Government in July 1918, No. 1 going to Swansea for conversion to carry oil and No. 2 to Penarth for conversion to carry water.[27] In March 1919 the PTR&D offered to sell them to the Ministry of Supply for £10,000 each, which was not accepted, and both were restored to their original condition at Government expense, No. 2 returning in February and No. 1 in May 1920.[28] Both barges were condemned in April 1927.[29]

Most sailing colliers arrived at Port Talbot in ballast; to speed up the discharge of this useful material the directors decided in March 1910 to purchase a 65-foot long Temperley Patent Transporter for this purpose. This was a type of overhead crane similar to a gantry crane and used to bunker steamships from barges or colliers lying alongside. At the same time the directors purchased the brig *Sonia*, 251 tons gross, for £390 from John Levantin Kjellberg of Gothenburg, Sweden, on which to mount the transporter and load the ballast.[30] The conversion of the *Sonia* to a transporter barge was undertaken by the Port Talbot Graving Dock Co. and was completed in October 1910.[31] Ballast was unloaded from the *Sonia* at Llewellyn's Quay for removal by rail.[32]

The dredger *Bollin* and the two steam hopper barges were laid up in October 1910 and the crews, apart from the dredger's engineer who was retained to carry out repairs, were discharged.[33] Exactly the same happened in December 1917.[34] Dredging resumed for three months from September to December 1918, when the plant was laid up again.[35] Roberts pointed out in March 1921 that the *Bollin* was then twenty-nine years old, twenty-two of them at Port Talbot – which was old as dredgers went – and that future maintenance was bound to be costly.[36] The *Bollin* disappeared around this time but in 1923 the *Don Frederico* was purchased by the GWR from the SHT and was listed at being at Port Talbot;[37] this bucket dredger was built in Glasgow in 1909, had been acquired by the SHT in 1920, and was broken up in 1947.[38]

LAUNCHES

The PTR&D owned at least three steam launches for use around the docks, *Nell*, *No. 3* and *No. 4*. One of their duties was to provide a ferry service between Llewellyn's Quay, North Bank, Talbot Wharf and the South Side of the New Dock. The Port Talbot

One of the PTR&D's steam launches, used to provide a ferry service in the dock area, is seen at a jetty on Llewellyn's Quay.   *Author's collection*

Graving Dock Co. built such a launch 25 feet long by 7 feet for £200 in 1908, and another was ordered from Messrs Vosper & Co. for £315 in December 1908, arriving the following February.[39] A secondhand launch with a new boiler and machinery was acquired from the Graving Dock Co. in November 1912.[40] All three were extant in 1923.[41]

NOTES

1. TNA: PRO RAIL 1058/1528/77.
2. WGAS D/D PRO/BRB/328.
3. TNA: PRO RAIL 1058/1528/154.
4. TNA: PRO RAIL 1058/1528/180, 182.
5. TNA: PRO RAIL 1058/1528/184.
6. TNA: PRO RAIL 1058/1528/238.
7. TNA: PRO RAIL 1058/1528/240.
8. Duncan Haws, *Merchant Fleets No. 24: Britain's Railway Steamers: Western & Southern Companies plus French and Stena* (TCL Publications 1993), p. 24.
9. Tim Nicholson, *Take the Strain: The Alexandra Towing Company and the British Tugboat Business 1833–1987* (The Alexandra Towing Co. Ltd 1990), p. 160.
10. *London Gazette*, 3 February 1899, 9 March 1900, 24 October 1905.
11. TNA: PRO RAIL 1058/1528/171.
12. See Chapter 11.
13. Cleaver, 'Alterations and Improvements', pp. 105–7, 169–70.
14. WGAS D/D PRO/BRB/312.
15. WGAS D/D PRO/BRB/323.
16. WGAS D/D PRO/BRB/310.
17. TNA: PRO RAIL 1058/1528/104, 105; WGAS D/D PRO/BRB/313.
18. Cleaver, 'Alterations and Improvements', pp. 111–12.
19. *The Times*, 13 August 1913.
20. WGAS D/D PRO/BRB/336.
21. WGAS D/D PRO/BRB/338.
22. TNA: PRO RAIL 1057/1528/236, 247.
23. TNA: PRO RAIL 250/317.
24. TNA: PRO RAIL 1057/1528/74, 78.
25. TNA: PRO RAIL 1057/1528/74, 78.
26. WGAS D/D PRO/BRB/337.
27. TNA: PRO RAIL 1057/1528/228, 229.
28. TNA: PRO RAIL 1057/1528/240, 242.
29. TNA: PRO RAIL 250/317.
30. WGAS D/D PRO/BRB/329.
31. TNA: PRO RAIL 1057/1528/147.
32. TNA: PRO RAIL 1057/1528/155.
33. TNA: PRO RAIL 1057/1528/198.
34. TNA: PRO RAIL 1057/1528/222.
35. TNA: PRO RAIL 1057/1528/229.
36. TNA: PRO RAIL 1057/1528/249.
37. TNA: PRO RAIL 253/338.
38. Haws, *Merchant Fleets No. 24*, p. 24.
39. TNA: PRO RAIL 1057/1528/131.
40. TNA: PRO RAIL 1057/1528/170.
41. TNA: PRO RAIL 253/338.

GWR 2-6-2T No. 4544 at Port Talbot Central on the 6.45 p.m. train to Blaengarw on 14th May 1919. This train called at Bryn, Maesteg, Cwmdu, Lletty Brongu, Bettws Llangeinor, Pontyrhyll and Pontycymmer, reaching its destination at 7.38 p.m., covering the seventeen and a half miles in 53 minutes. No. 4544 was shedded at Duffryn from April 1916 until an unknown date in 1920. The significance of the six-pointed star on the smokebox door is unknown. The first two carriages are PTR stock, the second apparently being one of the Composites, by this date downgraded to an all-Third.
Author's collection

16

Train Services[1]

PASSENGER TRAINS

DUFFRYN LINE

Passenger trains on the PTR commenced on Monday 14th February 1898.[2] At first trains started from Port Talbot Central station, but, following agreement with the R&SBR, Aberavon station, which was more convenient for the centre of Port Talbot, provided an alternative starting point from 1st June 1898. The trains ran only as far as Pontycymmer until 26th May 1902, when the line to Blaengarw and the station there was opened for passenger traffic. The initial service consisted of four return services daily, the first departing at 7.15 a.m., with an additional return train on Saturday afternoons. An evening return service on Saturdays was added as from 5th March 1898.

Several changes were made in October 1898 when the Saturday afternoon train was dropped. The first Up train of the day was altered to leave Aberavon at 5.55 a.m., running to Maesteg from where, after prompt station work, it returned to Bryn, reversed again and continued to Pontycymmer arriving at 7.05 a.m. From January 1899 this practice was discontinued and the train ran through to Pontycymmer arriving at 6.40 a.m. The return service left Pontycymmer at 8.05 a.m. and arrived at Port Talbot Central at 8.48 a.m. Thus was established a pattern of five return journeys daily taking about 45 minutes in each direction, with an additional return train late on Saturday evenings. All services were extended to Blaengarw when that station opened, the journey time typically being 53 minutes.

By 1907 the evening return was also being run on Wednesdays. More significantly, the new steam rail motor (SRM) was used for all passenger services to and from Blaengarw except for Saturdays and special occasions. This pattern of services, with slight alterations in departure times, continued until 1914, when the Wednesday and Saturday evening trains were retimed. The Wednesday train was moved from a 10.30 p.m. departure from Aberavon to an 11.00 p.m. departure from Central station. The 10.30 p.m. Saturday departure from Aberavon was discontinued and replaced by two trains, leaving Central station at 9.15 p.m. and 11.30 p.m. Additionally, ordinary passengers had the use of one carriage attached to the workmen's trains, as described below.

When the steam rail motor was removed from service in August 1915, all passenger trains reverted to locomotive haulage, probably by GWR engines shedded at Duffryn Yard. By 1920 Aberavon had been abandoned as a starting point and all passenger trains used the terminus at Port Talbot Central. There were now four return services daily to Blaengarw, and the Saturdays only evening service reverted to one departing from Port Talbot at 10.10 p.m. In addition there was a daily return service to Maesteg departing at 4.50 p.m.

A poster public timetable, dated 17th October 1921 and until further notice, proclaimed that the PTR was the shortest route between Blaengarw, Pontycymmer, Pontyrhyll, Maesteg and Port Talbot, Briton Ferry, Swansea and west thereof. No mention was made of the overall time taken and it could well have been quicker to travel via Bridgend for journeys involving the GWR. The timetable appears to have been arranged to suit connections with trains to and from Fishguard – otherwise there could be a lengthy wait at Port Talbot. For example, a passenger could depart Fishguard Harbour at 4.55 a.m., arrive at Port Talbot & Aberavon (GWR) at 9.04 a.m., depart Port Talbot (Central) at 9.20 a.m. and arrive at Blaengarw at 10.13 a.m. This timetable showed five return journeys Mondays to Saturdays, with the additional late evening return journey on

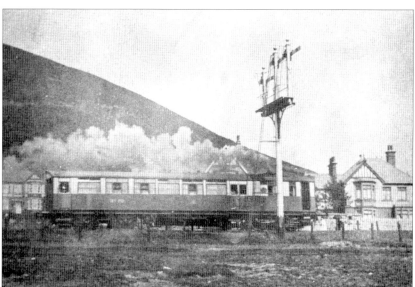

GWR SRM No. 20 at Tonygroes South Junction, heading for Duffryn Junction and the main line to Pontyrhyll. GWR SRMs were sent to Duffryn Yard as stand-ins when the PTR's model was at Swindon for repairs. No. 20 was at Duffryn Yard from 28th June to 15th August 1908.
Courtesy Byron Gage

Maximum Loads on Port Talbot Railway.

UP TRAINS.

From.	To.	No. of Wagons exclusive of Brake Van.	
		Loaded. (Mineral)	Empty.
†Tonygroes Junction ...	Cwmavon	10	20
Cwmavon	Tonmawr	8	15
North Bank	Copper Works	35	70
Grids and Margam Junction	Dyffryn Junction	—	*40
Aberavon	Dyffryn Junction	—	40
Dyffryn Junction	East End	—	18
East End	Pontyrhyll Junction ...	—	30
Margam Junction	Waterhall Junction... ...	—	45
Waterhall Junction	Pyle Sidings	40	—

DOWN TRAINS.

FROM.	To.	No. of Wagons exclusive of Brake Van.	
		Loaded. (Mineral).	Empty.
†South Wales Mineral Junction Line	Tonygroes Junction ...	25	30
Pontyrhyll	Maesteg ... ... }	18	—
Maesteg	East End of Tunnel ... }		
East End of Tunnel ...	Dyffryn Junction	30	—
Dyffryn Junction	Aberavon	30	—
Dyffryn Junction	Margam Junction and Grids	35	—
Copper Works	North Bank	35	50
Pyle Sidings	Waterhall Junction ...	—	45
Waterhall Junction ...	Margam Junction	45	—

These loads are for engines with 18 in. cylinders.

* The load for a 16 in. class of engine is 35.

† The load over the South Wales Mineral Junction Line is for 16 in. class of engine.

Tables of maximum loads on the PTR taken from the Working Time Table commencing 19th July 1920 and until further notice. Engines with 18-inch cylinders were the 0-6-2Ts, those with 16-inch cylinders the 0-6-0STs. Note that the 0-8-2Ts, Nos 17–21, only worked over the main line to and from Duffryn Junction, and that these engines could take a greater load up the gradient from Maesteg to the tunnel. These large engines were also allowed to take fifty empties to Ynysdavid and forty on to Tonmawr, and to bring thirty-five loads back down. It is not known if they were turned to work chimney first up to Tonmawr. Although not a common occurrence, only short loaded mineral trains were allowed up the SWMJnR. The loads given for GWR engines are somewhat cryptic. Presumably 2-6-0 engines refers to the '2600' and '4300' classes, and "ordinary" tender engines means the various 0-6-0 classes. Nos 99, 3121, 3151 and 3179 refer to the '3100' Class, 2177 and 2178 to the '4500' Class, and 1733 to the '1854' Class, these being the original numbers when these engines first appeared on the PTR.

MAXIMUM LOAD FOR G.W. TRAINS OVER THE P.T.R. & D. CO.'S O.V.E. LINE.

SECTION.		Number of Wagons exclusive of Brake Van.									Ordinary Engines.						
		2-8-0			2-6-2 T			2-6-0			Tender.			Tank.			
From	To	Coal	Goods	Empties	Coal	Goods	Empties	Coal	Goods	Empties	Coal	Goods	Empties	Coal	Goods	Empties	
Down Trains. Tondu ... ... Margam Junction ...		...	...	...	...	...	...	30	...	...	20	...	...	...	...	...	Assisted Tondu to Cefn Junction.
								50	...	...	40	...	...	...	...	...	
Up Trains. Margam Junction ... Waterhall Junction		...	...	...	...	...	...	...	...	70	...	...	45	...	...	...	
Waterhall Junction... Tondu		...	...	...	...	...	...	...	...	65	...	...	40	...	...	...	

MAXIMUM LOADS ON PORT TALBOT RAILWAY—*continued.*

The Load for Nos. 20 and 21 Engines (American) will be as under :—

*Dyffryn to East End	30	Empties.
West End to Pontyrhyll Junction ...	30	,,
Pontyrhyll Junction to Maesteg ...	30	Loaded.
Maesteg to East End	30	Loaded.
East End to Dyffryn	30	,,

The Sharpe Stewart Engines Nos. 17, 18, and 19, will work :—

Dyffryn to Pontyrhyll Junction ...	32	Empties.
Pontyrhyll Junction to Dyffryn ...	30	Loaded.

The loads for Great Western Engines working on Port Talbot Railway are as follows :—

	No. of Engine.	Class.	Up.	Down.
Duffryn Main Line.	99, 3,121, 3,151 and 3,179.	Class.	27 Empty and van.	26 Loaded and van (Mineral).
	2,178.	,,	21 ,, and ,,	20 ,, and ,, ,,
	1,733	,,	20 ,, and ,,	19 ,, and ,, ,,
Tonmawr.	2,177.	Class.	30 Empty to Cwmavon.	30 ,, and ,, ,,
			25 ,, from Cwmavon to Tonmawr Junction.	
Margam to Waterhall.	1,733.	Class.	45 Empty and van.	50 ,, and ,, ,,
Duffryn to Docks.	1,733.	Class.	45 Empty and van.	45 ,, and ,, ,,

Saturdays only. The afternoon return service to Maesteg had been dropped.

The line was not normally open on Sundays, but during August and September 1900 an experimental passenger train was run from Port Talbot to Pontycymmer on four successive Sundays at small profit,[3] but the practice was evidently not repeated. After the GWR had taken over the operation of the railway, arrangements were made to carry mail bags from Port Talbot to Bryn by the first train of the day and return by the last train. Other places further along the line were of course served more conveniently by the GWR in this regard.

Further changes to the timetabled service occurred after grouping. On the return trains to Blaengarw, the early morning train was withdrawn, leaving four daily and just one evening (Saturdays only) service. In a foretaste of changes to come, return trains to Maesteg were introduced: a daily morning service and four on Saturday afternoons and evenings. In addition, paying passengers were allowed to use the 9.45 p.m. workmen's service to Maesteg. By 1932 there were only three return services to Blaengarw, running on Fridays and Saturdays only, all other trains terminating at Maesteg. It would have come as no surprise when the passenger service between there and Blaengarw was withdrawn as from 12th September 1932.[4] The road from Maesteg to the lower Avon Valley via Bryn, the present-day B4282, had been improved in the 1920s, and in 1924 a bus service began plying the route between Maesteg and Port Talbot[5] which provided a far more convenient service. The number of tickets issued during 1925 at Port Talbot Central, 85,943, and Maesteg Neath Road, 71,296, fell to 23,950 and 9,131 respectively in 1932.[6] Consequently, in July 1933 the Traffic Committee of the GWR Board of Directors approved the recommendation of their general manager to withdraw the passenger service between Port Talbot and Maesteg as from 11th September 1933.[7]

SWMJnR

The inhabitants of Tonmawr first applied for a passenger service on the SWMJnR in May 1899. The general manager at the time, Probert, estimated that the cost of providing three stations, near the entrance to Cwmavon Sidings, at the north end of Pontrhydyfen Viaduct and at Tonmawr, was £600.[8] Nothing was done at the time, nor in response to two applications from the newly-formed Baglan Higher Parish Council in May 1913 and July 1914.[9] Eventually, in March 1920, Probert's successor Lowther saw a deputation of three councillors and asked to be informed of a suitable time for a train. Col Pringle's report on the proposed workmen's service, which commenced on 1st August 1920, had noted that demand for a passenger train would be forthcoming once a workmen's train was running.[10] The issue was brought before the PTR&D Board for the first time in January 1921. Lowther suggested that a market train might be run on Saturdays only, and it was agreed to refer the matter to the GWR and the Board of Trade. Major Hall reported in February 1921 that 80-foot long platforms had been provided at Cwmavon, Efail Fach, Tonmawr and Corrwg Merthyr for a workmen's service, and that if the platform at Tonmawr was increased to 120 feet to take a three-coach train, not more than one public train per day could be run from Port Talbot.[11] An undertaking was given to the Board of Trade to work this train under standard block regulations, and the service commenced on 23rd July 1921,

the fare being 11d single and 1s 10d return. The train departed from Tonmawr at 3.40 p.m. and ran non-stop to Tonygroes Junction, where it reversed and arrived at Central station at 4.00 p.m. The return train left at 9.00 p.m., giving those travelling five hours to savour the delights of Port Talbot. This service was fairly short-lived, and was withdrawn on 22nd September 1930.[12]

SWMR Cymmer–Glyncorrwg

Very little workmen's accommodation was available at Glyncorrwg. Most of them lived at Cymmer about two and a half miles away. In March 1908 the Clerk of Glyncorrwg UDC wrote to the Board of Trade pointing out the desirability of a passenger service between these two places and urging the Board to press the PTR to provide such facilities.[13] The Board of Trade, of course, had no jurisdiction in such matters and declined to become involved. A little later the Clerk wrote that prior to the transfer of the SWMR to the PTR, passengers were able to travel in carriages attached to mineral trains, but these were no longer provided, and in reply was reminded that the line was not equipped for passenger working.

A public passenger service between the two places was first considered by the Consultation Committee of PTR/GWR directors in May 1908. A road motor service had been suggested, with combined road and rail bookings, but this was subject to the GWR's motor expert being satisfied as to the conditions. Although the local authority had promised to improve the existing road if necessary, the idea was not pursued. The subject was revived in June 1913, by which date Glyncorrwg Colliery had closed but Ynyscorrwg Colliery was just opening. This time a rail motor service was proposed, and for this a platform on the GWR at the north end of Cymmer Tunnel was envisaged, connected by a long footbridge to the GWR and R&SBR stations, the route then traversing the high 1878 bridge over the River Avon to reach the SWMR. The cost of adapting these railways for passenger traffic was estimated to be £5,680, subsequently increased to £5,810. This scheme was approved by the SWMR directors in November 1913. In July 1914 it was agreed to proceed with the conversion scheme, each company bearing the cost of the works on its own land.

It was fortuitous that nothing was done on the ground immediately, because in April 1915 the GWR was informed that Glyncorrwg UDC no longer favoured the agreed scheme because of the distance between the proposed and existing stations at Cymmer; instead, they had revived the idea of a halt on the SWMR and suggested that a footbridge should be built across the intervening valley to the R&SBR station. The GWR officers concluded that this scheme would be better from the point of view of both the public and the railway companies, and that as the bridge would form a public thoroughfare the council should contribute towards its cost; this the council was disinclined to do and, as the PTR could do nothing owing to the war, the matter remained in abeyance for the duration.

Planning resumed in July 1917 following a meeting between Lowther and a deputation from Glyncorrwg UDC. A new plan for converting the Cymmer–Glyncorrwg section of the SWMR for passenger service was submitted to the Board of Trade in September 1917. Following a visit on 3rd October 1917, Col Pringle reported that the existing permanent way was in fair condition for moderate speeds, and that provided the electric train staff was extended from Tonmawr to Glyncorrwg with a pillar at Cymmer, and the

SWMR No. 5 with the 3.10 p.m. train to Glyncorrwg shortly after leaving Cymmer on 14th May 1919. The carriage is Great Western, the covered goods wagons are TVR and GWR.
Author's collection

connections at Glyncorrwg were coupled to a frame in a signal box, he could recommend the Board of Trade to authorise the passenger service at a maximum speed of 25 mph. The work was put in hand straight away, at an estimate cost of £1,825. In fact relaying at Glyncorrwg had already begun[14] and all works there apart from the platform were completed by December 1917.[15] The work at Cymmer was finished by February 1918[16] and brought into use straight away.[17] The net cost to the SWMR was only £370, the balance coming from the sale of materials recovered from the incline.[18] Col Pringle inspected the works in March 1918 and, subject to some minor matter requiring attention and a general speed limit of 25 mph, recommended the Board of Trade to approve the working of passenger trains on this section of the SWMR,[19] which was given on 30th March 1918. The minor matters concerned the starting signals at Glyncorrwg not being visible from the box – they were to be raised or indicated in the box – and the lack of level crossing gates at Cymmer, necessitating whistle boards 100 yards either side and a speed limit of 10 mph there. Passenger service was brought into use on Thursday 28th March 1918,[20] which was also the date of the first, and as far as is known the only, working timetable the SWMR issued. This showed four passenger trains each way daily and an additional evening train on Saturdays, Down trains taking 6 minutes and Up trains 8 minutes for the journey. The GWR Officers' Conference noted in March 1919 that the service had so far shown a favourable result, but that there had been no further developments regarding the footbridge over the River Avon at Cymmer.[21] By 1929 the service had been reduced to two trains each way on Friday evenings with a third late on Saturday evenings; it was withdrawn on 22nd September 1930.[22]

WORKMEN'S TRAINS

DUFFRYN LINE

The PTR was not under any obligation in its Acts to run workmen's trains between any points on it railways. However, in evidence to the Board of Trade in response to a Parliamentary Order of 8th June 1899 the company stated that the 5.55 a.m. train to Pontycymmer, retimed to 6.00 a.m., and the 5.58 p.m. return were run for the convenience of workmen and that special cheap weekly tickets were issued for the purpose. This type of ticket was also available between Maesteg and Bryn on the 8.5 a.m. from Pontycymmer and the 6.35 p.m. return. During 1899 a total of 10,632 workmen's tickets were issued at Port Talbot (Aberavon), Bryn, Maesteg and Garth. The type of carriage for use by workmen is not recorded, although by 1900 secondhand 4-wheel carriages were available for the purpose.[23] This seems to be the extent of the PTR's provision for workmen's trains for at least ten years. To make up for gaps in the timetable a weekdays late afternoon Down train from Bryn and a Saturdays excepted evening return to Maesteg were introduced in 1913. These trains were worked by the engine, coaches and guard working the ordinary evening passenger trains.

These workmen's trains were rationalised the following year. An early morning train left Port Talbot Central at 5.50 a.m. for Bryn and Maesteg, ran back to Bryn, returned to Maesteg, and finally departed from Maesteg at 7.10 a.m., arriving back at Central at 7.32 a.m. This cycle was repeated on weekday evenings except Saturdays, and, apart from the Bryn/Maesteg shuttle, in the afternoon. These trains were made up of the five SWMR workmen's coaches with one ordinary PTR coach attached for the convenience of ordinary passengers. Apart from discontinuing entirely the Bryn/Maesteg shuttle in 1920, this pattern of services continued until 1929 when the afternoon train was dropped. No workmen's services were run after September 1933. Although a platform was put in in 1920 for Celtic Lower Colliery, there is no indication in the Working Time Tables that any passenger or workmen's trains ever stopped.

SWMJₙR

Mercantile Colliery In January 1899 the directors agreed to run a workmen's train over the SWMJnR from Port Talbot Central to Mercantile Colliery, about one mile up the Whitworth Branch,[24] for which two ex-L&NWR coaches were purchased. Under the terms of an agreement dated 15th March 1899, Powley, Thomas & Co. were to pay a reduced rate of £1 per day for the service, which was to operate six days a week, and to indemnify the PTR against accidental injury or loss.[25] This service was discontinued when the colliery was abandoned in March 1903.

Whitworth Colliery Starting on 1st April 1907 a workmen's train was run once each way from Duffryn Junction via Port Talbot Central to Whitworth Colliery on the Blaenavon Branch in conjunction with the new sinking there.[26] The trains, which consisted of an engine and two coaches, departed at 5.45 a.m. and returned at 5.10 p.m., taking 40 and 35 minutes respectively, the coaches being stabled at Tonmawr Junction between times. These trains called at Tonygroes, Cwmavon Yard, Pontrhydyfen and Efail Fach. By May 1909 the service had been increased to two trains per day, Up trains departing at 6.00 a.m. and 4.30 p.m. and Down trains at 6.45 a.m. and 5.40 p.m. – suggesting that an overnight shift was being worked – plus an additional Saturdays only train departing at 1.00 p.m. and returning at 1.45 p.m. The service probably ceased when the colliery was abandoned in November 1911.

Corrwg Merthyr Colliery Early in 1920 the PTR sought Board of Trade approval to run three-coach workmen's trains over the uninspected portion of the SWMJnR from Tonygroes North Junction to Corrwg Merthyr Colliery at the top of the Whitworth Branch. Col Pringle's report dated 9th March 1920 stipulated that single platforms, 6 feet wide, one foot above rail level, of sufficient length to suit the number of coaches on the trains and with adequate approaches and lighting, were required at Cwmavon, Efail Fach and Corrwg Merthyr.[27] All the connections on the Whitworth Branch required facing point locks, and some sidings were required to be fitted with trap points. The report also stipulated speed limits of 25 mph between Tonygroes North Junction and Tonmawr Junction, and 15 mph between there and Corrwg Merthyr. Subject to these requirements being effected Col Pringle recommended approval of the service. With this report to hand the PTR directors and the GWR officers agreed in March 1920 to run a workmen's train leaving Port Talbot at about 6.30 a.m. and returning from the colliery at about 2.30 p.m., with the empty coaches being left at Tonmawr Junction in the interim. The colliery, which was to be charged £6 per day for an engine and two coaches for the double journey, signed the usual indemnity on 18th May 1920.[28] Relaying the Whitworth Branch and erecting the necessary platforms commenced straight away.[29] The work, which also included a platform at Tonmawr Junction,

was completed by the end of July. The train service commenced on 1st August 1920[30] and was presumably withdrawn by the GWR in early 1925 when the colliery was abandoned.

OVER

Baldwins first applied for a workmen's train service to run from Margam Steelworks to its Newlands and Cribbwr Fawr collieries in May 1915. This could not be entertained at the time and the matter rested until January 1918 when the directors approved a second application. The PTR&D erected a temporary platform in the Old Dock area near the Ffrwdwyllt Tinplate Works, which was completed in April 1918,[31] and Baldwins built the platforms at the two collieries.[32] Lowther wrote to the Board of Trade in April 1918 pointing out that hitherto the workmen had been conveyed by motor lorry and charabanc, and noting that the planned workmen's service was supported by the Coal Controller who desired the trains to start running on 6th May 1918 or the collieries would be idle as the road transport was to be stopped on the 4th.[33] Permission to run the service was granted on 3rd May, subject to inspection and a maximum speed of 25 mph, or less as the curves necessitated. The service consisted of three return journeys a day Mondays to Fridays, at a charge of £9 per day, and two on Saturdays *pro rata*.[34] For operating convenience the two-coach trains were run round at Waterhall Junction. The inspection was carried out by Col Pringle on 3rd December 1918;[35] the signalling and working arrangements were found to be adequate for workmen's trains, but improvements and further inspection were required for general passenger service. The maximum speed limit of 25 mph was confirmed, with a maximum of 15 mph on the unsignalled section between the Old Dock Platform and Copper Works Junction, over the curves from there to Margam West Junction, and on the bridge over the GWR. The service was withdrawn by July 1928, probably when Cribbwr Fawr Colliery closed.

SWMR

At first, requests for the provision of a workmen's service fared little better than those for a passenger service, although one was provided for in the December 1907 agreement between the Glyncorrwg Colliery Co. and the PTR. Lowther informed the Board of Trade in February 1914 that the PTR was being pressed by miners working at Glyncorrwg to provide facilities for conveying them from Cymmer to Glyncorrwg, as housing there was not nearly sufficient. His company was willing to run an engine plus two carriages from Cymmer to Glyncorrwg in the early morning and back in the afternoon. The Board of Trade replied that it could not sanction this, and the matter was initially deferred pending the adaptation of the line for passenger traffic – until the exigencies of the First World War brought about a change of attitude. In December 1916 the Blaencorrwg Colliery Co. asked the Board of Trade to authorise a workmen's service to its newly opened colliery some three miles from Cymmer to overcome a shortage of miners. The Mines Department of the Board of Trade considered the case to be a fairly strong one and in January 1917 the Board of Trade informed Lowther that it was prepared to reconsider the arrangements for working daily morning and evening service over the line for workmen only.[36] The train was to be worked on the one engine in steam basis, both engine and coaches were to vacuum fitted, and the colliery was to erect a

ABOVE: North Rhondda Halt circa 1950 with the workmen's train made up of old 4-wheel coaches which provided the service up to 1952. BR No. 9634 is standing next to the inlet connection for Glyncorrwg Colliery in the distance. *Author's collection*

BELOW: Glyncorrwg looking south on 1st April 1956. In the siding is the clerestory stock used for workmen's trains in the period between the withdrawal of the 4-wheeled coaches in 1952 and the introduction of ex-GWR "Main Line & City" stock in 1957/58. Also visible is a gas tank wagon used for replenishing these gas-lit vehicles. *Author's collection*

rough platform not less than 30 feet long and one foot above rail level. The PTR agreed to provide an engine and two coaches, one 5-compartment Third Class and one Brake Third, to carry ninety workmen for £2 per exclusive of insurance. As the proposed service would also benefit the nearby North Rhondda Colliery, the platform was erected about 70 yards short of the siding connections to the two collieries. On 23rd March 1917 both companies jointly signed an indemnity protecting the SWMR against all risks.[37] The service, which commenced on 5th March 1917, left Cymmer at 6.30 a.m. and after a stop at Glyncorrwg arrived at Blaencorrwg and North Rhondda Platform 15 minutes later. The return service departed at 3.40 p.m. Owing to the gradients encountered, and the lack of run-round facilities at the upper end, the trains were propelled up to the collieries. The coaches were stabled at Glyncorrwg overnight.

Glyncorrwg South Pit reopened in 1919 and in September 1920 a platform was erected there by the colliery.[38] Finishing touches were made by the SWMR and South Pit Halt was ready for use by November 1920.[39] A formal agreement between the three colliery companies and the GWR was made on 5th November 1923, whereby the railway company agreed as from 27th August 1923 to provide one to three workmen's trains per day from Cymmer to North Rhondda Halt, calling at Glyncorrwg station and Glyncorrwg South Pit Halt, at mutually agreed times.[40] This agreement was amended in 1925 and 1936 to reflect the changes in colliery ownership.[41] The workmen's service, latterly to South Pit Halt only, ended on 2nd November 1964.

GOODS AND MINERAL TRAINS

DUFFRYN LINE

Although the first mineral train had been run in August 1897, it was not until January 1898 that Pontyrhyll Junction was completed, permitting PTR trains to run into the Garw Valley.[42] The initial service was six daily return workings from Duffryn Yard, three as far as North's or Garth Colliery sidings at Maesteg, and three, which did not call at these places, to Pwllcarne at the head of the Garw Valley. One of the trains also handled traffic to and from the R&SBR at Aberavon Junction. No specific timings were given for traffic between Duffryn Yard and the docks, which "as far as possible" was worked by engine No. 1, the dock pilot engine. The same general pattern of services was in operation later that year, except that Up trains, "if required", alternatively started at Port Talbot Central, Aberavon Junction or Margam Junction, and all Down trains were timetabled through to Copper Works and Margam junctions. "Any Bank Engine that may be available", in addition to the dock pilot, was to work the traffic between these places and Duffryn Yard. One consequence of the agreement between the GWR and PTR made in 1903 concerning mineral traffic from the Garw Valley[43] was that mineral trains then terminated at North's siding, Maesteg.

By 1907 there were eight such trains daily which seemingly were worked through to and from No. 1 grid by the train engine, as there was no mention of the use of a dock pilot engine. This practice was stopped as from May 1909 when it was realised that only four of

From 1952 to 1958 old GWR clerestory coaches modified with end windows were used for the Glyncorrwg to North Rhondda workmen's services. The train, propelled by No. 7744, is standing at North Rhondda Halt, with new surface facilities for the eponymous colliery under construction in the background.

Courtesy W A Camwell

Courtesy H C Casserley

No. 9617 propelling a workmen's train over Glyncorrwg level crossing and up the gradient towards South Pit Halt on 11th July 1958.

the five 0-8-2 tank engines were required to work between Duffryn Yard and the collieries, onward traffic being handled by one pilot engine making ten double trips to the docks.[44] There were, in fact, ten mineral trains to Maesteg run over the main line at this time, three of which could be extended to Garth if required, and one pick-up goods and mineral train, principally for Garth and Gwernllwyn collieries, which could be extended to Pontyrhyll if required. With the opening of St. John's Colliery in 1911,[45] five of these eleven trains could run on to Cwmdu if required. This increased traffic necessitated the use of all five heavy engines. North's Navigation Collieries were the principal source of traffic on the line, such that ten of the twelve mineral trains run in 1920 were designated to run to North's Siding, Maesteg, and Cwmdu only. The other two were designated pick-up mineral trains, both of which served Bryn Navigation Colliery, with one being extended to Cwmdu or Garth if required and the other going on to Celtic Sidings for Celtic Lower Colliery. This set the general pattern of working until the last train ran from North's on 28th August 1964.

NORTH'S RUNNING POWERS

PTR and GWR Working Time Tables make no mention of North's working their own trains between Maesteg and Cwmdu as allowed for in the running powers agreement of 16th November 1910.[46] However, the February 1939 Appendix to Section 10 of the "Working Time Table, Margam Moors to Fishguard Harbour and Branches" states the following:

North's Collieries engines and trains are permitted to run and convey colliery traffic between North's Collieries and Cwmdu. The trains are worked with a brake van in the rear and must

be signalled and dealt with in accordance with the standard regulations.

North's Navigation Collieries have been granted permission to run double load trains not exceeding 40 wagons, 2 engines and van, formed with van in the rear and an engine at each end from Cwmdu to North's Navigation Collieries and vice versa on the understanding that the provisions of rule 133 are observed. A freight brake van may be propelled from North's Colliery Signal Box to Cwmdu during daylight and in clear weather only. The guard, or shunter, must ride in the brake van, keep a sharp look out, and be prepared to hand signal to the driver, who must be in possession of the electric train staff.[47]

These instructions had probably been in force since about 1910. It is not known how much use North's, or their successors the NCB, made of their running powers before 1964.

At the time St. John's Colliery opened, North's possessed at least seven engines for working traffic over its private railway.[48] In order to work between Cwmdu and Maesteg, it was necessary to register some of them with the GWR, although North's locomotives must have used the line prior to registration. Two 0-6-0 saddle tank engines, *Marian* (built by Hudswell, Clarke in 1909) and No. 855 (built by the GWR at Wolverhampton in 1877 and sold to North's in 1906) were registered in 1911, receiving the registration numbers 95 and 96 respectively.[49] These two apparently sufficed until the 1920s, when *JL15*, *Carmen* (both 1922), *Eileen* (1926), *Celia* and *Antonia* (both 1929) were registered. Additionally, GWR '2021' Class 0-6-0ST No. 2158 was on loan to North's between 20th April and 13th July 1912 and could have been used over this section without restriction. To work their trains North's also required brake

From 1958 to 1964, when the service was withdrawn, the Glyncorrwg to North Rhondda workmen's train was made up of ex-GWR "Main Line & City" stock, modified with a central droplight in the guard's van ends, which is seen at the reconstructed platform on 11th July 1958. The new building work at North Rhondda Colliery appears to be virtually finished. In the foreground is the tramway which ran from a stockyard on the site of Blaencorrwg Colliery down to Glyncorrwg Colliery.

Courtesy H C Casserley

PTR No. 20 with a train of empties for the Garw Valley near the 11½ milepost. A scene such this would have been unlikely after 1st June 1903 when all the Garw Valley traffic to or from Port Talbot was worked by the GWR via Tondu and the OVER. Gwyn Briwnant Jones used Pearson's photograph of the newly completed line (see Vol. 1, p. 93) as the setting for this painting.

Gwyn Briwnant Jones

vans. A number of GWR-style vans were ordered from Hurst, Nelson in 1913, but details are scant.

OVER

The OVER was opened for goods and mineral traffic in August 1898.[50] Initially only one morning train was run daily from Margam Junction to Cefn Junction, the engine doing the necessary shunting at Bryndu Colliery and Coke Ovens. During the return journey a trip was made to Pyle to exchange traffic with the GWR. A similar working was run as required in the afternoon. Early in 1899 the GWR began to make use of its running powers over this line, which, confusingly, it called the Port Talbot Dock Branch, an appellation that lasted at least until 1937. Initially these trains were run as untimetabled special trains, of which those destined for the docks were worked to No. 1 grid by GWR engines. The 1903 agreement with the GWR markedly increased the traffic over the OVER and by 1904 eleven GWR trains were scheduled seven days a week with a twelfth on Tuesdays to Saturdays. These trains originated at Blaengarw or Tondu and were destined for Port Talbot Docks, Swansea Eastern Depot, Landore, or New Milford (later Neyland), all via Margam Sidings, with balancing return workings. By 1907 the number of PTR trains had increased to three daily, Sundays excepted, reflecting the greater mining activity along the line, the engine being required to shunt at Bryndu, Ton Philip, Aberbaiden and Cefn Cribbwr collieries as well as work trips to Pyle. After the GWR had taken over the working of the PTR in 1908, its trains picked up and dropped off at Waterhall Junction all traffic from the collieries in the Bryndu area to and from destinations west of Margam Junction, which eliminated much remarshalling at Margam Junction. To expedite traffic from May 1909, empty wagons for Tondu could be dispatched by either the OVER or via Pyle and the Porthcawl Branch.[51] By 1913 both the PTR and GWR had resumed Sunday working over the OVER and this had increased to four trains by 1920. In the post-grouping period the GWR made extensive use of the OVER, including

Sunday evening working in the Up direction (towards Tondu), balanced by a similar number of Mondays excepted trains in the Down direction.

SWMJnR AND SWMR

The SWMJnR opened was opened for goods and mineral traffic on 14th November 1898.[52] Initially, one morning and one afternoon train were run, with the option of an early morning train as required. These trains ran from Duffryn Junction up to Tonmawr Junction where traffic was exchanged with the SWMR, doing any necessary siding work *en route*. If required, the train was propelled up to Mercantile Colliery on the Whitworth Branch and then returned, after a pause at Tonmawr, to Blaenavon Junction, from where an optional trip was made up the Blaenavon Branch, working the colliery sidings as necessary. The train then retuned to Duffryn Junction, the round trip taking about three and a half hours. A similar pattern of services existed in 1907, arrival at Tonmawr being timed to roughly coincide with those of SWMR trains, of which there were nominally three each way per day. The main changes were that the Blaenavon Branch was worked by a back shunt from Tonmawr, and that the train engine was required to work as necessary any traffic to the docks and to collect from the Old Dock any empty wagons for the SWMR.

The procedure for dealing with traffic at Tonmawr and beyond changed in 1909 after the PTR took over the working of the SWMR. An SWMR engine worked the four trains from Tonmawr to Glyncorrwg and return and also worked traffic on the Whitworth and Blaenavon branches. The PTR ran two trains daily between No. 1 grid and Tonmawr where traffic was exchanged. By 1913 the route of these two trains had been changed to run from Neath Junction via the R&SBR to Aberavon Junction and thence to Tonygroes Junction, where they reversed and proceeded to Tonmawr and finally Glyncorrwg, a journey time of three hours. Local traffic on the SWMJnR and the Whitworth and Blaenavon branches was then worked by two or three shunting trips from Duffryn Yard. One of the

RIGHT: One of the Sharpe, Stewart 0-8-2 tank engines with a Down coal train on the OVER near Margam Moors. Note the three headlamps on the engine. This view appeared in *Description of the New Welsh Coal Port* published by the PTR&D Co. circa 1904. *Author's collection*

BELOW: A poor but rare view of a PTR coal train descending the SWMJnR and approaching Cwmavon. *Courtesy Arthur Rees*

Neath to Glyncorrwg trains had been altered to start from Duffryn Yard by 1918 and a second such train was run in the evenings. By 1929 the goods train service operated to the earlier pattern, *viz.*: three return trains from Duffryn Yard to Glyncorrwg which called as required at collieries beyond Tonmawr, and two shunting trips to Tonmawr which also worked the branches, one of which had been dropped by 1932. After the closure of Gyfylchi Tunnel in July 1947 and of the Margam Forge to Oakwood section of the SWMJnR in May 1954,[53] trains from Duffryn Yard to Glyncorrwg ran over the R&SBR to Cymmer Afan where they drew forward, reversed through Cymmer General into Cymmer Tunnel and then crossed Cymmer Viaduct to join the SWMR at Cymmer Corrwg.

PTR MINERAL TRAINS TO SWANSEA AND WEST WALES

Starting in 1920, a mineral train was run between Duffryn Yard and Felin Fran on the Swansea District line via the R&SBR, carrying traffic from North's and other collieries for Bynea, Llanelly and Milford Haven, the latter having precedence. The train, which was worked by either a PTR 0-6-2 tank engine and brake van or a GWR 0-6-0 engine and brake van, left Duffryn at 6.10 p.m. and arrived at Felin Fran at 7.15 p.m. The return working, which conveyed empties for collieries on the PTR system, arrived back at Duffryn at 9.00 p.m. Also in 1920, PTR mineral trains were run as required between Duffryn Yard and Swansea Docks via either the R&SBR or the Vale of Neath line depending on the ultimate destination. These too were worked by PTR or GWR engines as arranged at the time. A version of this train was still running in 1937.

LOCOMOTIVE REQUIREMENTS

To work these services in 1920, including those on the SWMR, to shunt the dock grids and tips, to work trips in and around the docks, to provide pilots at Duffryn Yard and sidings and a banking engine, required twenty-six locomotives, plus seven to be available at fairly short notice to work those trains run as required. Twelve were remanned twice during the day and so were at work almost continuously, Sundays being the only day on which routine maintenance was possible. For example, the first New Dock shunting engine was required to be available at 6.00 a.m. and was remanned at 1.47 p.m. and again at 9.47 p.m. The total requirement of thirty-three engines represented a 75 per cent availability of the forty-five PTR, SWMR and GWR locomotives shedded at Duffryn Yard on 1st January 1921.[54]

The GWR introduced its system of targets at Port Talbot to identify various shunting engine duties. In 1929, No. 1 was the banking engine, Nos 2, 4, 6 and 8 worked trips, Nos 3, 5, and 7 shunted in the docks, and No. 9 worked at Copper Works Junction, all based at Duffryn Yard. In addition, Duffryn Yard provided target No. 1 at Margam Moors, C1 and C2 at Margam Junction, C4 at Port Talbot General, and Nos 1–3 at Aberavon. By 1932 these duties, apart from those at Aberavon, had been combined into one series: T1 banking, T2–T8 shunting and trip working, T9 and T10 at Copper Works Junction, T11 and T12 at Margam Junction, T13 and T14 at Port Talbot Yard, and T15 at Margam Moors. This pattern persisted with minor variations until Duffryn Yard shed closed in 1964.

A Down coal train passing 2-8-0T No. 5254 waiting in the double line section at Bryn with Up empties. Photographed from the brake van on 14th July 1959. *Courtesy H C Casserley*

NOTES

1. This chapter is based mainly on the following timetables and appendices:
   PTR&D Co. Working Time Tables: 17 January 1898, 1 October 1898, January 1899, 1 April 1907, 10 May 1909, 12 July 1913, 13 July 1914, 19 July 1920, Appendix October 1910; Poster Time Table 17 October 1921.
   SWMR Co. Working Time Table 28 March 1918.
   GWR Service Time Tables Section 6A May 1898 (Dragonwheel Speciality Reprints 2007).
   GWR Service Time Tables: July 1904, 8 July to 22 September 1929, 18 July to 11 September 1932.
   BR(WR) Sectional Appendix to the Working Time Table Swansea Operating District April 1958.
2. See Volume 1, Chapter 4.
3. TNA: PRO RAIL 1057/1528/59.
4. Michael Quick, *Railway Passenger Stations in Great Britain: a Chronology* (Railway & Canal Historical Society 2009).
5. David Holding and Tony Moyes, *History of British Bus Services: South Wales* (Ian Allan, 1986), p. 93.
6. TNA: PRO RAIL 266/63.
7. TNA: PRO RAIL 250/357.
8. TNA: PRO RAIL 1057/1528/45.
9. Jason Jarvis, 'The Saturday Only Passenger Train Service between Tonmawr and Port Talbot Central', *Welsh Railways Archive*, 5/6 (November 2012), pp. 134–5.
10. TNA: PRO MT 29/80 p. 19.
11. Michael Hale, 'Passenger Trains on the South Wales Mineral Junction Railway', *Welsh Railways Archive*, 1/9 (May 1994), pp. 265–6.
12. Quick, *Railway Passenger Stations*.
13. TNA: PRO MT 6/2481/10.
14. TNA: PRO RAIL 1057/1528/219.
15. TNA: PRO RAIL 1057/1528/221.
16. TNA: PRO RAIL 1057/1528/223.
17. TNA: PRO RAIL 1057/1528/224.
18. TNA: PRO RAIL 1110/430.
19. TNA: PRO MT 29/79 p. 144.
20. TNA: PRO RAIL 1057/1528/225.
21. TNA: PRO RAIL 242/3.
22. Quick, *Railway Passenger Stations*.
23. See Volume 1, Chapter 9.
24. See Volume 1, Chapter 5.
25. TNA: PRO RAIL 574/35.
26. See Chapter 21.
27. TNA: PRO MT 29/80 p. 19.
28. TNA: PRO RAIL 574/56.
29. TNA: PRO RAIL 1057/1528/243.
30. TNA: PRO RAIL 1057/1528/244, 245.
31. TNA: PRO RAIL 1057/1528/225.
32. TNA: PRO RAIL 1057/1528/226.
33. TNA: PRO MT 6/2494/3.
34. TNA: PRO RAIL 574/55.
35. TNA: PRO MT 29/79 p. 277.
36. TNA: PRO MT 6/2481/10.
37. TNA: PRO RAIL 639/19.
38. TNA: PRO RAIL 1057/1528/245.
39. TNA: PRO RAIL 1057/1528/246.
40. TNA: PRO RAIL 252/2030.
41. TNA: PRO RAIL 252/2056.
42. See Volume 1, Chapter 4.
43. See Volume 1, Chapter 6.
44. TNA: PRO RAIL 242/3.
45. See Chapter 11.
46. See Chapter 11.
47. TNA: PRO RAIL 1136/35.
48. Geoffrey Hill, *Industrial Locomotives of Mid & South Glamorgan* (Industrial Railway Society 2007), p. 81.
49. *Locomotives of the Great Western Railway, Part 13 Preservation and Supplementary Information* (Railway Correspondence & Travel Society 1983), pp. N19–23.
50. See Volume 1, Chapter 5.
51. TNA: PRO RAIL 242/3.
52. See Volume 1, Chapter 5.
53. See Chapter 20.
54. Ian Harrison, *Great Western Railway Locomotive Allocations for 1921* (Wild Swan 1984).

17

Finances of the Port Talbot Railway & Docks Company and the South Wales Mineral Railway Company

PTR&D Company[1]

This section outlines the steps taken by the PTR&D to raise capital and to arrange loans, and summarises the income generated by the traffic carried by the railway and handled at the docks. Major items of capital expenditure are mentioned elsewhere in this history, but the overall picture is discussed here. It will be seen that Miss Talbot played a major role in assisting the company financially in its early years, her holding of 4% preference shares at December 1907 being 27,356 (£273,560). At the grouping in February 1922, her estate held £138,050 of the ordinary shares (21.9 per cent of the total issued) and £153,560 of the preference shares (25.6 per cent).[2]

Capital and Loans

The railway and dock works authorised by the PTR&D's 1894 Act were estimated to cost £563,676 and, accordingly, the company's capital was set at £600,000 in shares of £10, with powers to borrow £174,000 on mortgage.[3] This capital was immediately reduced by the 5,000 shares (£50,000) vested in Miss Talbot in settlement of all debts owing to her and as compensation for the shares she held in the old company, and by the sixty shares (£600) awarded to John Felton and Edward Knox, the other shareholders in the old company. On the other hand, Miss Talbot was contracted by the Act to apply for 7,500 shares and, of these, 2,300 (£23,000) were applied for in September 1894. Not surprisingly for a new company, there was no interest from the general public when these shares were offered in January 1895, the only applicants being four directors who took a total of 800 shares (£8,000).

S Pearson & Son's contract price for the construction of the works authorised by the 1894 Act was £527,000. Sir Weetman Pearson's offer to take 20 per cent of this amount as 10,500 shares at par (£105,000) was accepted by the directors in January 1895. To ensure an adequate supply of working capital, Miss Talbot on 23rd January 1895 made an agreement with Sir Weetman and his father George Pearson by which she undertook to subscribe to not more than 30,000 (£300,000) of the shares not taken up in addition to the 7,500 contracted for.[4] The amount was fixed at 9,580 shares (£95,800) in March 1895 and Miss Talbot allotted these to three of her relatives (2,400 each), her solicitor's firm (1,480) and her agent (900). To provide a security for this investment, the title deeds of Sir Weetman's estate at Paddockhurst in Sussex were transferred to Miss Talbot. The contractor was required to redeem these shares within seven years and to pay Miss Talbot 3% interest, but was entitled to receive any dividend paid out. These shares were redeemed in January 1901.[5]

Clause 143 of the 1894 Act granted powers to pay interest out of capital on paid-up shares at a rate not exceeding 3% per annum during the period allowed for completion of the works (docks, etc. seven years; railways three years). This was on condition that interest would only accrue after two-thirds of the authorised capital had been issued, the aggregate amount of interest was not to exceed £75,000, and that the authorised borrowing powers would be reduced by one-third of the amount of interest paid. Following a report by Sir Douglas Dalton, the Board of Trade in May 1895 certified that 50,000 ordinary shares had been issued.[6] Consequently the PTR&D paid ordinary shareholders interest at 3% per annum from June 1895 until December 1899, amounting to £70,439 18s 9d and thereby reducing its borrowing powers by £23,480.[7] The works were not finished by then, but any further interest payments out of capital would have exceeded the £75,000 limit.

Capital expenditure up to June 1896 amounted to £381,702 (Figure 17.1). Shortly afterwards the company obtained powers to build the OVER and SWMJnR.[8] The respective Acts authorised the PTR&D to raise further capital totalling £330,000 and to borrow an additional £110,000. An extraordinary general meeting of shareholders held on 21st October 1896 authorised the directors to issue 3,000 ordinary shares (£30,000) and 30,000 4% preference shares (£300,000), these to be offered to existing shareholders at the rate of one for every two ordinary shares held. Miss Talbot was entitled to subscribe to 4,790 preference shares as a consequence of her agreement with Sir Weetman Pearson, of which 2,500 were transferred to him, and in due course she owned 9,435 of this issue.[9] It is not clear how successful this issue was, although the 4% dividend was paid, out of net income, in June 1897.

By June 1897 £763,258 of capital had been expended on the railways and docks, some £93,000 short of the combined estimates. For the first time the directors resorted to their borrowing powers and in August 1897 arranged a one-year loan from the London & Provincial Bank of £240,000, in two mortgages of £174,000 and £66,000,[10] although only the first of these was taken out in 1897. In September 1897 the directors were authorised to create 4% debentures totalling £273,000, almost all of the loan capital then granted, to be issued as security. The directors heard in March 1898 that the London & Provincial Bank was not willing to agree to a further loan, but Lloyds Bank had offered advances totalling £150,000 at ½% above bank rate, with a minimum of 4%, which was accepted. These advances were payable in stages between March and August 1898, £34,000 having been mortgaged by April 1898.[11] The directors signed an undertaking to Lloyds Bank in May 1898 as to the means of servicing this debt to the two banks.[12] The terms were revised in September 1898,[13] such that the £150,000 out of a maximum of £200,000 advanced to PTR&D and spent on new works would remain owing, but would be reduced by the transfer of the mortgage from the bank to Miss Talbot. To repay the balance the company would:

1 By 1st October 1899 issue £270,000 of 4% debentures at 120%, secured by mortgages totalling £240,000 held by the London & Provincial Bank and £34,000 held by Lloyds Bank and about to be transferred to Miss Talbot.
2 Call up £84,198 preference shares and recover the Parliamentary deposits for the 1896 Acts totalling approximately £26,000.
3 Furthermore, at least 75 per cent of further advances would be as Lloyds Bonds to be issued to contractors and creditors.

The mortgages held by the London & Provincial Bank were transferred to Miss Talbot on 8th August 1898, she paying the bank £240,278 12s 9d comprising the capital plus interest.[14] The £34,000 mortgage from Lloyds Bank was paid off by Miss Talbot on 14th October 1898 and assigned to her, the company paying her interest at 4%.[15] As a result of these transactions the PTR&D owed Lloyds Bank £116,000 and Miss Talbot £274,278 12s 9d.[16] Miss Talbot also notionally advanced a further £8,228, but retained this sum as interest owing to her. Some of these were redeemed, such that the total on 31st December 1898 was £374,174. This was in excess of the £284,000 authorised and the company's 1899 Act included powers to raise an additional £300,000 of capital, as preference shares if necessary, and to borrow a further £100,000.[17] The situation was such that the directors instructed that no more salaried or waged staff were to be taken on without the approval of the Board and that the services of seven, subsequently reduced to six, office staff were to be dispensed with.

To tide the PTR&D over, Lloyds Bank agreed in February 1899 to re-advance up to £60,000 of the money repaid as Lloyds Bonds payable on 30th June 1899.[18] The amount owing to Lloyds Bank on 19th September 1899 was £194,178, made up of £146,543 bonds, £41,875 cash, and £5,760 interest, the date for repayment having been extended. Although the shareholders had in August 1899 authorised the directors to issue the 30,000 (£300,000) 4% preference shares allowed by the recent Act, the state of the money market made such action unfavourable. The date for repayment of the bank loan was further extended to April 1900. Miss Talbot agreed in October 1899 to finance the company for six months provided her loan did not exceed £80,000, and extended it yet again for two months in April 1900.

By the 31st May 1900 Miss Talbot was owed £282,506 12s 9d plus interest on the securities she held, plus £83,269 8s 8d on the Lloyds Bonds she had taken up from company's creditors, a total of £365,776 1s 5d. Lloyds Bank was due £146,543 8s 1d on the bonds it had taken up from creditors, and £15,534 17s 5d plus interest was outstanding on the earlier loans. At Miss Talbot's request, to pay off the amounts due to her, the PTR&D, Miss Talbot and Lloyds Bank made an agreement dated 31st May 1900; under this, the directors were to issue £258,000 of Perpetual Debenture Stock and 25,800 (£258,000) of the 25,815 unissued 4% preference shares,[19] authority to do so being given at a special meeting of shareholders held on 25th July 1900. These stocks and shares were offered to existing shareholders on the condition that every applicant for

preference shares was entitled to debentures of equal value. All monies received were to be paid into a special bank account and belong to Miss Talbot and the bank in proportion to the sums then owing. Furthermore, at the PTR&D's request, Miss Talbot and the bank were to subscribe to all unapplied-for preference shares and debentures in the proportion 72:28.

On the same date, Miss Talbot and Lloyds Bank also agreed between themselves that she would be offered any preference shares and debentures taken up by the bank before their being otherwise disposed of, and that after three years all such unsold stocks and shares held by the bank would be bought by Miss Talbot. The principal agreement was soon put into effect, Lloyds Bank being issued with £25,000 of debentures in August 1900 against further advances requires by the PTR&D. Miss Talbot advanced £33,252 in January 1901, taking the equivalent in debentures, some of this money being used to pay Sir Weetman Pearson the £22,500 due to him under the arbitration settlement.[20] At the same time the guarantee fund of 2,000 (£20,000) preference shares was transferred to S Pearson & Son Ltd.

Miss Talbot continued to finance the PTR&D during 1901, a total of £48,500 being advanced as cash up to August that year against debentures issued as security. In June 1904 this loan was called in,[21] and Miss Talbot was authorised to sell the debentures instead of being repaid. In addition to the debentures she held, and the ordinary and preference shares she had subscribed to, Miss Talbot had also received £121,160 as ordinary shares: £50,600 for the Old Dock, £14,000 for the C&PR and £56,560 for land for the 1894 and 1896 railways.[22] Although Miss Talbot provided a further advance of £6,980 in April 1902, there was a limit to her willingness and ability to continue to do so. Dividend payments on ordinary shares had ceased in December 1899 and were not to resume until December 1905, whilst those on preference shares, although starting at 4% when issued, had dropped abruptly in December 1900 to 0.5% and only risen to 1% in December 1901. Consequently, in June 1902 it was announced that she would only make advances against Lloyds Bonds. Nevertheless, there was a market for the debentures; Miss Talbot sold £10,000 of them in November 1902 at 99.5% net. By then the PTR&D had practically exhausted its borrowing powers (£360,520) and in September 1902 the directors had resolved to submit to the 1903 Session of Parliament a Bill to raise £100,000 as debentures in order to raise funds to further improve and equip the undertaking. This largely financial Bill was passed in principle in March 1903 and with minor amendments received the Royal Assent on 21st July 1903.[23]

In January 1904 the directors sought to address the shortage of cash by applying for a £30,000 overdraft with Lloyds Bank. This was refused but in April 1904 the bank agreed to extend the existing £23,000 loan for one year and to advance a further £17,000 for twelve months at 5%. This sum was guaranteed by Col Wright who deposited 25,000 £1 Baldwins ordinary shares as security.[24] The date for repayment of the Lloyds Bonds held by Miss Talbot expired in May 1904 and debentures authorised by the 1903 Act for £12,880 were issued to her. The PTR&D's financial position was eased in November 1904 by the sale of £50,000 of debenture stock at 97%. The proceeds were used to pay off the loans from Lloyds Bank; the loan account was moved to the London, City & Midland Bank which allowed a £20,000 overdraft without security.

The year 1905 marked a notable improvement in the PTR&D's financial position. The bank loans had been paid off and to raise cash the company was able to issue 4% debentures which for the first time were quoted on the London Stock Exchange. A deal for the sale of another tranche (£50,000) of debentures in stages was agreed in December 1905. The dividends paid on the preference shares had gradually risen from the low of 0.5% of December 1900 until the full 4% was reached again in June 1905; this rate was maintained for the remainder of the PTR&D's existence. Also in December 1905 a 1% dividend on ordinary shares was declared, the first since December 1899. The ordinary shareholders of course had to wait until the preference shareholders had been satisfied. As the company's fortunes improved the ordinary share rate increased until it matched that of the preference shares in December 1907. Miss Talbot's outstanding loan was repaid in December 1906 by the issue of £14,170 in debentures. At this date the company's capital consisted of £623,830 in ordinary shares, £600,000 in 4% preference shares and £52,828 as 4% debentures.[25] The PTR&D was authorised by its 1907 Act[26] to raise additional capital for the general purposes of its undertaking as stocks or shares not exceeding £120,000 and to borrow in respect of this capital not more than £40,000 on mortgage. Six thousand (£60,000) ordinary shares were created by resolution of the shareholders in January 1908, but the other 6,000 ordinary shares and £40,000 of debentures were not created until August 1912.

The PTR&D's close association with the GWR as a result of the working and running powers agreements[27] had significant effects on both its capital and revenue accounts. These agreements were expected to improve the returns to the ordinary shareholders, but it took some time for the full benefits to be realised. The rate of dividend on the ordinary shares dropped to 3% in 1908 and 1909, but then increased steadily up to 1913 when 9% was reached and maintained thereafter. The funds available to pay dividends were enhanced by Miss Talbot's policy from June 1901 to December 1908 of waiving the royalties and land rent charges due to her. These were payable half-yearly and gradually increased to a high of £2,054 as the trade of the port grew. In February 1909 Miss Talbot was asked not to waive these charges as the ordinary share dividend had reached 3% and the practice then ceased.[28]

By October 1910 the overdraft at the London, City & Midland Bank was approaching the then limit of £50,000. Although the bank was prepared to grant an extension of a further £50,000 at 5%, the GW/PT Directors' Consultation Committee decided in November 1910 that the PTR&D should retain as much of the balance due to the GWR in February 1911 as required to meet the overdraft, being charged 4% on this short term loan, using the money for capital expenditure on the dock. This debt amounted to £57,024 in May 1911 and had risen to £121,640 by June 1912 when the committee noted that the PTR&D's capital assets were not sufficient to meet the capital expenditure authorised and contemplated. It was agreed that the company would apply for further capital powers so as to maintain a margin between the temporary loans from the GWR and the PTR&D's unexercised powers of raising money. The outcome was the PTR&D's Act 1913,[29] its last for financial purposes, which authorised the company to raise a further £375,000 of capital and to borrow a further £125,000, bringing the grand totals to £1.725m and £649,000 respectively. These amounts were never fully utilised. In all, £630,000 of ordinary shares and £600,000 of 4% preference shares, a total £1.23m, and £460,520 of 4% debentures were issued.

The debt to the GWR continued to grow and in December 1913 Lowther asked Whitelaw, the GWR's accountant, what security they would prefer. The response was that the arrangement was based on good faith, that his chairman was quite satisfied with the position, and at the moment there was no intention to ask for a security. Whitelaw also complimented the directors of the PTR&D as to the way they had carried out their part of the agreement.[30] The amount owing had risen to £367,949 when the subject was reviewed by the GW Chairman's Conference in October 1916, and a limit of £400,000 was set.[31] Viscount Churchill, the GWR chairman, later remarked that the agreement was in the best interests of that company. The debt had risen to £427,026 in March 1921, the last reported figure, and was written off by the GWR under the terms of absorption.[32]

CAPITAL EXPENDITURE

Although the railways authorised by the 1894 and 1896 Acts were finished and brought into use more or less on time, the dock works were much delayed and only approached completion in December 1899 after the expenditure of an overall total of approximately £1.43m of capital (Figure 17.1). Thereafter the rate of expenditure was much lower and was due mainly to the purchase of new rolling stock and improvements to the railways and dock as has been described in previous chapters. The total had reached £1.85m in December 1912. There were marked increases in 1913 and 1914 and somewhat less in 1915, mainly due to the expense of the new

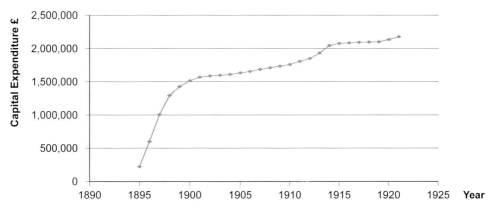

FIGURE 17.1:   PTR&D CAPITAL EXPENDITURE 1895–1921

TABLE 17.1: CAPITAL EXPENDITURE BY THE PORT TALBOT RAILWAY & DOCKS COMPANY

YEAR	RAILWAYS £	ROLLING STOCK £	DOCKS £	NON RAILWAY £	CUMULATIVE TOTAL £
Total to 1912	769,686	90,886	986,108	2,400	1,849,081
1913	9,424	0	75,616	0	1,934,122
1914	5,920	0	105,297	-875	2,044,465
1915	4,536	0	27,709	0	2,076,711
1916	-1,255	0	8,998	0	2,084,454
1917	1,041	0	7,502	0	2,092,999
1918	142	0	3,267	0	2,096,409
1919	-379	0	3,845	0	2,099,875
1920	-84	0	34,761	0	2,134,551
1921	1,078	0	40,458	0	2,176,089
Total to 1921	**790,111**	**90,886**	**1,293,566**	**1,525**	**2,176,089**

belt conveyors, but very little was spent during the remainder of the war. Capital expenditure was minimised after the war pending a Government decision on the future of the railways. Nevertheless, the rate of spending did increase then, mainly associated with the construction of Margam Wharf, although some of the increase must be ascribed to post-war inflation. The total capital expenditure to December 1921 was £2,176,089.

The form of railway accounts prior to 1912 makes it difficult to give an accurate breakdown of capital expenditure, but from then onwards the requirements of the Railway Companies (Accounts & Returns) Act 1911[33] make it possible to do so. The data for 1912 to 1921 is given in Table 17.1. Negative values are net of credits (for example, sale of land or materials) and the rolling stock figure is net of the sale of five locomotives and one workmen's coach in 1901/1903 (£10,191) and the value of twenty-three scrapped wagons in 1910 (£653).

TRAFFIC AND REVENUE
Although the PTR did not carry its first mineral traffic until 30th August 1897,[34] the PTR&D reported a modest gross income of £3,016 for the six months to June that year. This total was made up of coal carried £1,009, minerals £105, general merchandise £152, and dock charges £1,750, presumably all derived from traffic handled in the dock area. The working expenses for this period were £1,838. The gross receipts for the second half of 1897 were £5,499, largely accounted for by an increase in coal carried to £2,929, giving an annual gross income of £8,515, set against working expenses of £5,145. Livestock generated a trivial 3s 5d! The income generated by all these categories except dock charges rose approximately threefold in 1898 and the addition of passenger receipts pushed the total income up to nearly £23,000.

The tonnages of freight and mineral traffic handled by the railways and docks were first reported in 1899 when the New Dock opened. The annualised data for 1899 to 1907 is given in Figure 17.2. During this period the traffic carried by the railway rose from 870,000 tons to almost 2.81m tons. On average, 88 per cent of this traffic was coal; by no means was all of this shipped – only 44 per cent in 1899, rising to 70 per cent in 1906. The balance was used by local industries or taken further afield by rail. However, coal – the figures for which include coke and patent fuel

– made up most of the exports, other exports amounting in most years to about 20,000 tons. Unlike the trade of the old Port Talbot Company,[35] the exports of coal and related products from 1900 onwards were predominantly to foreign ports. Imports, mainly pit props and copper ore or precipitate, rose from 82,000 tons in 1899 to 196,000 tons in 1907. The drop of 20,000 tons in 1901 was due to the closure of Cefn Ironworks and the loss of ore imports.

Gross income rose in the same period from £49,645 to £136,545 (Figure 17.3). A major concern of directors of railway companies at the time was the ratio of working expenses to receipts as a measure of operating efficiency. This ratio improved from 69 per cent in 1900 to 53 per cent in 1906. An acceptable figure was one of the GWR's concerns when considering the working agreement.[36] Although the income from dock charges, and to a lesser extent coal traffic, increased noticeably, income from other sources levelled off: general merchandise at about £1,450 annually, mineral traffic £5,500, livestock a paltry £23, and passengers £4,500, which the introduction of Second Class in 1904 did nothing to improve.

The running powers and working agreement signed with the GWR in January 1908 was deemed to come into effect in January 1907.[37] As far a revenue was concerned, the agreement provided for the GWR to guarantee receipts to the PTR&D of £37,500 for 1907–10, £41,250 for 1911 and £45,000 per annum thereafter, plus 50 per cent of the excess profits. The GW/PT Consultation Committee of Directors further agreed in July 1908 that the PTR&D's proportion of competitive through traffic receipts would be 36.11 per cent. From 1908 onwards the PTR&D accounts showed the total amount received from the GWR for running the goods, mineral and passenger services under these terms, with no further breakdown. The sum received for 1908 was just over £37,000, rising to approximately £54,500 for 1912–21 (Figure 17.4). Every year up to at least 1918, the last for which information is available, the GWR was required to provide cash to make up the guaranteed receipts (Table 17.2).[38]

Dock charges continued to be the PTR&D's principal source of income. These rose from £64,400 in 1908 to a peak of £231,000 in 1920, falling off somewhat to £196,200 in 1921, the final full year of the company's independent existence. Gross receipts peaked in 1920 at £290,700. The mostly continual rise in receipts from 1908 to 1920 did not entirely reflect the traffic at the docks (Figure 17.5);

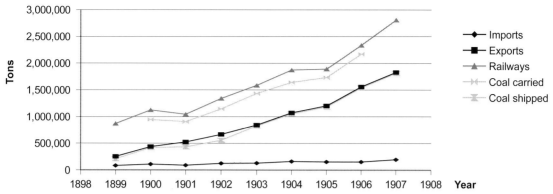

FIGURE 17.2:   PTR&D FREIGHT AND MINERAL TRAFFIC 1899–1907

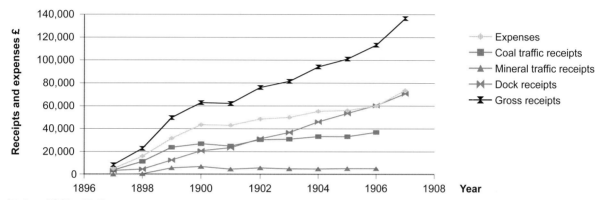

FIGURE 17.3:   PTR&D REVENUE 1897–1907

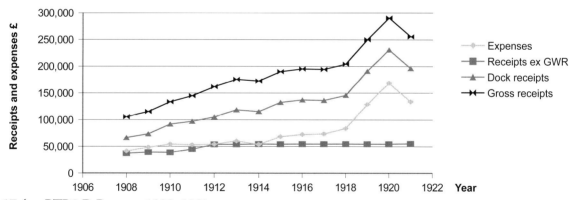

FIGURE 17.4:   PTR&D REVENUE 1908–1921

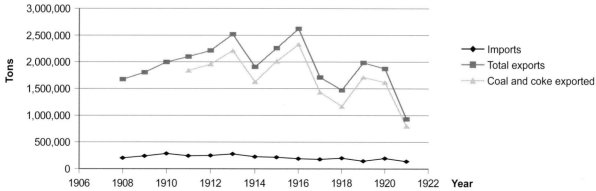

FIGURE 17.5:   PTR&D DOCK TRAFFIC 1908–1921

TABLE 17.2: GWR Contribution to Guaranteed Receipts

Year	GWR Contribution	Year	GWR Contribution
1907	£5,282	1913	£8,172
1908	£4,842	1914	£9,137
1909	£413	1915	£8,565
1910	£3,213	1916	£8,649
1911	£6,741	1917	£8,057
1912	£11,889	1918	£8,242

TABLE 17.3: Issued Stocks of the SWMR, 1921

Stocks Issued	Total	Held by GWR Value	Percent
Ordinary	£55,610	£46,350	83.3
Consolidated 3% Preference	£105,370	£97,792	92.8
3% A Debentures	£5,353	£5,353	100.0
3% B Debentures	£83,700	£64,109	76.6
Total	**£250,033**	**£213,604**	**85.4**

imports peaked at 278,000 tons in 1913 and then slowly declined. Exports were more affected by the First World War and reached their highest pre-grouping level of 2.33 million tons in 1916 followed by a general decline to a post-war low of 931,000 tons. These amounts reflected the trade depression of the time which was accompanied by rising costs.

SWMR Company[39]

By the time the PTR&D took control, the SWMR had finished reorganising its capital as authorised by the 1903 Act.[40] In all £55,610 of ordinary shares and £105,370 of consolidated 3% preference shares had been issued, on which no dividend ever was or would be paid. The loans had been restructured and increased to £5,023 of A debentures and £83,700 of B debentures. Further B debentures of £330 were issued in 1912, bringing the total issued capital to £250,033. Interest at 3% was paid on the A debentures throughout the PTR&D's period of control. Interest on the B debentures started at 1¾% in 1908, rising gradually to the maximum of 3% in 1911. The gross receipts of the SWMR never

exceed £15,000 between 1908 and 1922, peaking at £10,479 in 1914, and consequently the PTR&D retained 67½% as working expenses throughout as provided for by the working agreement.[41] The SWMR's proportion of the receipts was usually just sufficient to pay the declared interest on the debentures, but in 1911 and 1912 was it necessary for the PTR&D to augment its payments by £511 and £1,189 respectively.

At the end of 1921 the GWR held 85.4% of the issued stocks of the SWMR, as shown in Table 17.3.

Up to December 1868 the SWMR had expended £197,311 on capital projects, mainly the construction of the railways. A further £54,561 was spent up to 1907, and of this over £42,000 was debited to capital expenditure as a result of debt restructuring. The major item of expense in this period was £4,584 for the change of gauge. The net capital expenditure from 1908 to 1922 was only £803, a result achieved by the periodic sale of scrap materials. Thus £3,260 was spent in 1917/18 in equipping the line from Cymmer to Glyncorrwg for passenger service, against which was set material recovered from the incline valued at £2,890. The total capital expenditure on the SWMR to December 1922 was £251,503.

Notes

1. This section is based the PTR&D Co. Accounts 1895–1921, TNA: PRO RAIL 1110/384.
2. WGAS D/D PRO/BRB/41, 47.
3. See Volume 1, Chapter 3.
4. SML PEA 4/10.
5. SML PEA 4/7.
6. TNA: PRO MT 6/697/5.
7. PTR&D Co. 1903 Act, preamble.
8. See Volume 1, Chapter 5.
9. WGAS D/D PRO/BRB/47.
10. TNA: PRO RAIL 574/86–88.
11. TNA: PRO RAIL 574/85.
12. TNA: PRO RAIL 574/79.
13. TNA: PRO RAIL 574/80.
14. TNA: PRO RAIL 574/84.
15. TNA: PRO RAIL 574/83.
16. TNA: PRO RAIL 574/81.
17. See Volume 1, Chapter 6.
18. TNA: PRO RAIL 574/82.
19. TNA: PRO RAIL 574/95.
20. See Chapter 12.
21. TNA: PRO RAIL 574/97.
22. TNA: PRO RAIL 1057/1533.
23. 3 Edw. 7 c.cxiii.
24. TNA: PRO RAIL 574/96.
25. TNA: PRO RAIL 1057/2952.
26. 7 Edw. 7 c.xxix.
27. See Volume 1, Chapter 8.
28. TNA: PRO RAIL 1057/2539.
29. 3 & 4 Geo. c.xli.
30. TNA: PRO RAIL 1057/2952.
31. TNA: PRO RAIL 253/757.
32. See Chapter 19.
33. 1 & 2 Geo. 5 c.34.
34. See Volume 1, Chapter 4.
35. See Volume 1, Chapter 2.
36. TNA: PRO RAIL 1057/2952.
37. See Volume 1, Chapter 8.
38. TNA: PRO RAIL 242/1.
39. This section is based the SWMR Co. Accounts 1861–1922, TNA: PRO RAIL 1110/430.
40. See Volume 1, Chapter 7.
41. TNA: PRO RAIL 253/761; see also Volume 1, Chapter 8.

18

Directors and Officers

DIRECTORS

The PTR&D's 1894 Act provided for a minimum of five and a maximum of nine directors, any three being a quorum. Three directors were named in the Act, Col John Roper Wright (1843–1926), Sidney Hutchinson Byass (1862–1929) and Col Charles Richard Franklen, with powers to nominate two more. No explanation was given for the choice of Col Wright and Byass, although both were prominent local businessmen who had strongly supported the promotion of the Bill in Parliament, being chairmen of Wright, Butler & Co. Ltd and R B Byass & Co., respectively. It is probable they were encouraged to take on the role by Miss Talbot's agent, Edward Knox. Col Franklen represented Miss Talbot.

The nominated directors were Mr L Wood and Mr Thomas E Watson, chairman of Pyman, Watson & Co. Ltd and Ffaldau Collieries Co. Ltd.

Col John Thomas North (1842–96), chairman of North's Navigation Collieries Ltd, and the 4th Earl of Dunraven (1841–1926) were elected at the first shareholder's meeting held on 27th December 1894, thereby completing the first Board.[1] All subsequent directors were appointed by the Board and confirmed, without dissent, at a general meeting.[2]

Mr Wood did not remain for long, resigning in January 1895 over the issue of non-competitive tendering for the contract for the construction of the railway and new dock. Ivor Bertie Guest (1835–1914), the first Baron Wimborne, of the Dowlais iron dynasty, replaced Wood in June 1895. Col North, who died in May 1896, never attended any Board meetings and was replaced in May 1898 by Edward Knox (born circa 1861), Miss Talbot's agent and the erstwhile first secretary of the company.

At their meeting on 16th August 1899 the shareholders voted to increase the number of directors from seven to nine and at the same time confirmed the appointment of John Joseph Smith, the chairman of North's Navigation Collieries Ltd, as from June 1899. Richard Cory of Cory Bros, colliery proprietors and coal shippers, joined the Board in October 1901, making up the full complement of nine directors. Knox resigned as Miss Talbot's agent, and consequently as a director, in January 1901, and took up a similar position at Hylton Estates, Kilmersdon, near Radstock. Godfrey Lipscomb (born circa 1864), Knox's successor as Miss Talbot's agent, was immediately appointed a director and remained until the end. Lord Wimborne resigned in May 1902 and Col Franklen died in July 1903, but neither was immediately replaced.

The directors present at the first Board meeting on 26th September 1894 elected the Earl of Dunraven chairman. In his absence, Col Wright was elected deputy chairman and was effectively the chairman for the next fourteen years. The Earl of Dunraven offered to resign as a director in July 1896 owing to his other commitments

preventing him from attending Board meetings. He was informed that this step would not be conducive to the welfare of the company, and having been asked to reconsider, agreed to continue. The Earl's continued absence from Board and shareholder meetings eventually brought about his resignation as chairman in July 1908, when Col Wright was elected to that position in his stead, although he continued as a director until November 1916.

Col John Roper Wright (1843–1926) was deputy chairman of the PTR&D from 1894 to 1908, and chairman from then until 1922, during which time he was also chairman of the SWMR. Col Wright, who was created a baronet in 1920, was a major figure in the steel industry, having worked with Siemens on the development of blast furnaces in the 1860s before moving to South Wales to establish in due course the firm of Wright, Butler & Co., which was one of the businesses which merged in 1902 to form Baldwins Ltd. Col Wright was chairman of Baldwins from 1908 to 1925, when he handed over to his son, Col Sir William Charles Wright. *Courtesy Arthur Rees*

The Board was strengthened in February 1909 by the appointment of David Alfred Thomas, the prominent chairman of the Cambrian Combine,[3] as the eighth director. These gentlemen directed the affairs of the company, by now focussed on developing the docks side of the undertaking, up to the outbreak of the First World War. Cory died in September 1914, but it was not until November 1916 when the Earl of Dunraven resigned that a new director was appointed. This was Stanley Baldwin (1867–1947), son of Alfred Baldwin and founder of Baldwins Ltd whose current chairman and joint managing director was Col Wright. Baldwin's tenure was short-lived, being obliged to resign in April 1917 on taking a junior ministerial position in Lloyd George's coalition government. Lord Rhondda, as Thomas had by now become, similarly resigned in February 1917 on becoming President of the Local Government Board.

Smith's resignation in September 1919 due to ill health reduced the number of directors to a sub-minimum of four, and Henry Seymour Berry (1877–1928) and Col William Charles Wright were appointed to replace Lord Rhondda and Smith respectively. Berry was *inter alia* chairman of North's and Celtic collieries and later GKN.[4] Col W C Wright, the only son of Col J R Wright, was deputy chairman of Baldwins Ltd, becoming chairman in 1926 on the death of his father, and later chairman of the British (Guest Keen & Baldwin) Iron & Steel Co.[5] Coincidentally, Col J R Wright was created a baronet and Col W C Wright was knighted, both in 1920.

Sir Thomas Watson, who had been created a baronet in January 1918, was knocked down by a motor car in London on 1st May 1921 and died shortly afterwards,[6] but owing to the imminence of the grouping was not replaced. Of the five directors remaining in office at his time, two, Col Sir John Wright and Mr Sidney Byass, had served since the formation of the company in 1894.

The directors' remuneration was set at the second general meeting held on 1st August 1895 at a total of £1,400 per annum. In January 1908 the proprietors voted to increase this figure by £600, the total being allocated as follows: Col Wright, £500, Byass and Watson, £350 each, Lipscomb, £300, Smith and Cory, £250 each, the differences reflecting the various additional duties undertaken. The fees remained at these amounts until the grouping when the five directors shared the £12,500 voted by the proprietors for loss of office.[7]

Edward Knott, secretary. *Courtesy Arthur Rees*

Frederick Page, accountant.

Courtesy Arthur Rees

OFFICERS

During the first four years of its existence the PTR&D appointed a number of officers, some of whom proved unsuitable for their roles. However, among them were some very competent gentlemen who remained in their senior positions for the duration of the company's independent existence.

The resident engineer of the old Port Talbot Co. was Robert A Carr (born circa 1865). He continued in that position with the new company and took on the additional roll of traffic manger in March 1895. It is not clear what traffic there was to manage, and in July 1896 he was given three month's notice of dismissal, subsequently taking the position of engineer on the Burry Port & Gwendraeth Valley Railway.[8] Nothing was done to fill the position of resident engineer until June 1897 when the directors decided that Albert Havelock Case (1857–1940) would be appointed to the position *pro tem*, to become full time when the existing contracts were completed, his job being to maintain the completed works.[9]

Up to the end of 1900 the PTR&D also employed consulting engineers. The first of these was James Adair McConnochie (1835–95)[10] who had been engaged by Miss Talbot in 1890 to advise on the development of the Old Dock[11] and was retained by the new company to work on the design of the New Dock. The prominent mining and civil engineer Thomas Forster Brown (1835–1907)[12] contributed towards the design of the New Dock, the OVER and the SWMJnR, and was named as one of the engineers on the Deposited Plans for all three schemes. The third consulting engineer retained by the company in its early days was Patrick Walter Meik (1851–1910).[13] At the time he was in partnership with his father practising as Thomas Meik & Sons. Following the death of Meik senior the partnership was reformed with Patrick Meik and his brother Charles Scott Meik (1853–1923), whose early career had been blighted by the Tay Bridge disaster. Patrick Meik was involved in the design of, and supervised the construction of, all the new works carried out by the PTR&D, his services being dispensed with early in 1901 when construction had finished. Charles Meik was appointed the company's engineer in the dispute over Pearson's contract,[14] and was joint engineer with Sir William Matthews for the proposed dock improvements of 1914. A young engineer named William Halcrow joined the Meik brothers about 1901 and, although he left in

1910, he later rejoined Charles Meik, becoming a partner in 1922. In due course this firm became Sir William Halcrow & Partners Ltd, at the time of writing operating as Halcrow Group Ltd.[15]

A Mr Bloomfield was appointed book-keeper in March 1895, but must have proved unsatisfactory as he was dismissed in February 1896. The following month Edward Knott (1870–1933), who was previously employed as a clerk, was promoted to the newly created position of accountant. Edward Knox, who had been the company's secretary since September 1894,[16] gave three month's notice as from 1st February 1898 to terminate his appointment. Knott, who was described as tall, dark and handsome,[17] was appointed secretary in his place as from 1st May 1898 at a salary of £300 per annum, and remained in this position until the end of the of the company's independent existence, ending on a salary of £850 per annum.

The position of book-keeper remained vacant until May 1897 when Frederick William Page (born 1871) was appointed, with the additional role of debt collector, effective from 1st July. Page had previously been employed as a clerk at a local tinplate works. Following the appointment of Knott as secretary, Page was promoted accountant at a salary of £150 per annum, he too remaining to the end, his final salary being £550 per annum. Following the grouping, Page was transferred to Paddington where he worked as one of the two assistants to R Cope, the chief accountant of the GWR.

It was not until July 1896 that the company appointed its first general manager, when James Probert (born circa 1852) was recruited to the position at a salary of £500 per annum. Probert had started his railway career in November 1867 with the L&NWR at Swansea, rising to the position of chief clerk in the Coaching (Assistant Superintendent's) Department.[18] Probert resigned in February 1900, and the following month the directors decided to give him £250 and terminate his engagement immediately. No reasons were given by either party, although the tone of his internal correspondence suggests his views were not always popular. The 1901 census describes Probert as a broker and metal merchant in Swansea.

The lesser post of traffic manager was advertised at £500 per annum, with the stipulation that candidates should be under the age of forty. Eighty applications were received, from which six were selected for interview:

W P Dent	NER	Blyth Dock
Wm Harrison	NER	Percy Main
W J Holloway	Cardiff Railway	Cardiff
E Lowther	NER	Gateshead
J H Vincent	Barry Railway	Barry
J H Williamson	NER	Hull

The preponderance of applicants employed by the North Eastern Railway is noteworthy. The NER was the mineral carrier *par excellence*, a status to which the PTR&D aspired. Edward Lowther (1859–1945) stood out from this group, at the time being the Chief Inspector of the Mineral Department of the NER. In April 1900 the directors resolved to ask Lowther to obtain leave of absence for about two weeks to attend at Port Talbot so as to make himself thoroughly acquainted with the working of the traffic of the railway and dock, and, if he could see a way of reducing expenditure, to be appointed

traffic manager at £500 per annum plus RCH Superannuation, with three month's notice on either side. Despite being just over the age limit, Lowther was appointed traffic manager as from 1st June 1900. His performance evidently impressed the directors such that he was appointed general manager as from 1st January 1902, and asked to submit for Board's approval the authority he would suggest as necessary to carry out the working of the line. In effect he was invited to write his own job description. The results of his efforts have been noted throughout this history. In December 1904 Lowther's salary was raised from £500 to £750 per annum as a mark of the Board's appreciation of the satisfactory manner in which he had carried out his duties.

With the 1908 running powers and working agreements in operation, Lowther came more and more to the notice of the directors and senior managers of the GWR – so much so that by April 1916 his salary, ten twenty-thirds of which was paid by that company, had been raised to £2,000 per annum, with a further rise to £2,500 in July 1919. Charles Roberts, the chief goods manager of the GWR, retired on 30th June 1921,[19] and Lowther was appointed to this position as from 1st July 1921 at a salary of £3,750 per annum.[20] He continued as general manager of the PTR&D without additional remuneration, although there was little for him to do pending absorption. A final rise in July 1922 brought his annual

Edward Lowther, general manager.   *Courtesy Arthur Rees*

salary to £4,500. Lowther was due to retire in March 1924, but was invited to take charge of the GWR Docks Department at his existing salary, which he did until April 1925, when he left for a well-earned retirement in his native Cumberland on a pension of £3,000 per annum.[21] Locally, Lowther was a JP, a county councillor, a Pilotage Commissioner, founder and one-time president of the Port Talbot Chamber of Commerce and chairman of the Port Labour Tribunal.[22] A contemporary described Lowther as "a big, proud, important looking man, reminiscent of an Edwardian Cabinet Minister, especially when he wore his top hat, which was not infrequently".[23]

John R Cadman was appointed chief clerk in October 1900, reporting to the general manager. At the time of his death in March 1917 Cadman was acting as the traffic manager, and was replaced by R J Williams.

The position of locomotive superintendent was filled even later. At the Board meeting on 16th December 1896 Mr Watson proposed that Walter James Hosgood (1866–1943), then assistant chief engineer under his brother John Howell Hosgood (1860–1910) with the Barry Dock & Railway Company (BD&R), be engaged as locomotive and machinery superintendent, should enquiries prove satisfactory. Hitherto this role had been performed by Patrick Meik and it was suggested that in the meantime a Mr Nicholson, one of Meik's engineers, should do this work. Hosgood accepted the position as from 1st March 1897, his salary being £300 per annum. He took on the additional role of resident engineer in June 1899 at a salary of £450 per annum, following the resignation in May 1899 of Case who had accepted a Government engineering position.[24]

Hosgood had started his railway career as a telegraph clerk at Neath. He completed a four-year apprenticeship under T Hurry Riches, the locomotive superintendent of the TVR in 1887. Following this he went to sea for two years as a marine engineer and then spent one year in the drawing office of Sharp, Stewart & Co., Glasgow, before joining the BD&R.

Hosgood's time with the PTR&D could not be considered an unqualified success. The problems arising from the acquisition and performance of the Cooke-built locomotives have already been described,[25] and on at least two occasions he was reprimanded by the directors for slack office management. Hosgood tendered his resignation in December 1904 and left in March 1905 to take up the position of locomotive, carriage and wagon superintendent of Rhodesian

Albert Hertz, locomotive superintendent.
Courtesy Arthur Rees

Railways. The directors agreed to waive the usual six months notice, and were perhaps not unhappy to see him go. In Rhodesia Hosgood acquired the soubriquet of Togo, because being bearded he resembled the Japanese admiral of the time.[26] Hosgood retired from Rhodesian Railways in 1924 and returned to England where for six years he was a consulting engineer with the firm of Sir Douglas Fox & Partners.[27]

Following Hosgood's resignation, and on the recommendation of Lowther, the posts of resident engineer and locomotive and mechanical superintendent were separated. Consequently, Albert Holger Hertz (1857–1930) was appointed locomotive and mechanical superintendent on 1st April 1904 at salary of £225 per annum, reporting to the general manager. Hertz, who was born in Copenhagen and had taken British citizenship, had been engineer in charge of the PTR&D's hydraulic machinery and marine plant since 1894, having previously been a chief engineer on ocean going steamers. On taking his new position Hertz moved into Central Station House, living there until March 1914. As a consequence of the working and running powers agreements, Hertz transferred to the GWR in April 1908 and was appointed divisional locomotive superintendent, Port Talbot, at a salary of £300 per annum.[28] He retired in March 1922 having reached the age of 65, and was granted a GWR pension of £325 per annum,[29] he being too old to have joined the RCH Superannuation Scheme.

William Cleaver (1873–1951), who had been trained at the engineering works of Taylor & Sons, Briton Ferry, was appointed Case's draughtsman and chief assistant in September 1898, and remained as assistant when Hosgood assumed the role of resident engineer in June 1899. Following Hosgood's resignation, Cleaver was appointed resident engineer on 1st April 1904 at salary of £225 per annum, reporting to the general manager. He held this position until the PTR&D was absorbed by the GWR, and was responsible for the many improvements and extensions to the docks and railways. Following the grouping he was appointed resident engineer at Newport Docks, subsequently becoming, in January 1928, divisional district engineer covering Newport, Cardiff, Penarth and Barry. Cleaver, although described as having a lean and hungry look,[30] seemingly did not enjoy the best of health and in June 1916 was permitted by the directors to live in Bridgend for this reason. He retired in May 1931 due to ill health and was granted a GWR pension of £750 per annum.[31]

William Cleaver, engineer.
Courtesy Arthur Rees

The increasing numbers of mechanical and hydraulic appliances in the docks and the use of electricity to power some of them and to provide lighting led the PTR&D around 1908 to employ H J Roberts and H Morgan as mechanical and electrical engineer respectively. Both passed to employment with the GWR at the grouping, Roberts becoming the mechanical engineer at Barry Docks.

The envisioned development and expansion of the docks required a competent person to direct shipping within and approaching the area. Capt. Henry N Knox RN (circa 1832–1916) was appointed nautical advisor in May 1895 and apparently still held that position when he died in June 1916. William G Barron (born circa 1860), deputy harbour master with the old company, was appointed harbour master in December 1896, but was seemingly unsuited to the role and was moved to the position of debt collector in January 1898, relieving Page of this duty. In October 1900 this post was deemed to be unnecessary and Barron was given six month's notice of termination of his employment. Capt Humphrey Jones (born circa 1862), a master mariner then with the BD&R, was appointed harbour master in March 1898 and remained until the end of the company's existence.

Once Hosgood had left the only officers to attend Board meetings were the general manager, Lowther, and the secretary, Knott. When appropriate, the company's solicitor also attended. Charles Cheston of Cheston & Sons, London, who was also Miss Talbot's solicitor, held this position until his death in May 1906, when his firm became Broad & Sons, who continued to act for the company.

H J Roberts, mechanical engineer.
Courtesy Arthur Rees

H Morgan, electrical engineer.
Courtesy Arthur Rees

Capt Humphrey Jones, harbour master.
Courtesy Arthur Rees

Notes

1. See Volume 1, Chapter 3.
2. TNA: PRO RAIL 574/6.
3. Margaret Haig Mackworth, Viscountess Rhondda, *DA Thomas, Viscount Rhondda, by His Daughter and Others* (Longmans, Green & Co. 1921), chapters IX and X.
4. Edgar Jones, *A History of GKN, vol. 2: The Growth of a Business, 1918–45* (Macmillan 1990), pp. 76–89.
5. Jackson, *The Letter-Books of W Gilbertson & Co.*, p. 404.
6. TNA: PRO RAIL 1057/2952.
7. See Chapter 19.
8. *Historical Model Railway Society Journal*, Vol. 19 2008 p. 322.
9. Claude Stacey (ed.), *Men of the West* (Author 1926).
10. *Proc. Inst. Civil Eng.*, 1895–96, pp. 406–408.
11. See Volume 1, Chapter 2.
12. *Proc. Inst. Civil Eng.*, 1907–08, pp. 313–14.
13. *Proc. Inst. Civil Eng.*, 1910–11, pp. 328–30.
14. See Chapter 12.
15. *125 Years of Halcrow* (Halcrow Group Marketing 2003).
16. See Volume 1, Chapter 3.
17. J Ivor Hanson, *Profile of a Welsh Town* (Author 1969), p. 82.
18. TNA: PRO RAIL 410/1847.
19. *The Times*, 11 June 1921.
20. TNA: PRO RAIL 250/53; *The Railway Gazette*, 17 June 1921.
21. TNA: PRO RAIL 250/54; *Who's Who in Wales* (Western Mail, 1921); *Who's Who in Cumberland and Westmorland* (Who's Who in the Counties, 1937).
22. *The Railway Gazette*, 14 March 1924.
23. Hanson, *Profile of a Welsh Town*, p. 82.
24. ME Day, *The Engineers' Who's Who* (DMA Co., 1939).
25. See Volume 1, Chapter 9.
26. Anthony H Croxton, *Railways of Zimbabwe* (David & Charles, 1982), p. 260.
27. *Proc. Inst. Mech. Eng.*, 1944, p. 351.
28. TNA: PRO RAIL 250/49.
29. TNA: PRO RAIL 250/53.
30. Hanson, *Profile of a Welsh Town*, p. 82.
31. WT Pike, *British Engineers and Allied Professions in the Twentieth Century* (WT Pike, 1908); *Railway Gazette*, 15 May 1931.

Tonmawr signal box photographed in May 1954. This was the second box at Tonmawr, opened in September 1925 opposite the site of the original and closed in May 1954.

Author's collection

19

The Grouping

WAR WAS DECLARED ON 4th August 1914 and the Government took over the PTR&D's railways at midnight under the provisions of the Regulation of the Forces Act 1871, control being exercised through the Railway Executive Committee of the Board of Trade and, from August 1919, by the new Ministry of Transport. Capital expenditure, unless officially sanctioned, was stopped by the Board of Trade as from 19th May 1915, a policy only rescinded on 2nd June 1919. During the war compensation for loss of income, if any, was paid in monthly instalments based on pre-war receipts and later included the costs of arrears of maintenance.[1] As preliminary step in the political process that was to lead to the Railways Act 1921, the Government at the end of June 1920 issued a White Paper outlining proposals for the future organisation of transport in Great Britain.

PTR&D COMPANY

The White Paper formed the basis of subsequent negotiations with the PTR&D. Felix Pole, the GWR's assistant general manager, commented on a meeting with Lowther in August 1920 that the latter felt his directors would willingly discuss the absorption of the PTR&D by the GWR.[2] At a subsequent meeting in October 1920 between Lowther and Messrs Aldington, general manager, Bolter, secretary, and Cope, accountant, of the GWR, it was agreed that amalgamation was preferred to lease. If the latter course was adopted the PTR&D ordinary shareholders required a guarantee of 9% return, although the GWR was only prepared to go to 8%. Leasing turned out not to be an option.

At a meeting held on 17th November 1920 between Col Sir John Wright, Bart. (as he had become in the previous New Year's Honours) and Lowther for the PTR&D, and Lord Churchill (the GWR chairman) and Messrs Aldington, Bolter and Cope for the GWR, the following terms for the proposed amalgamation were agreed:

- £100 GWR 4% Debenture Stock for each £100 PTR&D 4% Debenture Stock.
- £8 GWR 5% Preference Shares for each £10 PTR&D 4% Preference Shares.
- £18 GWR 5% Guaranteed Stock for each £10 PTR&D Ordinary Shares.
- Capital overdraft to be assumed by the GWR.
- General reserve to be taken over by the GWR.
- Existing obligations of the PTR&D to be assumed by the GWR.
- Officers and staff to be taken over on terms not less favourable than they currently enjoyed.
- Deficiencies under the dock agreement to be written off by the GWR (circa £400,000).

It was also suggested that the directors should receive three years' fees for loss of office and retain their gold passes. Lowther was personally assured by Lord Churchill that he would not suffer under these arrangements, and was later informed that he would be given a role in the new GWR at a salary not less than he was then receiving. Sir John Wright enquired if there was a place for a former PTR&D director on the reconstituted GWR Board, and was informed that this privilege was reserved for constituent companies. All these terms were agreed and formally accepted at a Board meeting of the PTR&D directors held on 15th December 1920, except that they felt that three years' fees were not adequate compensation and suggested they should have at least five years, and that the position of the company's secretary should be clarified.

The group of GWR and PTR&D directors and officers met again on 11th January 1921 when it was recognised that the arrangement would have to be treated as provisional so that it could be carried through under the terms of the forthcoming Act, and as such it was to be regarded as confidential. It was decided that Knott would retain his position as secretary of the Pilotage Board and would be adequately compensated for loss of office as secretary of the PTR&D. A draft agreement was ready by 23rd March; this anticipated a date for the exchange of stocks and shares effecting absorption of 1st July 1921.

The introduction of the Railways Bill 1921 on 11th May 1921 caused this step to be delayed and Knott was requested to remain as secretary until absorption actually occurred. The PTR&D directors approved the draft agreement on 18th May. Government control of the railways ended on 15th August 1921, four days before the Railways Act 1921[3] received the Royal Assent. Under this Act the PTR&D was designated a subsidiary company to be absorbed into the Western Group, in which the six principal Welsh companies were amalgamated with the GWR. Matters then went quiet until the Railways Amalgamation Tribunal started work towards the end of November 1921.[4]

In January 1921 the directors felt it advisable to recommend the shareholders not to sell their holdings in view of the approaching completion of negotiations with the GWR. The PTR&D was included in the GWR (Western Group) Preliminary Absorption Scheme (No. 1),[5] which was not approved by the Tribunal until January 1923,[6] by which date the new Western Group was for the most part complete. Absorption of the PTR&D was deemed to have taken effect on 1st January 1922.

The directors decided in February 1922 that if they were awarded £12,500 for loss of office, this amount would be divided between them proportionally to their present fees, and also that until their services were no longer required they would continue to carry out their duties at the existing rate of fees. This sum, to be paid out of the assets of the company, was approved at an extraordinary meeting of shareholders held on 6th April 1922. The compensation was divided as follows: Col. Sir John Wright £3,541 13s 4d, Mr S H Byass and Mr G Lipscomb £2,500 each, and Col Sir Charles Wright and Mr H Seymour Berry £1,979 3s 4d each. A special general meeting held on the same date unanimously approved the Absorption Scheme, and without further ado the PTR&D Company passed into history.

The Railway Act also provided for the payment of outstanding compensation arising from the period of Government control. In the case of the PTR&D this amounted to £41,820 plus £113 accrued interest. This sum was paid out by the Government in five tranches between December 1921 and February 1923, the monies going to the GWR as the absorbing company.

SWMR COMPANY

Although the directors of the SWMR discussed the 1921 Railways Bill in June that year, it was not until November 1922 that the GWR put forward its terms for absorption:

- £10 cash for each £100 of Ordinary Stock.
- £25 cash for each £100 of Preference Stock.

- The equivalent in 4% GWR Stock for the 3% A and B Debenture Stock.

These terms were recommended to the proprietors at a special general meeting held on 13th December 1922 and accepted unanimously. As the GWR already held 85.4 per cent of the issued stocks of the SWMR,[7] the upshot was that it acquired the outstanding stock for the cash equivalent of £17,513 15s 0d.

In view of the special nature of preparing conversion lists and the absence of staff, Knott was instructed to obtain the assistance of G Gething, formerly of the PTR&D's secretary's office and by then in the docks superintendent's office, outside of his usual hours and to pay him reasonable remuneration.

The SWMR was included in the GWR (Western Group) Preliminary Absorption Scheme (No. 3),[8] which was approved by the Railways Amalgamation Tribunal in July 1923.[9] Absorption of the SWMR was deemed to have taken effect on 1st January 1923. The GWR allowed the three Port Talbot directors, Col Sir John Wright, Mr Byass and Mr Lipscomb, £569 2s 0d compensation for loss of office, to be divided equally between them. This too was approved at the final, extraordinary, general meeting, also held on 13th December 1922.

NOTES

1. W E Simnett, 'Railway Amalgamation in Great Britain', *The Railway Gazette*, 1923.
2. TNA: PRO RAIL 253/757.
3. 11 & 12 Geo. 5 c.55.
4. Simnett, 'Railway Amalgamation in Great Britain'.

5. *The London Gazette*, 11 April 1922.
6. *The London Gazette*, 2 January 1923.
7. See Chapter 16.
8. *The London Gazette*, 15 December 1922.
9. *The London Gazette*, 2 July 1923.

Tonygroes South Junction was renamed the East Junction by 1947 and is seen here on 23rd March 1962. Beyond the junction is the site of the signal box and further on is the North, later West, Junction. The short connection to Aberavon Junction, the left-hand line from North Junction, had been taken out of use in June 1961. The right-hand line up to Margam Forge was closed in March 1963.   *Courtesy C H A Townley*

20

Post Grouping and the British Railways Period

RAILWAYS

Following absorption into the new Great Western system, the relatively short PTR and SWMR lines were incorporated into the Swansea Division for passenger traffic and the Swansea District for goods traffic. Very few changes were made to any of these lines until the 1940s. The release crossover and signal box at Port Talbot Central had been removed by 1920 and the lines there worked as a siding from Tonygroes Junction signal box. In 1923, 2,300 square yards of land in Port Talbot were purchased for the construction of the central station authorised by the GWR's 1914 Act serving the GWR, PTR and R&SBR lines.[1] This was the last mention of this scheme, which if implemented would have transformed the centre of Port Talbot. To avoid confusion with the nearby GWR station in Castle Street, the PTR station at Maesteg was renamed Maesteg Neath Road in July 1924. The most expensive single improvement to the network pre-1939 was the reconstruction in 1927 of Water

Street bridge at the 3¾ milepost on the OVER at a cost of £5,490.[2] The width was increased from 15 to 34 feet, possibly with the intention of doubling the line between the Newlands Loop and the connection to Newlands Colliery, although this was never done. Closure of Ffoes Bank signal box and shortening of the loop on the Porthcawl Branch at the nearby Cefn Junction were authorised in March 1929,[3] all movements there being worked from Cefn Junction signal box. In August 1929 the PTR's Aberavon Junction signal box was closed and the double line from there to the junction singled.

Somewhat against the general trend, a platform known as Duffryn Mills Halt was opened on 14th February 1931. This halt was sited on the Up side at a point adjacent to the Glenhafod Colliery siding connection – a short distance up the line from Duffryn Junction – and was constructed at the expense of Port Talbot Corporation to serve the cemetery at nearby Goitre. The platform was 75 feet long and formed of old sleeper walling filled with ash. The halt

A short train of coal, or pit waste, from Garth (Tonmawr) Colliery heading off the Whitworth Branch in May 1958. Evidence of track alterations here are apparent. Garth Tip is level with the engine, with the tip dropping down to the right bank of the River Pelenna. *Courtesy Hugh Davies*

ABOVE: Although passenger trains ceased in September 1933 Port Talbot Central station continued in use as a goods depot, particularly for coal as seen here on 13th August 1953. The station building survived in remarkably good condition. *Author's collection*

BELOW: Maesteg station in September 1951, long after passenger services had been withdrawn and the shelter on the Up platform removed. *Courtesy W A Camwell*

was used in the Down direction only,[4] and although it appeared in the Service Time Tables no train times were given and it was presumably used as required.

On the SWMR, further improvements to the signalling and layout at Glyncorrwg were made in 1923 and 1925 to improve the running of the workmen's trains.[5] The station at Cymmer was renamed Cymmer Corrwg in September 1926 to avoid confusion with the R&SBR and GWR stations in the village. In June 1936 approval was given for a siding at the west end of the passing loop at Tonmawr to provide rail access to a new tipping ground for Garth Tonmawr Colliery.[6] This siding was extended in the reverse direction in 1959 and was used until the colliery closed. The original signal box at Tonmawr was closed in September 1925 and was replaced by a standard GWR box, from Carne Point on the Fowey Branch, on the opposite side of the tracks. Minor alterations in the track layout at the junction of the Whitworth Branch were made at the same time. The second signal box lasted until May 1954, when it too was replaced, this time by three ground frames, one at the west end of the original loop and two at the east end.

CLOSURES

Passenger trains between Port Talbot and Maesteg – including, one imagines, the funeral service – were withdrawn as from 11th September 1933.[7] Economic downturn and colliery closures resulted in a gradual loss of traffic and the line beyond Lletty Brongu on the Duffryn line was closed in stages. The section between Lletty Brongu and Celtic Colliery was given over to wagon storage in March 1939; traffic from this colliery was worked out via Pontyrhyll until it too was closed in 1942. This policy of closures continued after nationalisation. The section between Celtic Lower Colliery and Bettws was removed in March 1948, followed by the line between there and a point about a quarter of a mile short of Pontyrhyll Junction in 1949, although this was not approved by the British Transport Commission until February 1950.[8] The track between Cwmdu and Lletty Brongu was removed in June 1959.

By 1964 St. John's Colliery was the only one south of Maesteg still working. Early in 1964 the decision was taken to close the PTR from a short distance above Duffryn Junction to its then termination at Cwmdu as from 31st August 1964, and to remove all signal boxes and other equipment.[9] The line from a point at 7 miles 42 chains, a short distance north of Maesteg Neath Road station, to Cwmdu was still being used by the National Coal Board to work traffic between St. John's Colliery and the exchange sidings and washery at Maesteg under agreements dating from 1910.[10] In July 1964 this length of line was offered to the National Coal Board for a nominal £100, but the perceived need to obtain an Act of Parliament to effect this sale resulted in the line being leased instead. In Port Talbot itself, Central station was closed as a goods yard in February 1960 followed by the short connection from Tonygroes Junction to Aberavon in June 1961. The short section from Tonygroes Junction to Duffryn Junction was closed in March 1963. Following the closure of the PTR main line, the layout at Duffryn Junction was reduced to a loop off which ran four engineers' sidings. The whole was worked as a siding from Copper Works Junction signal box until the Dock Branch between the two junctions was closed on 6th February 1967.

The SWMJnR faired no better. The final quarter of a mile of the Whitworth Branch above Bryn Corrwg Colliery was removed circa

An Up empty mineral train on the R&SBR approaching Oakwood Junction and the 1953 connection to the SWMJnR near Pontrhydyfen Viaduct. Below the train is the track bed of the SWMJnR which was removed in 1954. This section of the R&SBR was closed in 1964. The rough ground in the centre of the view is the site of Oakwood Ironworks.   *Author's collection*

1946. The colliery wagon storage loops put in at Tonmawr Junction in 1921 were closed in 1951 and removed in 1955. By March 1952 the condition of a river bank retaining wall and the girder bridge over the R&SBR at Ynysdavid were causing concern. To obviate the need for repairs costing an estimated £26,110, the Railway Executive proposed to close a two and a half mile length of the SWMJnR between the ¾ milepost above Margam Forge and the 3¼ milepost near Pontrhydyfen Viaduct.[11] At this time Garth Colliery on the Whitworth Branch, and Marine and Fernland collieries on Blaenavon Branch were producing 62,000 tons of coal annually creating £31,000 of revenue; it was proposed to deal with this traffic via a new 286-yard connection to the former R&SBR at an estimated cost of £4,792. The new connection was in place by September 1953, but the affected SWMJnR section was not removed until July 1954. The new connection was put into use on 27th June 1954 and traffic from the Tonmawr direction then reached Port Talbot Docks via Aberavon and Burrows Junction or, until June 1961, a reversal to Duffryn Junction. The new junction on the R&SBR, worked by a ground frame and known as Oakwood Junction, was inspected by Col McMullen in February 1955 when it was noted that only two goods trains a day, limited to twenty-five wagons, worked on the SWMJnR.[12] After the provision of additional catch points at Cwmavon to protect the level crossings further down in the event of a runaway, the work was approved. The Blaenavon Branch, and probably also the connection to the SWMR, were closed entirely on 1st December 1958, leaving the SWMJnR as a straggling four miles

long line to Garth Tonmawr Colliery. The Cwmavon to Port Talbot section of the former R&SBR was taken out of use in July 1963 resulting in a very circuitous journey for traffic from this colliery via Oakwood Junction and Cymmer to reach the outside world. The last train from Garth Tonmawr Colliery ran in July 1964 and this route as far as Duffryn Rhondda Colliery in the Avon Valley was closed in the following November. The lower part of the SWMJnR from Tonygroes Junction to Margam Forge serving the wagon repairs siding there was closed in March 1963.

The short section of the former SWMR from the top of the disused incline to 2m 52ch near Crythan Platform was removed shortly after the abandonment of Eskyn Colliery in 1920. The line from there to 4m 11ch near Tonmawr, over which there was no traffic, was closed in May 1950, saving an estimated £308 annually.[13] More significant was the closure of Gyfylchi Tunnel on 13th July 1947 due to a landslip at its western end. From then on the most direct way out for traffic from the eastern end of the line was via Cymmer Tunnel, Maesteg and Tondu. The SWMR from 4m 11ch to 5m 31ch (Tonmawr West Junction), and from 5m 62ch (west end of Gyfylchi Tunnel) to 8m 61ch (Abercregan) was closed in May 1951, resulting in an annual saving of £366.[14] This closure included a total of 1m 17ch of sidings, including Blaenavon Loop and the storage sidings at Tonmawr, although the latter were still in use in June 1954. The signalling at Tonmawr and Cymmer Corrwg was altered to suit the new arrangements. A small amount of coal was taken out from Abercregan siding and the line between there

The landslip on 13th July 1947 at the western end of Gyfylchi Tunnel caused the closure of the SWMR at this point. The left-hand siding, an extension of the loops at Tonmawr, was used in the 1950s as a loading point for North End Colliery half a mile up Cwm Pelenna off to the left.

Courtesy Michael Hale

RIGHT: An undated, post nationalisation view of an Up empty wagon train passing through Cymmer Corrwg, as the station had been named since 1926.
Author's collection

BELOW: No. 9736 on the road leading to the disused Glyncorrwg Colliery Co.'s engine shed at Glyncorrwg, with its former offices beyond. Following the purchase of the SWMR by the PTR&D in 1907, the Glyncorrwg Colliery Co. was given free use of the shed and continued to use it until circa 1926. As a result, the water tank was the only facility used here by railway companies after 1907.
Courtesy C H A Townley

The repositioned South Pit Halt alongside the reconstructed pithead looking Down the line towards Glyncorrwg on 2nd July 1960.

Courtesy P J Garland

and Cymmer Corrwg was not closed until May 1961. The topmost quarter mile of the SWMR at the closed North Rhondda Colliery was sold to the National Coal Board in 1965. Glyncorrwg Colliery closed on 2nd May 1970. The last train on the truncated SWMR ran on 26th June 1970 and the remaining section down to Cymmer Corrwg, and the line over Cymmer Viaduct to the north end of Cymmer Tunnel, were closed two months later.

ENGINE SHEDS

At the grouping, Duffryn Yard engine shed was added to those making up the Neath Division of the Locomotive, Carriage and Wagon Department of the GWR. The former SWMR engine shed at Glyncorrwg was used by the Glyncorrwg Colliery Co. until circa 1926,[15] after which it was relegated to being a watering point only. The water tank there was repaired in October 1936.[16] Seventeen of the twenty-two PTR and two of the five SWMR engines taken over by the GWR, together with twenty-five GWR locomotives, were shedded at Duffryn Yard on 1st January 1922. This total of forty-four tested the capacity of the five-road engine shed and the rather limited siding accommodation and facilities outside. Furthermore, the former R&SBR shed closed in November 1922 and some of its allocation were transferred to the nearby Duffryn Yard.

Economic conditions in the years following the First World War were not conducive to unnecessary capital expenditure, but by 1929 rising unemployment forced the Government to act. That year a Development (Loans Guarantees and Grants) Act was passed,[17]

the purposes of which were to authorise the Treasury to guarantee loans raised in connection with public utility undertakings, and to authorise the giving of financial assistance in respect of expenditure incurred or loans raised for development works, all with the intention of relieving unemployment. The railway companies were the main beneficiaries of this Act although they could not take advantage of the first of these options as they had already borrowed to the limits determined by their share capital. By October 1929 the GWR had developed a list of new works expenditure totalling £3,973,000, of which £3 million qualified for a grant.[18] The total reached nearly £4.5 million by December 1929,[19] covering a wide range of works across the entire system throughout the depression of the 1930s.[20] In October 1929 the directors of the GWR approved improvements at Duffryn Yard estimated to cost £25,000,[21] of which £14,000 qualified for a grant at 2.5% over five years. All the facilities at the depot were altered to a greater or lesser extent. A sixth shed road was added, new offices and boiler house were built onto the rear of the shed, and the lifting shop was enlarged. The old flat-deck turntable was removed and replaced by a 45-foot well type turntable to the rear of the shed. This enabled the old ground-level coaling stage to be replaced by a typical GWR elevated coaling stage with a ramp approach. This work was completed in 1931. Duffryn Yard was allocated the shed code 87B by British Railways in August 1950 and was closed on 2nd March 1964 upon the opening of a new diesel depot at Margam. The remaining steam locomotives were transferred to Neath. *(Continued on page 399)*

Two views of the top end of the SWMR on 28th July 1957 after North Rhondda Colliery had closed and the area was in use as a stockyard. The 1 in 22 gradient is very apparent. The engine is No. 9799. Note the short siding for the brake van, and the tramway (in the foreground below) which connected the stockyard to the colliery.

Both courtesy Hugh Davies

One of a number of views of Duffryn Yard and Junction taken on Tuesday 1st June 1926, nineteen days after the end of the general strike. This general view of the yard shows still only five roads leading into the shed. Former SWMR No. 1, having resumed its earlier GWR number, 1811, and been fitted with pannier tanks in May 1925, is at the coal stage. A PTR 0-6-0ST and, unusually, a tender engine are on shed. *BR/OPC*

MAIN PICTURE: A general view of Duffryn Junction and Yard looking towards Port Talbot Steelworks on 1st June 1926. Although taken on the same date as the previous view, a certain amount of locomotive movement has occurred. The coal miners were still on strike which probable accounts for the large number of wagons held in the loops, although both running lines are clear. At least two former PTR coaches are held in the further carriage siding. Duffryn No. 1 signal box is to the right of centre with the carriage shed behind. *BR/OPC*

INSET: Also in 1926, but not necessarily same date, this view shows more clearly the double junction at Duffryn No. 1 and the pairs of loop sidings on either side of the main line. This whole area is now a housing estate. *Courtesy Arthur Rees*

The rear of the carriage shed and the slightly elevated engine shed viewed from the bridge carrying the road towards Chapel of Ease Crossing over the River Ffrwdwyllt. There were three short sidings in the carriage shed yard; the left-hand 4-wheel carriage has been grounded for use as accommodation. *BR/OPC*

The approach to Duffryn Junction from the Tonygroes direction with the Up loop sidings diverging to the left, 1st June 1926. *BR/OPC*

ALLOCATION

By January 1934, fifty-seven engines were allocated to Duffryn Yard and the number remained more or less at this figure until closure. Locomotives acquired at the grouping were still fairly common at this time. Eight examples each from the PTR and R&SBR were present, together with twenty-five 0-6-0 tank engines and two 'Aberdare' Class 2-6-0 tender engines.[22] The 0-6-2 tank engine was the most popular type on the railways of South Wales and in 1924 Collett designed the '5600' Class to replace or augment the non-standard pre-grouping engines of this type there. Two hundred were produced in batches up to 1928, of which eight were allocated to Duffryn Yard in January 1934. Also present in 1934 were six of the '4200' Class 2-8-0T type introduced by Churchward in 1910 for heavy mineral traffic in South Wales. Although the PTR would seem to have qualified on this basis, the first to be allocated to Duffryn Yard was No. 4238 in October 1923.[23] At nationalisation there were fifty-five engines at Duffryn Yard, all tank engines: eight of the 2-8-0T wheel arrangement, fifteen of the 0-6-2T type (including

the ex-PTR No. 9 and seven other pre-grouping examples) and thirty-two of various classes of 0-6-0 pannier tank.[24] By the time the shed closed in March 1964 the allocation had been reduced to twenty-four steam engines, three of '4200' Class, four of the 2-8-2T '7200' Class, and seventeen pannier tanks – fifteen of the '8750' Class and two of the modern '9400' Class.[25] The last mineral train on the PTR, on 28th August 1964, was pulled by 2-8-0T No. 5213, which at the time was shedded at Neath.

In due course steam engines allocated to Duffryn Yard carried the shed code PT on the valance behind the front buffer beam, altered to DYD in 1941.[26] In BR days the shed code 87B was carried on the smokebox door.

Although never officially a diesel depot, three standard BR diesel shunters 13264–6, later D3264–6, TOPS 08194–6, went new to Duffryn Yard in August 1956. These soon moved away, but in May 1958 seven new ones arrived, D3432–8, TOPS 08361–8. Six of these moved to Margam diesel depot when Duffryn Yard closed.[27]

(Continued on page 407)

ABOVE: The interior of the carriage shed on 1st June 1926, by this time used for wagon repairs. Note the pre-cut lengths of timber. *BR/OPC*

ABOVE: The nondescript office and workshops to the rear of the carriage shed. The unkempt appearance suggests they were not used that much. Holy Cross Church can be made out in the right background. *BR/OPC*

LEFT: Duffryn Yard, photographed on 9th May 1939, with all six shed roads in use. Note the unidentifiable tool van in the far siding. *Author's collection*

ABOVE: Former R&SBR No. 7 as GWR No. 806 shunting alongside Duffryn No. 2 signal box. No. 806 was withdrawn from Duffryn Yard in April 1940. Briton Ferry Collieries Ltd owned Cwmmawr Colliery at Cwmavon which closed circa 1938. By 1930 this colliery company also owned Maesmelyn Colliery at Cwmavon. *Author's collection*

BELOW: A general view of Duffryn Yard on 29th August 1948, nine months after nationalisation. Note all six shed roads in use, and a former Rhymney Railway engine at the far left. Otherwise only standard GWR classes are visible, with no sign of new ownership. The '4200' Class 2-8-0T on the right appears to still be in wartime livery. The Duffryn No. 1 signal box Down starter visible has arms, from the left, for the Dock Branch, Duffryn Sidings loop, and Tonygroes Junction. *Author's collection*

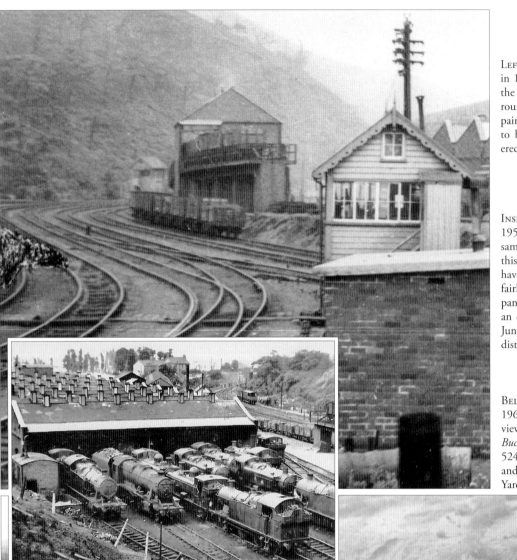

LEFT: The south end of Duffryn Junction in 1954, showing No. 1 signal box and the double track main line running round to No. 2 box in the distance with pairs of loop sidings on either side. Also to be seen is the elevated coaling road erected at Duffryn Yard in 1931.
Author's collection

INSET: Duffryn Yard on 7th April 1955, photographed from much the same viewpoint as the other views of this location. The standard GWR types have been joined by examples of the fairly recent '94XX' Class of 0-6-0 pannier tanks, and on this occasion by an ex-LMS '8F'. The line to Tonygroes Junction passes under the bridge in the distance. *Author's collection*

BELOW: Duffryn Yard photographed in 1963, about a year before closure. On view are Nos 4265, 1001 *County of Bucks*, 9633, 4970 *Sketty Hall*, 6691, 5248, 7229 and 5787. Nos 4970, 5787 and 9633 were withdrawn from Duffryn Yard later that year. *Author's collection*

ABOVE: The '5600' Class of 1924 was also designed specifically for use in South Wales. The first allocated to Duffryn Yard was newly-built No. 6690 in October 1928. No. 6616, built in December 1927 and withdrawn in September 1962, is seen here near Duffryn No. 2 signal box on 8th September 1951. *Author's collection*

Most types of GWR tender and tank engines were to be seen at Duffryn Yard from 1922 onwards, the exception being the largest passenger classes. Prominent were tank engines of the standard two-cylinder classes. No. 4207, photographed there in 1946, is representative of the '4200' Class of 2-8-0 tank engines introduced in 1910 for heavy mineral traffic in South Wales. This particular locomotive was built in February 1912 and withdrawn in October 1961. *Author's collection*

ABOVE: The depression of the 1930s resulted in some of the '4200' Class 2-8-0 tank engines being surplus to requirements. Accordingly, between 1934 and 1939, fifty-four members of this class were rebuilt as 2-8-2 tank engines, becoming the '7200' Class suitable for main line duties. Only a few were allocated to Duffryn Yard, but the shed was convenient for servicing them between duties on the main line. No. 7244, which had been rebuilt from No. 4216 in March 1938 and was withdrawn in February 1965, is seen at Duffryn No. 1 box heading back towards Copper Works Junction on 14th July 1959.

Courtesy R M Casserley

BELOW: Swindon ceased building 'large' 0-6-0 tank engines in 1901. These were all saddle tank engines, and most were sooner or later converted to pannier tanks. Building resumed in 1929 with the '5700' Class of pannier tank engines, which with the modified '8750' Class eventually reached a total of 863 locomotives. Two hundred and fifty were built by outside contractors, including No. 7704 by Kerr, Stuart in 1930, as revealed by the plate on the front splasher. This engine went new to Duffryn Yard in March that year and was photographed there on 2nd August 1931. No. 7704 was withdrawn in December 1960.

Author's collection

The '9400' Class was the ultimate design of pannier tank engine. Only the first ten were built by the GWR in 1947; the remaining 200 were built by contractors during 1950–56. No. 9456, build by R Stephenson in September 1951 and sent new to Duffryn Yard, was photographed alongside the coaling stage on 25th August 1962, with Nos 5230, 4287 (both '4200' Class) and '9F' 2-10-0 No. 92218 behind. No. 9456 was withdrawn in April 1964. *Author's collection*

With clouds of smoke drifting across the yard, a '2800' Class 2-8-0, a '4300' Class 2-6-0 and an 0-6-0 pannier tank are seen at Duffryn Yard coaling stage circa 1950. *Courtesy Bert Pember*

The top end of Duffryn Sidings, mainly occupied by BR steel mineral wagons. Just visible in the sidings alongside the erstwhile carriage shed is what appears to be the former PTR 12T travelling hand crane No. 1, later GW213. Postcard, postally used 31st August 1960.
Author's collection

Probably not a common visitor, ex-LMS '8F' No. 48308 at the throat of Duffryn Yard on 16th April 1955. The siding behind the prominent signal was the designated storage road for the Duffryn Yard breakdown train. The chimney of Glenhafod Colliery is visible in the background. *R E Vincent, The Transport Treasury*

DOCKS

The docks of course constituted the major part of the PTR&D's undertaking, being one of the six principal coal exporting ports in South Wales. R J Williams, the erstwhile traffic manager,[28] was appointed dock superintendent, Port Talbot, in July 1922,[29] reporting to chief docks manager, J H Vickery, the former general manager of the Alexander (Newport & South Wales) Docks & Railway Co., who was based in Cardiff. G L Gibson was appointed resident dock engineer, replacing William Cleaver, who had moved to Newport.[30] T R Herbert replaced Roberts as mechanical engineer.[31]

The GWR spent considerable sums of money in maintaining the infrastructure of the docks. In 1922 the training wall was restored to its original height at an estimated cost of £3,000 in order to help keep the entrance channel clear. Both breakwaters were susceptible to damage by storms and collisions. In 1923 £25,000 was spent in repairing the north breakwater.[32] Up to 1947, repairs to this breakwater amounted to almost £37,000, although as it was also a pier used by the public some of the expense was defrayed by Port Talbot Corporation. In the same period a total of £20,000 was spent keeping the south breakwater in good repair. In December 1929 the Docks & Steamboats Committee of GWR directors, which oversaw all the company's docks, recommended the extension of the north and south breakwaters by 500 feet and 1,000 feet respectively.[33] The company's application for a grant of £350,000 under the Development (Loan Guarantees & Grants) Act 1929 to meet the estimated cost was approved in March 1930, the terms being 5% for ten years and 3.75% for a further five years. Authority to construct such extensions had been granted by the PTR&D's lapsed

1914 Act[34] and steps were immediately taken to revive and extend these powers. The Parliamentary Notice announced the intention to seek an Act to this effect, and also to authorise the GWR to construct a new lock at Swansea.[35] The Great Western Railway (Docks) Act 1930,[36] which gained Royal Assent on 4th June 1930, extended the completion date for the works at Port Talbot to June 1933 – but in October 1930 the directors decided to defer them for the time being because of the Government's attitude to dock charges. The Government planned to lower them to cover working expenses only, with no allowance for capital expenditure, making the £17,500 annual interest charge difficult to justify, and a year later the breakwater extensions were abandoned as unlikely to be remunerative.

Port Talbot Corporation naturally desired to see the docks developed so as to benefit the locality generally. In October 1929 the corporation proposed that a second lock entrance, also authorised by the PTR&D's 1914 Act, should be provided, with financial assistance from the Development (Loan Guarantees & Grants) Act. This proposal was not adopted at the time and was abandoned a year later. This potential revival of the 1914 Act attracted the attention of Messrs Coode, Wilson, Mitchell & Vaughan-Lee, the firm the original consulting engineer, Sir William Mathews deceased, had belonged to.[37] This firm pressed their claim to be involved in the work but were politely informed that their services would not be required. The inner lock gates were renewed in 1934 at a cost of £10,000.[38]

No more dockside industries were established in the 1920s beyond those instigated by the PTR&D.[39] However, six sites were available and these were promoted by the GWR in 1932,[40] as shown in Table 20.1. None of these was particularly large and not surprisingly none

TABLE 20.1:   DOCKSIDE SITES PROMOTED IN 1932

	LOCATION	APPROXIMATE AREA (ACRES)
1	Right bank of River Avon above the Corporation bridge	1.86
2	Right bank of River Avon below the Corporation bridge	3.72
3	Between graving dock and No. 7 tip	2.15
4	Between Nos 3 and 4 tips	1.76
5	Between Nos 4 and 9 conveyor	1.01
6	Between Phoenix Wharf and No. 11 conveyor	1.96

TABLE 20.2:   ADDITIONAL DOCKSIDE SITES PROMOTED IN 1939

	LOCATION	APPROXIMATE AREA (ACRES)
6	All land east of Rio Tinto Wharf and approach sidings	37.2
7	Land north-west of Margam Wharf	3.0
8	Between the Steelworks grids and Messrs Calder's works	5.0
9	Principality Wagon Works site alongside the R&SBR near Seaside station	1.85
10	Llewellyn's Quay	10.0
11	Adjacent to the Docks Hotel	0.3

was taken up at the time. In 1939 site 6 was greatly expanded and a further five were added,[41] see Table 20.2. This time there was more interest. Site 6 was occupied by South Wales Metal Refiners (1941) Ltd and a Ministry of Fuel and Power Briquetting Plant;[42] site 11 was taken by Metallurgical Industrial Processes Ltd.

DOCK RAILWAYS

The principal addition to the dock railways post grouping was the construction in 1924 of the third grid near Burrows Junction, envisaged originally as part of the new exchange sidings with the R&SBR.[43] This would have been grid No. 10 in the PTR&D's scheme, but at an unknown date the GWR renumbered some of the grids as shown in Table 20.3 and it became No. 9.[44]

The new No. 9 grid, situated between No. 10 grid and the running line from Old Dock Junction to Burrows Junction, was intended for steelworks traffic. The six sidings had a capacity of 240 wagons, bringing the total number of wagons that could be berthed on the former PTR&D's lines in the dock area to 9,000. Associated with this work, the bridge over the dock feeder at Burrows Junction was reconstructed in 1925 and widened so as to permit a double line of rails running from the Old Dock Junction direction. At the same time the short connection from the former R&SBR line to North Bank was removed and in 1927 additional sidings for Wagon Repairs Ltd were laid across the site.[45] In 1924 a molten slag line was laid for Baldwins between their Port Talbot and Margam steelworks to obviate using the running lines.[46] Few changes were made to the railways and grids on the South Side of the New Dock in the post-grouping period, the principal addition being two more sidings for crippled wagons at No. 4 grid which were put in 1923.[47]

JETTIES AND TIPS

Through William Cleaver, the PTR&D was a pioneer in the use of reinforced concrete, or ferro-concrete as it was known at the time, for the construction of wharves and jetties.[48] However, timber was used for tip jetties Nos 1-3 and 5-7 before he was appointed engineer, and from 1922 onwards these required repair or reconstruction. No. 7 was partially reconstructed in 1922–23[49] and No. 5 was repaired in 1924.[50] This work turned out to be inadequate and in 1925 both jetties were rebuilt in reinforced concrete by Sixild & Partners for £9,747.[51] No. 2 jetty was reconditioned in 1938[52] and Nos 3 and 5 were reconstructed in 1946.[53]

Some of this reconstruction work was associated with the replacement of existing coal tips by ones of higher capacity. In May 1925 the GWR directors approved the tender of Armstrong Whitworth & Co. to supply and erect five 30-ton fixed coal hoists at Port Talbot, Barry and Newport for £54,655.[54] Two of these were destined for Port Talbot and became the new Nos 1 and 7 tips, completed in 1927. Advantage was taken in 1930 of the 1929 Development (Loan Guarantees & Grants) Act to fund the replacement of Nos 3 and 5 tips with hoists of 30-ton lift capacity. These were provided by the East Ferry Road Engineering Works Co. Ltd at a cost of £28,450.[55] In June 1923 the directors approved the reconstruction of No. 10 belt conveyor so that it could deal with 20-ton wagons.[56] The work was carried by the original makers, Messrs Spencer & Co., at a cost of £13,500 and completed in 1925. Other improvements included the fitting of anti-breakage devices to tips Nos 3–5, and equipping conveyors Nos 9 and 10 with 'Norfolk' diggers to dig small washed coal out of wagons. These various improvements rendered No. 6 tip redundant and it was removed in 1934, followed by No. 11 conveyor by 1937.

These higher capacity tips required more hydraulic power than was currently available. New and more powerful steam driven pumping engines were provided in the South Side hydraulic power house with assistance under the terms of the Development (Loans Guarantees and Grants) Act. In December 1945 the GWR directors approved in principle replacing these two steam-driven pumps with electric-driven pumps at an estimated cost of £83,000. Nothing was done until February 1947 when the work was put in hand at a revised cost of £97,500. After nationalisation this scheme was inherited by the Docks & Inland Waterways Executive. The GWR had negotiated a supply of electricity from the Margam Works to power these pumps, but the increased demand there resulted in the necessary electricity being provided by the South Wales Electricity Board (SWEB).[57] These new pumps were put into use early in 1950. The electricity generating station erected by the PTR&D to power the conveyors had been closed in 1937 and arrangements made to take a supply from Port Talbot Corporation, later the SWEB.

20-TON COAL WAGONS

These improved tipping facilities resulted in Port Talbot Docks being equipped with eight appliances capable of handling 20-ton capacity coal wagons, which themselves had a tare weight approaching 10 tons. This was in turn associated with a strong effort by the GWR management to persuade colliery proprietors and coal shippers to use these larger wagons as a more economical means of transport. The arithmetic was quite simple: 600 tons of coal in 10-ton wagons necessitated a train length of 1,080 feet with a tare weight of 369 tons, whereas the same load in the larger wagons resulted in a train length of 735 feet and a tare weight of 288 tons. To encourage uptake, a discount, typically 5 per cent, was offered on the rate for conveyance.

The first 550 wagons were assigned to collieries shipping coal at Port Talbot and Swansea. North's Navigation Collieries Ltd signed an agreement with the GWR on 23rd September 1924 under which 200 of these 20-ton wagons were "appropriated" to colliery use for the conveyance of coal from Caerau, Coegnant and St. John's collieries to Kings Dock, Swansea, and Port Talbot.[58] North's agreed to modify their screens to accommodate the larger wagons and were granted a 5 per cent reduction in rates, but charged 2½ to 5d ton for the use of the wagons, depending on usage and subject to a minimum of fifty-two journeys per wagon per year. In November 1924, North's took a further fifty wagons on the same terms. The first North's coal was tipped at Port Talbot from a 20-ton wagon on 27th August 1924. A similar agreement was signed on the same date with the Vale of Neath Colliery Co. Ltd for 300 20-ton wagons to convey coal from Aberpergwm Colliery at Glyn Neath to Kings Dock, Swansea, and Port Talbot.[59] This agreement was transferred to Amalgamated Anthracite Collieries Ltd in July 1929. A third such agreement was signed with Messrs Stockwood, Rees & Co. Ltd in October 1924 for their exclusive use of twenty-five 20-ton wagons to carry coal from Glyncorrwg, or any other colliery by arrangement, to Milford Haven, for eight years.[60] Possibly due to the Glyncorrwg Colliery Co. being unwilling to modify its screens, this agreement was not put into effect and in September 1925 was noted as being "finished with." All these wagons were painted in standard GWR livery with the assignees names on the sides, but only those for North's and the VoN Colliery Co. were marked with a return destination, to Maesteg and Glyn Neath respectively.

The only other colliery on the former PTR to utilise these large wagons was Glenhafod Colliery in the Duffryn Valley. This was on a different basis in that Glenhafod Collieries Ltd took fifty wagons on redemption hire for ten years from 30th January 1934 at a rent of £23 0s 9d per annum, with an option to purchase after ten years.[61] The agreement required the colliery company to break up existing wagons of a total capacity of not less than 1,000 tons by 30th June 1934. These wagons were built by Charles Roberts & Co. Ltd as part

TABLE 20.3: PORT TALBOT GRIDS

PTR No.	LOCATION	GWR No.
1	Copper Works Junction	1
2	Grid for No. 9 conveyor	
3	Grid for Nos 1–3 tips	3
4	Grid for No. 10 conveyor	2
5	Sandhills	4
6	Reception grid South Side (nearest Copper Works Junction)	7
7	Reception grid South Side	6
8	Reception grid South Side (furthest from Copper Works Junction)	5
9	Near PT Steelworks	
10	Near PT Steelworks (post grouping)	9
11	Near PT Steelworks	10
12	Near PT Steelworks	11

The first 20-ton wagon tipped in South Wales, Port Talbot, 27th August 1924. Wagon 110024 was one of 250 assigned to North's Navigation Collieries. *Author's collection*

409

Although intended mainly as a coal exporting dock, Port Talbot could handle all classes of traffic as these two cargo liners in the dock demonstrate. Postcard, postally used July 1957. *Author's collection*

of the 5,000 constructed by various outside contractors and were painted in the colliery's usual livery. In April 1937 these wagons were transferred to Stephenson, Clarke & Associated Companies Ltd, the well-known coal factors which had already acquired 2,000 such wagons from new. Stephenson, Clarke purchased these wagons from the GWR on 1st January 1944 at the end of the ten-year hire period. In total, 5,950 of three types of 20-ton wagons were built by the GWR and outside contractors for use by larger concerns.[62]

WHARVES

Talbot Wharf was the main import wharf at the docks. Although the works carried out by the PTR&D were not extended, approximately £20,000 was spent in repairing and reconstructing the wharf in reinforced concrete up to 1941. Two 3-ton movable hydraulic cranes from Vickers Armstrong were added in 1931, one on Talbot Wharf Extension and one on Steelworks Wharf, and eight of the fifteen hydraulic cranes were converted from fixed to luffing jibs in 1936. Also in 1936, the 15-ton fixed crane on Steelworks Wharf was transferred to Talbot Wharf. Three more hydraulic cranes were added in 1937, and a further six in 1940. Two hydraulic accumulators were erected on Talbot Wharf in 1928 and 1936 to store power for the increased number of cranes there.

Following the dismantling of the Crown Preserved Coal Co.'s works in 1938, Crown Wharf, which had been reconstructed in 1927, was in 1941 adapted for use by the War Department.[63] Quayside sidings were laid in and connected via loop sidings and a long, almost semicircular, line to the Dock Branch west of Copper Works Junction. After the war two 3-ton cranes by Barry Dock were installed in Crown Wharf.[64] One of the 1½-ton hydraulic cranes installed by the old Port Talbot Company on North Bank was moved in 1923 to a new position alongside the 12-ton hand crane near the old lock entrance.[65]

MARGAM WHARF AND ABBEY WORKS HOT STRIP MILL

The work done at Margam Wharf up to 1926[66] satisfied the needs of the steelworks there until 1941. In April 1941 the GWR directors authorised the expenditure of £13,868 on siding alterations at Margam Wharf associated with the import of iron ore. In the meantime these works had undergone a change of ownership as part of the ongoing effort to rationalise the UK steel industry.[67] In 1930 the heavy steel interests of Baldwins and Guest, Keen & Nettlefolds were merged to form the British (Guest, Keen, Baldwins) Iron & Steel Co. Ltd (the British was dropped in 1936) comprising the Port Talbot, Margam, Dowlais and Dowlais-Cardiff works.[68] The new company initially concentrated its efforts on rebuilding Dowlais-Cardiff,[69] leaving Port Talbot and Margam much as they had been. The other parts of Baldwins, including tinplate manufacture, were acquired by Richard Thomas & Co. Ltd in 1944 to form Richard Thomas & Baldwins Ltd. Further consolidation occurred in 1947 when Guest, Keen, Baldwins and Richard Thomas & Baldwins merged to form the Steel Company of Wales (SCoW).

Even before this merger took place, the two companies concerned agreed in October 1945 to build a hot strip mill at Port Talbot adjacent to Margam Steelworks. Test piling began in January 1946.[70] In the same month the GWR directors tentatively agreed that their company would carry out works estimated to cost £750,000, including doubling the OVER, diversion of lines leading to the docks, and the provision of sidings; the steel company contributing 50 per cent of the cost of the railway works. Some of these works required Parliamentary powers. A preliminary notice appeared in the *London Gazette*,[71] followed shortly afterwards by a concise summary of the Bill in *The Times*.[72] The deposited plans showed a deviation railway for the OVER, 1 mile 66 yards in length, commencing near Copper Works Junction and terminating at the 1m 7ch point on that railway.[73] The Great Western Railway Act 1946,[74] which gained

ABOVE: A 1920s postcard showing the West Curve running off the bottom of the view from Copper Works Junction to re-emerge and join the GWR main line under the PTR overbridge next to Margam Gas Works in the right corner. The long sidings on the near side of the Dock Branch are the reception sidings for Margam Steelworks. *Author's collection*

The girder bridge erected in 1948/49 to carry the deviated Dock Branch over the GWR main line, looking north towards Port Talbot circa 1952. The old PTR bridge crossed the main line approximately at the centre of the approaching train. The Taibach Loop left the Dock Branch at Overbridge Junction off to the left and descended over the arches to join the main line round the bend. The signals are for Ramp Line Junction just beyond Overbridge Junction, left for the Ramp Line, right for Copper Works Junction. *Kidderminster Railway Museum*

MARGAM STEEL WORKS, PORT TALBOT

An early 1950s postcard view showing the diversion of the PTR Dock Branch around the expanded Margam Steelworks by carrying it on new bridges over the main road and GWR main line. By this time there were four blast furnaces at Margam. *Author's collection*

W 7197

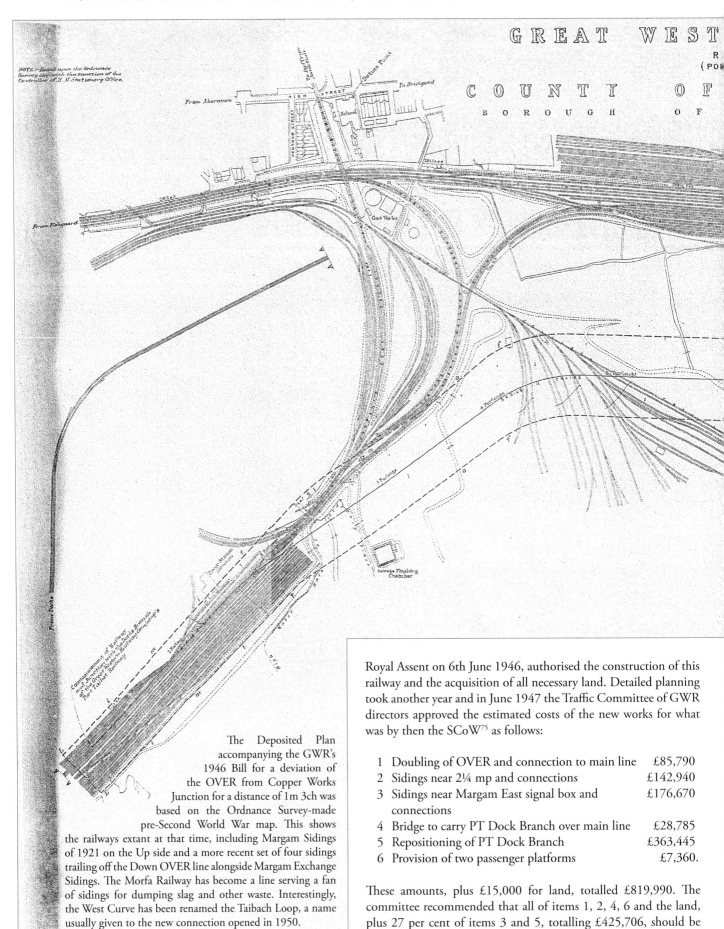

The Deposited Plan accompanying the GWR's 1946 Bill for a deviation of the OVER from Copper Works Junction for a distance of 1m 3ch was based on the Ordnance Survey-made pre-Second World War map. This shows the railways extant at that time, including Margam Sidings of 1921 on the Up side and a more recent set of four sidings trailing off the Down OVER line alongside Margam Exchange Sidings. The Morfa Railway has become a line serving a fan of sidings for dumping slag and other waste. Interestingly, the West Curve has been renamed the Taibach Loop, a name usually given to the new connection opened in 1950.

Royal Assent on 6th June 1946, authorised the construction of this railway and the acquisition of all necessary land. Detailed planning took another year and in June 1947 the Traffic Committee of GWR directors approved the estimated costs of the new works for what was by then the SCoW[75] as follows:

1	Doubling of OVER and connection to main line	£85,790
2	Sidings near 2¼ mp and connections	£142,940
3	Sidings near Margam East signal box and connections	£176,670
4	Bridge to carry PT Dock Branch over main line	£28,785
5	Repositioning of PT Dock Branch	£363,445
6	Provision of two passenger platforms	£7,360.

These amounts, plus £15,000 for land, totalled £819,990. The committee recommended that all of items 1, 2, 4, 6 and the land, plus 27 per cent of items 3 and 5, totalling £425,706, should be

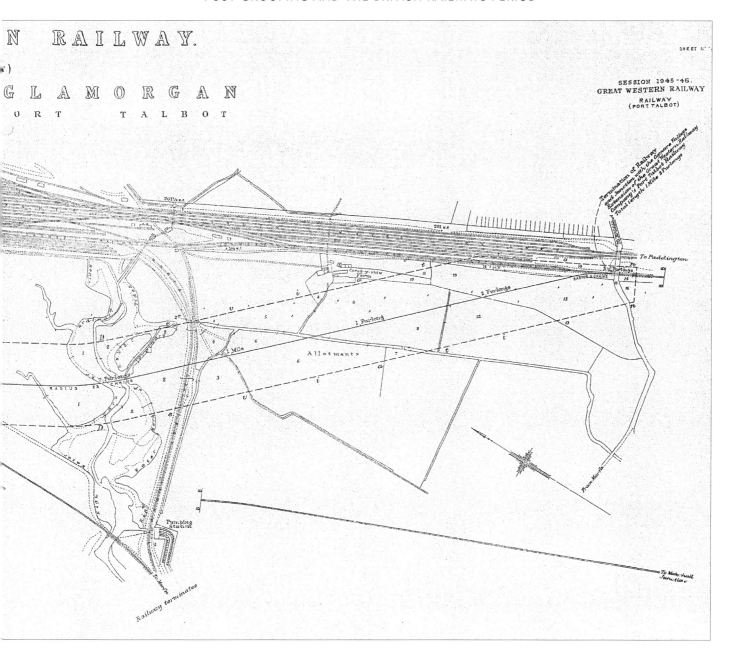

borne by the GWR, and the remainder by the SCoW. These sums were approved by the full GWR Board on 13th June 1947. Works estimated to cost £405,000 were put out to tender and that of Sir Robert McAlpine & Sons (South Wales) Ltd for £443,388 17s 3d was accepted in July 1947. Extra work required the subvention of a further £9,500 in December 1947.

These levels of expenditure presaged major changes to the lines in the neighbourhood of Copper Works Junction and to the OVER. The PTR Dock Branch from Copper Works Junction to beyond the bridge over the GWR main line, the Margam West Curve of 1917, the OVER as far as the 1m 11ch point, and the double line to Margam Wharf were all removed. The double track OVER deviation railway commenced on the Port Talbot Dock Branch adjacent to the end of No. 7 grid (GWR numbering), curved to the south-east, and maintained a straight course parallel to and about 250 yards distant from the old route for half a mile before tending left to rejoin the original line, which itself was doubled

to the 2¾ milepost. The OVER was connected to the GWR main line by new double junctions – in the easterly direction at Margam Moors at the 198¾ milepost and in the westerly direction near the 200 milepost. The old exchange sidings with the GWR were greatly extended and became the GWR Down Yard. A range of new sidings, Margam Abbey Works Yard, was laid alongside the OVER between the 2 and 2½ mileposts, bringing the total of new sidings to approximately 24 miles. Running parallel to the Down Yard and commencing near where the new OVER joined the old, a single line, known as the Ramp Line, was constructed which climbed up to a junction with the repositioned Dock Branch, a double line from here down to a new Copper Works Junction with the deviated OVER. In the opposite direction this double line branched off and dropped down to join the GWR main line, a stretch known as Taibach Loop. The elevated junctions were known as Ramp Line Junction and Overbridge Junction, and were worked from a new Copper Works Junction signal box situated halfway between these

415

LEFT: A view looking along the deviated Dock Branch circa 1952. Copper Works Junction is off to the right, with the 1949 signal box obscured by the structures in the middle ground. The Ramp Line climbing up from Margam to Ramp Line Junction is on the left with, in the distance, the coal sidings for the expanded steelworks. *Kidderminster Railway Museum*

BELOW: The diverted Dock Branch ran through the steelworks to reach the repositioned Copper Works Junction seen at the left centre of this view. The coal tipplers feeding the coke ovens are prominent in the centre, with the new junction signal box on stilts just above the left-hand one. *Author's collection*

ABOVE: Looking south-east towards Margam Halt circa 1952. This area was controlled by Margam East signal box, opened 1950 and closed 1963. The OVER is the two tracks on the far right, having been doubled from Margam Sidings as far as the 2¾ milepost as part of the 1948/49 alterations.

Kidderminster Railway Museum

RIGHT: Margam Abbey Works East signal box was situated at 2m 42ch on the OVER and opened in March 1949 to control entry to Margam Abbey Works Yard to the north and to the new double line which joined the GWR main line at Margam Moors Junction to the south. This view dated 23rd June 1984 is looking in the down direction towards Port Talbot with the main line behind the box, which was closed in November 1987.

Author's collection

two and the eponymous junction. The Port Talbot Dock Branch was diverted to join these new railways at Overbridge Junction, crossing the main road by a new, curved, concrete bridge and the GWR main line by a new girder bridge. The connection from Copper Works Junction to the O&SSR on Margam Wharf was removed and replaced by a double-line connection from the tracks of No. 1 grid. These works were completed in stages during 1948/49. The space between the Ramp Line and the repositioned OVER was occupied by the coal and ore sidings for the expanded steelworks. The platforms referred to (item 6, above) were for Margam Halt on the main line for use by steelworkers, which opened in February 1948 and closed in November 1964.[76]

DOCKS TRAFFIC

Exports recovered from the post-war slump early in the post-grouping period and reached an all-time high of 2.81 million tons in 1923, almost all of this coal (Figure 20.1). As a consequence of the 1926 national coal strike, coal exports dropped to less than 1 million tons for the first time since 1901, and although there was some recovery up to 1930, the trade depression of the following decade and then the start of the Second World War led to a new low in 1940. Slight rises in the following two years could not hide the general trend, and in the last year of GWR ownership coal exports had fallen to 262,000 tons. On the other hand, imports tended to increase during the inter-war period until halted abruptly

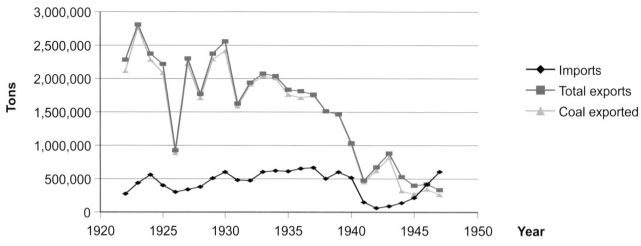

FIGURE 20.1: PORT TALBOT DOCKS IMPORTS AND EXPORTS 1922–1947

by the war. Port Talbot Docks were used as an assembly point for equipment for the invasion of France in 1944, but it is not known if the data used in Figure 20.1 include this material. Imports picked up after the war and exceeded imports for the first time in 1947.

NATIONALISATION

The railway works associated with the new Abbey Works were commenced during 1947, the year of the Transport Act which led to the nationalisation of inland public transport, docks and inland waterways.[77] The Act, which came into force on 6th August 1947, created the British Transport Commission which exercised its powers through various executives, notably the Railway Executive trading as British Railways (later British Rail) and the Docks & Inland Waterways Executive (D&IWE) which operated as British Transport Docks. The railway companies were nationalised on 1st January 1948 and between these two dates they were not permitted to undertake works costing more than £50,000. The establishment of these two executives resulted in the former PTR&D's undertaking being divided between them, the PTR

and SWMR inevitably becoming part of British Railways Western Region. The whole of the dock area – except the land occupied by the Port Talbot and Margam steelworks and by the Mansel, Taibach and Ffrwdwyllt tinplate works – was transferred to the South Wales Division of the D&IWE on 1st July 1948. This included Margam Wharf, both breakwaters and all the dock railways apart from the line leading to the former R&SBR Docks station. Grids 1 and 4–7 (GWR numbering) within this area were initially regarded as "railway" for accountancy purposed, but this was soon dropped.[78] Nationalisation was a political football and both activities were eventually privatised, the docks in 1982 as Associated British Ports, and the railways as a plethora of companies in 1994–97.

The continued expansion of the Margam and Abbey works of the SCoW led to a decision to construct an extensive hump yard to the east of Margam Moors to deal with the increased traffic.[79] The yard was opened in April 1960 and closed for traffic in October 1987, being replaced by Margam Knuckle Yard at the eastern end of the Abbey Works. The only part of the former PTR that was involved in the hump yard scheme was the extension of the doubling of the OVER from Margam Moors to the eastern end of the Newlands

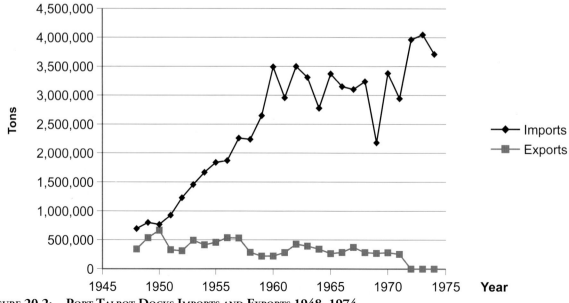

FIGURE 20.2: PORT TALBOT DOCKS IMPORTS AND EXPORTS 1948–1974

Margam Wharf in the 1950s, by then equipped with four ore unloading gantries. *Author's collection*

DOCKS AND STEELWORKS, MARGAM
W 5696

passing loop and the connection of the OVER directly to the main line by a line known as the Newlands Loop. This section of the OVER was singled again in 1975, and then singled back as far as the western end of the Knuckle Yard in 1987. All the connections at Waterhall Sidings were taken out in 1965 leaving just a single line. At the time of writing the OVER still sees occasional use as a diversionary route.

MARGAM WHARF AND THE TIDAL HARBOUR

In February 1947 the GWR directors provisionally approved the expenditure of £92,500 on the extension of Margam Wharf, having the previous December authorised dredging at Port Talbot during 1947 costing £150,000. Owing to the moratorium on expenditure nothing was done until October 1948 when the D&IWE, from whom the SCoW now leased the wharf, revived the scheme and proposed to extend the wharf at its northern end from 878 feet to 953 feet with the intention of allowing larger vessels to be berthed there to offload the increased quantities of ore required.[80] Unusually, the cost of the extension was less that the original estimate – amounting to £63,277, shared equally with the SCoW, including the permanent way and dredging the frontage. Imports of iron ore increased from 594,171 tons in 1948 to 1.03 million tons in 1952 (Figure 20.2). In November 1952 the SCoW announced that a further £40 million was to spent on the development of the sheet steel and tinplate industry in South Wales, of which £28 million was for new plant in the Port Talbot area.[81] A fourth large blast furnace and ninety additional coke ovens were planned for the Margam Works, together with extensions to the melting shop and rolling mills at the Abbey Works. After

completion the aggregate inward and outward traffic were estimated to be 3.8 million and 1.45 million tons respectively. The extensions entailed considerable works, particularly at Margam. To handle a total of between 2.25 million and 2.5 million tons of imported iron ore annually, Margam Wharf was extended northwards by a further 325 feet and a fourth unloading gantry was installed. In March 1953 the BTC authorised the D&IWE to contribute £60,000 towards the total estimated cost of £275,000. The old Port Talbot Steelworks were gradually run down whilst Margam and Abbey expanded.

A growing problem with Port Talbot Docks was the entrance lock, which limited the size of vessel able to reach Margam Wharf to about 8,000 tons deadweight, and the need to keep the entrance channel clear. Ore carriers with square-sided holds were introduced which led to reduced unloading times and faster turn-round so that maximum use could be made of locking opportunities. By 1964 the limits of this system were reached with annual imports of about 3 million tons of ore. In 1964 British Transport Docks Board obtained Parliamentary powers to construct a tidal harbour to the south of the existing docks at Port Talbot.[82] This harbour is protected to the south by a main breakwater one and a quarter miles long and to the north by a 1,500-foot extension to the old south breakwater, and contains a specialised ore unloading jetty 1,700 feet long. A conveyor belt system carries the ore to stockyards on reclaimed land to the south of Margam Works and to a railway ore terminal established alongside the old south dock approximately on the line of the Port Talbot Dock Branch. With additional dredging the tidal harbour can accept ore carriers of about 160,000 tons deadweight. The tidal harbour and facilities there were opened by

HM The Queen on 12th May 1970. Over 4 million tons of iron ore were imported through this new facility in 1973.

CLOSURE AND REOPENING OF PORT TALBOT DOCKS

Coal exports declined almost continually from approximately 2.5 million tons in 1930 to 262,000 tons in 1947. This trend continued during the nationalisation period to just 47,000 tons in 1962 and coal shipments stopped in October that year.[83] Although coal shipments had ceased, British Transport Docks Board improved the facilities on Talbot Wharf where most of the steel exports were handled. Furthermore, ten cargo lines serving foreign ports used Port Talbot in 1965, five of them on a regular basis and the others as traffic required.[84] This business was not enough to sustain the docks and they were closed to shipping in 1971.

Although not unknown, the reopening of old docks to commercial traffic is unusual, but Port Talbot became fortunate in this regard in early 1998 when the docks were reopened for the shipment of 400,000 tons annually of treated slag produced by Cambrian Stone, a British Steel/Tarmac joint venture, to Purfleet in Essex. The docks were formally reopened on 13th March 1998. Since then the general cargo berths have handled a variety of traffics, including processed slag, sand, cement, steel and heavy-lift cargoes. There are also jetties for liquid-bulk handling and areas of open storage for cargo handling.[85]

NOTES

1. TNA: PRO RAIL 250/354; see also Chapter 11.
2. TNA: PRO RAIL 250/180.
3. TNA: PRO RAIL 250/356.
4. TNA: PRO MT 29/66 p. 214.
5. TNA: PRO RAIL 250/353, 354; MT 29/83 p. 246.
6. TNA: PRO RAIL 250/357.
7. See Chapter 16.
8. TNA: PRO AN 13/1676.
9. TNA: PRO RAIL 252/2400.
10. See Chapter 11.
11. TNA: PRO AN 13/1756.
12. TNA: PRO MT 29/99 p. 76.
13. TNA: PRO AN 13/1696.
14. TNA: PRO AN 13/1744.
15. See Volume 1, Chapter 7.
16. TNA: PRO RAIL 250/278.
17. 20 Geo. 5 c.7.
18. TNA: PRO RAIL 250/55.
19. *Hansard*, 24 December 1929.
20. R Tourret, *GWR Engineering Work 1928–1938* (Tourret Publishing, 2003).
21. TNA: PRO RAIL 250/277.
22. Nigel Pocock and Ian Harrison, *Great Western Railway Locomotive Allocations for 1934* (Wild Swan, nd).
23. TNA: PRO RAIL 254/81.
24. E T Lyons, *An Historical Survey of Great Western Engine Sheds 1947* (Oxford Publishing Co., 1972).
25. Tony Walmsley, *Shed by Shed, Part 6* (St. Petroc Infopublishing, 2009).
26. Lyons, *Great Western Engine Sheds 1947*.
27. Jim Grindlay, *British Railways Locomotive Allocations 1948–1968, Part Six: Diesel & Electric Locomotives* (Transport Publishing, 2007).
28. See Chapter 18.
29. TNA: PRO RAIL 250/5.
30. See Chapter 18.
31. TNA: PRO RAIL 253/338.
32. TNA: PRO RAIL 250/54.
33. TNA: PRO RAIL 250/56.
34. See Chapter 12.
35. *The London Gazette*, 28 March 1930.
36. 20 & 21 Geo. 5 c.lxxvii.
37. TNA: PRO RAIL 258/465.
38. TNA: PRO RAIL 250/316.
39. See Chapter 14.
40. *Sites for Works at the South Wales Docks and Plymouth* (GWR, 1932).
41. *Sites for Works at the South Wales Docks and Plymouth* (GWR, 1939).
42. See Chapter 14.
43. See Chapter 13.
44. TNA: PRO RAIL 1033/245.
45. TNA: PRO RAIL 250/317.
46. TNA: PRO RAIL 250/354.
47. TNA: PRO RAIL 250/316.
48. See Chapter 12.
49. TNA: PRO RAIL 250/179.
50. TNA: PRO RAIL 250/317.
51. TNA: PRO RAIL 250/54.
52. TNA: PRO RAIL 250/57.
53. TNA: PRO RAIL 250/62.
54. TNA: PRO RAIL 250/54.
55. TNA: PRO RAIL 250/318.
56. TNA: PRO RAIL 250/54.
57. TNA: PRO AN 13/261.
58. TNA: PRO RAIL 252/2088.
59. TNA: PRO RAIL 252/2089.
60. TNA: PRO RAIL 252/2130.
61. TNA: PRO RAIL 252/2268.
62. Atkins, A G, W Beard and R Tourret, *GWR Goods Wagons* (Tourret Publishing, 1998) pp. 242–58.
63. TNA: PRO RAIL 250/58.
64. TNA: PRO RAIL 250/62.
65. See Chapter 12.
66. See Chapter 14.
67. Protheroe-Jones, *Welsh Steel*; John Vaizey, *The History of British Steel* (Weidenfeld & Nicolson, 1974).
68. *Guest Keen Baldwins Iron & Steel Co. Ltd.* (ETW Dennis & Sons Ltd, 1937).
69. *The Iron & Coal Trades Review*, 16 October 1936.
70. TNA: PRO RAIL 250/183.
71. *The London Gazette*, 12 February 1946.
72. *The Times*, 15 February 1946.
73. PA HL/PO/PB/3/plan1945-1946/G2.
74. 9 & 10 Geo. 6 c.xxiv.
75. TNA: PRO RAIL 250/359.
76. Quick, *Railway Passenger Stations in Great Britain*.
77. A J Mullay, *Railways for the People* (Pendragon Publishing, 2006).
78. TNA: PRO RAIL 1033/245.
79. *Margam Marshalling Yard* (British Railways Western Region, c.1960); *Margam Marshalling Yard* (AEI, c.1960).
80. TNA: PRO AN 13/399.
81. W F Cartwright, 'Steel Company of Wales: Developments at Port Talbot', paper to BR(WR) London Lecture and Debating Society, paper no. 401, 29 January 1953.
82. *The Times*, 29 November 1963; British Transport Docks Act 1964 Eliz. 2 c.xxxviii.
83. *Port Talbot Docks* (British Transport Docks Board, 1966).
84. *Cargo Liner Services* (British Transport Docks Board, August 1965).
85. Associated British Ports: Port Talbot, www.abports.co.uk/custinfo/ports/port accessed 16 February 2010.

21

Along the Port Talbot Railway
and the South Wales Mineral Railway

Most of the PTR and all of the SWMR have long gone. This account describes what would have been encountered during a journey along these lines when developed to their fullest extent, and the industries – principally collieries – which were or had been at one time served by them. For both these railway companies, as with other South Wales lines, Up trains went up the valleys away from the coast, whereas the GWR Up trains were headed, nominally at least, in the direction of London, although it is not clear when this designation was applied to the PTR and SWMR post grouping. Distances are given in miles (m) and chains (ch) from the official zero points. Most of the lines were worked by electric train staff and pillars were provided in signal boxes as appropriate for the sections on either side. In GWR days, token exchanging apparatus was provided at Newlands

signal box. The sections between Duffryn No. 1 and No. 2 signal boxes and between Copper Works and Margam East Junctions were worked as double line block sections. The Blaenavon, Whitworth and Pyle branches, and the lines from Tonygroes Junction to Port Talbot Central, from Glyncorrwg to North Rhondda Colliery and from Tonmawr to Incline Top were worked by one engine in steam with a train staff.

PORT TALBOT TO PONTYRHYLL

PORT TALBOT CENTRAL AND TONYGROES JUNCTION
For passengers Port Talbot Central would have been a convenient starting point, being a short walk from the GWR station. The original basic layout consisted of a platform line with run-round

A view across Port Talbot Central station circa 1905. Clearly visible are the water tank, signal box and the two long goods sidings, the further one of which served the goods lockup. The line can be seen climbing and curving round the sports ground to reach Tonygroes Junction signal box faintly visible in the centre of the view. The Oakwood Railway runs across the bottom left-hand corner, with the route of the short-lived connection to the PTR also clearly visible. On the far right is a rare glimpse of one of the PTR's three cattle wagons. *Author's collection*

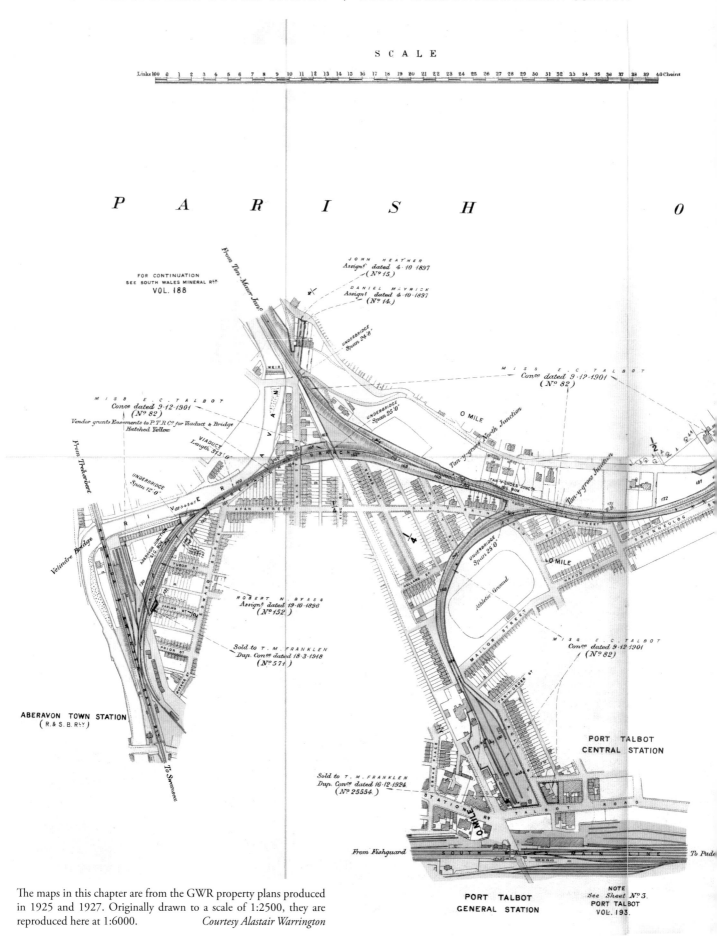

SCALE

PARISH O

The maps in this chapter are from the GWR property plans produced in 1925 and 1927. Originally drawn to a scale of 1:2500, they are reproduced here at 1:6000.

Courtesy Alastair Warrington

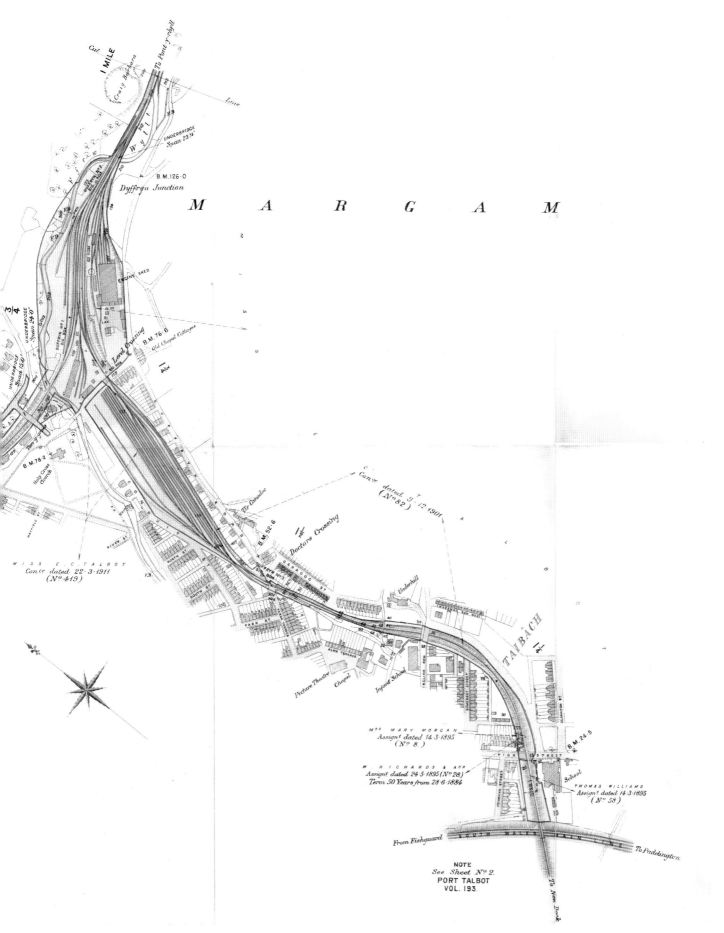

NOTE
See Sheet No 2.
PORT TALBOT
VOL. 193.

loop and two goods sidings, one of which served a cattle dock, all worked by a signal cabin containing seven levers. By 1920 the release crossover and signal box had been removed, the whole then being worked as a siding from Tonygroes Junction cabin. The zero milepost was situated by the buffer stop on the platform line.

On leaving the station the line passed the site of a short-lived trailing connection to the Oakwood Railway, which at one time ran along nearby Oakwood Lane, and then climbed at 1 in 40 whilst making a 90 degree turn round Aberavon rugby ground. At 0m 22ch the line became double in order to make a double junction at Tonygroes South Junction (0m 30ch), about halfway along the 565 feet long loop there. The lines to Aberavon and Tonmawr diverged at the North Junction. All was worked by Tonygroes Junction signal box which contained twenty-four working levers, and like all PTR boxes in GWR days was open continuously from early on Monday morning until after the last train on Sunday. The gradient eased to 1 in 100 through the junction and then to 1 in 927 for the single line stretch from 0m 36ch to Duffryn Junction (0m 63ch).

ABERAVON TO TONYGROES JUNCTION

An alternative starting point was the R&SBR's Aberavon station, which was nearer the town centre and from which about half the passenger trains originated up to about 1920.[1] This station went through a number of name changes, starting with Aberavon Town, then Aberavon Port Talbot, Port Talbot (Aberavon) and finally Aberavon Town again. The double junction for the line to Tonygroes Junction was situated at the north end of the platforms at 13m 44ch (R&SBR mileage) and curved to the right, passing the R&SBR's engine shed and carriage sidings. The first 6 chains were over R&SBR metals, the PTR line commencing at 0m 40ch from Tonygroes South Junction. The line climbed gradually, passing the PTR's Aberavon Junction signal box (0m 36ch) and became single at 0m 32ch. This McKenzie & Holland box contained twenty-three levers, and was the block point for the short single line section from Tonygroes Junction. Traffic for exchange with the R&SBR was left either in a siding behind Aberavon station or, failing that, on the Down line opposite the signal box. Still climbing, the line was carried by the curved 513 foot long, thirteen-span Aberavon Viaduct across the site of the former Margam Tinplate Works and over the outside edge of a bend in the River Avon. This viaduct consisted of steel girders resting on piers of brick and concrete, five of the twelve being set in the river bed. The line then crossed the erstwhile Oakwood Railway by a girder bridge before falling slightly to reach the westerly fork of the double line at Tonygroes North Junction (0m 12ch).

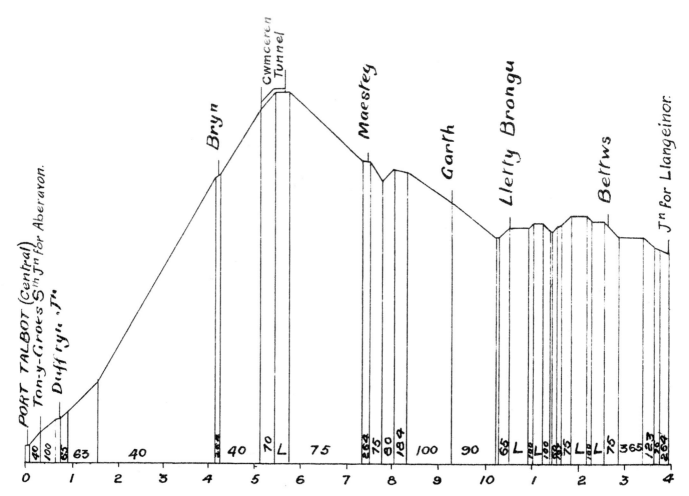

Gradient diagram of the PTR main line from Port Talbot Central via Duffryn Junction (Duffryn Valley), Maesteg (Llynvi Valley) and Pontyrhyll (Garw Valley). The scale of all the diagrams reproduced in this chapter is ½ inch to 1 mile horizontally and 1inch to 160ft vertically. This set was issued circa 1908.

Aberavon Town station viewed from the footbridge at the southern end of the platforms. The junction for the PTR, which was controlled by Plough Junction signal box behind the photographer, is immediately beyond the platforms. Postcard, postally used 26th November 1928. *Author's collection*

Tonygroes Junction, showing the line curving round to Central station in the left background with Port Talbot Steelworks behind, and the line to Aberavon and Tonmawr running off to the right, the junction signal for which is just visible. *Author's collection*

FACING PAGE, TOP: The north end of Tonygroes Junction where the lines to Aberavon and Tonmawr diverged. Postcard, postally used 12th August 1942.
Author's collection

FACING PAGE, BOTTOM: Tonygroes Junction signal box 1937. The gentleman on the left wearing the bowler hat is Harry Borkett.
Courtesy Roy Evans

LEFT: The interior of Tonygroes Junction signal box with signalman E Davies.
Author's collection

BELOW: The Gwar-y-Cae area of Port Talbot with, in the left corner, a PTR Brake Third carriage parked in one of the loops at Tonygroes Junction. Note the footbridge painted in the same style as those at the stations.
Author's collection

PORT TALBOT & ABERAVON, GENERAL VIEW.

This postcard shows the area just west of Duffryn Junction. The line to Tonygroes Junction comes from behind the carriage shed and curves round to the right. The Dock Branch is out of sight in the foreground. Chapel of Ease Crossing cabin is visible near the bottom right. The open area is the site of Duffryn Sidings which were laid in in 1907. Alongside the carriage shed are PTR open wagons painted grey and three bogie coaches painted cream and brown on the coloured original; whether these are correct liveries or artistic licence is not known. *Author's collection*

BELOW: Duffryn Junction No. 2 Signal Box eventually acquired a full nameplate, as seen on 1st July 1961. *Author's collection*

DUFFRYN JUNCTION

Duffryn Junction was the focal point of the PTR. From here radiated lines to the docks, to Tonygroes Junction, and to Maesteg and Pontyrhyll, and here also was Duffryn Yard engine shed. The junction itself consisted of a loop 600 feet long with Up and Down lines, with the lines to Tonygroes Junction and the docks diverging at a double junction (0m 63ch) at the western end. The carriage shed sidings made a trailing connection to the Up line from the docks in the V of this junction. Adjacent was Duffryn No. 1 signal box (0m 59ch) with sixteen levers which worked all the points and signals at this end of junction. Duffryn No. 2 box (0m 71ch) with twelve working levers at the other end controlled all the tracks which converged to a single line at 0m 78ch. On the Up side a pair of loops referred to as marshalling sidings ran from the Tonygroes Branch to join the running lines at Duffryn No. 2. Three sidings – holding eight, sixteen and thirty-one wagons respectively, which mainly seemed to be used for wagon storage – occupied the land between the loops and the River Ffrwdwyllt. Similarly a pair of loop sidings which connected with the Dock Branch near Duffryn No. 1 were provided on the Down side. Duffryn Yard engine shed was adjacent to these loops with a connection to the running lines at Duffryn No. 2. The extended headshunt for all the sidings on the Down side was used to stable the breakdown train.

The gradient through Duffryn Junction was 1 in 65, changing to 1 in 63 which continued to 1m 47ch where the four-mile 1 in 40 climb to the western portal of Cwm Cerwyn Tunnel commenced. Four collieries and one factory were at one time or another served by the PTR along this lower section of the main line. All were close

LEFT: Looking up the Duffryn Valley near Duffryn (woollen) Mills towards Goitre. Visible to the left is Duffryn No. 2 home signal where the loops at Duffryn Junction commenced. Postcard, postally used 18th August 1911. *Author's collection*

BELOW: The same view in the 1920s. The sidings put in for Glenhafod Colliery in 1920, the chimney of which peers over the trees, can be seen in the centre. Duffryn Mills Platform was situated behind the tree in the foreground. *Author's collection*

enough to Duffryn Junction to be worked by propelling wagons from there with the guard travelling on the leading wagon or brake van.

GLENHAFOD COLLIERY (1M 4CH)
In February 1920 the directors approved the application of W F Gibb of Glenavon Garw Collieries Ltd for a siding connection about 100 yards up the main line from Duffryn Yard for a new colliery sinking at the old Goitre level. At that time this colliery company, which had been formed in 1907, owned Glyncymmer and Glenavon collieries at Cymmer, Nantewlaeth Colliery near Glyncorrwg, Corrwg Rhondda Colliery at Blaengwynfi and Glengarw Colliery at Blaengarw. Instead of adding directly to this list, a new company, Glenhafod Collieries Ltd., was registered in September 1920 with a capital of £250,000.[2] £100,000 of preference shares were

divided equally between Glenavon Garw Collieries Ltd, the Briton Ferry Steel Co. Ltd and the Llanelly Steel Co. 1907 Ltd, which perhaps suggests where much of the output was destined. R Gibb and the two steel companies received substantial allocations of the £150,000 of ordinary shares. Glenhafod Colliery siding connection was completed by November 1920,[3] but not inspected by the Board of Trade until the following September.[4] A siding agreement was concluded on 6th May 1921 and terminated on 30th June 1963, the colliery having closed in 1959.[5]

DUFFRYN MILLS PLATFORM (1M 6CH)
This platform was put in in 1931 and was passed on the Up, left-hand side, although it was used by untimetabled Down trains only. It was situated near a convenient footbridge over the River Ffrwdwyllt for the short walk up to the cemetery at Goitre.

Cwm Duffryn Colliery (1m 16ch and 1m 32ch)

The directors approved siding connections not far from the top end of Duffryn Yard in November 1917 for this colliery which was established on the opposite side of the valley to the old Goitre level.[6] The siding agreement was signed in January 1918.[7] This siding was originally intended to take the form of an extended loop, but only the lower end was installed initially and this was completed by March 1918.[8] The connection was not inspected and sanctioned until September 1921, one of the conditions being that it should be worked by loads not exceeding five wagons being propelled from Duffryn Yard.[9] The upper connection was laid in by 15th March 1924 and inspected in the following May.[10] This short-lived colliery company was acquired in July 1929 by the nearby Glenhafod Colliery Co., which was no doubt more interested in the mineral rights than working this slant. The connections were rendered inoperable in 1931.

The English Celluloid Co.'s works looking down the valley. These works were used as a prisoner of war camp during the First World War. The PTR can be discerned to the right of the view.

Author's collection

430

Cwm Gwynea or Lewis Rhondda Colliery (1m 20ch)

Shortly after the 1894 railway opened for traffic in February 1898 an estimate was prepared for J Lewis of Pontypridd for a siding connection a quarter of a mile up the valley from Duffryn Yard, apparently to serve a proposed colliery in Cwm Gwinea.[11] The siding agreement required Lewis to pay off the installation costs by the payment of 1½d per ton on all traffic, with a minimum of £10 per year. By June 1900 the PTR had tired of Lewis' non-payment of his accounts and his obligations were forwarded to R Gibb at Glyncymmer Colliery, Cymmer, whom it was hoped would take over the matter. This did not happen, and in August 1907 Cleaver reported that the connection, which had never been used and had been left out when the main line was renewed, would be relaid as Lewis was restarting operations.[12] This work was completed the following month,[13] but was not inspected by the Board of Trade, presumably in the belief that the original inspection sufficed, although this had never occurred either. The connection served the colliery via a three-quarters of a mile long tramroad. It is not clear

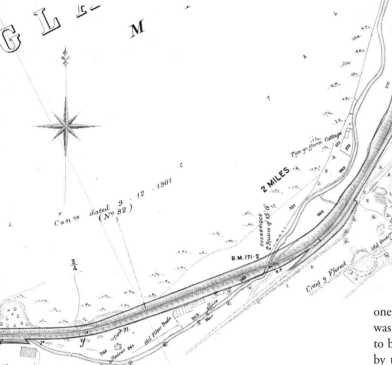

when this siding connection was put into use. The colliery is listed as Lewis Rhondda Colliery in the 1908 list of mines, but does not appear in the 1918 list, and appears in the Working Time Tables from 1909 to 1914.

English Celluloid Co. (1m 40ch)

In August 1901 an agreement was signed with the English Celluloid Co. for a siding connection on the main line about half a mile up the valley from Duffryn Yard. This company had been formed in 1900 for the manufacture of celluloid, a highly-inflammable thermoplastic made from nitrocellulose and camphor with a wide variety of uses including photography.[14] The majority of directors and shareholders were French, although by 1904 Richard Cory,

one of the PTR&D's directors, was vice chairman. The company was not a commercial success and in April 1906 passed a resolution to be voluntarily wound up. The business was eventually acquired by the Aflectite Celluloid Syndicate Ltd which had been formed in 1910,[15] who in turn sold it to the Argonite Non-Flammable Celluloid Co. Ltd. This company had been formed in 1911, again with a large number of foreign shareholders.[16] The prospectus, dated 18th February 1911, announced that this company would purchase from the Syndicate a large modern factory near Port Talbot, with a valuation of £56,690, a factory at Bow, London, valuation £5,000, and a secret process for the manufacture of non-flammable celluloid film, all for £65,000 cash and £4,000 in fully paid up shares. However, although some of the disputes between the numerous parties involved were resolved by expensive litigation, failure to pay interest on its debentures led to a receiver being appointed in March 1913 and the company was wound up in December 1914. The connection was ready for use in October 1901,[17] and inspected by Major Druitt later that month.[18] In view of the troubled history it appears not much traffic was carried. The site was used as a prisoner of war camp during the First World War.

Cwmgwyneu Colliery (2m 26ch)

In February 1917, F E Jacobs applied for a siding connection to be laid in for a new colliery sinking in Cwm Wernderi. Jacobs was acting on behalf of W Gilbertson & Co. Ltd,[19] which in January 1920 jointly with Richard Thomas & Co. Ltd registered a subsidiary named Cwmgwyneu Collieries Ltd with a capital of £80,000.[20] The connection was made at the same point as that put in for the construction of Cwm Wernderi reservoir.[21] The connection was ready for use by July 1917[22] and was inspected in February 1921.[23] The colliery closed in 1927[24] when a receiver was appointed, and the company was wound up in September 1929. The property reverted to Margam Estates and the GWR allowed the sidings to

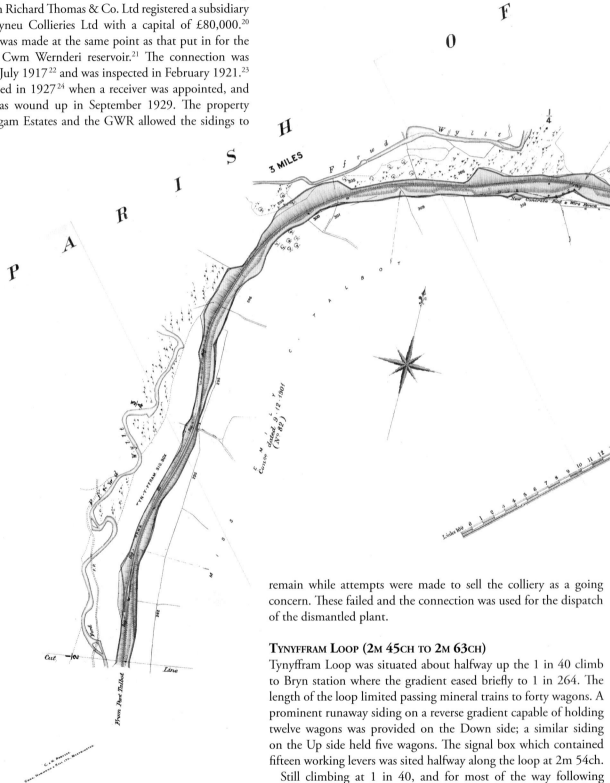

remain while attempts were made to sell the colliery as a going concern. These failed and the connection was used for the dispatch of the dismantled plant.

Tynyffram Loop (2m 45ch to 2m 63ch)

Tynyffram Loop was situated about halfway up the 1 in 40 climb to Bryn station where the gradient eased briefly to 1 in 264. The length of the loop limited passing mineral trains to forty wagons. A prominent runaway siding on a reverse gradient capable of holding twelve wagons was provided on the Down side; a similar siding on the Up side held five wagons. The signal box which contained fifteen working levers was sited halfway along the loop at 2m 54ch.

Still climbing at 1 in 40, and for most of the way following closely the River Ffrwdwyllt, the line reached the connection for Bryn Navigation Colliery (3m 79ch). Owing to the gradient, traffic for this colliery was worked into the sidings either by the banking engine if one had been provided or working traffic back down from

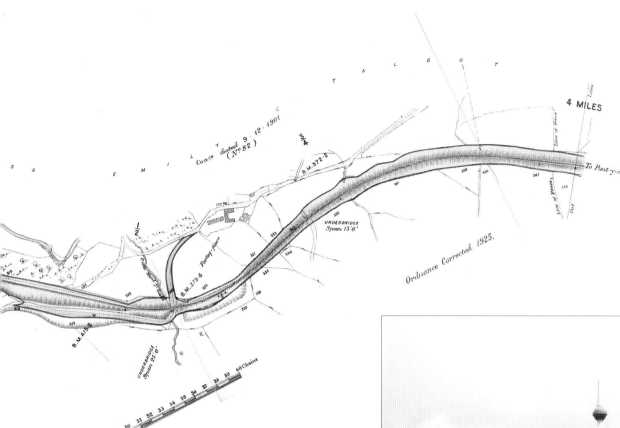

Bryn Up home signal on 29th May 1954. To the left is part of the railway system which served Baldwins' Bryn Navigation Colliery about half a mile away via a reversal and was worked by steam locomotives.
Courtesy P J Garland

Bryn station – an engine at the lower end being one of the working arrangements insisted on by the Board of Trade. Brake vans holding trains on the main line were required have their wheels chained and padlocked.

BRYN NAVIGATION COLLIERY (3M 79CH)

It appears that part of the line had been in use for some months before the official opening, as on 21st November 1896 the directors agreed that Pearson's could haul coal from Bryn to Port Talbot, the wayleave being 3d per ton. Coal had been worked at Bryn since at least 1841 as part of the English Copper Company's operations.[25] Activities had suffered following that company's demise, but resumed in 1896 when Messrs Morris, Jacobs & Jones, trading as Bryn Navigation Colliery Co., leased the minerals there from Miss Talbot.[26] Jacobs was also managing the coal working at the Cwmavon Works, which were by then owned by Wright, Butler & Co. The directors of the PTR had deferred an application for a siding for Bryn Colliery in July 1896, but in February 1897, Meik, its engineer, proposed a branch from the east end of Bryn station to serve the colliery and which would allow for future extension up Cwm Drysiog to the north-east.[27] This was rejected on the grounds of cost, as was a narrow gauge line, presumably matching that of the old Bryn Tramroad. The general manager recommended a direct connection costing £300,[28] and the directors resolved on 15th September 1897 that this should be constructed by Pearson's as part of their contract. The draft agreement included a clause to the effect that the colliery company would pay 10s per week towards the expense of a signalman at Bryn. The directors declined to entertain the colliery company's application for a revision of the wayleave charge prior to the full opening of the line. The siding agreement, which was eventually made on 18th March 1898, provided that the colliery would refund the cost of the junction and sidings previously constructed by the PTR by paying a surcharge on all traffic.[29]

Bryn Navigation Colliery Co. Ltd, which was registered in February 1898 with a capital of £25,000 and had acquired the colliery at that time,[30] was in effect a wholly owned subsidiary of

Wright, Butler & Co. Ltd.[31] The colliery company was one of those which constituted Baldwins Ltd in April 1902, the colliery being sold to the new company for £22,000. The siding agreement was somewhat belatedly transferred to Baldwins in December 1924 and terminated on 5th December 1963 when the colliery closed.

CEFN-Y-BRYN AND PARC-Y-BRYN COLLIERIES
The headshunt of Bryn Navigation Colliery Co.'s private siding was extended circa 1903 into Cwm Drysiog to serve the screens of Cefn-y-Bryn Colliery and, a little further on, Parc-y-Bryn Colliery.

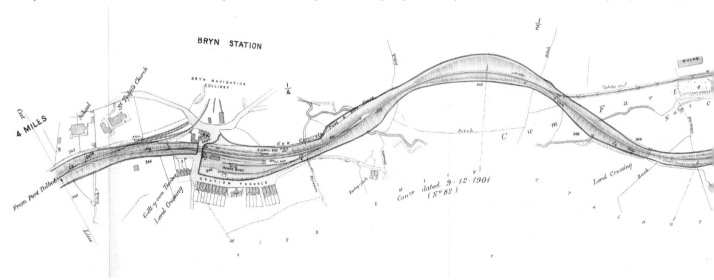

This general view of Bryn shows the dominating position of Bryn Navigation Colliery, the private siding for which connected to the PTR by the gate on the far right. Bryn station is mostly hidden by the church. Postcard, postally used 31st August 1910. *Author's collection*

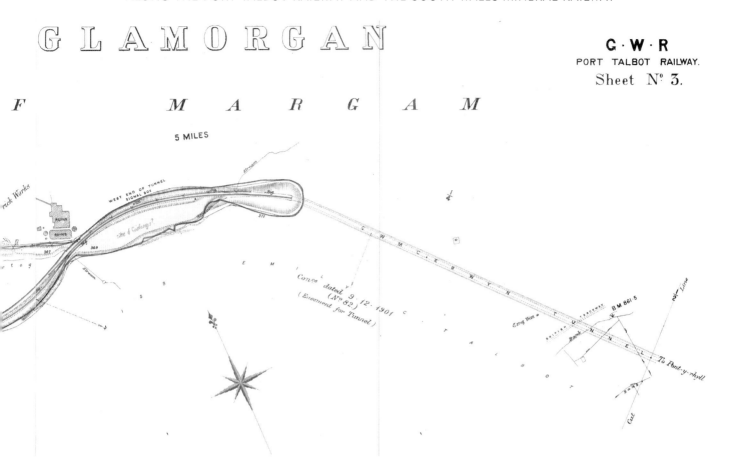

Cefn-y-Bryn Colliery Company Ltd was formed in August 1908 to acquire the mineral leases first granted by Miss Talbot in September 1902.[32] The seams were abandoned in 1924, and the lease and business sold in 1925 to Wern-y-Bryn Colliery Co. Ltd which continued production until circa 1935, Baldwins having declined to take over the colliery.[33] The GWR consented to Baldwins permitting Wern-y-Bryn Colliery Co. to use the junction and sidings at Bryn in 1926, no doubt superseding an earlier unreported arrangement, and the consent was only terminated when the main siding agreement ended in 1963.

Parc-y-Bryn Colliery Company Ltd was formed in July 1907 to acquire the mineral leases first granted by Miss Talbot in October 1905.[34] Two of its directors had earlier been involved in starting Bryn Navigation Colliery. The slant at Parc-y-Bryn was connected to the screens by a half mile long tramway. This was not a very successful venture and the colliery closed in 1925. Shortly after Miss Talbot's death in 1918 the Trustees of the Margam Estate proposed that the PTR should take over the maintenance of the private line from Baldwin's siding to the screens, but the directors would not entertain this.

BRYN

The main line reached the commencement of the double track section through Bryn station at 4m 8ch, still climbing at 1 in 40 until an abrupt change at 4m 11ch to 1 in 264 past the platforms. There was a public level crossing at the lower end leading from the village to Station Terrace and the goods yard, supplemented by a footbridge connecting the two platforms. The main station

Passenger service was withdrawn between Port Talbot and Maesteg on 11th September 1933 although the station buildings at Bryn were not demolished until circa 1956. This view looking north shows 2-8-0T No. 5254 passing through the closed station towards Cwm Cerwyn Tunnel on 14th July 1959 with empties for the collieries at Maesteg.
Courtesy H C Casserley

435

Baldwins' Bryn Navigation Colliery circa 1920. This colliery comprised one shaft and one slant, this acting as the upcast. This view shows the loaded side of the screens. *NM&GW*

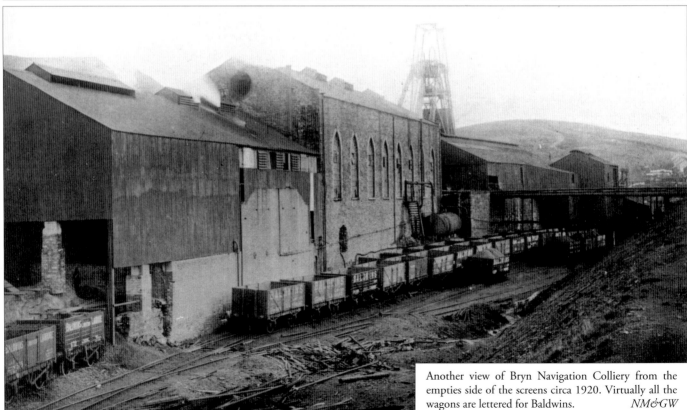

Another view of Bryn Navigation Colliery from the empties side of the screens circa 1920. Virtually all the wagons are lettered for Baldwins. *NM&GW*

building and two goods sidings were on the Down side, although the outer siding, which could hold sixteen wagons, was used only as a runaway siding. The Down home signal was kept at danger until the signalman was assured that a Down mineral train was under control. Bryn signal cabin with eleven working levers was on the Up side at 4m 17ch.

The single line recommenced at 4m 26ch and continued the climb up to West End of Tunnel Loop, skirting round the sites of Varteg Colliery and Bryn Brickworks.

VARTEG COLLIERY (4M 42CH)

In May 1900 Hosgood applied to the Board of Trade for provisional sanction to put in a connection just above Bryn at milepost 4½ for Messrs R B Byass & Co. who proposed to reopen some old coal workings in Cwm Varteg.[35] This was granted, with the proviso that as the proposed refuge siding was about 150 yards from the main line, a trap point was needed near the junction. The works, which cost £450, were reported as finished on 8th June and were inspected on 14th August, by which date coal was being taken out by rail.[36] This siding made a through connection with the Bryn Brickworks siding over the site of old mineral workings.

BRYN BRICKWORKS (4M 71CH)

During May 1898 a connection was laid in for Messrs R B Byass' Bryn Brickworks Co. near the west portal of Cwm Cerwyn Tunnel, apparently without having been considered by the Board.[37] The siding – which left the main line on a falling 1 in 100 gradient and was provisionally sanctioned by the Board of Trade on condition that every train had an engine at the lower end – was reported to have been completed in December 1898. The works were not inspected until May 1899, when Col Yorke confirmed the need for the condition. Shortly afterwards, the directors approved the construction of an Up Loop at West End[38] and the connection had to be moved back a short distance.

The directors approved the Varteg Colliery siding agreement at their meeting on 27th February 1901. This agreement was somewhat unusual in that it provided for the first 200 yards of the siding to be maintained by the PTR and permitted the railway company to use the siding for what was termed "temporary shunting" whenever there was room.[39] Owing to a lack of an alternative, workmen were permitted to walk along the line between Bryn and the colliery. This colliery was short-lived, however, and in November 1902 the general manager informed the secretary that although it had closed, the junction was to remain as it was convenient to the company. Both junctions served the brickworks but Messrs Byass were debited with only one half of the total cost of working them.[40] The lower connection was restored in August 1921 to allow the Eagle, Bryn & Cwmavon Brick Works Ltd, which had been formed in 1912 to consolidate four brickworks in Bryn and Cwmavon into one business,[41] to remove the old machinery.[42] The sidings had been abandoned by December 1923, but the lower connection was not removed until August 1927.

WEST END OF TUNNEL LOOP (4M 67CH TO 5M 5CH) AND CWM CERWYN TUNNEL

West End Loop was very similar to that at Tynyffram, the main difference being that the runaway siding, for which the points were normally set, was long enough to hold sixteen wagons. The 1911 signal box,[43] at 4m 75ch, had seventeen working levers. The 1 in 40 gradient continued right up to the mouth of the 1012-yard Cwm Tunnel at 5m 8ch, where it eased to 1 in 70 until the middle of the tunnel was reached at an elevation of about 700 feet and level running was achieved. Down mineral trains were required to run "cautiously" through the tunnel and to come to a stand at the western end to allow sufficient brakes to be pinned down so that they could be brought to a standstill on West End Loop, where further brakes were pinned down to control the journey down to Bryn and Duffryn Junction.

Cwm Cerwyn Tunnel was aligned approximately north-west–south-east. On leaving the tunnel the line ran through End East Loop and then turned through a semicircle to head north, passing a siding laid in for Maesteg UDC, falling all the way at 1 in 75 to reach Maesteg in the Llynvi valley.

EAST END OF TUNNEL LOOP (5M 59CH TO 5M 77CH)

This loop, at 754 feet, was the shortest between Duffryn Yard and Maesteg. A short mileage siding trailed off the Maesteg end of the Down line[44] and from this at one time ran a temporary siding for reservoir construction.[45] The loop signal cabin was situated on the Down side at 5m 65ch with all twelve levers in use. The working instructions stipulated that Down mineral trains were not to be brought to a stand at the Down home signal unless they had a banking engine at the rear.

TON HIR COLLIERY (5M 53CH)

In March 1903 the directors agreed to the application by Henry Walters of Bryn for a colliery siding connection to the Down line at East End of Tunnel. By then the directors had become wary of making these connections for businesses with uncertain prospects and insisted on a deposit of £200, £85 on completion and the balance of the estimated cost of £370 at 3d per ton on all traffic. The connection was in progress by the following month, although Hosgood reported that work by the colliery was slow and that no traffic could be expected for at least two months.[46] The connection was completed in May 1903[47] and inspected by Major Druitt in July.[48] Major Druitt was not impressed with the signalling arrangements, as two discs were worked by one lever, giving conflicting signals. As there was no spare lever in the cabin, it was agreed to do away with the entry disc and work by hand signals, and the works were sanctioned with this modification. The siding agreement was signed on 1st July 1903. A further siding was laid in for Walters at his expense in May 1905.[49]

Ton Hir Colliery was a level situated some distance to the north of Cwm Cerwyn Tunnel on land leased from Miss Talbot in February 1903,[50] and connected by tramway to the screens at East End. Walters turned his business into a limited company in May 1905, which was carried on by his son until 1927 when it was voluntarily wound up and the siding connection was removed.

MAESTEG UDC (6M 49CH)

A temporary junction and short siding were laid in at the 6m 49ch point on the north side of the main line in September 1920 for a Maesteg UDC housing scheme.[51] The connection was inspected in September 1921[52] and taken out of use in March 1935.[53]

Maesteg station more or less as first constructed looking Up the line towards North's junction pre 1908 when the signal box was raised. The buildings appear to be painted in the GWR style of light and dark stone. Note Charles Bazzard wagon No. 10 in an early version of their livery in the siding and the PTR covered goods wagon in the goods shed. *Author's collection*

PARISH OF MARGAM

6 MILES

SCALE

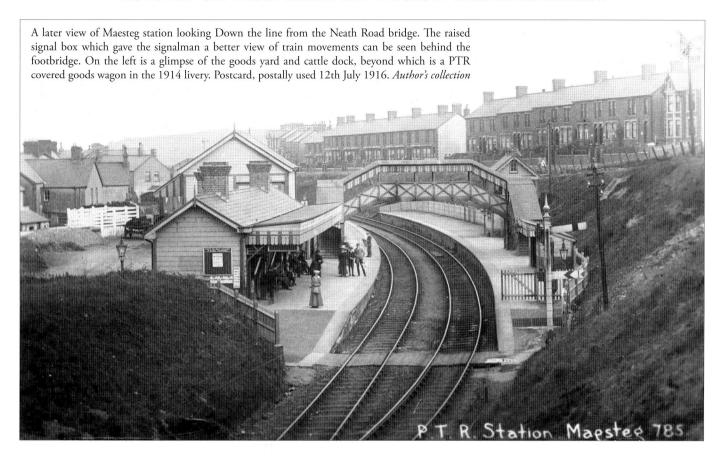

A later view of Maesteg station looking Down the line from the Neath Road bridge. The raised signal box which gave the signalman a better view of train movements can be seen behind the footbridge. On the left is a glimpse of the goods yard and cattle dock, beyond which is a PTR covered goods wagon in the 1914 livery. Postcard, postally used 12th July 1916. *Author's collection*

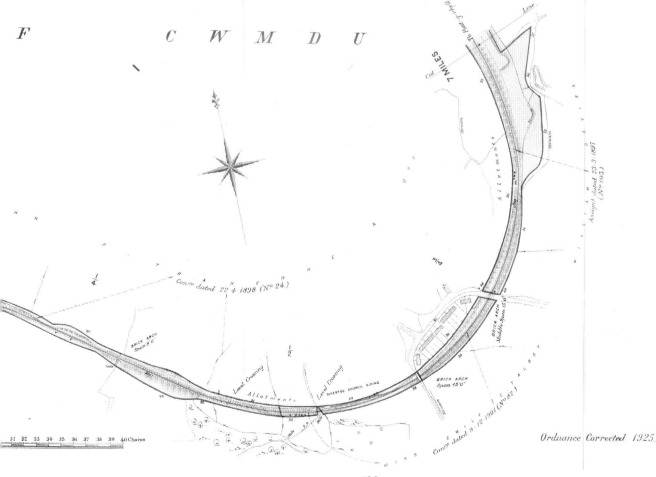

MAESTEG

The PTR entered the 800-foot double track section through Maesteg station at 7m 20ch. The track layout here resembled that at the other stations, in that there was a small goods yard with two sidings trailing off the Down line, holding ten wagons on the goods shed line and eight on the other which served a loading dock and cattle pens. The main station building was also on the Down side, which was linked by a footbridge to the shelter and signal box (with nine levers in use) on the Up platform. The PTR station was about a quarter of a mile from Maesteg town centre down Neath Road and Talbot Street, whereas the GWR station was only 175 yards distant.

From Maesteg the line passed under Neath Road and curved quite sharply to the right, initially through the remains of Llynvi Ironworks, such that in three-quarters of a mile it reached the 8 milepost, half a mile distant across the Llynvi Valley heading approximately south-east. To get there the line dropped at 1 in 75 to cross the River Llynvi and then climbed more gently to cross the GWR Llynvi Valley line on a high embankment built originally to link the Llynvi and Maesteg Ironworks. From hereon the line dropped at 1 in 100 through the old Maesteg Ironworks site to reach Cwmdu. This section contained the two major connections to North's Navigation Collieries.

LEFT: Postcard view of Maesteg signal box circa 1912, noticeably not carrying a name board. *Author's collection*

Another postcard view of Maesteg circa 1912, this one showing the Maesteg station staff. *Author's collection*

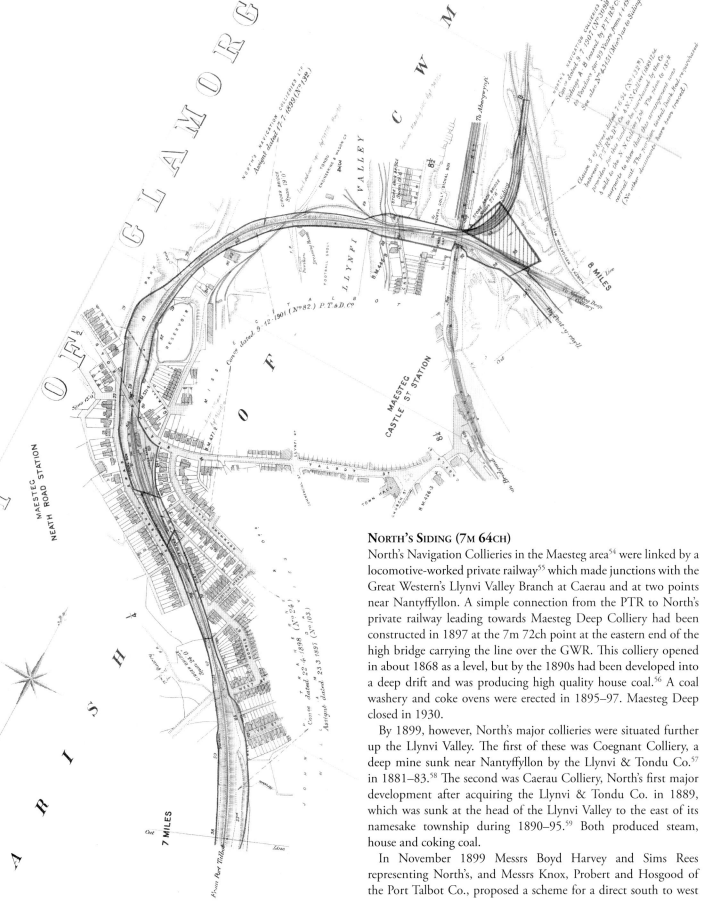

NORTH'S SIDING (7M 64CH)

North's Navigation Collieries in the Maesteg area[54] were linked by a locomotive-worked private railway[55] which made junctions with the Great Western's Llynvi Valley Branch at Caerau and at two points near Nantyffyllon. A simple connection from the PTR to North's private railway leading towards Maesteg Deep Colliery had been constructed in 1897 at the 7m 72ch point at the eastern end of the high bridge carrying the line over the GWR. This colliery opened in about 1868 as a level, but by the 1890s had been developed into a deep drift and was producing high quality house coal.[56] A coal washery and coke ovens were erected in 1895–97. Maesteg Deep closed in 1930.

By 1899, however, North's major collieries were situated further up the Llynvi Valley. The first of these was Coegnant Colliery, a deep mine sunk near Nantyffyllon by the Llynvi & Tondu Co.[57] in 1881–83.[58] The second was Caerau Colliery, North's first major development after acquiring the Llynvi & Tondu Co. in 1889, which was sunk at the head of the Llynvi Valley to the east of its namesake township during 1890–95.[59] Both produced steam, house and coking coal.

In November 1899 Messrs Boyd Harvey and Sims Rees representing North's, and Messrs Knox, Probert and Hosgood of the Port Talbot Co., proposed a scheme for a direct south to west

General View. Maesteg.942

This general view of Maesteg provides a rare glimpse of the goods yard with PTR, GWR and Elder's wagons present. The GWR station can be discerned in the centre background with Maesteg Deep Colliery and coke ovens above and to the right. In the left background a train of wagons is standing near the connection of North's sidings to the PTR.

Author's collection

A view looking north-east from the Neath Road bridge where the PTR passed between No. 1 blast furnace and the blast engine house of the old Llynvi Ironworks, with a Down mineral train conveying North's coal heading towards Port Talbot. North's Junction signal cabin can be made out above the grandstand on the edge of the rugby ground, and above that a train movement heading from North's sidings onto the private railway. North's engine shed is behind the house in the foreground. Postcard, postally used 3rd December 1906.

Author's collection

ABOVE: North's Junction signal box on 14th July 1959, with 2-8-0T No. 5264 shunting wagons in North's Sidings. *Courtesy H C Casserley*

BELOW: North's Navigation Collieries were a source of considerable traffic for the PTR. Caerau Colliery, begun in 1890, was the most northerly. This view circa 1905 is looking south with the North Pit on the right and the South Pit opposite. The sinking rig for No. 3 pit, opened in 1906, is in the centre. Caerau Colliery closed in 1977. *Author's collection*

connection from the Caerau and Coegnant pits to the PTR. Two ways of proceeding were suggested:

1   that North's would prepared the ground and the Port Talbot Co. would lay the permanent way, or
2   that one of the companies should do all the work with North's paying for it, and the Port Talbot Co. would buy it back at the rate of 10 per cent on all traffic until the amount was cleared, after which the sidings were to belong to the railway company. The colliery company would maintain the sidings and have use of them on payment of a nominal sum.[60]

The Port Talbot directors resolved to accept the second option at their meeting on 15th November 1899. Boyd Harvey confirmed this arrangement of behalf of North's on 28th November, but declined to pay towards the costs of a signalman should one be necessary, as the original agreement between the companies gave them free access to the PTR.[61] Boyd Harvey also asked Knox to arrange for a lease of the required land from Miss Talbot. The agreement confirming the arrangements was made on 5th April 1900 and included a rebate to be allowed on the increased shipment that would ensue. The sidings were reported to be finished and ready for use by February 1901 and the rebate came into effect on 1st February.

The connection took the form of four sharply-curved loop sidings and a crossover connection to the PTR main line, controlled by a covered ground frame at 7m 69ch. The reason for the fairly lengthy time for construction could have been that it was necessary to build a bridge to carry the new sidings over a section of North's internal railway. The connection was provisionally sanctioned by the Board of Trade on 19th February, but not inspected and passed for use until October 1901.[62] At some point, possibly as early as 1910, the ground frame was replaced by a small signal box which became a block point between Maesteg and Cwmdu. The original connection was taken out in December 1905.[63]

After arrival at Maesteg, trains with empty wagons for North's were run round and propelled about a quarter of a mile along the main line to the junction and then into the sidings. Drivers were instructed to push wagons as far up the sidings as possible so that following trains would not be required to propel an excessive number round the curves. In April 1901 Hosgood reported that the curves in the new sidings were too sharp for the company's 0-6-2 tank engines and that North's were altering them accordingly.[64] The sidings were back in use by July 1901, although the curves were still very sharp. In November Hosgood reported that the American engines were at risk of being derailed, and as the new Sharp, Stewart engines were now being delivered it was necessary to alter the company's end of the junction so that all classes could work in safely.[65] This time Hosgood sought permission from North's for the Port Talbot Co. to do the work.[66]

North's costs for constructing the interchange sidings amounted to £3,000 9s 9d, and were paid off by mid 1905 by means of the rebate.[67] The directors on 24th January 1906 resolved that according to the terms of the agreement plans were to be prepared for the conveyance by North's of the land on which the sidings were situated and for the lease of the sidings to North's for ninety-nine years at £1 per annum. The leased started from 1st January 1906 but the conveyance and lease documents were not finalised until July 1907, the PTR&D thereby acquiring ownership of about 1,200 yards of sidings.

Caerau, Coegnant and Maesteg Deep Collieries were served by North's private railway which had connections with the GWR at Caerau, Coegnant Sidings, Nantyffyllon and Llynvi Junction, and with the PTR at North's Junction, Maesteg. This view shows North's railway approaching Caerau Colliery circa 1910.
Author's collection

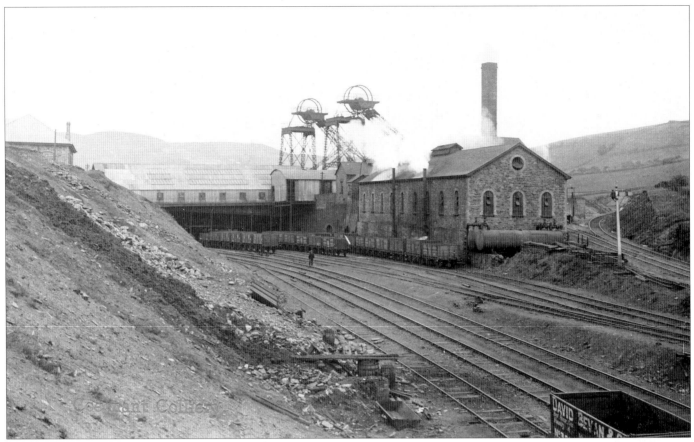

ABOVE: Coegnant Colliery after remodelling of the surface workings in 1903/4. North's private line from Caerau Colliery further up the valley comes in from the right and was apparently signalled. Coegnant Colliery closed in 1981. *Author's collection*

BELOW: A closer view of Coegnant Colliery with the fan house in the centre and the South and North pits behind. Note the North's wagon in the simplified livery. Postcard, postally used 2nd February 1914. *Author's collection*

ABOVE: Maesteg Deep Colliery was at the southern end of North's private railway and was situated to the east of, and close to, North's sidings. This view dates from circa 1915. This colliery closed in 1930. *Author's collection*

BELOW: A view circa 1915 of the coke ovens and washery erected near Maesteg Deep Colliery in 1895–97, the site later being used for Maesteg Central Washery. *Author's collection*

Maesteg coke ovens with the coal washery in the left centre. As fully developed this plant had two sets of ovens set at right angles to each other.
Author's collection

NORTH'S TEMPORARY CONNECTION (8M 17CH)

Circa 1911 a new siding connection was put in for North's Navigation Collieries at 8m 17ch on the main line, and inspected by the Board of Trade in March 1912.[68] The purpose of this siding is not clear, although it was close to North's Maesteg Deep Colliery, possibly in conjunction with some construction work there. It does not appear in any of the Working Time Tables and was seemingly removed by 1914.

MAESTEG SLAG SIDING (8M 18CH)

A siding connection near the 8¼ milepost for Mr Holman of Messrs M J Stonehouse Ltd was agreed in June 1915.[69] This business, which had earlier operated near Cefn Ironworks on the OVER, exploited the slag from the old Maesteg Ironworks site to produce tar macadam. The connection was ready by February 1916,[70] and during the next eight months the PTR made up at Holman's expense the ground on which an internal loop was laid.[71] A second connection was agreed in 1921, but never laid in. The sole connection was inspected in September 1921.[72] This company went into liquidation in November 1932 and the siding agreement was cancelled in December 1932.

BRYN RHYG (8M 47CH)

In May 1921 the directors approved the application of H P Herdman of Bridgend for a siding connection for a new colliery being opened near Cwmdu by Bryn Rhyg Collieries Ltd.[73] The upper, inlet, end of this siding was connected to the main line at 8m 47ch and worked by a ground frame. The lower, outlet, end made an end-on junction with the nearby Cwmdu Loop and was worked from the existing signal box. The connections were laid in by October 1921,[74] and were reported to be in use by December.[75] Despite notification to the Board of Trade in November 1921 that the works were completed, they were not inspected until 23rd February 1928.[76] A second loop siding within the colliery company's boundary and repositioned screens were agreed by the GWR in May 1925. This colliery company went into voluntary liquidation in October 1930 and was taken over by Bryn Rhyg Collieries (1930) Ltd. This concern failed in September 1933 and Port Talbot Trading & Transport Ltd, acting as receivers, agreed to the GWR taking over the sidings, weighbridge and other material in lieu of the amount owing.

CWMDU AND GARTH

Cwmdu was reached at 8m 58ch. The construction of this station and the siding connection for St. John's Colliery were described earlier.[77] The signal box was placed on the Down side at 8m 69ch and contained twenty-three levers. Passenger trains were not permitted to cross here, but a passenger and a goods train could do so provided the latter was held in the goods loop. The single line resumed at 9m, passed over Heol Fain level crossing and the direct connection to St. John's Colliery exchange sidings at 9m 1ch, it then curved though 90 degrees to reach the site of Garth station at 9m 34ch, still falling at 1 in 100. The signal box at 9m 37ch, which contained thirteen levers,[78] was closed in January 1916 and

A postcard view of PTR No. 17 just to the south of Maesteg station. It is seen in original condition apart from the plated-in bunker.

Author's collection

the passing loop from 9m 29ch to 9m 47ch was probably removed a the same time.

GARTH MERTHYR COLLIERY (9M 36CH AND 9M 72CH)

Garth Merthyr Colliery[79] and the nearby Oakwood Colliery, which was served by the GWR, were purchased in 1900 by Sir Alfred Jones, chairman of the well-known shipping firm Elder Dempster, to supply his large fleet of steamers with bunker coal.[80] This coal mining subsidiary traded as Elder's Navigation Collieries Ltd. The pit was substantially deepened and new coke ovens and a washery were established on the surface. Sir Alfred Jones died in 1909 at a time when Elder's Navigation Collieries was being run at a loss.[81] Garth and Oakwood collieries closed on 31st May 1910 but, new pay rates having been negotiated with its workmen, reopened in November 1910. That year control of the Elder Dempster shipping line passed to Lord Kylsant and the mining subsidiary was reorganised as Elder's Collieries Ltd. The name was changed to Celtic Collieries Ltd in March 1915 and in 1916 this enterprise was sold on to Lord Rhondda's Cambrian Combine. After four very profitable years the entire share capital was purchased by North's Navigation Collieries, which itself had become part of the Cambrian Combine in October 1916. As a result of poor trading conditions Celtic Collieries was put into receivership in March 1930 and Garth Colliery closed the following September.[82]

The first connection for this colliery was put in by Pearson's in 1897 during the construction of the line,[83] but was later relaid by the PTR to make it easier to work. The PTR had use of this siding although the colliery company was required to pay for its maintenance, the arrangements confirmed by an agreement dated 21st June 1899.[84] This connection was worked originally by a ground frame, but from 1907 by the nearby Garth signal box. The second connection, trailing to the Up direction, was constructed in July 1907, and confirmed by an agreement date 14th June 1913.[85] The two were connected within the colliery property to form an internal loop. This connection was belatedly inspected and sanctioned in 1912.[86] Traffic for this colliery could be worked in and out at both connections. Owing to the gradient, an engine or 20-ton brake van was required to be at the lower, Lletty Brongu, end during shunting operations. The siding agreement was renegotiated in July 1924 and terminated on 11th November 1930 when the sidings were sold by the receiver of the colliery company to George Cohen, Sons & Co. Ltd for dismantling the surface plant.[87]

The line continued to fall at 1 in 90 to reach Lletty Brongu or Pontrhydycyff Viaduct (10m 20ch to 10m 24ch). This eight-arch brick-built structure crossed Nant Cwmdu at a height of 73 feet and the sidings of the nearby Llynvi Valley Colliery. From here to Pontyrhyll Junction the line undulated with little change in elevation, following the 400-foot contour.

GELLIHIR COLLIERY (10M 32CH AND 10M 55CH)

In March 1905 a siding connection was put in just beyond Lletty Brongu Viaduct at a cost of £185 for a new level being developed by Messrs Llewellyn, Phillips & Walters.[88] Major Druitt inspected the works in August 1905 and the connection was sanctioned

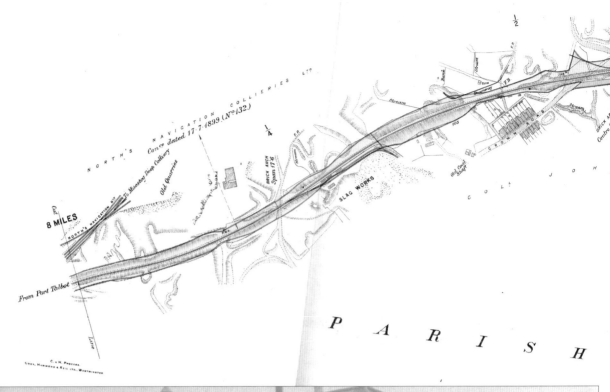

ABOVE: The GWR-design signal box erected at Cwmdu in connection with the provision there of a loop and junction for North's new St. John's Colliery.
Author's collection

FACING PAGE: St. John's Colliery circa 1916. The line down to the exchange sidings at Cwmdu runs off from the bottom left of the view. Note that most of the wagons are in North's simplified livery. The engine is ex-GWR No. 855 which was sold to North's in 1906.
Author's collection

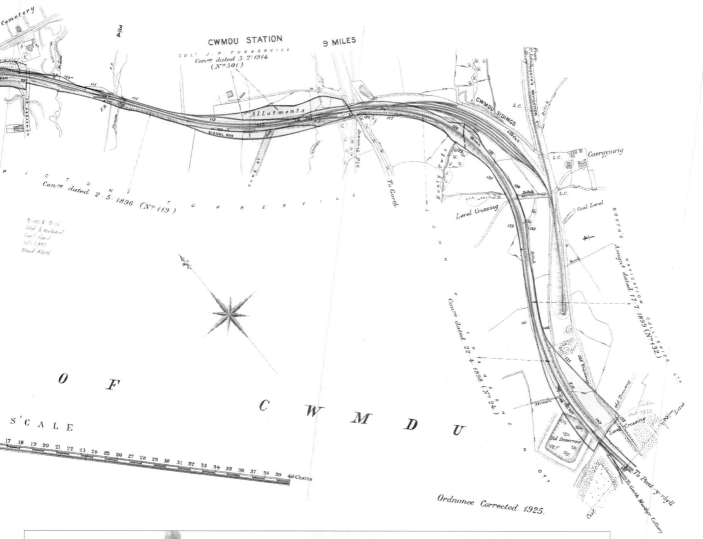

ABOVE: Garth Colliery, with the PTR in the foreground before Garth loop was constructed in 1906. *NM&GW*

BELOW: Garth Colliery circa 1906 viewed from the east where the PTR ran past the workings. Note the PTR wagon partly hidden by the fountain.
Author's collection

ABOVE: Garth Colliery, by now renamed Elder's Navigation Colliery, viewed from the other direction looking up the valley circa 1906. The washery is in the centre of the view, with the 1900/1906 coke ovens on the far left and No. 1 pit headgear to the right. Note the industrial locomotive on the private line which connected this colliery with Maesteg Merthyr (Oakwood) Colliery which was served by the GWR.   *Author's collection*

BELOW: Lletty Brongu Viaduct, with Llynvi Valley Colliery and its siding in the foreground.   *Courtesy John Ryan*

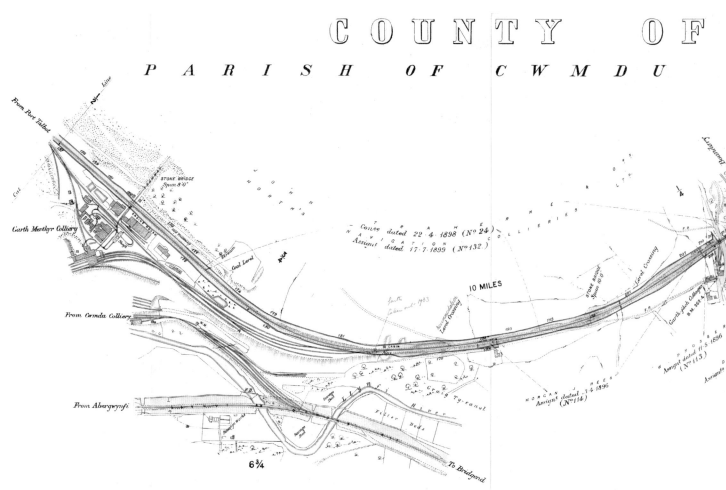

COUNTY OF

PARISH OF CWMDU

Lletty Brongu or Pontrhydycyff Viaduct circa 1905. Llynvi Valley Colliery, the chimney of which can be seen, was connected to the GWR which ran across the centre of the view.

Author's collection

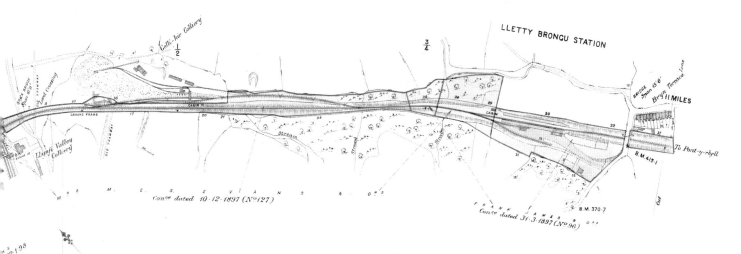

provided traffic was worked with the engine at the lower, viaduct, end.[89] The colliery siding was extended into a loop in August 1907[90] when a second connection was laid in near Lletty Brongu station at a cost of £140 "particularly for berthing empty wagons".[91] This connection was not inspected and sanctioned until March 1912. Following two serious runaways in 1908, catch siding were laid in at Gellihir Colliery at the colliery's expense.[92] A new siding agreement was made on 1st January 1908 with Gellihir Colliery Co. Ltd[93] which had been formed in October 1906 to acquire the business.[94] By November 1911 the majority of the issued shares were held by Swansea Navigation Collieries Ltd, Llanelly. By January 1913 the business had been acquired by O H Thomas Ltd and a new siding agreement was made with these owners on 15th August 1919. Although Thomas had died in 1917,[95] his company at last had siding connections with the PTR. The siding agreement was terminated by the NCB on 30th April 1953.

LLETTY BRONGU

Shortly beyond the second connection for Gellihir Colliery the line reached Lletty Brongu station. Following the construction of Garth Loop in 1906 this had been reduced to one platform, although the original Up platform remained in a derelict state. The typical goods yard contained two sidings, the ground frame for which was at 10m 62ch, one siding serving a goods shed and the other a loading bank. Between Lletty Brongu and Bettws Llangeinor there were connections to a number a small collieries, some of which lasted for only a short time.

Thomas Rees, station master at Lletty Brongu, circa 1912.
Author's collection

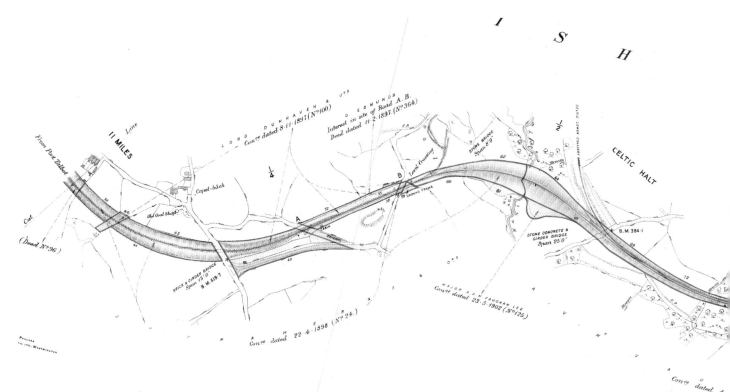

Lletty Brongu was one of three stations specified in Pearson's contract for the construction of the 1894 railway, the others being Bryn and Maesteg. All were of similar design with goods sheds built of timber framing and boarding on a brick base, 40 feet long and 22 feet wide inside. This view shows the goods yard circa 1912. The posed group appears to consist mainly of wagon repairers with possibly two lengthsmen on the right. Second left is the station master, Thomas Rees. The wheelbarrow is lettered "Johnston Davie, Lletty Brongu". Among the wagons visible in the mileage siding are those lettered for Horton Lime Works, Llewellyn & Co., Argoed Colliery, Cynonville R&SBR, and West Rhondda, Lletty Brongu.

Author's collection

LLETTY BRONGU COLLIERY (11M 20CH)

On 19th April 1899 the directors approved Messrs Morrish & Co.'s application for a siding connection for their recently opened colliery at milepost 11¼. The following October the directors agreed with Probert's recommendation that the colliery company be allowed to pay off the balance of the cost of the siding, then £239, at £50 per annum. The siding connection, which was worked by a covered ground frame, was sanctioned for use by the Board of Trade on 22nd June 1899, a condition being that if trains exceeded fifteen wagons the engine was to be at the lower end.[96] A year later the directors learned that this colliery was about to be closed and moved to a site served by the GWR only. Despite an outstanding balance for the siding of £108, they resolved in November 1900 to accept £100 in quarterly payments provided the whole of the westward traffic from the new colliery was sent via the OVER. By the following June £82 was still owing and in July 1901 the general manager was authorised by the directors to take possession of the siding, whose value exceeded the outstanding debt. There is no evidence this colliery produced much coal or was re-established elsewhere.

Lletty Brongu station circa 1912, by which date the passing loop had been removed and the Up platform taken out of use. The general similarity to Bryn and Maesteg is apparent.
Author's collection

The PTR entered the Garw Valley near Llangeinor on a ledge about 100 feet above the GWR, as seen in this view of Llangeinor station. The PTR's Bettws Llangeinor station was a short distance off to the left. *Author's collection*

CEDFYW RHONDDA OR WEST RHONDDA COLLIERY (11M 30CH)

In April 1906 Cleaver applied to the Board of Trade for approval to lay in a siding about half a mile beyond Lletty Brongu station for T Walters' Cedfyw Rhondda Colliery.[97] This was granted but, as the main line at this point was on a slight down gradient towards Pontyrhyll, the siding was required to be worked with the engine at the lower end. This, of course, was an operational nonsense, but the Board of Trade waived the condition on learning that the siding was to be worked by empties being propelled from Garth with a 20-ton brake van leading, and that this was quite capable of holding the number of wagons likely to be placed against it. As with a number of other works approved around this time, this siding was not inspected and sanctioned until March 1912.[98] Walters sold this small colliery to the newly formed West Rhondda Colliery Co. Ltd, in which he was the principal shareholder, in December 1909.[99] This company failed to pay interest on some of its debentures and a receiver was appointed in August 1914. Although the debenture holders were paid off, all the capital had been lost and the company ceased to trade, being dissolved in November 1917. The business was sold to the Cedfyw Rhondda Colliery Co. Ltd which had been formed in July 1915,[100] and a new siding agreement was signed on 24th March 1917.[101] This colliery worked until September 1927 when the company resolved to be voluntarily wound up. The liquidator disclaimed the agreement and the siding was taken out of use early in 1928.

CELTIC HALT AND SIDINGS (11M 49CH AND 11M 53CH)

In addition to further developing Garth and Oakwood collieries, Celtic Collieries made a new sinking in Cwm Cedfyw for Celtic Lower Colliery and a siding connection was approved in May 1917. The colliery had asked the PTR to contribute to the cost of the bridge necessary to carry the three-quarters of a mile long siding to the mine over an intervening road, but this was not entertained. Eventually, in November 1918, an arrangement was reached whereby the PTR would construct the connection, which consisted of two junctions off the main line connected so as to form a very short loop, a siding holding thirty wagons, and the bridge, for an estimated total of £5,000.[102] These works were reported to be ready for use in September 1919.[103] The site was fairly remote and the colliery company erected a 100-foot long by 8-foot wide platform at 11m 46ch for use by its miners. The platform – which was reported to be in use in January 1920[104] – and connections were inspected in September 1921 when all was found to be in order.[105] The PTR agreed on 20th August 1921 to register the name of the platform as Celtic Lower Halt.[106] A new siding agreement was made with Dunraven Estates Co. Ltd in August 1932 when the earlier colliery company went into liquidation, this agreement was terminated on 31st May 1942 once all the private sidings had been removed.[107]

MOELGILAU OR BETTWS LLANTWIT COLLIERY (12M 9CH)

At their meeting on 24th January 1900 the directors approved the application of W H Morgan of Bridgend for a siding connection to be put in near milepost 12 for his new colliery. The terms were 50 per cent of the cost of £150 as cash, the balance to be paid off at 3d per ton on all coal sent out. Major Pringle found the works to be satisfactory when inspected on 14th August 1900.[108] Three days later the general manager reported that the colliery had commenced

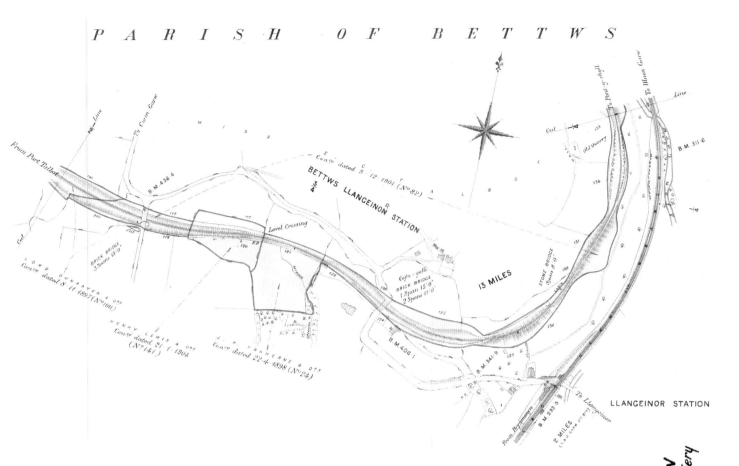

to put coal onto rail.[109] The siding was relaid for the use of "a new company" in 1907,[110] possibly referring to the fact that Morgan disposed of his property in 1909 to the Bettws Llantwit Colliery Co. and the colliery was renamed accordingly.[111] This colliery closed circa 1911.

Gwernllwyn Colliery (12m35ch)

Morgan also had an interest in a mining property about a quarter of a mile nearer Bettws Llangeinor station. A siding connection was approved in 1902 and although never inspected it appeared in later Working Time Tables. In November 1908 these mineral and mining rights were acquired by John Walters, who already possessed a number of small mining properties in the Llynvi Valley, and the Bettws Colliery Co. was formed to achieve this end.[112] This company soon failed and a receiver was appointed in February 1910, the colliery having been idle since 3rd August 1909. The siding and connection were recovered in July 1911.

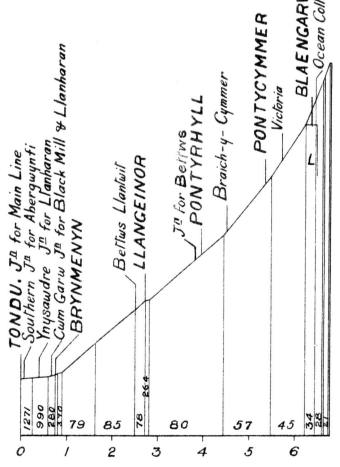

Right: The PTR joined the Garw Valley Branch, over which it had running powers, on a 1 in 80 gradient at Pontyrhyll, steepening to 1 in 45 for passenger trains and 1 in 21 for mineral trains at the top end.

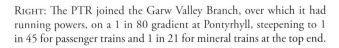

459

About half a mile further up the valley at Tylagwyn, the Garw Valley narrowed noticeably and from here the PTR and GWR, doubled by the date of this postcard view, ran parallel to each other until Pontyrhyll Junction was reached. *Author's collection*

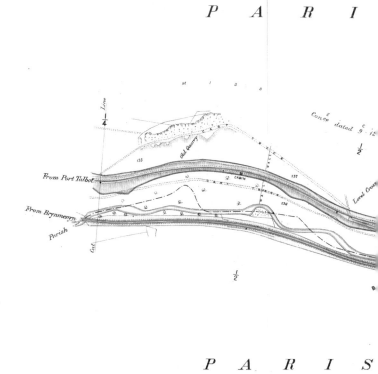

BETTWS LLANGEINOR

A quarter of a mile further on the remote unstaffed platform at Bettws Llangeinor was reached at 12m 60ch. Shortly beyond this station the line abandoned its roughly easterly direction and curved round to head north up the Garw Valley, running parallel to the Garw Valley Branch of the GWR. When first encountered, the PTR was about 100 feet above the GWR and dropped only slightly to the junction at Pontyrhyll. There were no siding connections along this section. A request for one to be put in for Cefn Gelli quarry near the 13¼ milepost was refused after the general manager reported on 11th June 1897 that it was uncertain that the annual charge of £40 would be paid.[113] The loop sidings at Pontyrhyll commenced at 13m 57ch, the main line only becoming double just before the junction at 14m 1ch, which was 3m 8ch from Brynmenyn junction. PTR running powers extended from there to the termination of the Garw Valley Branch beyond Blaengarw station, at 5m 74ch.

(Continued on page 467)

Pontyrhyll had a staggered platform arrangement and this view shows the Up platform looking down towards the junction with the PTR, the signals for which are visible beyond the platform end. Also prominent is the 1898 signal box opened in conjunction with the alterations necessary for the new junction.

Author's collection

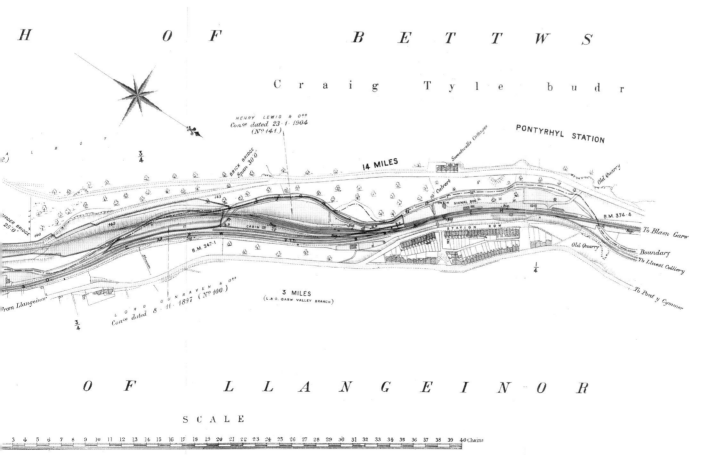

This general view circa 1908 shows Pontycymmer after the line to Blaengarw had been doubled in 1900–1902. Prior to doubling, Pontycymmer had a single platform, which is just visible to the left of the overbridge in this view, becoming the Down platform (GWR terminology) in the new arrangement. Pontycymmer became another station with staggered platforms, the new Up platform is visible below Ffaldau Colliery. Prior to opening the line to Blaengarw for a passenger service PTR passenger trains terminated at Pontycymmer and made a smart turnaround in order not to block the line. The tracks across from the platform are the outlet roads for Ffaldau Colliery. Postcard, postally used 28th August 1909.   *Author's collection*

ABOVE: Ffaldau Colliery was an important source of traffic for the PTR, not only due to the amount of coal shipped but also because the colliery had guaranteed this traffic in its early years. The colliery company supported the PT Co.'s 1894 Bill in Parliament and for a long time its managing director was a director of the railway company. PTR mineral trains ceased to work in the Garw Valley in 1903, the traffic being worked by the GWR as a result of the 1903 agreement. In this busy scene mainly empty wagons lettered for Pyman, Watson (the owners of Ffaldau Colliery) are on the screen roads, and an Up goods train is being marshalled in the Up platform line. *Author's collection*

BELOW: Blaengarw station was built by the GWR as a result of pressure from the PTR, opening for passengers in May 1902. The PTR, and later the GWR, operated a passenger service between Port Talbot and Blaengarw from May 1902 to September 1932, with a journey time of about 53 minutes for the seventeen and a half miles. *Author's collection*

ABOVE: The GWR continued for a further half mile beyond Blaengarw station, terminating round the bend and out of sight in this view. On either side were marshalling sidings for International Colliery, top left, and Ocean Colliery, approached by the incline and off to the right.

Author's collection

BELOW: The large International Colliery at the head of the Garw Valley was a further important source of traffic for the PTR. This colliery relied on rope haulage and gravity to move wagons around its workings, the sole connection was via the incline seen here. International Colliery closed in 1968. Postcard, postally used March 1909.

Author's collection

Glenavon Colliery, later Glengarw Colliery, was situated just to the east of Blaengarw station and was connected to the GWR main line nearby. This colliery closed in 1959. Postcard, postally used December 1919. *Author's collection*

Ocean Colliery, later named Garw Colliery, was part of David Davies' Ocean Coal Co. It was situated to the east of Blaengarw and reached by a lengthy connection from the marshalling sidings. Unlike the other collieries at Blaengarw, this one employed steam locomotives to work its internal traffic. Garw Colliery closed in 1985. Postcard, postally used 30th October 1908. *Author's collection*

TONYGROES TO TONMAWR

The SWMJnR took the more northerly fork at Tonygroes North Junction (see p. 422) and distances were measured from that point. Apart from a short climb at 1 in 44 on the approach to the bridge over the R&SBR at Ynysdavid, the SWMJnR followed the left bank of the River Avon on fairly easy gradients as far as Oakwood. Beyond Oakwood the gradient stiffened noticeably, the line climbing at 1 in 40/42 for over two and a quarter miles, with a slight easing through Efail Fach, before easing again to join the SWMR at Tonmawr West Junction (5m 55ch). Like the main line to Pontyrhyll, siding connections were to be found at frequent intervals along the SWMJnR.

CRAIGAVON COLLIERY (CIRCA 0M 30CH)

A connection was put in for Craigavon Colliery near the Upper Forge Works following an application in July 1898 from Messrs Jenkins & Sons, who guaranteed traffic worth £300 per annum.[114] The siding agreement, belatedly made in February 1906, was terminated in February 1909 and the siding was removed.[115]

MARGAM FORGE (0M 49CH)

The Margam Tinplate Works at Upper Forge had closed in 1893[116] and the Oakwood Railway as far as the level crossing over the GWR main line fell out of use, apart from a short section to Oakwood Junction where the SWMJnR joined its route.[117] This portion became a long storage siding holding seventy-three wagons. The junction was renamed Margam Forge by 1913. By about 1932 the siding was being used by the Marcroft Wagon Co.

MAESMELYN COLLIERY (1M 74CH)

In December 1916 the directors agreed to a siding connection for Maesmelyn Colliery, Cwmavon, which was being established on a site opposite Cwmavon Yard by Herbert Hudson Ltd. This company, which had been formed in August 1916,[118] acquired a lease of Measmelyn Colliery Co. Ltd[119] and a sublease of the minerals being worked by the nearby Ynys Avon Colliery. The agreement with Herbert Hudson Ltd called for two connections,[120] but only one was laid in and this was ready for use in March 1917.[121] A receiver appointed in June 1927 disclaimed the agreement in January 1928 and it was terminated by the GWR. Empty wagons were delivered to this siding either by being worked back from Ynysdavid Yard or shunted in by a banking engine. Measmelyn Colliery was acquired by Briton Ferry Collieries Ltd by 1930, but closed by 1938.

CWMAVON YARD AND CWMAVON WAGON REPAIR SHOP (1M 78CH)

A mileage siding was put here on the river side of the railway during the construction of the SWMJnR;[122] access from Cwmavon across

The former Oakwood Railway near Upper Forge in use as a siding. Postcard, postally used 31st August 1910. *Author's collection*

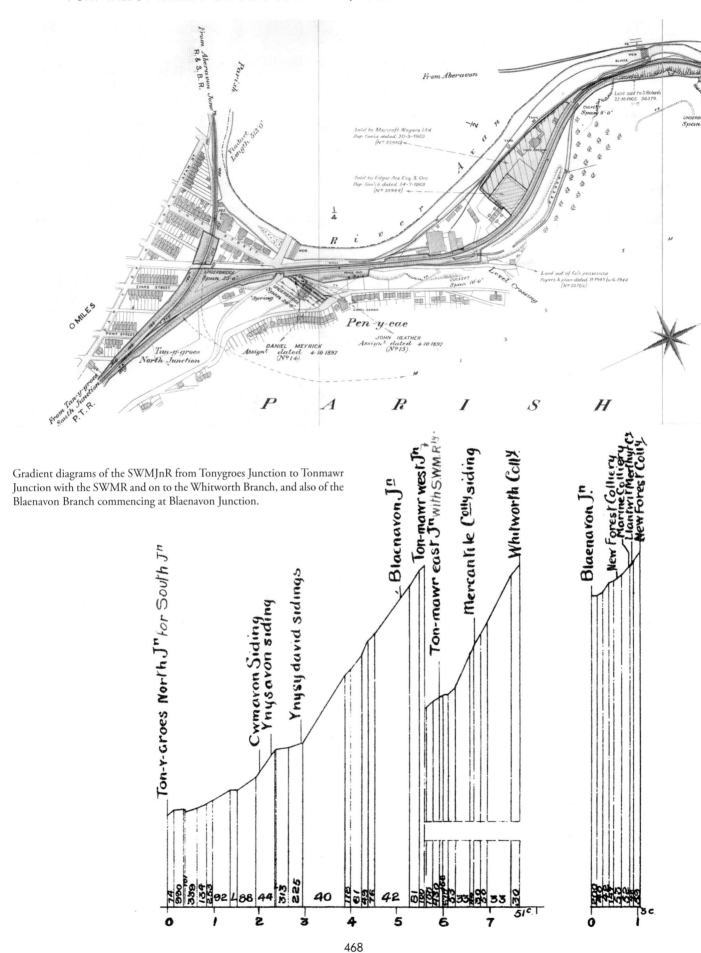

Gradient diagrams of the SWMJnR from Tonygroes Junction to Tonmawr Junction with the SWMR and on to the Whitworth Branch, and also of the Blaenavon Branch commencing at Blaenavon Junction.

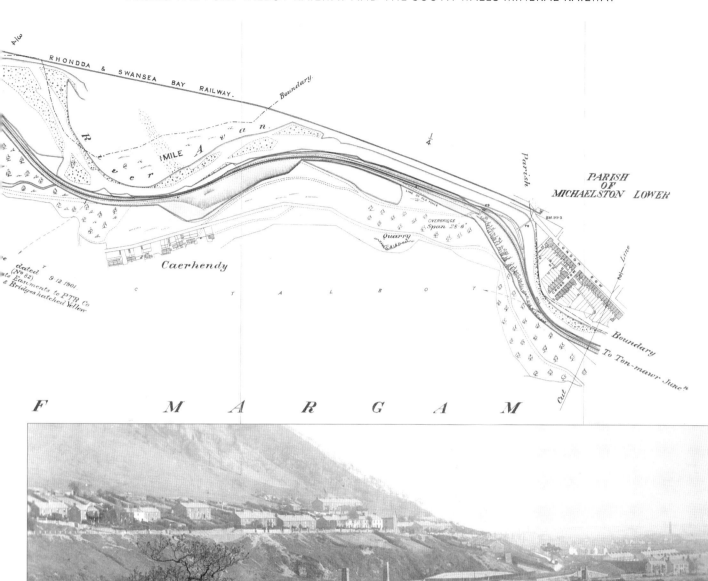

Looking down the Avon Valley with Penycae on the hillside. In the centre is the disused Margam Tinplate Works at Upper Forge with the SWMJnR skirting round to the left and across the bottom of the view. The row of wagons by the river is standing on what used to be the Oakwood Railway, by then a long siding which connected to the SWMJnR at Oakwood Junction a little further up the valley. Postcard, postally used 18th August 1911.

Author's collection

The Avon Valley closes in for a short distance at Corlanau, and here the R&SBR, on the left, and the SWMJnR run close to each other on opposite sides of the river, with Cwmavon in the distance. Postcard, postally used 5th February 1909. *Author's collection*

the river was via the bridge built for the Bryn Tramroad.[123] A second connection for Messrs Hudson was agreed in November 1920, this one for a wagon repairing and repainting shop in Cwmavon Yard. The agreement dated 3rd March 1921 provided for the PTR to slew the existing mileage siding towards the river and to construct the connection, a slag wall and a protective fence to the rear of the recently opened Cwmavon Halt at 2m 7ch.[124] As with Maesmelyn Colliery, this agreement was also disclaimed by the receiver of Herbert Hudson Ltd in January 1928 and was terminated.

YNYS AVON COLLIERY (2M 20CH)

A siding connection for Ynys Avon Colliery was put in during the construction of the SWMJnR.[125] This siding was extended in August 1901, the cost being paid off by coal supplied to Duffryn Yard in PTR wagons at 12s per ton.[126] The siding connection was taken over by the Eagle Brick & Tile Co. Ltd in March 1908[127] which established a brickworks there. Ynys Avon Colliery was owned by Ynysavon Colliery Co. Ltd from 1914 to 1916,[128] and Ynysavon (1916) Colliery Co. Ltd from 1916 to 1920,[129] before passing to the Ynyslas Colliery Co. By 1925 only the brick company remained, lasting until 1950 when the siding agreement was terminated.

YNYSDAVID SIDINGS (2M 48CH)

The SWMJnR crossed the R&SBR and its Tymaen Sidings by a two-span lattice girder bridge (2m 24ch to 2m 71ch), and curved to the right to reach the block post at Ynysdavid Sidings. The five sidings were at a slightly lower level and were served by a trailing

connection off the SWMJnR via a short (220 feet) loop. The sidings, with a total capacity of seventy-eight wagons, were connected by a short incline down to Baldwins' private railway which divided into two. One lengthy line passed under the SWMJnR, crossed the river and eventually reached Cwmmawr Colliery and Cwmavon coke ovens. The other line served Oakwood Colliery, a quarter of a mile distant and situated between the PTR and the R&SBR. Not more than twelve loaded or thirty empty wagons were allowed to be pushed through the loop, and for some reason "GWR side tank engines", presumably the '4500' Class, were not allowed to propel wagons from the sidings.

The 167 yards long Pontrhydyfen Viaduct was reached 3m 30ch. This ten-arch viaduct of brick construction was built on a slight curve on the 1 in 40 gradient and crossed the River Avon at a height of 70 feet to reach the west side of Cwm Pelenna at an elevation of about 300 feet.

TEWGOED COLLIERY (3M 41CH AND 3M 51CH)

In February 1907 the directors approved connections for loop sidings for Rhydavon Colliery just beyond Pontrhydyfen Viaduct; these were completed and in use by June 1907.[130] Rhydavon Colliery was reported to have been abandoned by 1908 and the mine was taken over by the Tewgoed Colliery Co. The siding agreement was transferred to T Hughes on behalf of the Craiglyn Colliery Co. in February 1913. This business was turned into a limited company in December 1917, but ceased trading in August 1930 and all the assets were sold.[131]

CWMAVON, GLAM.

This bridge was built circa 1841 for the tramroad connecting the coal workings at Bryn with the English Copper Co.'s works at Cwmavon. The SWMJnR in the foreground follows the route of the Oakwood Railway. The end of Cwmavon mileage siding is visible on the left. A small wagon repair works was established between the siding and the main line in 1921.

Author's collection

The SWMJnR curved round to cross the R&SBR and Baldwins' Tymaen Sidings by a two-span girder bridge. The PTR's Ynysdavid Sidings are at a higher level in front of the farther embankment. The tall chimney marks the site of the Eagle Brick & Tile Company's works, which were served by a private siding off the SWMJnR, and beyond which was Ynysavon Colliery. *Author' collection*

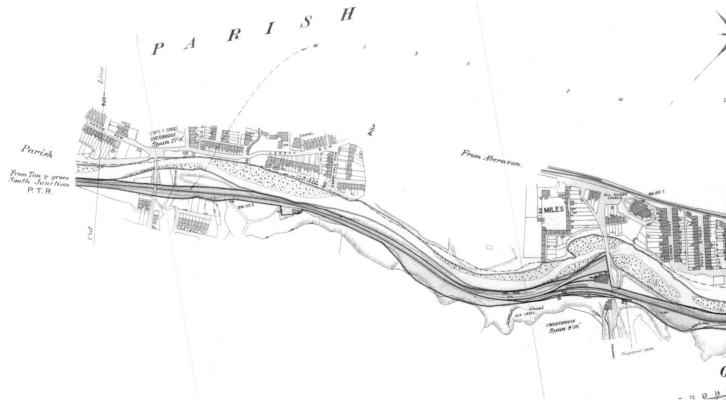

The girder bridge at Ynysdavid carrying the SWMJnR over the R&SBR and Baldwins' Tymaen Sidings viewed from the other direction. These sidings were connected to the R&SBR at Tymaen Junction, the roof of the signal being visible to the left of the bridge. *Courtesy Arthur Rees*

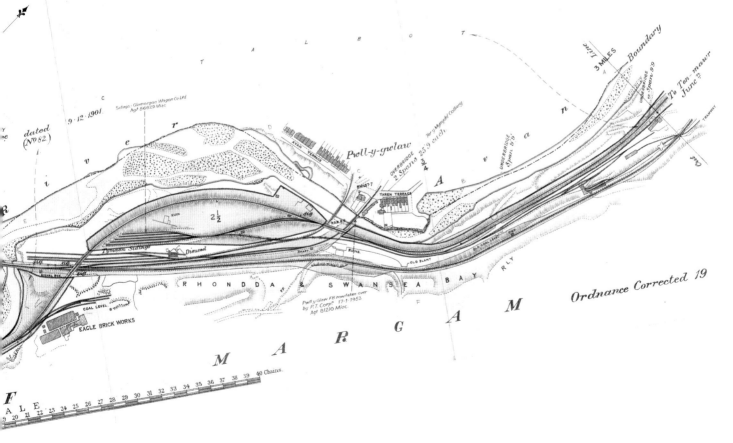

Part of the complex of railways at Ynysdavid. The SWMJnR runs left to right across the foreground, crossing, first, the long private siding seen curving round behind the cottages to Baldwins' Cwmavon Colliery off to the left and, second, the R&SBR branch to Tewgoed or Torymynydd Colliery off to the right. These two lines came together at Baldwins' Tymaen Sidings, off to the lower left. Just visible to the left of the left-hand bridge is the junction for the PTR's Ynysdavid Sidings.

Author's collection

ABOVE: Another view of the bridges seen above. The screens for Tewgoed Colliery are directly above the left-hand bridge. *Author's collection*

BELOW: Pontrhydyfen Viaduct. Postcard, postally used 19th August 1913. *Author's collection*

This postcard view, looking up the Pelenna Valley, shows the screens and sidings for Rhydavon Colliery under construction just beyond the north end of Pontrhydyfen Viaduct, dating the view to 1907.

Author's collection

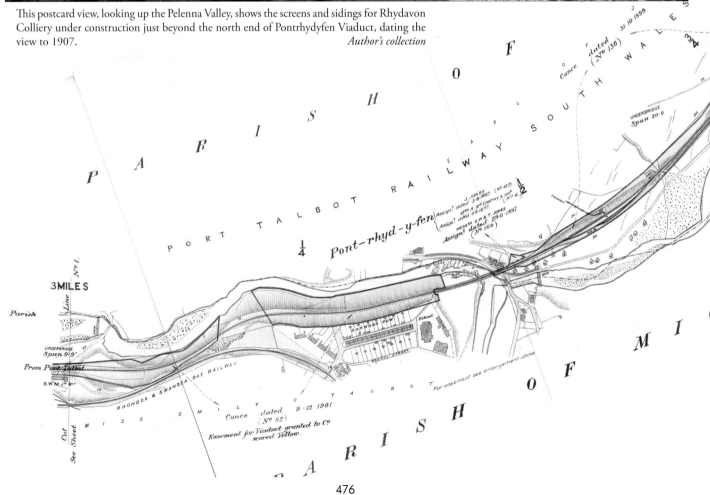

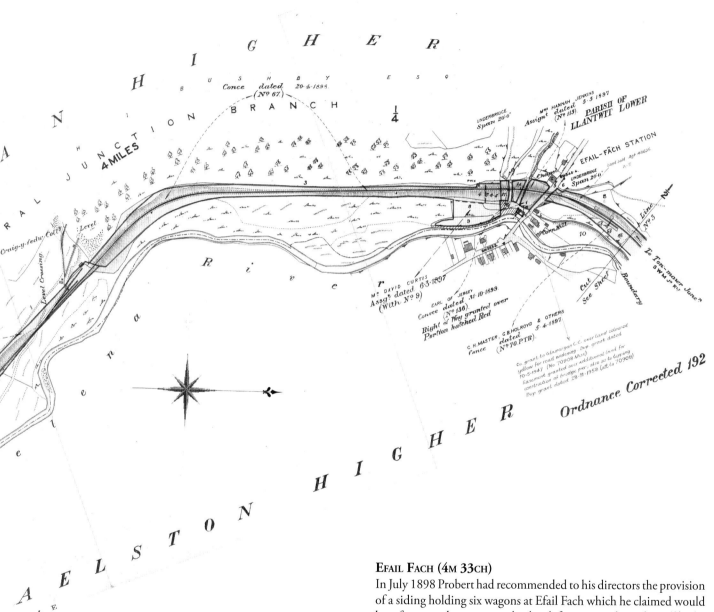

PENSTAR COLLIERY (3M 69CH)

A siding connection for Penstar or Craigyfedw Colliery was approved in March 1905 and put in immediately.[132] This colliery eventually became part of the small empire owned by Herbert Hudson Ltd, which included Maesmelyn Colliery and a wagon works at Cwmavon. As with the other collieries, the siding agreement was terminated in January 1928.[133]

EFAIL FACH (4M 33CH)

In July 1898 Probert had recommended to his directors the provision of a siding holding six wagons at Efail Fach which he claimed would be of great advantage to the local farmers and residents.[134] The directors were not persuaded, and the matter rested until March 1900 when the local inhabitants of Efail Fach applied for a mileage siding. Again the directors demurred, but offered the necessary land at a reasonable rental and suggested the applicants paid the cost of the siding. In the event, the PTR decided in September 1907 to put in the siding itself, although it was not completed until the following September.[135] The platform at Efail Fach at 4m 38ch was erected opposite the siding. Empties for this siding and those at Tewgoed and Penstar Collieries could be propelled from Ynysdavid if necessary.

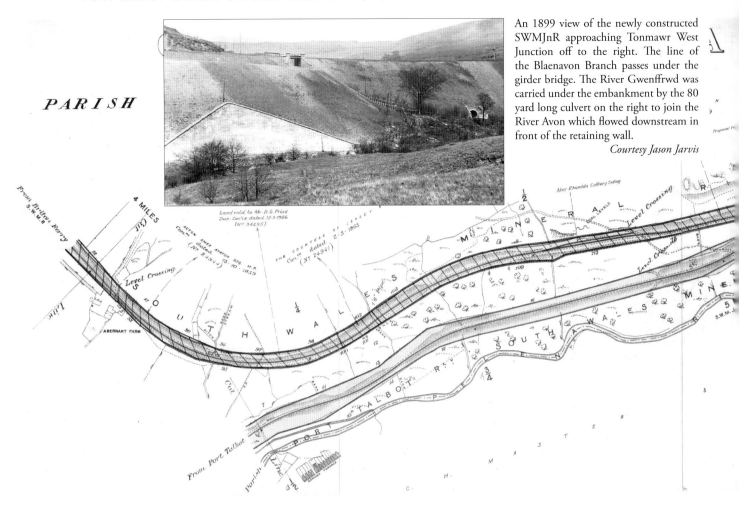

An 1899 view of the newly constructed SWMJnR approaching Tonmawr West Junction off to the right. The line of the Blaenavon Branch passes under the girder bridge. The River Gwenffrwd was carried under the embankment by the 80 yard long culvert on the right to join the River Avon which flowed downstream in front of the retaining wall.

Courtesy Jason Jarvis

BLAENAVON JUNCTION

Near the 4½ milepost the SWMJnR encountered the SWMR about 50 feet higher up on the left, and the two ran in parallel to the junction. The Blaenavon Branch commenced at Blaenavon Junction (5m 7ch), for most of its life worked by a ground frame.[136] The SWMJnR crossed this branch by a girder bridge at 5m 22ch and the River Gwenffrwd shortly after at 5m 25ch, although this was hardly visible, being carried in a culvert through the embankment under the full width of the tracks here.

TONMAWR SIDINGS (5M 24CH)

None of the collieries connected to the Blaenavon or Whitworth branches had sufficient land on which to increase their siding accommodation. Consequently, the directors proposed in July 1920 that the PTR should provide the land and sidings at an estimated cost of £2,500, this to be redeemed by the colliery companies paying an additional 8d per ton on all coal consigned away. This scheme was approved by the GWR Officers' Conference in October 1920, and an agreement to that effect between the PTR, the SWMR and the eight participating colliery companies was signed on 8th November 1920.[137] Those involved were the Blaenmawr, Bryngrugos, Bryngwyn, Merthyr Llantwit and Oakland companies on the Blaenavon Branch and the Corrwg Merthyr, North End and Torybanwen companies on the Whitworth Branch. Under the terms of the agreement the two railway companies were to provide approximately one acre of land, lay down the sidings

and maintain them at a cost shared proportionally to the colliery companies' traffic. The plan included in the agreement shows two loop sidings with capacities of forty-seven and fifty wagons lying between the SWMJnR and SWMR, but connected only to the SWMR. The required land was made available by slewing both railways sufficiently to provide space for three loop sidings, this task being completed by March 1921.[138] In addition to these storage sidings the PTR laid in, at a further cost of £1,500, a shunting loop holding forty-eight wagons for its own use which was connected to the SWMR at its eastern end and to both railways at the western end (at 5m 24ch on the SWMJnR and 4m 78ch on the SWMR). The work was completed by August 1921[139] and following Board of Trade approval the sidings were brought into use in October 1921,[140] although the new connection to the SWMJnR was not inspected until February 1928.[141]

Six of the above colliery companies signed memoranda in 1928 that their portion of the sidings had been transferred to the GWR, which had purchased their interest for £479.[142] Corrwg Merthyr Colliery Co. had gone into receivership in 1922 and no one was available to execute an assignment. North End Colliery Co. (1928) Ltd wished to retain their interest and a Memorandum of Agreement dated 20th December 1928 assigned for its use a length at the Briton Ferry end of the northernmost siding holding twelve wagons. These agreements were disclaimed by the liquidator of the North End Colliery Co. in November 1931 and, as this company was in debt, the GWR exercised its power of lien on that part of the siding.

ORGAN

SOUTH WALES MINERAL JCN. R
AND SOUTH WALES MINERAL R
Sheet Nº 3.

PARISH OF BAGLAN HIGHER

A view from the SWMR bridge taken on 2nd June 1954 showing the Blaenavon Branch passing under the Blaenavon Loop and heading into Cwm Gwenffrwd. The tracks converged behind the bushes in the centre.

Courtesy Desmond Coakham

Left: Blaenavon Junction photographed on 2nd June 1954. The Blaenavon Branch curves right then left to pass under the PTR line to Tonmawr by a bridge just visible to the left of the water crane.
Courtesy Desmond Coakham

Below: Looking east towards the junction of the PTR, on the right, and the SWMR, on the far left, beyond the road bridge in the distance. In between are the sidings laid in in 1921 to provide wagon storage for collieries on the Whitworth and Blaenavon branches. This area is now the site of Tonmawr Sports Centre and an industrial estate. The Glyncorrwg Mineral Railway ran along what is now Abergwenffrwd Road on the hillside. Photographed 2nd June 1954. *Courtesy Desmond Coakham*

The same scene as above viewed from the other direction. In the left centre can the seen the PTR line dropping down towards Pontrhydyfen, the course of the SWMR line continuing to Incline Top, and just above it, a rock face marking the site of Tycoed Colliery, later Tonygregos Quarry, which were served by a siding off the SWMR. Note the Iron Mink on the right.
Courtesy Desmond Coakham

TONMAWR JUNCTION

Tonmawr Halt was erected at 5m 49ch adjacent to the bridge which carried Tonmawr Road over the SWMR and SWMJnR. Although only used by passenger trains between 1921 and 1930,[143] the derelict platform remained until the 1950s. A short distance further on the SWMJnR joined the SWMR at Tonmawr West Junction (5m 55ch on SWMJnR, 5m 31ch on SWMR). The passing loop (holding forty-six wagons) and two loop sidings (holding thirty and forty wagons) put in by the PTR in 1898[144] commenced immediately

beyond the junction and converged at 5m 50ch (SWMR mileage). The Whitworth Branch commenced at Tonmawr East Junction (5m 51ch). In GWR days the passing loop became the Up line, but little change was made to the track layout except at the East Junction where a crossing was put in to allow trains from the Whitworth Branch to run directly to the Down line. There were two signal boxes here; the original one on the north side of the loops with eighteen levers was replaced in 1925 by a GWR box alongside the Down line.

LEFT: A view of the Tonmawr area circa 1950 looking towards the 1925 signal box. The left-hand prominent track is the connection for Garth tip siding seen on the right. The bracket signal controlled, from right to left, the siding connection, the SWMJnR to Tonygroes junction, and the SWMR to the terminus at the top of Ynysmaerdy Incline. The junction point for the latter is just visible at the far left of the view.

Courtesy Jason Jarvis

The junction of the PTR (left) and SWMR lines at Tonmawr West Junction on 2nd June 1954 viewed from just beyond the passing loops. The remains of Tonmawr Platform can be seen near the bridge, which was later demolished to make way for a road improvement scheme. The tracks on the left are Garth Tip Siding and its connection to the SWMJnR. The appearance of this part of Tonmawr has changed greatly due to tip reclamation work.

Courtesy Desmond Coakham

SLS Special at Tonmawr East Junction on 29th May 1954. The view is facing to the west. The train is standing on what was by then the Up line. The point in the left foreground was a crossing which enabled trains from the Whitworth Branch to reach the Down line. The point under the engine marks the start of the loop sidings. Railway Terrace can be seen in the upper right. Tonmawr's second signal box, visible in the middle distance, was removed shortly afterwards. *Courtesy Desmond Coakham*

The east end of the loops at Tonmawr where they converged with the main line. The defunct signals controlled the junction to the Whitworth Branch. 2nd June 1954.

Courtesy Desmond Coakham

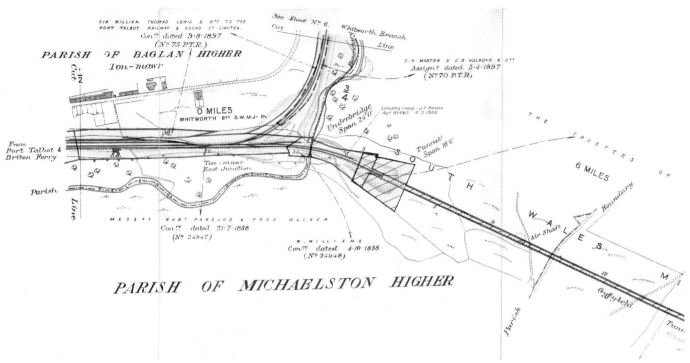

The east end of Tonmawr on 2nd June 1954 with the Whitworth Branch curving away to the left. As originally built the branch joined the track in the foreground before it fanned out into the passing loop and loop sidings. The layout was altered to that shown in 1925.

Courtesy Desmond Coakham

WHITWORTH BRANCH

The Whitworth Branch served a number of small collieries located in remote upland country. It extended for 1m 56ch, although railway maintenance ended at 1m 44ch. The line was steeply graded, including four stretches at 1 in 30/33, to reach an elevation of approximately 700 feet at the terminus. All the points were operated by ground frames and the line was worked by one engine in steam.

GRAIG-DDU COLLIERY (0M 3CH AND 0M 18CH)

The line curved sharply northwards from Tonmawr East Junction to enter upper Cwm Pelenna, initially along the right bank of the river, and immediately reached the loop siding for Graig-Ddu Colliery. Connections existed on the old Whitworth Railway,[145] but these were absent from the list produced for the GWR Officers' Conference in November 1908. The colliery was acquired by the newly formed Tonmawr Collieries Ltd in 1913.[146] Coal was struck at the wrong place and, having spent all the capital, the workings were abandoned on 24th January 1914. The mine was acquired by the Graig-Ddu Colliery Co. Ltd which had been formed in 1922[147] and shared directors with Port Talbot Trading & Transport Ltd.[148] One of the shareholders in the new colliery company was William Cleaver, the PTR's erstwhile engineer. Graig-Ddu Colliery Co. ceased trading in 1933 and the works were abandoned. The loop later became a railway-owned siding.

NORTH END COLLIERY (0M 35CH AND 0M 50CH)

The PTR directors approved an application of John Beamand in July 1911 for a siding connection 35ch up the Whitworth Branch for a new sinking known as North End Colliery, with the stipulation that the colliery sidings were to be arranged so as to obviate the necessity for engines to cross the bridge over the River Pelenna, the colliery being on the left bank. This connection was completed within one month[149] and the siding agreement was made on 28th August 1911.[150] An agreement for a second connection for empty wagons further up the branch was agreed in March 1913.[151] The working instructions forbade engines crossing either of the bridges, the colliery being responsible for all wagon movements on its side of the river. Both connections were transferred to North End Colliery Co. Ltd, which was registered in April 1914 with John Beamand as managing director.[152] This company underwent capital reorganisations in 1920[153] and 1928,[154] and the siding agreement was transferred to the reformed companies.[155] North End Colliery Co. (1928) Ltd went into voluntary liquidation in February 1931 and the agreement was terminated on the 21st of that month. The GWR exercised its lien on all colliery company plant within its boundary and the remainder was acquired by T Jenkins & Sons, of Briton Ferry, for dismantling. A new agreement was made with this firm in March 1932 for the use of both connections and the viaduct over the river.[156] This agreement was terminated in June 1933, but the lower connection remained in use until at least August 1934, the upper junction having been spiked over as the viaduct was unfit for any traffic.

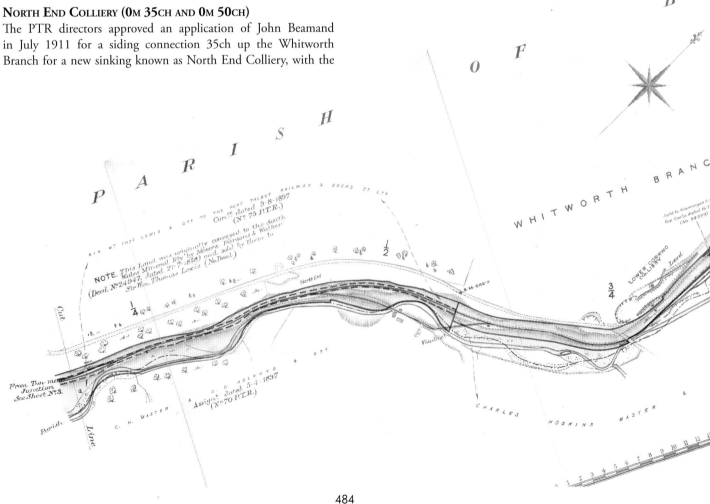

Washout below Blaenmawr, later Garth Tonmawr, Colliery on the Whitworth Branch following a prolonged period of torrential rain in October 1928, viewed from Fforchdwm Viaduct. The small hut is for the weighbridge, with the screens beyond. The colliery sidings consisted of a pair of loops connected at the upper and lower ends to the main line, which hereabouts was on a gradient of 1 in 30. The arches, at the time of this view carrying a minor road, are possibly remnants of Dugdale Houghton's short-lived railway constructed in the 1860s (see Volume 1, Chapter 1). *Courtesy Jason Jarvis*

BLAENMAWR COLLIERY (0M 63CH AND 1M 7CH)

At the ¾ milepost the Whitworth Branch passed under the remains of the three-arch Fforchdwm Viaduct which formerly carried the Glyncorrwg Mineral Railway across the valley. This viaduct was demolished in 1979 as it was considered to be a danger to the public.[157] Mercantile Colliery nearby,[158] to the right of the line, was reported in November 1908 to be unused, but in April 1914 the PTR directors agreed to a new connection for this mine near the ¾ milepost, the old ones seemingly having been taken out. The siding agreement, made with the Mercantile Colliery Co. in July 1914, was transferred in August 1921 to the Blaenmawr Colliery Co. Ltd,[159] which had acquired the colliery in April 1920.[160] A second, inlet, connection was added just above the one milepost by 1925. The Blaenmawr Co. went into receivership in July 1929. By November 1930 the business had been taken over by Garth Collieries Ltd; the original siding agreement was terminated and a revised one made in October 1931.[161] The colliery, latterly known as Garth Tonmawr, was destined to become the last working mine in Cwm Pelenna, the siding agreement being terminated on 27th October 1964.

Garth Tonmawr Colliery on the Whitworth Branch, 1st July 1961. Coal had been worked at this site since at least the 1840s; Fforchdwm Row, just visible above the colliery, dates from that period. The colliery was purchased by Garth Collieries Ltd from the previous owners, the Blaenmawr Colliery Co. Ltd, in 1930 and closed in 1964.

Courtesy Michael Hale

LOWER CORRWG COLLIERY (0M 65CH)

A trailing siding connection for Lower Corrwg Colliery, which was on the left just beyond Fforchdwm Viaduct, was approved by the directors in May 1909. This colliery was also acquired by the newly formed Tonmawr Collieries Ltd in 1913. Attempts to open a new level at Lower Corrwg failed; the workings were abandoned in January 1914 and the leases surrendered.

BRYN CORRWG COLLIERY (1M 11CH AND 1M 20CH)

The GWR approved sidings for this new level in May 1926,[162] although the two connections had been put in about two years earlier. A siding agreement was made in October 1927.[163] This colliery, renamed Graigavon Colliery, was owned by Messrs Jones & Bevan by 1940 and closed in March 1959. The sidings agreement was terminated in June 1961.

TORYBANWEN COLLIERY (1M 31CH AND 1M 45CH)

Another new sinking was for Torybanwen Colliery at the top end of the Whitworth Branch, for which the PTR directors approved a connection in May 1917. This was laid in by March 1918,[164] although the agreement with Torybanwen Collieries Ltd, when it was made in June 1918, provided for two junctions.[165] Work to lay in the second, upper connection for empty wagons began in December 1918,[166] although it was not ready for use until February 1920.[167] Torybanwen Collieries Ltd, which was registered in May 1918,[168] went into liquidation in May 1925 and this business and siding agreement were transferred to the New Glenraven Colliery Co. Ltd. This company too went into liquidation; the agreement was deemed to have been terminated and the sidings were removed by the GWR by January 1931.

CORRWG MERTHYR COLLIERY (1M 38CH)

Further repairs to the upper end of the branch between Mercantile Colliery and the old Whitworth Colliery were authorised by the PTR directors in March 1900 at the request of the Cwm Pelenna Colliery Co., who had acquired the latter colliery and were opening a new level there. This colliery went through several changes of name and ownership until it was purchased by East Kootenay Consols Ltd in October 1916.[169] This company, which was formed in 1898 to prospect for gold in Canada, latterly traded as Cwm Corrwg Merthyr Navigation Collieries, giving rise to the final name of the colliery as Corrwg Merthyr. An agreement with this company dated 29th June 1920 provided for new junctions and sidings at the top end of the Whitworth Branch, all to be put in by the PTR at the colliery's expense.[170] The platform for the workmen's train service to this colliery,[171] provided in 1920, was erected at 1m 34ch. Like several other colliery companies hereabouts this business failed and in August 1922 was in the hands of a receiver. The colliery was abandoned in March 1925 and the junctions and sidings were recovered by the GWR in 1926.

BLAENAVON BRANCH

Although shorter at 0m 79ch than the Whitworth Branch, the Blaenavon Branch served a similar number of collieries, and was worked in the same way. From Blaenavon Branch Junction the line fell slightly and then passed in quick succession under the SWMJnR, the SWMR and the Blaenavon Loop, climbing at 1 in 40/42/147 to a junction with the latter line at 0m 33 ch.[172] This burrowing line was more in keeping with the network of railways in the South London suburbs than a moderately-used branch line in South Wales. The Blaenavon Loop was part of the original Blaenavon Railway and joined the SWMR at Blaenavon Loop Junction (4m 73ch, SWMR mileage). Beyond the junction with the loop the Blaenavon Branch followed the right bank of the River Gwenffrwd over lesser gradients than on the Whitworth Branch, the steepest being 1 in 46 approaching the top end, near to the route of the erstwhile Glyncorrwg Mineral Railway.

Forest Isaf colliery on the Blaenavon Branch looking down the valley towards Blaenavon Junction in 1905. The level was reached by a tramroad on the upper level heading towards the hill on the right.

Courtesy Jason Jarvis

CEFN MORFYDD COLLIERY (0M 34CH AND 0M 47CH)

By 1899 New Forest Colliery[173] had been renamed Forest Isaf Colliery. This had closed by 1906 and part of the site was used for New Forest Quarry, which was itself renamed Tynycwm Quarry in 1909. The colliery workings were reopened by the Cefn Morfydd Colliery Co. Ltd, which was registered in January 1914.[174] The PTR directors agreed to a loop siding with two connections to the Blaenavon Branch in May 1914.[175] The colliery was sold on to the Bryngwyn Colliery Co. Ltd in March 1918,[176] but this was another short-lived business and on 31st December 1926 the GWR deemed the tenancy to have ceased. The colliery was revived by Wenallt Colliery Ltd, which in late 1930 was permitted by the GWR to use a (re)movable tramway of not more than 2ft 10in gauge across the railway at 44ch for conveying spoil from the colliery on the west side of the line by manpower to the east side, and also to use the existing sidings, loading bank and chute.[177] This was an extremely short-lived business, which failed before the agreements could be exchanged, these being terminated on 17th February 1931. Undaunted, the agreements were revived in December 1933, but the colliery closed for good in April 1935 and the tenancy was terminated 26th September 1936.[178]

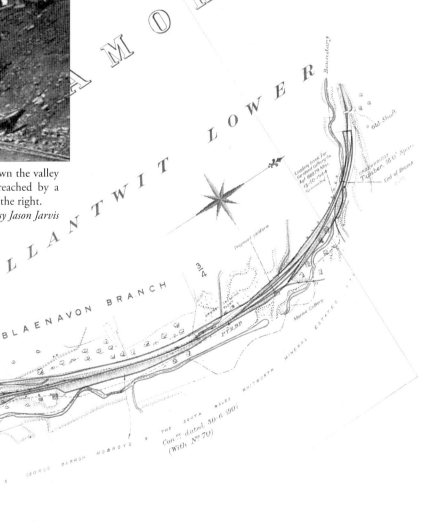

GWENFFRWD QUARRY (0M 56CH)

A siding connection for Gwenffrwd Quarry was authorised by the directors in May 1898. The cost of £90 was to be paid off by an additional 2d per ton on all traffic in and out, implying nearly 11,000 tons. By March 1899 only 134 tons had been carried.[179] The quarry closed circa 1931.

BRYNGRUGOS COLLIERY (0M 60CH AND 0M 70CH)

The two connections put in pre 1899 for Marine Colliery[180] remained unchanged until final closure in 1955, although successive owners tended to change the name, becoming successively Avon Merthyr, Talbot Merthyr, Bryngrugos and finally Marine again. Avon Merthyr Colliery was purchased by the Talbot Merthyr Colliery Ltd in March 1905, which worked the mine until June 1914 when the company went into voluntary liquidation.[181] The colliery was acquired by the Bryngrugos Colliery Co. Ltd in March 1918,[182] thereby giving rise to its fourth name. This business ceased trading circa 1927. The colliery was taken over by John Faraday and worked under the original name of Marine Colliery. A revised loop siding for this colliery was put in by the GWR in 1931.[183] The siding agreement was terminated in December 1955, when it was noted that no traffic had passed for a considerable time.

MERTHYR LLANTWIT COLLIERY (0M 62CH AND 0M 74CH)

Llantwit Merthyr Colliery was on the opposite side of the valley to Bryngrugos Colliery and was accessed by bridges over the river. Likewise, the two connections put in pre 1899[184] remained unchanged until closure, although here too the name changed with the owner, becoming in turn Merthyr Llantwit and finally Blaenavon.[185] George William Baker, the final owner, terminated the siding agreement on 30th April 1931.[186]

WHITWORTH COLLIERY (CIRCA 0M 68CH)

The prospect of significant colliery development in Cwm Gwenffrwd was heralded by the registration in September 1905 of Whitworth Collieries Ltd, with a nominal capital of £600,000. The objects of this company were to enter into an agreement with South Wales Whitworth Mineral Estates Ltd to acquire its surface and mineral properties of 3,697 and 6,526 acres respectively, and to carrying on business as colliery proprietors.[187] Most of the shareholders were German; Col Wright was a director for the first year of the new company's existence. The proposed connection of the new Whitworth Colliery to the Blaenavon Branch was approved in May 1906, although the plan, which included slewing the bridge carrying the SWMR over the Blaenavon Branch, was not finalised until the following December. The relaying of the upper portion of the Blaenavon Branch adjacent to the connection was approved in November 1907.

An agreement dealing with shipping rates and the junction was sealed on 23rd January 1907.[188] The latter provided for a "temporary railway for the purposes of construction," completed in April 1907, which was to be followed by a permanent connection.[189] The agreement also prohibited the colliery from making a connection to "some other railway" – that is, the SWMR – unless the PTR was unable to take the traffic. The PTR directors were informed in March 1907 that the SWMR would agree to the bridge under its tracks being altered to provide convenient access to the colliery; the agreement was, however, on condition that the PTR did not object to the SWMR making its own connection from their line to the colliery for the purpose of taking traffic for Briton Ferry and beyond. No doubt reluctantly, the condition was agreed. It is not certain that the bridge was in fact altered.

Sinking the first shaft commenced in April 1907, but steam coal of the Rhondda No. 2 seam was not reached until February 1911.[190] Problems with drainage and finance resulted in a receiver being appointed in December 1911. Whitworth Collieries ceased carrying on business in November 1913 and was finally dissolved in January 1915.[191] The temporary siding trailed off the Blaenavon Branch, crossed the river and ran back down the valley for about 600 yards to the workings.

TYNYCWM COLLIERY (0M 76CH)

Starting in 1912, attempts were made to open up a colliery at the top end of the Blaenavon Branch, above the point where it crossed the river by a wooden underbridge. In April that year the directors approved an agreement for a siding connection for Tynycwm Colliery which had been entered into with Thomas Hughes on 17th February 1912, apparently on behalf of Brynafon Colliery Co. Ltd.[192] After some delay apparently caused by Hughes' uncertainty as to proceeding, the connection was completed in March 1913.[193] However, nothing further was done and the siding connection was removed, the colliery company having gone into voluntary liquidation.[194] The siding agreement was eventually cancelled by the GWR in 1925.

OAKLAND COLLIERY (0M 76CH)

The connection was reinstated for the Oakland Colliery Co. in July 1914,[195] but the sidings were never laid in as planned. The GWR deemed this particularly agreement to have been terminated on 30th June 1925. The third and final agreement was made in September 1915, this time with the Oakland Colliery Co. Ltd.[196] This company purchased the colliery in June 1914 and worked it until it ceased trading in January 1926.[197] The business and siding agreement were acquired by Ton yr Rhondda Colliery Ltd,[198] as from 1st October 1927, and the colliery was renamed accordingly. This colliery company failed in June 1928 and in December 1929 the GWR recovered the siding material in lieu of the amount it was owed.

A poor but probably unique view looking east of Merthyr Llantwit Colliery near the top end of the Blaenavon Branch in 1905. This colliery was situated about 70 yards back from the branch and connected to it by a curvaceous loop which crossed the intervening River Gwenffrwd twice. *Courtesy Jason Jarvis*

PORT TALBOT DOCK BRANCH

The Dock Branch consisted of that part of Railway No. 1 authorised by the 1894 Act from where it commenced in the dock area, which was the zero mileage point, to Duffryn Junction, a distance of 2m 1ch. The branch was easily graded, dropping in elevation from about 70 feet at the junction to 25 feet at the docks. The tracks from the junction converged into single line opposite the carriage shed and immediately passed over Chapel of Ease level crossing, which was operated from a small cabin alongside.

DUFFRYN SIDINGS

These sidings were located immediately south of Chapel of Ease Crossing (see pp. 422–3 for the map of the route from Duffryn Sidings to the crossing of the South Wales main line) and comprised four loop sidings for marshalling trains holding thirty-one to thirty-three wagons each, six storage sidings holding thirty to forty-two wagons, an engineering siding holding forty-two wagons and a siding which could hold up to thirty-six crippled wagons. The outlet for these sidings at the southern end was controlled by Duffryn

No. 3 signal cabin (1m 52ch). This box also controlled the oblique level crossing over Varna Terrace known as Doctor's Crossing. A short shunting neck was provided so that engines did not block the crossing.

COPPER WORKS JUNCTION

The line then curved round Taibach, crossed the High Street (the present-day A48) by a brick-arch bridge and then the GWR main line by a lattice-girder bridge to enter the dock area. At 1m 3ch the line became double track, then crossed the Morfa Railway by a girder bridge and dropped down to Copper Works Junction. This junction had been completely remodelled in 1915 and a new signal box provided at 0m 64ch with forty-eight levers, replacing the earlier one at 0m 61ch.[199] From hereon the Dock Branch was quadruple tracked, with Up and Down 'Fast' lines flanked by 'Slow' lines. The main reception grids, Nos 6–8 (PTR numbering) were on the left, and No. 1 on the right. The Dock Branch Extension commenced beyond the zero mile point, leading to the empty-wagon grid on Morfa Newydd and to the grids serving the tips and conveyors on the South Side of the dock.

RIGHT: Chapel of Ease Crossing, photographed on 30th May 1958. This small cabin contained four levers for working the crossing gates and locks which were released by Duffryn No. 1 signal box nearby. The bracket signal controlled the entrance to Duffryn Sidings just beyond the crossing. *Author's collection*

BELOW: Duffryn Sidings circa 1930. The main line is nearest the camera with the four loop sidings beyond, in one of which is a train of pit props. A GWR pannier tank engine is standing in the dead-end sidings. *Author's collection*

PORT TALBOT DOCKS

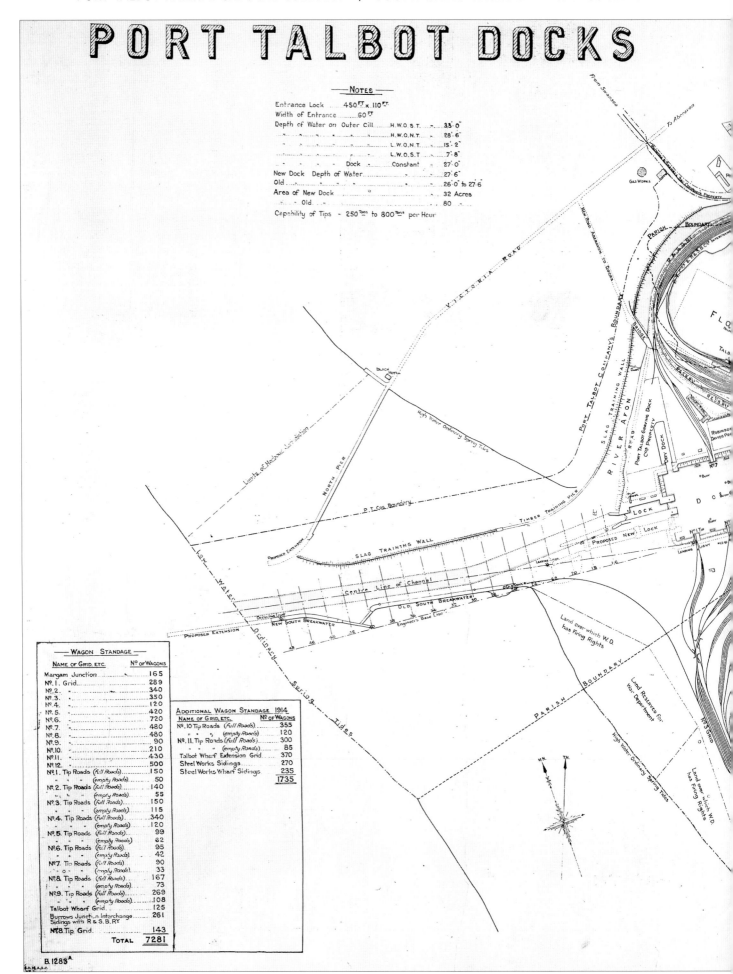

NOTES

Entrance Lock	450 FT x 110 FT
Width of Entrance	60 FT
Depth of Water on Outer Cill ... H.W.O.S.T.	33' 0"
" " " " " H.W.O.N.T.	28' 6"
" " " " " L.W.O.N.T.	15' 2"
" " " " " L.W.O.S.T.	7' 8"
" " " Dock ... Constant	27' 0"
New Dock Depth of Water	27' 6"
Old " " " "	26' 0" to 27'.6"
Area of New Dock "	32 Acres
" " Old "	80 "
Capability of Tips - 250 Tons to 800 Tons per Hour	

WAGON STANDAGE

NAME OF GRID, ETC.	No OF WAGONS
Margam Junction	165
No. 1. Grid	289
No. 2. "	340
No. 3. "	350
No. 4. "	120
No. 5. "	420
No. 6. "	720
No. 7. "	480
No. 8. "	480
No. 9. "	90
No. 10. "	210
No. 11. "	430
No. 12. "	500
No. 1. Tip Roads (Full Roads)	150
" " (empty Roads)	50
No. 2. Tip Roads (Full Roads)	140
" " (empty Roads)	55
No. 3. Tip Roads (Full Roads)	150
" " (empty Roads)	115
No. 4. Tip Roads (Full Roads)	340
" " (empty Roads)	120
No. 5. Tip Roads (Full Roads)	99
" " (empty Roads)	62
No. 6. Tip Roads (Full Roads)	95
" " (empty Roads)	42
No. 7. Tip Roads (Full Roads)	90
" " (empty Roads)	33
No. 8. Tip Roads (Full Roads)	167
" " (empty Roads)	73
No. 9. Tip Roads (Full Roads)	269
" " (empty Roads)	108
Talbot Wharf Grid	125
Burrows Junction Interchange Sidings with R & S.B. RY	261
No. 8 Tip Grid	143
TOTAL	**7281**

ADDITIONAL WAGON STANDAGE 1914

NAME OF GRID, ETC.	No OF WAGONS
No. 10 Tip Roads (Full Roads)	355
" " (empty Roads)	120
No. 11. Tip Roads (Full Roads)	300
" " (empty Roads)	85
Talbot Wharf Extension Grid	370
Steel Works Sidings	270
Steel Works Wharf Sidings	235
	1735

B.1283 A

This map of Port Talbot Docks stamped 6th July 1922 shows the extent of developments there at the time of the grouping, the most prominent new feature being Baldwins' Margam Steelworks. The tables at the bottom left-hand corner reveal that the docks had standage for a total of 9,016 wagons. *Author's collection*

SCALE OF FEET

Duffryn Sidings in BR days, showing Doctor's Crossing and Duffryn No. 3 signal box at the bottom left of the view.

Author's collection

ABOVE: Duffryn Yard was the last shed of GWR No. 296, the former TVR 'O4' Class 0-6-2T No. 94, which is seen passing over Doctor's Crossing heading towards Copper Works Junction on 24th June 1948. Duffryn No. 3 signal box is visible above the cab. This engine was withdrawn in September 1949. *Courtesy R K Blencowe*

BELOW: The second Copper Works Junction signal box of 1914 was situated at a fairly isolated position where the Dock Branch, the West Curve and the OVER converged on the main line running through the New Dock area. A train from the Duffryn Junction direction may just be discerned to the right of the box. This view with Margam Steelworks in the background was taken from a position alongside the Military Road on 30th April 1946, just prior to commencement of the major alterations associated with the new Abbey Works. *Author's collection*

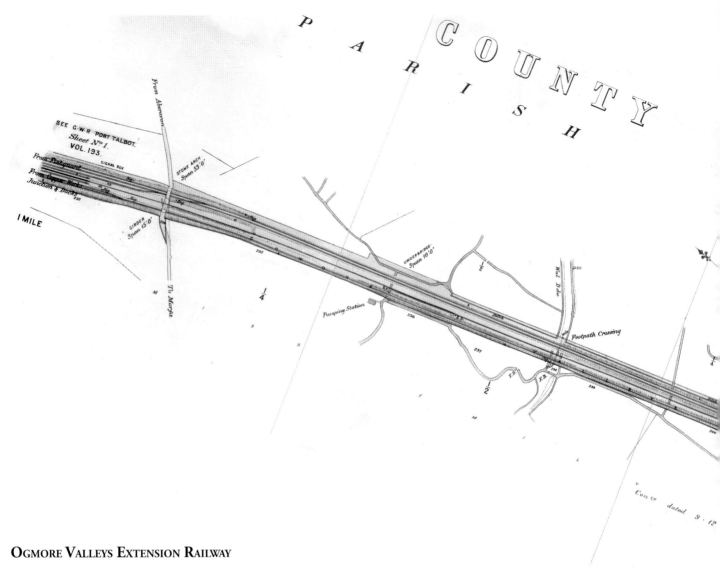

Ogmore Valleys Extension Railway

The OVER commenced at Copper Works Junction and followed a fairly level route until 4m 52ch, where it began to climb steadily at about 1 in 70 to Cefn Junction with the Porthcawl Branch of the GWR. The line from Newlands onwards served a number of collieries which worked the Southern Outcrop.

The double track OVER shortly passed the site of Morfa Crossing Halt erected at 0m 17ch, in conjunction with the use of German prisoners of war in the construction of Margam Steelworks,[200] and then crossed the Morfa Railway on the level to reach the connection with Margam West Junction on the GWR (0m 30ch). This junction was the western outlet for Margam Exchange sidings which, prior to the GWR working the PTR, were designated as shown in Table 21.1.

After 1908 the use of Nos 3 and 4 was changed to handle traffic from the GWR intended for the docks, the Duffryn Valley and the SWMJnR. A connection was made at 0m 48ch on the OVER with Margam East Junction on the GWR for eastbound traffic, and at 0m 66ch there was a direct connection for westbound traffic off the OVER. The OVER became single track at 1m 7ch and ran parallel to the GWR main line until the 2½ milepost where it curved away, then swung back to cross the GWR near the 3¼ milepost and reach Newlands Loop (3m 36ch to 3m 62ch).

Newlands Colliery (3m 65ch)

In February 1913 Baldwins Ltd, through Cribbwr Fawr Collieries Ltd, applied for a siding connection for a new sinking with an estimated daily output of 2,000 tons being contemplated near the 4 milepost on the OVER. The connection was eventually agreed to in April 1914, but the outbreak of the First World War precluded much being done to develop this colliery. Work commenced towards the end of the war. A temporary siding was laid in in February 1918[201] and removed in October 1921.[202] An agreement for a permanent connection at 3m 76ch, made on 19th June 1920, stipulated that the three loop sidings nearest the OVER were for loaded wagons and the fourth, leading to the rear of the colliery, was for empties.[203] The connection was laid at a cost of £790 and brought into use by 14th January 1921,[204] although not inspected by Col Pringle until September 1921, when he stipulated that trains were to be taken off the main line before shunting commenced.[205] The connection remained in use until the agreement was terminated on 31st March 1968, the NCB having announced the closure date of the colliery to be 23rd January 1968. Newlands Colliery Halt, for workmen's trains, was situated at 4m 18ch.[206]

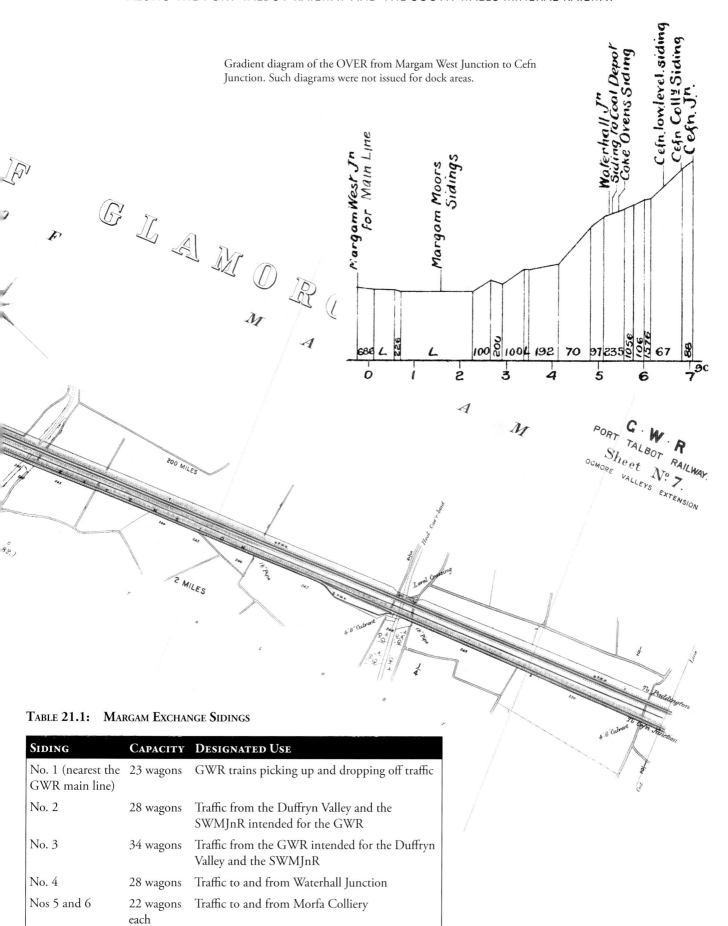

Gradient diagram of the OVER from Margam West Junction to Cefn Junction. Such diagrams were not issued for dock areas.

TABLE 21.1: MARGAM EXCHANGE SIDINGS

SIDING	CAPACITY	DESIGNATED USE
No. 1 (nearest the GWR main line)	23 wagons	GWR trains picking up and dropping off traffic
No. 2	28 wagons	Traffic from the Duffryn Valley and the SWMJnR intended for the GWR
No. 3	34 wagons	Traffic from the GWR intended for the Duffryn Valley and the SWMJnR
No. 4	28 wagons	Traffic to and from Waterhall Junction
Nos 5 and 6	22 wagons each	Traffic to and from Morfa Colliery

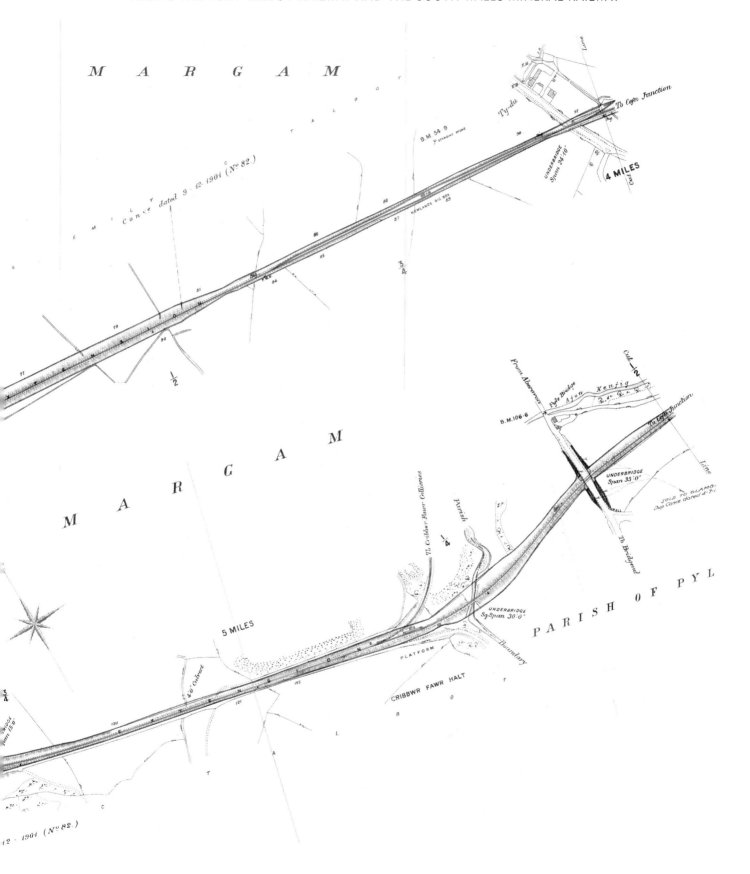

CRIBBWR FAWR COLLIERY (4M 76CH)

Small-scale coal working commenced at Coalbrook about one mile north of Pyle circa 1903. Initially the coal was taken by road to the coal yard at the western end of Waterhall Sidings, a practice which generated a succession of complaints from Penybont Rural District Council to the agents, Messrs D. Treharne and Co. of Swansea, regarding damage caused to the highway.[207] The colliery was acquired by Cribbwr Fawr Collieries Ltd in 1905, who set about a major expansion. It changed hands again in 1916, when Baldwins acquired it to ensure a supply of coking coal to its Margam coke ovens.[208] The PTR directors approved a siding connection in November 1905 near the 5 milepost on the OVER, and somewhat unusually agreed to construct the junction, the half mile long connection and all the associated sidings at the colliery, for the sum of £1,420. This work was reported to be complete in October 1906,[209] and the sidings, which were capable of taking any of the company's larger engine, were handed over the following month. The standard siding agreement between the two companies was sealed on 21st May 1907.[210] This colliery was abandoned in January 1928 but the siding connection was not taken out of use until April 1961. A halt for workmen's trains was constructed at 5m 0ch near the siding connection.[211]

Newlands Colliery, Pyle

LEFT: Work to develop Newlands Colliery started following the end of the First World War and this postcard view dated circa 1920 shows the surface workings under construction. The colliery consisted of slants and one shaft, the headgear for which is visible in the distance.
Author's collection

BELOW: Cribbwr Fawr Colliery circa 1908, after being taken over by Cribbwr Fawr Collieries Ltd. Postcard, postally used 14th August 1916.
Author's collection

Cribbwr Fawr Colliery, Pyle

ABOVE: A later view of Cribbwr Fawr Colliery than on the previous page, seen here after it had been taken over by Baldwins in 1916. By this date a number of changes to the surface workings are apparent. *Author's collection*

BELOW: Baldwins' Cribbwr Fawr Colliery circa 1921. Most of the coal wagons present belong to the colliery owner or associated companies, but there are at least three lettered for Ton Phillip. *NM&GW*

WATERHALL JUNCTION

Waterhall Junction with the Pyle Branch was reached at 5m 50ch and was situated at the western end of Waterhall Sidings. These consisted of long loops on both the Up and Down sides, each with a trailing crossover to the main line at about the mid point, and a further loop on the Up side. All but the eastern entry to the Down loop at 6m 4ch were worked from Waterhall Sidings signal box on the Down side at 5m 57ch. Entry to the Down Loop was worked by a ground frame. The sidings for the former Bryndu Colliery and coke ovens at 5m 58ch were adapted and extended to provide five marshalling sidings, a siding for crippled wagons, and a goods siding. A two-road coal yard running off the Down Loop, sometimes wrongly identified as the site of Penylan engine shed, was situated adjacent to Waterhall Junction.

The 75-chain Pyle Branch ran for the most part on the track bed of the old C&PR to reach exchange sidings with the GWR at Pyle. There were no industries on this line, the only distinguishing feature being Apple Tree Level Crossing over Kenfig Road in Pyle. A daily return service was scheduled in the early days, but by 1907 trains ran as necessary, on a one engine in steam basis. The loops at the Pyle end were extended by the GWR and the branch was used for wagon storage. The portion from Waterhall Junction as far as the 60ch point was lifted in 1958 and the remainder closed in 1965.

BRYNDU COLLIERY (5M 68CH)

Bryndu Colliery had been in existence since 1839[212] and, together with Cefn Colliery near Cefn Junction, was by 1898 owned by Bryndu & Port Talbot Collieries Ltd. Following an agreement dated 1st June 1898, William Blindell had purchased these collieries and coke ovens from Miss Talbot[213] and later that year sold them to this newly registered company in which he was to become the major shareholder.[214] Mr Knox, Miss Talbot's agent, was one of the original subscribers, possibly as her nominee. Before the OVER had opened for traffic the colliery company had enquired if the railway would provide two sidings to accommodate its traffic if it guaranteed 500 tons of coal per day.[215] This request was declined as being excessive, but in April 1900 it was reported that the two sidings for dealing with the colliery traffic at their adjacent coke ovens were in very bad state of repair and required to be relaid at once, as the rails and sleepers were worn out, having been in use since 1875.[216] This task was completed by September 1900.[217]

Bryndu & Port Talbot Colliery Co. was not a commercial success. In March 1902 the colliery company asked for a reduction in the rate from the colliery to its Cefn coke ovens. This was declined, but a discount was offered provided accounts were paid promptly, the outstanding balance was cleared and excessive shunting at the coke ovens ceased. The following month the directors resolved that if the arrears were not paid forthwith traffic would not be handled. In June 1902 Blindell was informed that if the monthly account was not paid he would be asked to pay as guarantor, failing which the colliery traffic would be stopped and coal and wagons seized as lien. By September 1903 the directors' patience was exhausted and they decreed that there would be no further haulage unless an advance to cover the estimated monthly account was paid. Other creditors had also had enough and the colliery company was wound up by a High Court order on 10th November 1903.[218]

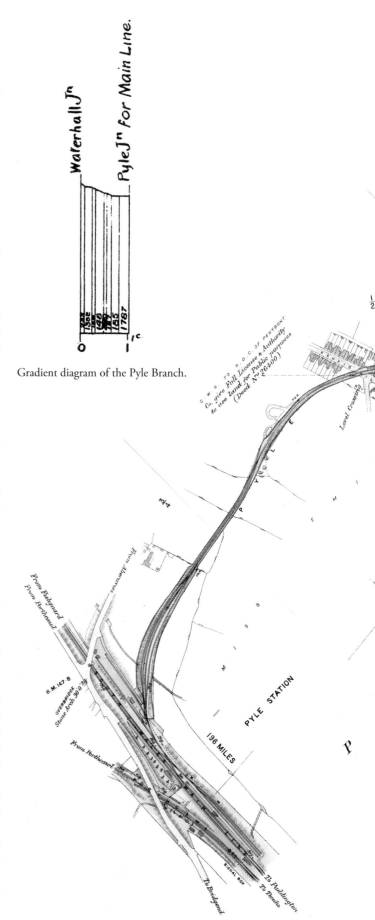

Gradient diagram of the Pyle Branch.

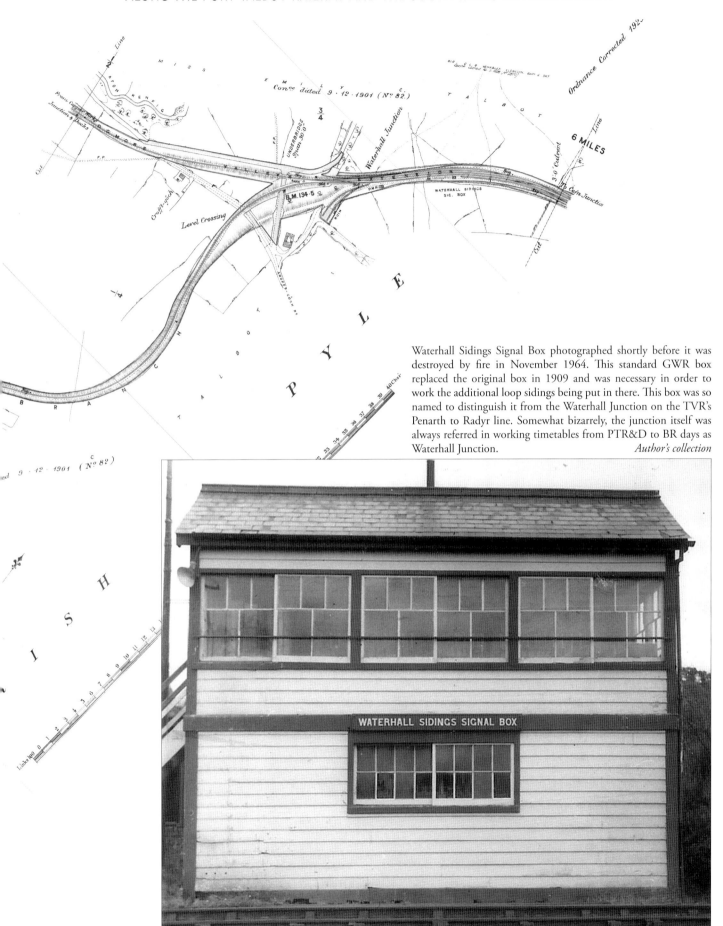

Waterhall Sidings Signal Box photographed shortly before it was destroyed by fire in November 1964. This standard GWR box replaced the original box in 1909 and was necessary in order to work the additional loop sidings being put in there. This box was so named to distinguish it from the Waterhall Junction on the TVR's Penarth to Radyr line. Somewhat bizarrely, the junction itself was always referred in working timetables from PTR&D to BR days as Waterhall Junction. *Author's collection*

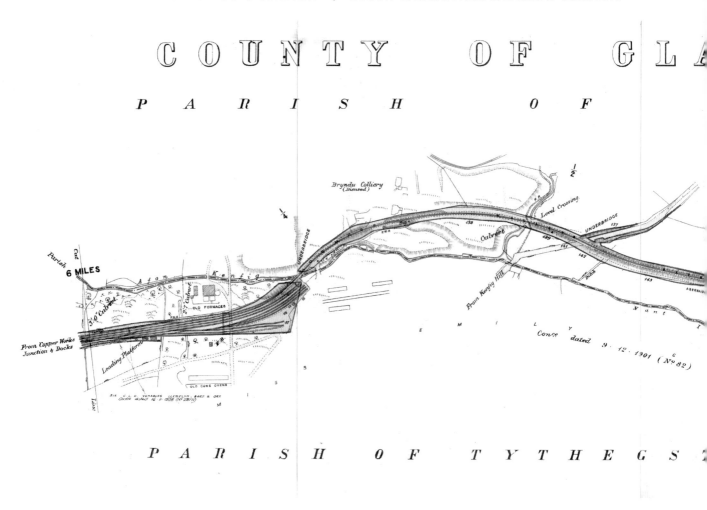

Surprisingly, this was not the end. Production continued and a new siding connection was laid in in January 1909.[219] The colliery finally became idle in February 1914 when the company was wound up. It was then revealed that Miss Talbot had endeavoured to keep this unremunerative colliery working and ensure the jobs of 500 employees, at a personal loss of nearly £100,000.[220]

ABERBAIDEN COLLIERY (6M 40CH AND 6M 56CH)

A connection to Cefn Low Level Siding, as the line to the former Cefn Ironworks was known, for Aberbaiden Colliery was approved in May 1900 and in use by the following August.[221] This colliery was owned by Wright, Butler & Co., and became part of Baldwins in 1902. In 1905 the existing loop siding was extended westwards and two new connections were laid in.[222] The loop was also extended eastwards to connect with Cefn Low Level Siding which served Ton Philip Colliery. By 1920 the traffic generated here required the provision of an electric train staff pillar so that shunting could take place clear of the main line. Aberbaiden Colliery was served by a three-quarters of a mile long private railway, the first third of which was double track. The colliery also worked Pentre Slant, connected by a half mile long tramway. Both were closed in January 1959. Maintenance of the Low Level Siding passed to the Margam Estate in October 1931.[223]

TON PHILLIP COLLIERY (6M 65CH)

Ton Phillip Rhondda Colliery Co. Ltd was registered in October 1898 with an initial capital of £5,000.[224] By June 1914 Baldwins Ltd owned half the shares and the directors had been replaced by Baldwins' directors.

The Ton Phillip Rhondda Colliery Co. began a new sinking near Cefn Ironworks in 1898 and its request for a connection to Cefn Low Level Siding was approved by the railway's directors in April 1899.[225] This siding required relaying, and the siding and new connection were reported to be in use in January 1900.[226] A new junction was laid in in 1907 in conjunction with improvements at the colliery.[227] The colliery was one mile to the east of Aberbaiden and was connected to the OVER by a one and a quarter mile siding. About halfway along, this siding split to make a connection to the colliery company's Tytalwyn Colliery which was situated midway between Aberbaiden and Ton Phillip. To works these long sidings a total of three engines were acquired.[228] Ton Phillip and Tytalwyn collieries closed by 1945, but the latter was resurrected by the Tytalwyn Colliery Company (1942) Ltd and worked with Aberbaiden Colliery until closure in 1959.

Cefn Low level Siding also served Mill Pit, which was owned by Bryndu & Port Talbot Collieries Ltd. Mill Pit was closed in 1913 but retained as a pumping station. Mill Pit, or Kenfig Disposal

502

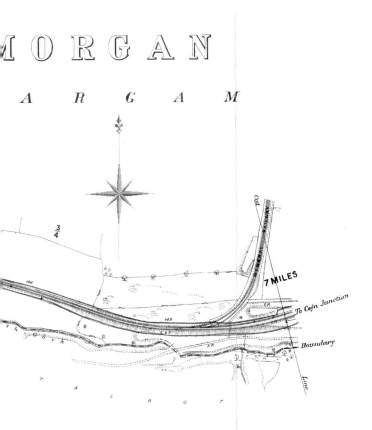

Point, was established on the site in the 1950s. Associated with this scheme, BR obtained powers in 1990 to deviate the OVER hereabouts for a distance of about 650 yards.[229]

MARSHALL STONEHOUSE (6M 66CH)

In July 1905 the directors approved a siding for Messrs Marshall Stonehouse near Cefn Ironworks to permit the removal of slag, the agreement being dated 18th September 1905.[230] Some of the slag was taken onwards by the GWR via the C&PR and Pyle Junction and points were relaid there in anticipation.[231] Marshall Stonehouse informed the PTR in May 1914 that they had no further use for this siding and offered it to the railway for £100. This was accepted and a further £100 was spent in converting it into storage sidings which were needed there.

CEFN JUNCTION

The OVER then ran past the disused Cefn Ironworks and Cefn Colliery, latterly owned by Bryndu & Port Talbot Collieries Ltd and which had closed in 1912. The line became double track at 7m 24ch, later extended back to 7m 10ch, in order to make a double junction with the loop on the Porthcawl Branch of the GWR at Cefn Junction (7m 40ch).

Baldwins' Aberbaiden Colliery looking south, with the entrance to the slant going underground at the bottom right. The tramroad from Pentre Slant comes in from the right. This colliery used wire haulage to bring up empties along the three-quarters of a mile long siding from the OVER.

Author's collection

Mill Pit was sunk by the Bryndu & Port Talbot Colliery Co. circa 1900 and was reached by a connection off Cefn Low Level Siding. This colliery closed in 1913 due to poor geological conditions. *NM&GW*

NM&GW

Mill Pit viewed from the other side. After closure this pit was used as a pumping station for the nearly Ton Phillip Colliery.

Tytalwyn Colliery was situated about halfway between Aberbaiden and Ton Phillip collieries and was served by a long siding connection from the OVER. Colliery-owned locomotives worked this private railway, as seen here. Postcard, postally used 12th August 1912.

Author's collection

CEFN CRIBWR COLLIERY. KENFIG HILL.

NM&GW

Cefn Colliery and the junction of the OVER with the GWR at Cefn Junction. The colliery appears to be abandoned, putting the date post-1912.

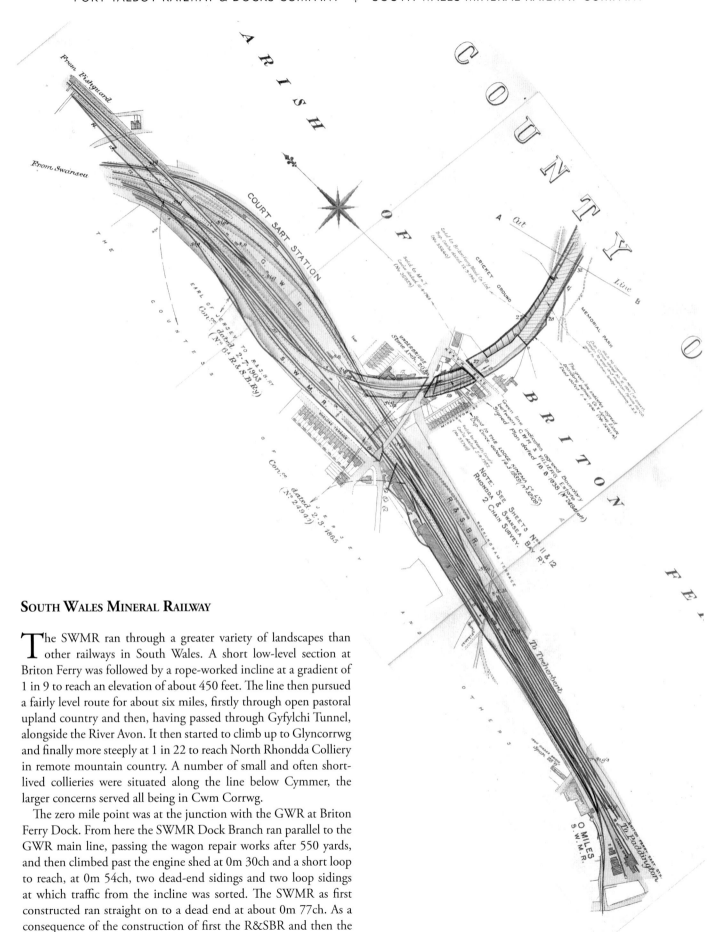

SOUTH WALES MINERAL RAILWAY

The SWMR ran through a greater variety of landscapes than other railways in South Wales. A short low-level section at Briton Ferry was followed by a rope-worked incline at a gradient of 1 in 9 to reach an elevation of about 450 feet. The line then pursued a fairly level route for about six miles, firstly through open pastoral upland country and then, having passed through Gyfylchi Tunnel, alongside the River Avon. It then started to climb up to Glyncorrwg and finally more steeply at 1 in 22 to reach North Rhondda Colliery in remote mountain country. A number of small and often short-lived collieries were situated along the line below Cymmer, the larger concerns served all being in Cwm Corrwg.

The zero mile point was at the junction with the GWR at Briton Ferry Dock. From here the SWMR Dock Branch ran parallel to the GWR main line, passing the wagon repair works after 550 yards, and then climbed past the engine shed at 0m 30ch and a short loop to reach, at 0m 54ch, two dead-end sidings and two loop sidings at which traffic from the incline was sorted. The SWMR as first constructed ran straight on to a dead end at about 0m 77ch. As a consequence of the construction of first the R&SBR and then the

Gradient diagram of the full length of the SWMR from the junction with the R&SBR at Neath Junction via Briton ferry and the incline to North Rhondda.

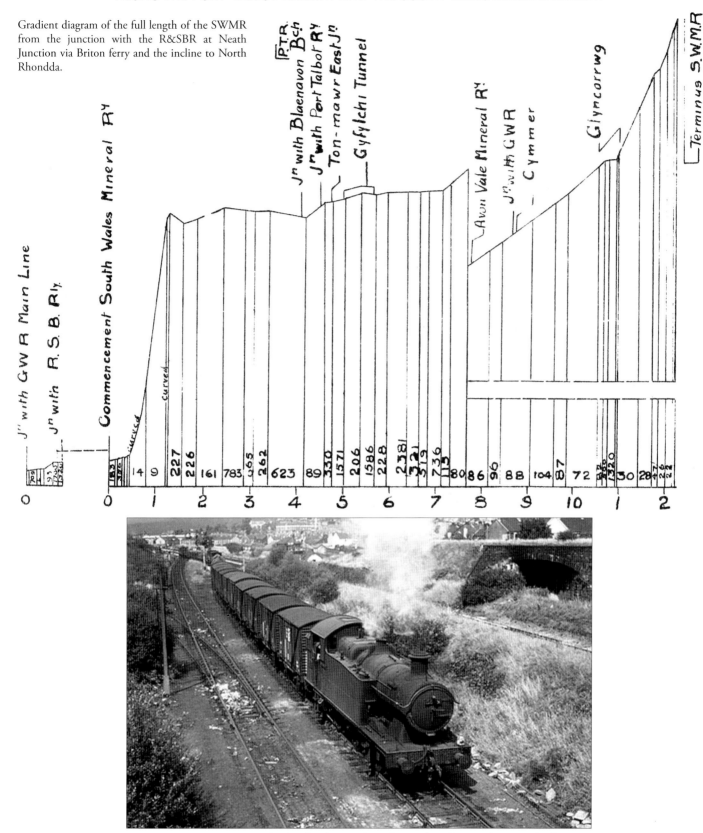

Ex-GWR 0-6-2T No. 5675 heads a freight train from the South Wales main line onto the former SWMR at Court Sart Junction circa 1964. The engine is close to the site of the former SWMR engine shed. The partially dismantled bridge on the right carried the SWMR over the main line, the R&SBR, and latterly the Up flying loop, towards the bottom of Ynysmaerdy Incline. The track layout hereabouts underwent several alterations over the years, firstly in conjunction with the construction of the R&SBR, then with the flying loops, and finally simplification under BR. Court Sart Down Junction signals are just visible above the second van. *Author's collection*

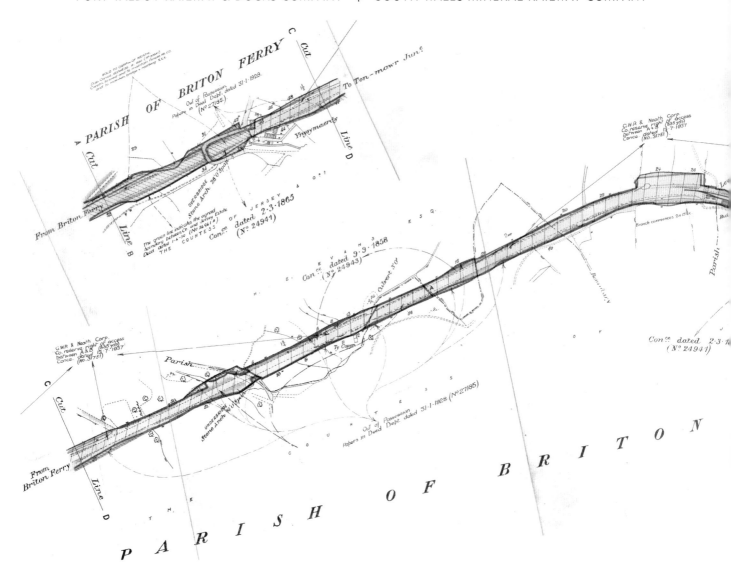

flying junction with the GWR at Court Sart, the SWMR curved round to join the R&SBR at Neath Junction (18m 28ch from Treherbert).[232] The SWMR main line curved back away from the Dock Branch at the southern end of the marshalling sidings, crossed over the GWR and R&SBR, opened out to two and then four tracks at the bottom of Ynysmaerdy Incline (1m 20ch), these tracks being protected by two short run-off sidings. When the track was removed from the closed incline, the line was severed in the two-track section just before the bridge over Neath Road, Briton Ferry. The two sidings and release crossover that remained were known as Balls Yard, although not on the GWR Property Survey.

The two-track incline was just under one mile long and at the top end ran through a deep rock cutting. The brake house at the top, the foundations of which are still visible, was situated on the north side of the tracks and operated a 21 feet diameter brake drum with a 12 feet diameter guide sheave.[233] Three loop sidings were provided for dividing Down trains into suitable lengths for descending the incline and recombining Up trains. These loops were at the western end of the main part of the SWMR; a single road engine shed, which housed one engine in 1907, was erected here near the 2¼ milepost. Following the closure of the incline the SWMR terminated at the 2m 14ch point.

Eskyn Colliery (2m 40ch)

Two further loop sidings were provided just beyond the top of Ynysmaerdy Incline between 2m 25ch and 2m 40ch. These saw little use after the closure of the incline and in April 1913 Gilbertson & Co.'s application to use the most southerly siding to load coal from its new level at Eskyn Colliery was agreed to at an additional 2d per ton. Later that year the SWMR agreed to a short siding being put in by the colliery at its own expense, presumably to allow more convenient loading of the coal, although an agreement was not signed until April 1915.[234] The colliery became a limited company in 1919, but restricted itself to hiring out wagons, the level having been idle since 1918, and ceased all operation in December 1920.[235] The siding and connection were removed shortly afterwards.

Crythan Platform (2m 54ch)

This platform was situated alongside the bridge which carried the old Cwmavon to Neath mountain road over the SWMR. A lockup/shelter was provided which presumably served the nearby farms and the unofficial passengers travelling to and from Neath when the Glyncorrwg Colliery Co. worked the SWMR. There is nothing to suggest it was used once the PTR took over working the line.

Eskyn Colliery level was opened in December 1910 by a Mr E L Davies. This 1911 view shows the entire workforce of sixteen underground men and one at the surface, presumably the boy, with the foreman Tom Llewellyn on the far left. *Courtesy Roy Evans*

Crythan Platform at 2m 54ch on the SWMR. The road bridge was seemingly built wide enough to span two tracks. *Author's collection*

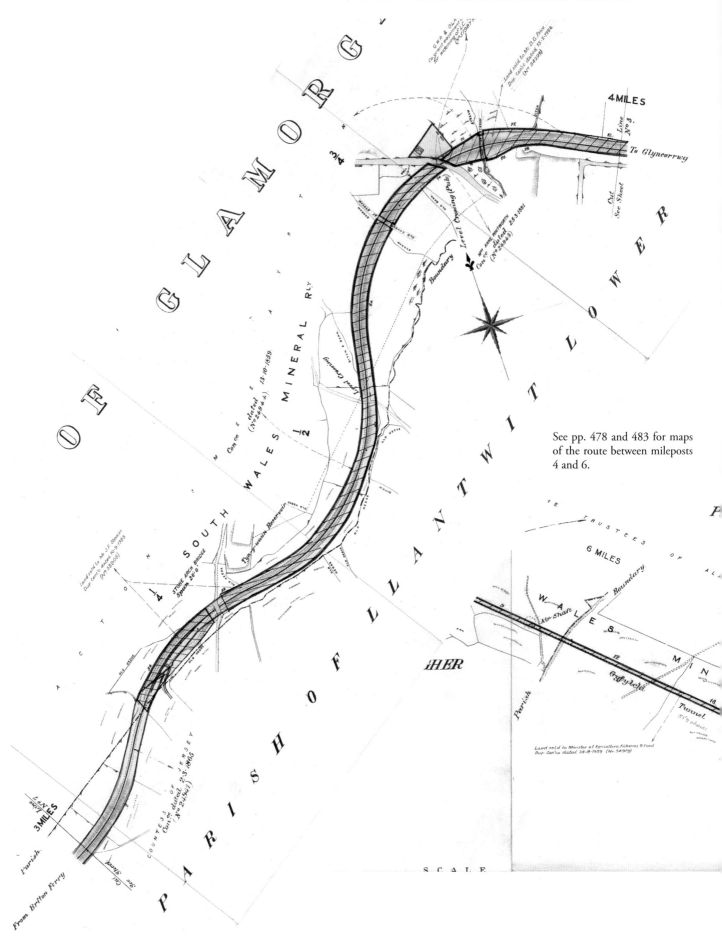

See pp. 478 and 483 for maps
of the route between mileposts
4 and 6.

BWLCH COLLIERY (3M 21CH)

Bwlch Colliery Co. Ltd was formed in November 1917 to take over and work some mineral leases previously owned by Messrs Baldwins.[236] A siding connection was under construction in November 1919,[237] subsequently formalised in an agreement dated 10th January 1920.[238] The agreement required the colliery company to lay in a siding holding ten wagons leading to two screen roads, each holding five loaded wagons and five empties. A second junction nearer Briton Ferry was to be put in when called for by the PTR. This was another colliery company that failed in the 1920s, being wound up in March 1926, the receiver being appointment by the Oaklands Colliery Co. as a result of a default on debentures totalling £8,000. The GWR cancelled the siding agreement on 29th September 1927.

ABERNANT QUARRY (4M 32CH)

A short-lived siding for Abernant Quarry was put in in 1909 for a Mr Morris and taken out of use the following year.[239]

ABER RHONDDA COLLIERY (4M 40CH)

An agreement was signed on 16th February 1920 with Messrs Davies & Sons for a siding connection at this point; the colliery was intended to work old levels there. The colliery company was required to lay in a siding holding twenty wagons.[240] The siding agreement was taken over by Messrs Bevan and McCarthy in August 1925, but

two months later McCarthy had surrendered his interest and Bevan was bankrupt. The GWR regarded the tenancy as expired on 30th June 1925, but retained the siding in anticipation of the colliery being reopened. This became increasingly unlikely and in October 1940 decided to remove the junction and siding.

TONYGREGOS QUARRY (4M 66CH)

This quarry was situated on the site of Tycoed Colliery and was in existence by December 1896,[241] but had closed by 1930.

BLAENAVON AND TONMAWR JUNCTIONS

The SWMR then reached in quick succession Blaenavon Loop Junction (4m 73ch), the connections for the loops that made up Tonmawr Sidings (4m 78ch and 5m 20ch), and Tonmawr West Junction (5m 31ch) as already described (see p. 478). Beyond Tonmawr East Junction (5m 51ch) for the Whitworth Branch the SWMR crossed the River Pelenna and entered the 1,109-yard Gyfylchi Tunnel (5m 64ch to 6m 35ch). The line emerged into the Avon Valley about 150 feet above the river and passed the site of the junction with R&SBR's railway No. 8 at 6m 70ch.[242] The SWMR maintained a level course until the 8 milepost where the gradient increased noticeably to typically 1 in 80 all the way to Glyncorrwg.

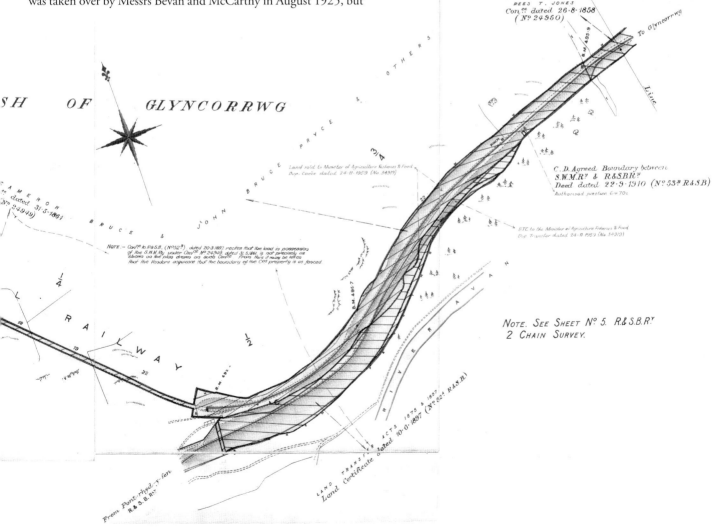

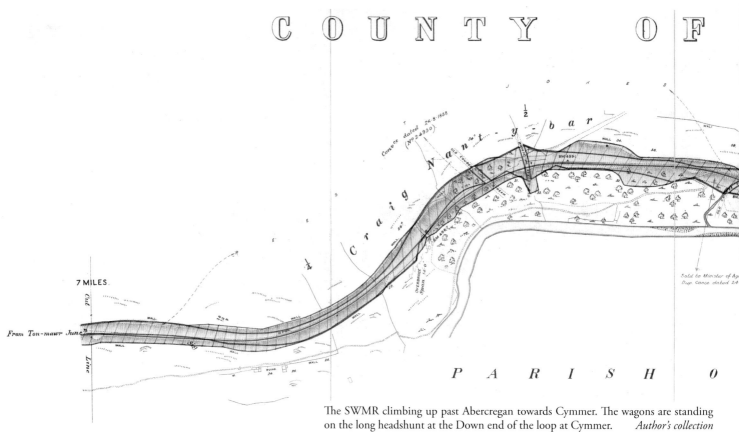

The SWMR climbing up past Abercregan towards Cymmer. The wagons are standing on the long headshunt at the Down end of the loop at Cymmer.   *Author's collection*

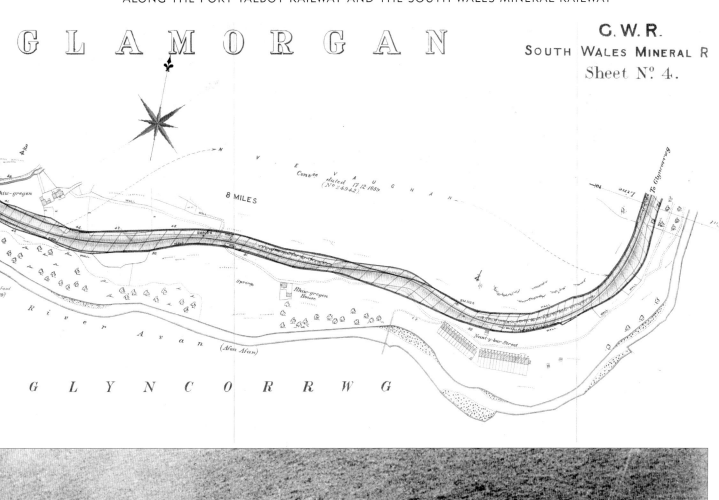

G L A M O R G A N

8 MILES

Convce dated 17 12 1855 (No 24942)

Rhiw-gregen House

Nant-y-bar Street

River Avan (Afan Afan)

G L Y N C O R R W G

NORTH RHONDDA

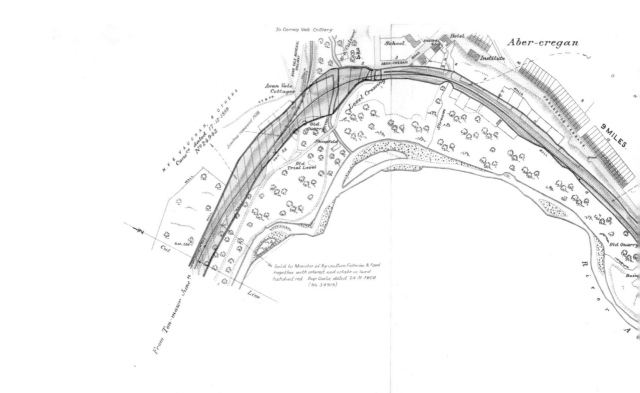

The loops and junction at Cymmer, SWMR, were little photographed until a passenger station was established there. This view looking down on the southern end of the loops also shows part of the circuitous pedestrian route up to the R&SBR and GWR station off to the right. *Author's collection*

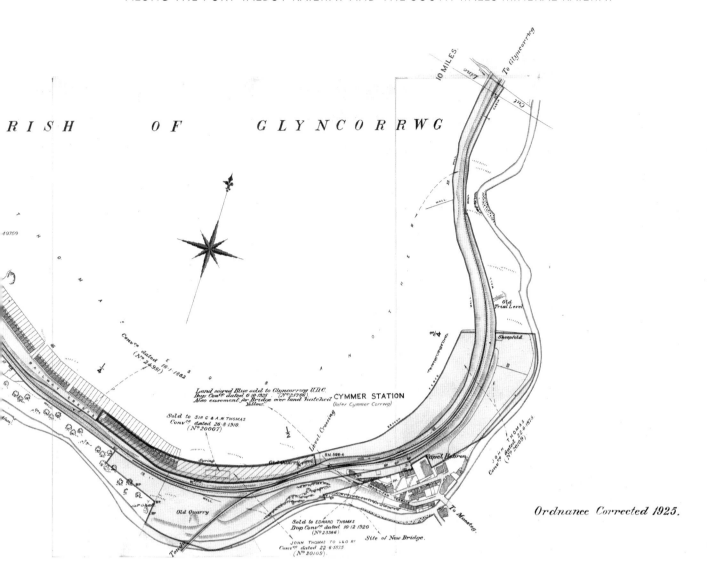

Ordnance Corrected 1925.

CORRWG VALE COLLIERY AND AVON VALE QUARRY (8M 51CH)

A siding connection had been in use since circa 1863, latterly serving the Avan Vale Mineral Railway. In April 1910 agreements were signed with the two companies using this railway, Corrwg Vale Colliery Ltd and Avon Vale Quarry Co., to the effect that the SWMR was the owner of the junction and that the two companies were allowed to use the junction and siding for their traffic.[243] The quarry ceased working in September 1918 and that tenancy was cancelled. The colliery closed circa 1925 and the GWR regarded the tenancy as terminated on 31st December 1926.

ABERCREGAN QUARRY (8M 66CH)

The Cefn-y-Fan-Estate & Fforchlais Quarry Co. Ltd was formed in August 1909 to acquire the lease of a quarry in Cwm Cregan and a right of way through Abercregan Farm to reach it.[244] An agreement with the SWMR dated 11th February 1911 provided for

a siding connection near the 8¾ milepost, with the quarry company laying down a siding parallel to the main line.[245] The quarry was abandoned by mid-1914 and the SWMR took possession of the siding as from 1st August in liquidation of the £35 10s 0d owing for the easement and tolls. The agreement was cancelled on 15th January 1915, but the siding remained in use for ordinary traffic purposes until circa 1961.

CYMMER

Just beyond Cymmer North Junction with the GWR (9m 40ch), the SWMR abandoned its generally eastwards direction and turned to head north up Glyn Corrwg. Cymmer station (9m 48ch), renamed Cymmer Corrwg in 1926, consisted of a platform 114 feet long with a small waiting room/office. About half a mile beyond the inlet ground frame for the Cymmer passing loop (9m 61ch), the SWMR reached the first major colliery it served.

The SWMR entered Cwm Corrwg some height above the river. Empty private owner wagons, most for Glyncorrwg and Glenavon collieries, are stored in the loop, circa 1914. *Author's collection*

General View, Cymmer. 880.

AVONDALE HOTEL.

NANTEWLAETH COLLIERY (10M 14CH, 10M 56CH AND 10M 57CH)

The PTR's engineer, William Cleaver, reported in April 1913 that a temporary siding connection had been laid in at the 10m 47ch point on the west side of the SWMR for Robert Gibb and brought into use.[246] A belated agreement between the SWMR and Gibb's Navigation Collieries Ltd for a siding and junction for a new sinking at Nantewlaeth at a cost of £166 was signed on 31st December 1913.[247] This company had been registered in July 1913 with a capital of £120,000[248] to carry on business as colliery proprietors and to give effect to various agreements with North's Navigation Collieries, Miss Talbot, the Earl of Dunraven and Glenavon Garw Collieries Ltd, another of Gibb's companies.[249] The latter had been registered in August 1907 with a capital of £100,000[250] and by October 1915 owned 50 per cent of the Gibb's Navigation shares, acquiring the remainder in 1917 when Gibb's Navigation was wound up.

In October 1915 the directors of the PTR agreed to two connections on the river side of the SWMR to form the inlet and outlet junctions to the new colliery sidings, and also to a bridge over the railway to carry coal from the pits to the new screens. Three new connections were reported to have been laid in by January 1916,[251]

the third being a repositioning of the original connection serving the shaft side of the colliery to a point nearer the inlet junction. An agreement covering these three connections was signed on 3rd April 1917, the colliery having to pay a £10 per year easement for sidings laid on SWMR property.[252] A supplemental agreement was made in November 1939 between the GWR and the Ocean Coal Co. Ltd regarding moving the outlet junction about 80 yards down the line to 10m 9ch, to make room for further sidings which served a new briquette works. The GWR's general manager reported to the Traffic Committee in November 1939 that a halt at Nantewlaeth Colliery for workmen had been authorised, the cost of £130 being borne by the colliery company.[253] This halt was sited just south of the colliery screens, and was served by trains working the Cymmer–North Rhondda service.[254]

Nantewlaeth Colliery starting producing coal in 1919, was taken over by the Ocean Coal Co. in 1938 and closed by the National Coal Board in 1949 – although the washery and briquette works continued until the 1960s. The siding agreements were terminated on 31st December 1965 and the connections removed shortly afterwards.

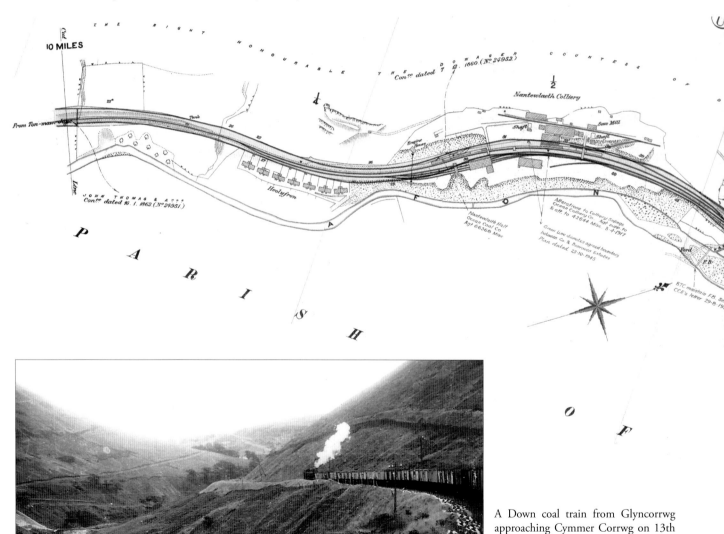

A Down coal train from Glyncorrwg approaching Cymmer Corrwg on 13th July 1959. The gradient hereabouts was 1 in 104.
Courtesy H C Casserley

Cymmer Corrwg looking up the valley, photographed in August 1951, showing the mixed construction of the platform. The running loop commenced here and continued round the bend. The third line on the right was a short siding.
Author's collection

ABOVE: The surface workings of Nantewlaeth Colliery, circa 1916, shortly after completion. The SWMR passed behind the colliery on the way to Glyncorrwg off to the right.

Author's collection

BELOW: Nantewlaeth Colliery Halt looking up the line towards Glyncorrwg on 13th July 1959. The colliery has a disused look, having ceased production in 1949, although the washery and briquette works situated about 400 yards behind the photographer continued in use until the 1960s.

Courtesy R M Casserley

The connection for the three loops at Glyncorrwg was reached at 11m 38ch. The passenger station was a little further on at 11m 54ch and the signal box at 11m 58ch, adjacent to the level crossing. The siding for the engine shed, which abutted the Glyncorrwg Colliery Co.'s office building, joined the main line in front of the signal box.

HENDREGARREG COLLIERY (11M 50CH)

The Hendregarreg Colliery Company Ltd was formed in 1919 to reopen some of the levels in Cwm Corrwg Fechan at Glyncorrwg previously worked by the Welsh Main Coal Co. Ltd.[255] An agreement with Messrs Griffiths & Co. on behalf of the colliery company dated 4th October 1920 provided for a connection to the main line just south of the platform and a siding running past the rear of the station to two screen roads and a tail shunt, each with a capacity of twelve wagons, on the site of the earlier exchange sidings.[256] Like the earlier line, this siding crossed Castle Street on the level and the colliery was required to provide a watchman whenever an engine and/or wagons were passing over. The siding was completed in November 1920[257] and brought into use the following month.[258] The siding agreement was transferred to the Llwynyffynon Colliery Co. in November 1924 and terminated on 12th November 1935 when mining ceased.

YNYSCORRWG COLLIERY (11M 60CH)

As allowed for in the December 1907 working agreement,[259] the Glyncorrwg Colliery Co. in February 1911 asked the directors of the PTR for assistance in providing sidings for its new sinking at Ynyscorrwg south of Glyncorrwg. In due course Lowther reported

the estimated cost of the connection to the SWMR and the quarter mile long siding, which required a two-span bridge over the river, to be £1,200, and proposed that the colliery company should pay one-third in advance and the balance at 3d per ton in addition to the rates for conveyance, plus interest. This expense was too onerous for the colliery and in December 1911 the SWMR's contribution was reduced to providing the siding connection only. The terms were embodied in a siding agreement dated 22nd November 1912, under which the colliery company would pay in advance one-third of the estimated £150 cost of the new connection, the balance being liquidated by an additional 3d per ton on all traffic to and from colliery.[260] The colliery was allowed to use its own engine to take outward traffic to the sidings at Glyncorrwg and remove all empty wagons, and to use that part of the SWMR necessary to do this and the sidings free of charge, but the sidings were not to be used for storage. This trailing connection was built across the level crossing, a development which eventually led to the provision of crossing gates.[261] Ynyscorrwg Colliery closed in 1924, but the siding was not removed by the GWR until 1928 when the Glyncorrwg Colliery Co. was in liquidation.

Following the introduction of a passenger service between Cymmer and Glyncorrwg in March 1918 the line beyond Glyncorrwg was known as the North Rhondda Blaencorrwg Branch.[262] The line climbed at an average gradient of 1 in 29, the steepest being a short section at 1 in 22 up to North Rhondda Colliery at the upper end at an elevation of about 1,000 feet. Not surprisingly, all traffic was required to be propelled from Glyncorrwg. By 1925 there were two short trailing connections along the fairly straight section beyond

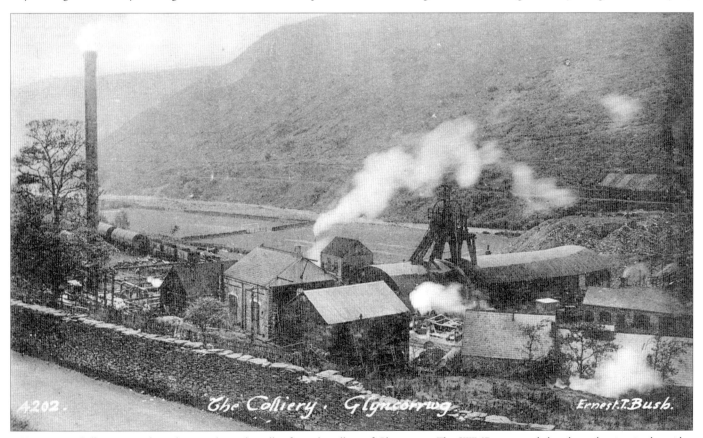

Ynyscorrwg Colliery was a short distance down the valley from the village of Glyncorrwg. The SWMR ran on a ledge above the river in the mid distance. *Author's collection*

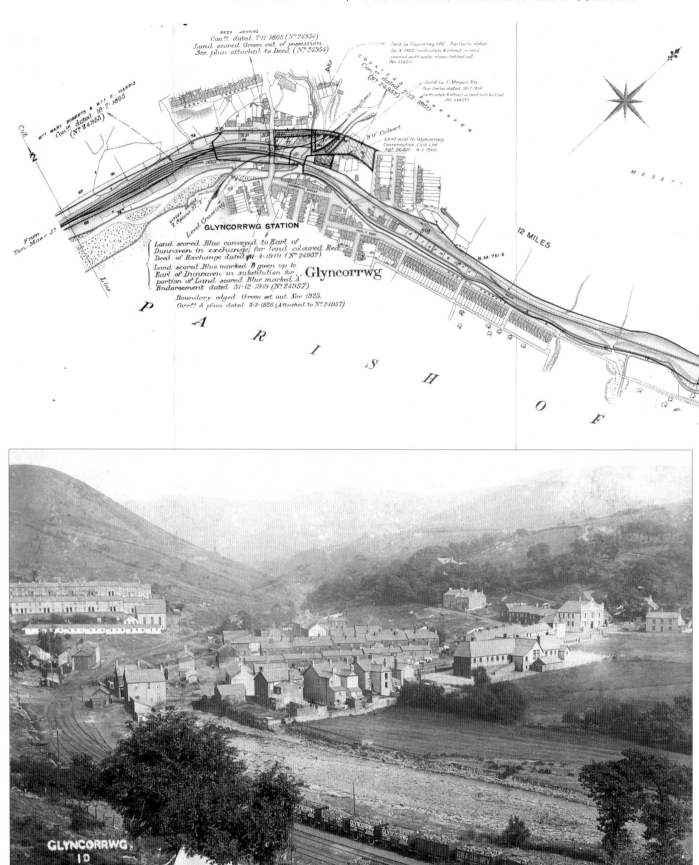

The presence of what look like new Glyncorrwg private owner wagons suggests that this postcard view of Glyncorrwg was taken at about the time North and South pits commenced working circa 1906, when the Glyncorrwg Colliery Co. was working the SWMR. The engine shed, with the company's offices behind, is visible at left centre.

Author's collection

Glyncorrwg at 12m 0ch and 12m 39ch, at least one of which was a runaway siding.[263] By this date a facing siding connection at 12m 7ch leading to a quarry on the other side of the river had been removed. This connection predated the PTR working agreement but was put in after 1900 and replaced an earlier tramway which ran down to Glyncorrwg.

GLYNCORRWG NORTH AND SOUTH PITS (12M 40CH AND 12M 64CH)
Both these pits, which were sunk in 1902 and 1904 respectively,[264] were idle from 1912 to 1919 and it is possible that the rearrangement

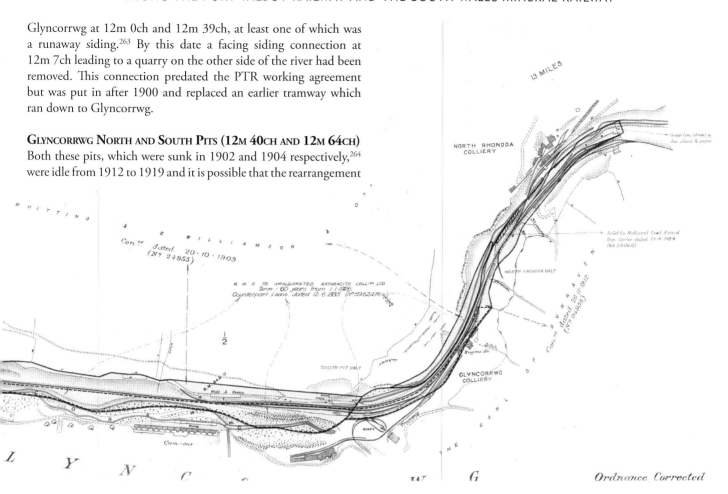

of the sidings at North Pit approved in February 1912 by directors of the SWMR were not carried out at the time. In connection with the reopening, Cleaver reported in May 1919 that the junctions were being relaid at the colliery company's expense so as to improve the arrangements generally.[265] This work was not completed until May 1920,[266] so that there were then only three connections, two at

the inlet end near North Rhondda Platform and one for the outlet at the 12½ milepost. Circa 1925 a receiver of the Glyncorrwg Colliery Co. was appointed on the petition of Messrs Norton, Rose & Co. acting for the Railway Debenture & Trust Co. Ltd and all other debenture holders.[267] The workings were acquired by Glyn Neath Collieries in 1926 and in 1928 became part of Amalgamated

The Glyncorrwg Colliery Co.'s offices at Glyncorrwg, circa 1906. Note the company's full name written across the lower windows. *Author's collection*

F. Bach photo

Looking down on Glyncorrwg from the east, with the engine shed and offices on the right and one of the Glycorrwg Colliery Co.'s engines taking water. Postcard, postally used 25th July 1907. *Author's collection*

GLYNCORRWG.

ABOVE: Glyncorrwg after the siding connection for Ynyscorrwg Colliery (off to the right of this picture) had been laid in (1913) but before the passenger station was completed (1917). One of Glyncorrwg Colliery Co.'s engines is on the shed road. Postcard, postally used 1917. *Author's collection*

BELOW: Glyncorrwg after the station building had been removed, showing the signal box opened in March 1918. *Author's collection*

LEFT: Glyncorrwg signal box circa 1955. *Author's collection*

BELOW: Cwm Cas with the surface workings of Cwm Cas level (worked 1888, or earlier, to 1907) on the left and the headgear for South Pit under construction in the centre background. This area was devastated by severe flooding on 28th September 1909. Postcard, postally used 30th June 1905. *Author's collection*

Anthracite Collieries Ltd. South Pit was further developed in the 1930s, for which new inlet and outlet connections were provided and for which a new sidings agreement was made.[268] The pithead was totally reconstructed by the NCB in 1955/56. The colliery sidings were altered and lengthened to suit these developments, and the SWMR main line was realigned. These works required yet another siding agreement, backdated to 1st January 1956, which was terminated on 31st July 1970 after the colliery had closed.[269] The Glyncorrwg Colliery Co. continued to use its own locomotives up to 1926[270] and these were presumably stabled in the engine shed at Glyncorrwg. The later owners of the colliery did not use standard gauge locomotives; the NCB employed narrow gauge diesel mechanical units both above and below ground.[271]

South Pit Halt (12m 49ch) was located between the outlet and inlet connections for Glyncorrwg Colliery and moved about 130 yards down the line in 1956 to a new position at 12m 43ch close to the new pithead. North Rhondda Halt (12m 68ch) was just above the upper connection, and the line terminated at 12m 71ch, although the SWMR owned land to beyond the 13 mile point which was occupied by part of Blaencorrwg Colliery's surface workings.

GLYNCORRWG PITS.

Glyncorrwg South Pit, with North Pit in the distance, circa 1906.

Author's collection

ABOVE: Glyncorrwg Colliery photographed on 25th May 1970 at about the time of its closure. The inlet connection on the SWMR is in the centre of the view. The tramway from the stockyard at the site of North Rhondda Colliery enters at bottom left and becomes mixed gauge with a colliery siding. *Courtesy J A Peden*

BELOW: North Rhondda Colliery under construction 1908. The drift entrance was at the top of the incline. *Author's collection*

The first coal at North Rhondda Colliery was raised on 3rd November 1909. Postcard, postally used 9th November 1909. *Author's collection*

NORTH RHONDDA COLLIERY (12M 71CH)

Corrwg Fechan Coal Co. Ltd was registered in August 1880 with a capital of £30,000[272] and developed the eponymous colliery on a site on the west side of the river about one-quarter of a mile above Glyncorrwg Colliery. This business failed and went into voluntary liquidation in February 1888, although the company was not dissolved until April 1946. An attempt to transfer the assets to the New Corrwg Fechan Coal Co. Ltd in January 1886 fell through[273] and the colliery fell into disuse. The North Rhondda Colliery Co. Ltd was registered in June 1908 with a capital of £20,000 to acquire a sublease of the property from, *inter alia*, the Corrwg Fechan Coal Co. Ltd.[274] New headings were driven and the first coal was raised on 3rd November 1909. This colliery was far more successful than its predecessor, remaining open until 29th July 1960.

Plans for sidings for the new colliery were ready by October 1908,[275] but an agreement allowing the colliery company to alter the existing, disused, siding and to lay down others was not made until 18th May 1909.[276] A further agreement, dated 28th October 1921, permitted the colliery to extend the sidings at its own expense.[277] These works required a new bridge across the river[278] and were brought into use in December 1920.[279] A new agreement between BR(WR) and the National Coal Board was made on 1st January 1956 and terminated on 31st July 1970.

BLAENCORRWG COLLIERY (12M 71CH)

The Blaencorrwg Colliery Co. Ltd was registered in September 1913 to acquire the lease of certain mines and plant at Blaencorrwg, including part of the old Corrwg Fechan Colliery, and was close to North Rhondda Colliery on the other side of the river.[280] An agreement for a siding connection was signed on 12th August 1914, in effect a continuation of the SWMR, and the sidings and screens were partly installed on railway company land.[281] The Blaencorrwg Co. sold all its assets to the East Rhondda Colliery Co. Ltd in April 1924 and then ceased trading. The siding agreement was transferred to the new owners in May 1925; another, concerning catch points on the outlet siding, was made in December 1928. The siding agreement was terminated in May 1956 – this, like its near-neighbour, being another long-lived colliery.

NOTES

1. See Chapter 15.
2. TNA: PRO BT 31/37286/170147.
3. TNA: PRO RAIL 1057/1528/246.
4. TNA: PRO MT 29/80 p. 216.
5. TNA: PRO RAIL 574/65.
6. See Volume 1, Chapter 1.
7. TNA: PRO RAIL 574/64.
8. TNA: PRO RAIL 1057/1528/224.
9. TNA: PRO MT 29/80 p. 219.
10. TNA: PRO MT 29/82 p. 72.
11. TNA: PRO RAIL 1057/2509.
12. TNA: PRO RAIL 1057/1528/114.
13. TNA: PRO RAIL 1057/1528/115.
14. TNA: PRO BT 31/9026/66784.

15. TNA: PRO BT 31/19686/112216.
16. TNA: PRO BT 31/13499/113729.
17. TNA: PRO RAIL 1057/1529/55.
18. TNA: PRO MT 6/1037/15.
19. See Chapter 13.
20. TNA: PRO BT 31/25439/162643.
21. See Chapter 12.
22. TNA: PRO RAIL 1057/1528/217.
23. TNA: PRO MT 29/80 p. 223.
24. TNA: PRO RAIL 574/57.
25. See Volume 1, Chapter 1.
26. TNA: PRO BT 31/7842/56131.
27. TNA: PRO RAIL 1057/1529/14.
28. TNA: PRO RAIL 1057/1528/5.
29. TNA: PRO RAIL 574/29.
30. TNA: PRO BT 31/7842/56131.
31. See Chapter 13.
32. BT 31/18522/99232.
33. TNA: PRO COAL 12/97.
34. TNA: PRO BT 31/18145/94063.
35. TNA: PRO MT 6/961/2.
36. TNA: PRO RAIL 1057/1528/59.
37. TNA: PRO MT 6/880/2.
38. See Volume 1, Chapter 6.
39. TNA: PRO RAIL 574/38.
40. TNA: PRO RAIL 1057/2540.
41. TNA: PRO BT 31/20420/119757.
42. TNA: PRO RAIL 574/70; RAIL 1057/1528/252.
43. See Volume 1, Chapter 10.
44. See Volume 1, Chapter 4.
45. See Volume 1, Chapter 6.
46. TNA: PRO RAIL 1057/1528/69.
47. TNA: PRO RAIL 1057/1528/70.
48. TNA: PRO MT 6/1388/1.
49. TNA: PRO RAIL 1057/1528/86.
50. TNA: PRO BT 31/17463/84658.
51. TNA: PRO RAIL 1057/1528/245.
52. TNA: PRO MT 29/80 p. 225.
53. TNA: PRO RAIL 574/59.
54. See Volume 1, Chapter 3.
55. Hill, *Industrial Locomotives of Mid & South Glamorgan*, p. 81.
56. Lewis, *Coal Industry*, p. 110.
57. See Volume 1, Chapter 1.
58. Lewis, *The Coal Industry*, p. 98.
59. Lewis, *The Coal Industry*, p. 93.
60. TNA: PRO RAIL 1057/1528/51.
61. TNA: PRO RAIL 1057/2658.
62. TNA: PRO MT 6/1037/16.
63. TNA: PRO RAIL 1057/1528/94.
64. TNA: PRO RAIL 1057/1529/49.
65. TNA: PRO RAIL 1057/1529/56.
66. TNA: PRO RAIL 1057/2658.
67. TNA: PRO RAIL 1057/2658.
68. TNA: PRO MT 6/2083/4.
69. TNA: PRO RAIL 574/51.
70. TNA: PRO RAIL 1057/1528/202.
71. TNA: PRO RAIL 1057/1528/209.
72. TNA: PRO MT 29/80 p. 220.
73. TNA: PRO RAIL 574/58.
74. TNA: PRO RAIL 1057/1528/254.
75. TNA: PRO RAIL 1057/1528/255.
76. TNA: PRO MT 29/84 p. 36.
77. See Volume 1, Chapter 10.
78. See Volume 1, Chapter 6.
79. See Volume 1, Chapter 1.
80. Lewis, *The Coal Industry*, p. 48.
81. Lewis, *The Coal Industry*, p. 53.
82. TNA: PRO BT 31/31818/65244.
83. See Volume 1, Chapter 4.
84. TNA: PRO RAIL 574/77.
85. TNA: PRO RAIL 574/45.
86. TNA: PRO MT 6/2083/2.
87. W&SHC 2515/210 Box 225/4.
88. TNA: PRO RAIL 1057/1528/84, RAIL 574/67.
89. TNA: PRO MT 6/1399/4.
90. TNA: PRO RAIL 1057/1528/114.
91. TNA: PRO MT 6/2074/10.
92. TNA: PRO RAIL 1057/1528/123.
93. TNA: PRO RAIL 574/67.
94. TNA: PRO BT 31/11687/90464.
95. *The London Gazette*, 23 July 1918.
96. TNA: PRO MT 6/887/8.
97. TNA: PRO MT 6/2074/12.
98. TNA: PRO MT 6/2083/3.
99. TNA: PRO BT 31/18964/104489.
100. TNA: PRO BT 31/22921/141089.
101. TNA: PRO RAIL 574/52.
102. TNA: PRO RAIL 574/66.
103. TNA: PRO RAIL 1057/1528/236.
104. TNA: PRO RAIL 1057/1528/238.
105. TNA: PRO MT 29/80 p. 222.
106. TNA: PRO RAIL 1057/2636.
107. W&SHC 2515/210 Box 262/6.
108. TNA: PRO MT 6/961/1.
109. TNA: PRO RAIL 1057/1528/59.
110. TNA: PRO RAIL 1057/1528/118.
101. TNA: PRO RAIL 1057/2487.
112. TNA: PRO BT 31/12591/100582.
113. TNA: PRO RAIL 1057/1528/6, RAIL 1057/2517.
114. TNA: PRO RAIL 1057/1528/20, 25.
115. TNA: PRO RAIL 574/30.
116. See Volume 1, Chapter 1.
117. See Volume 1, Chapter 5.
118. TNA: PRO BT 31/23364/144565.
119. TNA: PRO BT 31/21573/129877.
120. TNA: PRO RAIL 574/68.
121. TNA: PRO RAIL 1057/1528/214.
122. See Volume 1, Chapter 5.
123. See Volume 1, Chapter 1.
124. TNA: PRO RAIL 574/69; see also Chapter 15.
125. TNA: PRO RAIL 1057/1528/12.
126. TNA: PRO RAIL 1057/2591.
127. TNA: PRO RAIL 574/39.
128. TNA: PRO BT 31/14237/135304.
129. TNA: PRO BT 31/23280/143917.
130. TNA: PRO RAIL 1057/1058/112.
131. TNA: PRO BT 31/23916/149221.
132. TNA: PRO RAIL 1057/1058/84.
133. TNA: PRO RAIL 574/68.
134. TNA: PRO RAIL 1057/2535.
135. TNA: PRO RAIL 1057/1058/126.
136. See Volume 1, Chapter 10.
137. TNA: PRO RAIL 574/61.
138. TNA: PRO RAIL 1057/1528/249.
139. TNA: PRO RAIL 1057/1528/253.
140. TNA: PRO RAIL 1057/1528/254.
141. TNA: PRO MT 29/84 p. 37.
142. TNA: PRO RAIL 250/355.
143. Chapter 15.
144. See Volume 1, Chapter 5.
145. See Volume 1, Chapter 1.
146. TNA: PRO BT 31/21192/126789.
147. TNA: PRO BT 31/32528/182828.
148. TNA: PRO BT 31/35870/166143.
149. TNA: PRO RAIL 1057/1528/156.
150. TNA: PRO RAIL 574/41.
151. TNA: PRO RAIL 574/44.
152. TNA: PRO BT 31/22200/135114.

153. TNA: PRO BT 31/26090/169243.
154. TNA: PRO BT 31/30273/232242.
155. W&SHC 2515/210 Box 225/3.
156. W&SHC 2515/210 Box 261/6.
157. Jason Jarvis, *Pelenna Valley: A Pictorial History of Tonmawr and Pontrhydyfen* (Pelenna Community Council 1996), p. 13.
158. See Volume 1, Chapter 5.
159. TNA: PRO RAIL 574/48.
160. TNA: PRO BT 31/25757/165827.
161. W&SHC 2515/210 Box 260/7.
162. TNA: PRO RAIL 250/355.
163. W&SHC 2515/210 Box 242/2.
164. TNA: PRO RAIL 1057/1528/224.
165. TNA: PRO RAIL 574/71.
166. TNA: PRO RAIL 1057/1528/232.
167. TNA: PRO RAIL 1057/1528/239.
168. TNA: PRO BT 31/24060/150472.
169. TNA: PRO BT 31/15990/57509.
170. TNA: PRO RAIL 574/63.
171. See Chapter 15.
172. See Volume 1, Chapter 5.
173. See Volume 1, Chapters 5 and 6.
174. TNA: PRO BT 31/21972/133279.
175. TNA: PRO RAIL 574/47.
176. TNA: PRO BT 31/23986/149820.
177. W&SHC 2515/210 Box 257/2; 257/4.
178. W&SHC 2515/210 Box 271/4.
179. TNA: PRO RAIL 1057/2553.
180. See Volume 1, Chapter 5.
181. TNA: PRO BT 31/11083/84338.
182. TNA: PRO BT 31/23978/149749.
183. TNA: PRO RAIL 788/904, RAIL 250/356; W&SHC 2515/210 Box 259/5.
184. See Volume 1, Chapter 5.
185. TNA: PRO BT 31/26208/170498.
186. W&SHC 2515/210 Box 243/5.
187. TNA: PRO BT 31/11236/85822.
188. TNA: PRO RAIL 574/34.
189. TNA: PRO RAIL 1057/1528/110.
190. Jarvis, *Pelenna Valley*, p. 9.
191. *The London Gazette*, 8 January 1915.
192. TNA: PRO RAIL 574/42.
193. TNA: PRO RAIL 1057/1528/173.
194. *The London Gazette*, 11 September 1914.
195. TNA: PRO RAIL 574/42.
196. TNA: PRO RAIL 574/50.
197. TNA: PRO BT 31/22386/136632.
198. TNA: PRO BT 31/30067/226740.
199. See Volume 1, Chapter 10.
200. See Chapter 13.
201. TNA: PRO RAIL 1057/1528/223.
202. TNA: PRO RAIL 1057/1528/254.
203. TNA: PRO RAIL 574/62.
204. TNA: PRO RAIL 1057/1528/248.
205. TNA: PRO MT 29/80 p. 212.
206. Chapter 15.
207. TNA: PRO RAIL 1057/2490.
208. *British Coal, Iron and Steel: A Brief Survey of the Productions of Baldwins Limited* (E J Burrow & Co., 1934).
209. TNA: PRO RAIL 1057/1528/104.
210. TNA: PRO RAIL 574/31.
211. See Chapter 15.
212. Riden, John Bedford, p. 109.
213. See Volume 1, Chapter 1.
214. TNA: PRO BT 31/8023/57728.
215. TNA: PRO RAIL 1057/1528/23.
216. TNA: PRO RAIL 1057/1528/56.
217. TNA: PRO RAIL 1057/1529/42.
218. TNA: PRO BT 31/8023/57728.
219. TNA: PRO RAIL 1057/1528/130.
220. Hughes, 'Emily Charlotte Talbot', p. 93.
221. TNA: PRO RAIL 1057/1528/59.
222. TNA: PRO RAIL 1057/1528/94.
223. W&SHC 2515/210 Box 261/2.
224. TNA: PRO BT 31/16070/59232.
225. TNA: PRO RAIL 1057/1528/34.
226. TNA: PRO RAIL 1057/1529/36.
227. TNA: PRO RAIL 1057/1528/118.
228. Hill, *Industrial Locomotives of Mid & South Glamorgan*, p. 125.
229. British Railways Act 1990, Eliz. 2 c.xxv.
230. TNA: PRO RAIL 574/37.
231. TNA: PRO RAIL 1057/1528/95.
232. See Volume 1, Chapter 7.
233. William Cleaver Letter Book, Arthur Rees Collection.
234. TNA: PRO RAIL 639/18.
235. TNA: PRO BT 31/24504/154035.
236. TNA: PRO BT 31/23872/148877.
237. TNA: PRO RAIL 1057/1528/237.
238. TNA: PRO RAIL 639/22.
239. TNA: PRO RAIL 1057/1528/135.
240. TNA: PRO RAIL 639/23.
241. WGAS D/D Xra 10.
242. See Volume 1, Chapter 1.
243. TNA: PRO RAIL 639/12, 13.
244. TNA: PRO BT 31/18972/104551.
245. TNA: PRO RAIL 639/27.
246. TNA: PRO RAIL 1057/1528/174.
247. TNA: PRO RAIL 639/16.
248. TNA: PRO BT 31/21619/130218.
249. Roger L Brown, 'Coal Mining in the Upper Afan Valley, Part IV: Joseph, Gibb and the Great Western Railway' *Afan Uchaf*, 8 (1985), pp. 25–31.
250. *South Wales Coal Annual 1908*, p. 35.
251. TNA: PRO RAIL 1057/1528/201.
252. TNA: PRO RAIL 639/20.
253. TNA: PRO RAIL 250/466.
254. See Chapter 15.
255. TNA: PRO BT 31/25062/159173.
256. TNA: PRO RAIL 639/24.
257. TNA: PRO RAIL 1057/1528/246.
258. TNA: PRO RAIL 1057/1528/247.
259. TNA: PRO RAIL 574/33.
260. TNA: PRO RAIL 639/15.
261. See Volume 1, Chapter 7.
262. SWMR WTT, 28 March 1918.
263. BR(WR) Sectional Appendix to the Working Time Table Swansea Operating District April 1958.
264. See Volume 1, Chapter 7.
265. TNA: PRO RAIL 1057/1528/235.
266. TNA: PRO RAIL 1057/1528/242.
267. TNA: PRO BT 31/15048/30591.
268. W&SHC 2515/210 Box 275/7.
269. W&SHC 2515/210 Box 317/4.
270. Potts and Green, *Industrial Locomotives of West Glamorgan*, pp. 71–2.
271. Potts and Green, *Industrial Locomotives of West Glamorgan*, pp. 151–2.
272. TNA: PRO BT 31/34165/14369.
273. TNA: PRO BT 31/3778/23592.
274. TNA: PRO BT 31/37253/98333.
275. TNA: PRO RAIL 1057/1528/127.
276. TNA: PRO RAIL 639/11.
277. TNA: PRO RAIL 639/25.
278. TNA: PRO RAIL 1057/1528/245.
279. TNA: PRO RAIL 1057/1528/247.
280. TNA: PRO BT 31/21720/131171.
281. TNA: PRO RAIL 639/17.

22

Private Owner Wagons on the Port Talbot Railway and the South Wales Mineral Railway

PRIVATE OWNER WAGONS WERE a prominent feature of the pre-nationalisation scene on British railways. As the name implies, they were owned by businesses using the railways to transport their raw materials and products, predominantly by colliery companies. These wagons generated a considerable income for the railway companies, which kept a close eye on their condition and movements.

Private owner wagons were much in evidence on the PTR and SWMR, travelling to and from their owners' premises or awaiting shipment at the docks. Collected here, in the order encountered in Chapter 21, are builders' photographs of wagons made for colliery companies and other businesses whose works were served by the PTR or the SWMR, supplemented by pertinent information. As with the rest of South Wales, these wagons were built principally by the Gloucester Railway Carriage & Wagon Co. Ltd.[1] Further information on thirteen of these wagon fleets can be found in the series of books written by Keith Turton and published by Lightmoor Press.[2]

Glenhafod Collieries owned 155 wagons in August 1935, all mortgaged to Lloyds Bank. Illustrated are three 10-ton wagons in the number range 2251–2270 at Duffryn Yard in 1926. These were built by the Lancashire & Yorkshire Wagon Co. in 1898 and, judging by the numbers, may well have been transferred from the associated Glenavon Garw Colliery Co. Most of the other wagons were secondhand, built by Hurst, Nelson, and the British Wagon Co., but fifty new 12-ton wagons came from Hurst, Nelson in 1923.   *Author's collection*

NOTES

1. Chris Sambrook, *British Carriage & Wagon Builders & Repairers 1830–2006* (Lightmoor Press 2007), pp. 77–84.
2. Keith Turton, *Private Owner Wagons* (Lightmoor Press):
    A Second Collection (2004), p. 54, Elders Navigation; p. 67, Glyncorrwg.
    A Fourth Collection (2005), p. 35, Cleeves; p. 146, Brader; p. 181, Glyncorrwg.
    A Fifth Collection (2006), p. 170, Elders Navigation.
    A Sixth Collection (2007), p. 25, Blaenmawr; p. 48, Cribbwr Fawr; p. 70, Garth; p. 72, Glenavon Garw; p. 113, North Rhondda; p. 115, North's Navigation.
    A Seventh Collection (2008), p. 157, Glenavon Garw, Glenhafod, North's Navigation.
    An Eighth Collection (2009), p. 118, North End.
    A Ninth Collection (2010), p. 154, Glenavon Garw.
    A Tenth Collection (2011), p. 37, Bwlch.
    An Eleventh Collection (2012), p. 13, Baldwins; p. 28, Charles Bazzard; p. 64, Craiglyn.

ABOVE: The best known Glenhafod wagons are the fifty 20-ton vehicles hired from the GWR in 1934, although they remained with Glenhafod for only three years. These wagons were built by Charles Roberts & Co. Ltd to GWR diagram N32. They were numbered 2271–2320, numbers reflecting the then size of the Glenavon Garw fleet, and were transferred to Stephenson, Clarke, the well known coal factors, in April 1937. *HMRS*

RIGHT: Baldwins Ltd in due course acquired a large wagon fleet. In the early days at least they were lettered for the subsidiary they served. 10-ton wagon number 144, one of a batch ordered from Gloucester RC&W Co. in February 1903 shortly after the company was formed, was assigned to Bryn Navigation Colliery. *GRC&WCo*

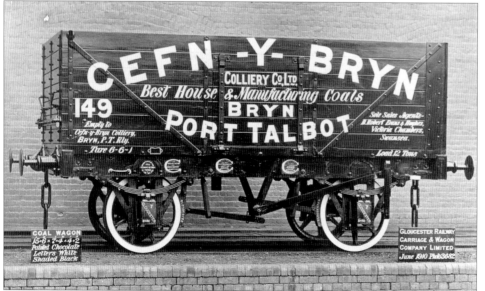

Cefn-y-Bryn Colliery Co. purchased 12-ton wagons from Gloucester RC&W Co. in 1908 and 1910, as seen here. The livery was chocolate with white lettering shaded black. Forty-eight secondhand wagons came from Gloucester in 1911. The wagons were branded to return empty to "Cefn-y-Bryn Colliery, Bryn, P.T.Rly.", and the sole sales agents were named as "D Robert Evans & Hughes, Victoria Chambers, Swansea", the original lessees of the colliery. *GRC&WCo*

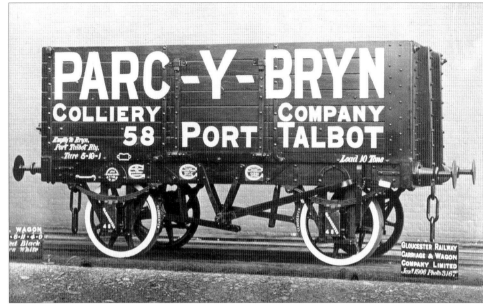

Parc-y-Bryn Colliery Co.'s wagons were less elaborately painted than those of its near neighbour, the Cefn-y-Bryn Colliery Co. 10-ton wagon number 58, one of ten supplied by Gloucester RC&W Co. in January 1906 before the business became a limited company, was painted black with white lettering. Return was to "Bryn, Port Talbot Rly."   *GRC&WCo*

12-ton wagon number 217 was one of a batch of twenty-five supplied by the Gloucester RC&W Co. to the Ton Hir Colliery Co. in July 1908. The wagon was painted in the simple livery of black lettered white, with the return address given as "Ton Hir Sidings, Maesteg, Port Talbot Ry. & Docks." The size of this colliery company's wagon fleet is not known; a further twenty-five 12-ton wagons were ordered from Gloucester in 1911 and this firm also had a contract for the repair of eighty-six 10-ton wagons.   *GRC&WCo*

Although North's Navigation Collieries had connections to the PTR at Maesteg and Cwmdu, none of its large fleet of 10-ton and 12-ton wagons, upward of 3,000 vehicles, was initially lettered for return to either place. Up to circa 1911 the wagons were painted red and elaborately lettered white shaded black, as exemplified by 10-ton No. 2197 ordered from Gloucester RC&W Co. in 1897.   *GRC&WCo*

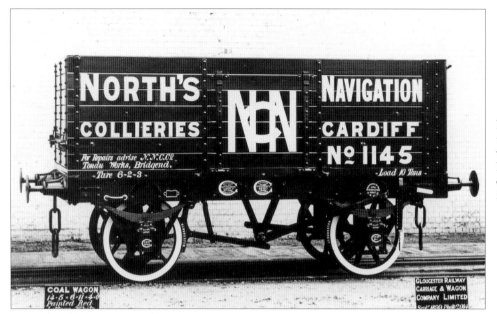

North's address was changed from Bridgend to Cardiff circa 1898, as shown on 10-ton wagon No. 1145 ordered in September 1899. North's established a wagon repair works on the site of the old Tondu Ironworks, as indicated on the wagon side. *GRC&WCo*

One of the final batch of wagons ordered from Gloucester RC&W Co. in December 1911, 12-ton number 3000. Later wagons were ordered from the Cambrian Wagon Co. Ltd. *GRC&WCo*

One of an unknown number of 14-ton brake vans ordered by North's from Hurst, Nelson & Co. Ltd, Motherwell, in 1913, presumably in accord with the running powers agreement over the PTR between Maesteg and Cwmdu. *Author's collection*

ABOVE: After 1912, North's wagons were (re)painted in a simplified livery, black with white lettering, and the apostrophe was dropped. *Carmen*, Hawthorn, Leslie 2396 of 1898, is shunting on North's private railway near Maesteg circa 1925. *Author's collection*

In 1924 North's signed two agreements with the GWR under which 250 20-ton coal wagons built to diagram N23 were assigned to its sole use. These wagons were built by the Birmingham RC&W Co. and given GWR numbers 110001–110250. No. 110071 is painted in GWR grey and lettered for Norths (note the missing apostrophe).
Author's collection

The Swansea & District Railwaymen's Direct Coal Association ordered two 10-ton wagons from Gloucester RC&W Co. No. 1, of September 1902, was painted black with white lettering and written to return empty to "North's Navigation Maesteg Deep Colliery, via G.W.R. & Port Talbot Rly. & Dock Co". *GRC&WCo*

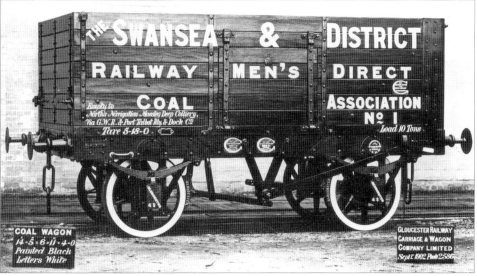

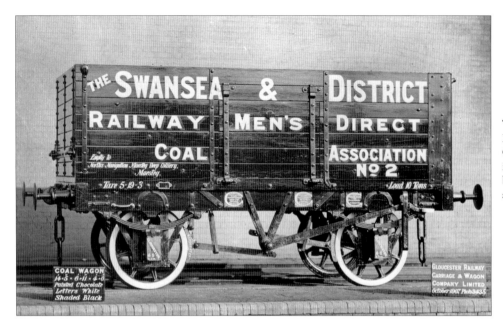

The Swansea & District Railwaymen's Direct Coal Association's No. 2, supplied in October 1907, was more elaborately painted in chocolate with white lettering shaded black, but the return instructions were simplified, no route being specified.

GRC&WCo

Elders Navigation Collieries owned Garth Merthyr Colliery near Cwmdu, which was connected to the PTR, and Oakwood Colliery, which was connected to the GWR near Maesteg, the two being joined by an internal railway. In the early days at least, wagons were lettered specifically for return to one or the other. The example illustrated here, built by Hurst, Nelson, was branded to return to "Cwmdu Sidings, Maesteg" – those concerned being required to know these were on the PTR. It is shown in photographic livery, the reverse of that usually applied. Confusingly, one end states "For Repairs Return to Colliery", the other "Repairs advise North Central Wagon Co., Cardiff." After 1915 Elders' wagons were gradually relettered Celtic to reflect the new ownership. *Author's collection*

The first wagons ordered for North End Colliery in 1911 were painted black with the full name in white lettering. 12-ton wagon No. 42, ordered in May 1912, shows the revised, more prominent style, with the lettering shaded in red, the wagon number on the opening end door, and the return address given as "North End Colliery, Tonmawr Junction, Port Talbot Railway."

GRC&WCo

North End wagon No. 110 of 1914 was identical to No. 42 except the number and return address are transposed. The colliery's wagon fleet totalled 100 vehicles with others hired as required. *GRC&WCo*

Having acquired Mercantile Colliery on the Whitworth Branch in 1920, the Blaenmawr Colliery Co. purchased a total of sixty-five wagons from three builders. 12-ton wagon number 163 was one of a batch of twenty-five built by Gloucester RC&W Co. in 1923, all of which were recovered by them when the colliery company went into receivership in 1929. *GRC&WCo*

The Garth Colliery Co. possibly took over some the Blaenmawr Colliery Co.'s wagons when it acquired the colliery in 1930. Twenty secondhand wagons were purchased in 1931. In the 1930s a total of forty-five 12-ton wagons was ordered from Gloucester RC&W Co., of which number 211 of 1937 is typical. *GRC&WCo*

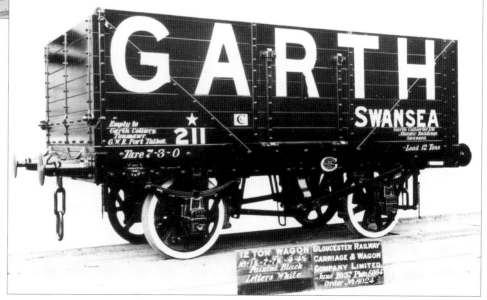

Prior to 1914, E A Cleeves & Co. of Swansea was a major distributor and exporter of anthracite and other coals. The small Merthyr Llantwit Colliery on the Blaenavon Branch evidently produced coal of sufficient quality and quantity to further this trade and in 1898 fifty 10-ton end-door wagons were ordered from the Gloucester RC&W Co. Unusually for a coal wagon, it was painted lead colour, with white letters shaded black, indicating return to this colliery on the SWMR. This was an error, as by this date the Blaenavon Branch was part of the PTR, although, as recounted in Volume 1, Chapter 6, the SWMR claimed the right to work the traffic, a situation not resolved until November 1902. Cleeves began acquiring its own collieries in 1914 and then traded as Cleeves' Western Valleys Anthracite Collieries Ltd. Cleeves' collieries formed part of the new Amalgamated Anthracite Collieries Co. Ltd in 1923 and the coal merchants' business continued as a wholly-owned subsidiary of Amalgamated Anthracite Collieries until the 1930s.

GRC&WCo

Almost any serviceable wagon could have been used to convey coal from Morfa Colliery over the one and a half mile Morfa Railway to Vivian's works alongside the GWR main line at Taibach. 10-ton wagon No. 142 was one of a batch of twenty-five ordered from Gloucester RC&W Co. in 1897 for main line use. These wagons were painted black lettered white and were written to return empty to Margam Sidings, Port Talbot, this being the exchange point for the colliery.

GRC&WCo

The Craiglyn Colliery Co. acquired Tewgoed Colliery in February 1913 and shortly afterwards ordered a batch of ten 12-ton wagons from Gloucester RC&W Co. No. 108 of May 1914 was painted black with white lettering indicting that the Sales Agent was T Sydney Bevan of Morriston, and written "Empty to Craiglyn Colliery Sidings, Near Cwmavon, Port Talbot Rly." A fleet of twenty-eight wagons seemingly sufficed for this small concern, the company's receiver recording the sale of twenty 12-ton wagons in July 1930 and eight 10-ton wagons a month later.

GRC&WCo

Cribbwr Fawr Collieries ordered fifty 12-ton wagons from Charles Roberts & Co. of Wakefield in 1907. These were painted red with white lettering shaded black, at least initially, unlike their Gloucester counterparts which dispensed with the shadowing.
Author's collection

Cribbwr Fawr Collieries number 412 was one of a batch of fifty purchased from Gloucester RC&W Co. in December 1909. The company name was given in full on these wagons and a less ornate script was used for the empty instructions. *GRC&WCo*

Below: W Brader was one of the small number of coal merchants known to have lettered their wagons for return to a colliery served by the PTR or SWMR, in this case Cribbwr Fawr Colliery on the OVER. No. 1 was one of two 12-ton wagons supplied by Gloucester RC&W Co. to Brader in 1911.
GRC&WCo

Charles Randall of Llanelly was another coal merchant who obtained coal from a named colliery served by the PTR. 10-ton wagon No. 6 was one of two ordered from Gloucester RC&W Co. in September 1907. This wagon had the common black bodywork with white lettering livery, and was written for return to "Bryndu Colliery, Via Margam, Jctn, P. T & D. Rly." Randall also ordered six 10-ton wagons from the Cambrian Wagon Co. in 1912 and was in business until at least 1938. *GRC&WCo*

ABOVE: Later Baldwins' wagons had slightly simplified lettering and gave the company's address as Landore, where its Swansea Hematite Iron & Steel Works was located. Nevertheless, a large number of wagons, such as 12-ton wagon number 1176 ordered in 1909, were lettered for return to "Aberbaiden Colliery, Bryndu, P.T. Rly."

GRC&WCo

A shunter and a team of gangers standing in front of Baldwins wagons near the siding connection for Aberbaiden Colliery.

Courtesy Barrie Flint

ABOVE: Most of Ton Phillip Rhondda Colliery Co.'s wagons were supplied by Gloucester RC&W Co., new and second-hand, in both 10-ton and 12-ton forms. 10-ton wagon number 277 of February 1902 displays the full company name with the head office at Swansea. The return address is given as "Bryndu, Port Talbot Rly." *GRC&WCo*

LEFT: Later Ton Phillip wagons carried a shortened, more prominent name and indicated what the colliery produced. 10-ton wagon number 343 of November 1904 was in the same livery of black with white lettering and was branded for return empty to "Bryndu Sidings, P.T.R." The office address is given as 8 Cambrian Place, Swansea, but this had changed to a Port Talbot address by 1918. *GRC&WCo*

RIGHT: Charles Bazzard (circa 1844–1926) was general manager of Avan Hill Colliery. Abergwynfi, until it closed circa 1898. He later set up a business at Briton Ferry as colliery agents and coal exporters, which was still in existence in 1926 run by his son. The size of the Bazzard wagon fleet is not recorded, but 12-ton wagon No. 200 built in 1908 is an example in a later style of livery. The return destination is given rather vaguely as "S.W.M.R. Briton Ferry", but the firm had no known siding there.

GRC&WCo

Twenty 12-ton wagons were ordered by the Bwlch Colliery Co. from Gloucester RC&W Co. in February 1923, of which wagon number 206 was one, lettered for return to "Bwlch Colliery Sidings, Ton Mawr, Port Talbot, G.W.R." What wagons, if any, were used before this date is not known. Twenty more came from the Ince Wagon Works in 1924. *GRC&WCo*

Glenavon Garw Collieries Ltd was formed in 1907 with various members of the Gibbs family as principal shareholders. Among the several collieries owned were Glenavon and Glyncymmer – both were at Cymmer and connected to the R&SBR – and Nantewlaeth, which was near Cymmer and served by the SWMR. Most of the eventual 2,200-strong wagon fleet seems to have been obtained secondhand, but number 689 was one of a batch ordered from R Y Pickering of Wishaw. It is lettered for return to "Cymmer, G.W.R. & R&S.B.Ry", which would have been near enough for onward movement to Nantewlaeth Colliery on the SWMR. *Author's collection*

Having such a large fleet meant that Glenavon Garw wagons carried a number of livery variations. 12-ton wagon number 1451 was one of a batch built in 1923 by the Fir Tree Wagon Co. of Wigan. Despite the date it is still lettered for return empty to "Cymmer R.&S.B. & G.W. Rlys South Wales"! 150 wagons, Nos 1451 to 1600, were built by Fir Tree Wagon for Glenavon Garw in 1923/24. *Author's collection*

Corrections and Addenda to Volume 1

CORRECTIONS

Chapter 1, p. 25 The penultimate sentence should read "The short goods siding on the right at one time also served a rail mill on the site of the defunct Cwmavon Iron Works."

Chapter 9, p. 239 The wagon length given in T L Jones' drawing is incorrect; it should be that of an ex-GWR 3-plank wagon, 15 feet 6 inches.

ADDENDA

Chapter 2, p. 64 The dock improvements were evidently completed by 1st September 1875 when an advertisement appeared in the *Western Mail* offering for sale at Port Talbot: "Fifty to sixty waggons, including 2 [cubic] yard end-tip waggons, 4 [cubic] yard ballast or coal waggons, with doors; stone trolleys; 20 tons rails; wrought iron swing bridge for carrying railway across, 45 feet span; steam crane, travelling crane, and sundries."

Chapter 2, p. 64 The *Cardiff Times* reported on 10th June 1876 that Mr Talbot had ordered from Messrs Llewellyn and Cubitt, of the Rhondda Engine Works, Pentre, coal staithes of the balance type for erection at Port Talbot.

Chapter 2, p. 70 The *South Wales Daily Post* reported on 2nd April 1894 that James Allan of Cardiff had secured a contract for erecting a new engine-house, accumulator and tip at the dock.

Chapter 6, p. 133 Imports of copper ore for Rio Tinto resumed in May 1899 as noted in a paragraph in *Engineering* dated 12th May 1899: "Port Talbot: The Rio Tinto copper ore trade, amounting to

The Glyncorrwg Colliery Co. owned at least 1,400 wagons, most if not all coming from the Gloucester RC&W Co. No. 101, of 10-ton capacity, is a typical example, delivered in May 1904 at the time of the opening of Glyncorrwg South Pit. The general style of lettering remained fairly constant throughout, although there are subtle variations in the positioning of some words. It is strange that the general manager's address is given as Briton Ferry, since the company's offices were at Glyncorrwg. Note that no return destination is given, presumably to allow for the options of Glyncorrwg SWMR or the company's colliery at Abergwynfi R&SBR. Most were plated to be repaired at the colliery company's own wagon works.
GRC&WCo

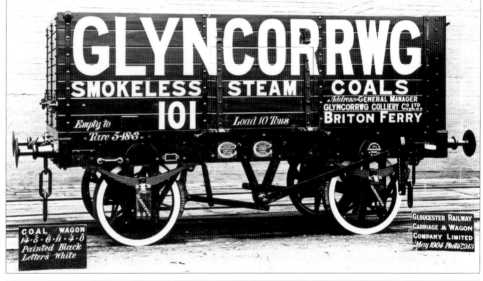

Although the first coal was taken away in Glenavon wagons, the North Rhondda Colliery Co. eventually owned 154 wagons, all apparently hired or purchased from the Gloucester RC&W Co. A typical example is 12-ton end-door wagon No. 109 purchased in October 1912.
GRC&WCo

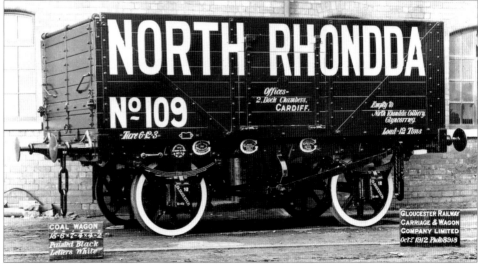

about 40,000 tons per annum, which for the last two years has been dealt with via Swansea, has now been secured to Port Talbot Docks, and delivery is direct to the works by the PTR&D Company's trains. The first boat, the steamship *Rosslyn*, belonging to Messrs John Corey & Sons Ltd., arrived at Port Talbot Docks on Thursday afternoon [11th May] with 912 tons precipitate and 234 tons matte; she was discharged in thirty hours."

Chapter 7, p. 156 It should be noted that the name of the private siding up Cwm Cregan as the Avan Vale Mineral Railway is found only on the OS survey of 1897 and subsequent editions. No information regarding this appellation has been found, and it may be a grandiose title used by the then proprietors, the Corrwg Vale Colliery Co.

Chapter 7, p. 156 In February 1873 the GWR directors approved the provision of additional siding accommodation at Briton Ferry at an estimated cost of £1,446, plus a further £1,500 for locking the points and signals [TNA: PRO RAIL 250/25]. These two sidings were located alongside the SWMR Dock Branch to the north of the station with trailing connections to the Up and Down SWR main line. No justification was given for these sidings, but they would have facilitated the interchange of the increasing traffic on the SWMR, and may have been a goodwill gesture following the GWR's refusal to compensate the SWMR for its enforced change to the narrow gauge. The connections to the main line were controlled by a new Briton Ferry No. 1 signal box alongside the Up Main connection. The works were inspected by Col. Yolland in October 1873 and approved with the proviso that a means of communicating with the trailing connection to the Down Main, which apparently was worked by a ground frame, was installed [TNA: PRO RAIL 639/36]. The question of which company should pay for the working of the junction was resolved by arbitration in December 1875, when it was declared that the GWR would pay two-thirds and the SWMR one-third of the costs [TNA MT 6/107/18]. The signal box, later known as Briton Ferry West Signal Box, and sidings lasted until 1915, when the area was remodelled by the construction of Up and Down goods loops [see Chapter 11, p. 277].

PTR&D No. 24 at Duffryn Yard seemingly as newly delivered from Hudswell, Clarke in 1901. Note the number on the chimney, the headlamp, the three-link coupling and safety chains, and the stone deflectors on the guard irons. On the original photograph it is possible to discern that the locomotive is lined out as per the builder's photograph (Volume 1, p. 211). Compare this with the view of the locomotive in its final condition (Volume 1, p. 214).
Author's collection

Bibliography

Books Consulted

125 Years of Halcrow, Halcrow Group Marketing 2003

Adams, D John, *Glimpses of Margam Life 1830–1918*, West Glamorgan County Council 1986

Adams, D John, and Arthur Rees, *A Celebration of Margam Park and Gardens*, West Glamorgan County Council 1989

AEI, *Margam Marshalling Yard*, c.1960

Atkins, AG, W Beard and R Tourret, *GWR Goods Wagons*, Tourret Publishing 1998

Atkins, Philip, *The Golden Age of Steam Locomotive Building*, Atlantic Transport Publishers 1999

Barnett, AP and D Wilson-Lloyd, *The South Wales Coalfield*, The Business Statistics Co. 1921

Barrie, DSM, *The Barry Railway*, Oakwood Press 1978

Barrie, DSM, *A Regional History of the Railways of Great Britain, Vol. 12, South Wales*, David & Charles 1980

Beche, Henry T de la, 'First report on the Coals suited to the Steam Navy', *Memoirs of the Geological Survey of Great Britain*, Vol. 2 part 2, 1848

Bevan, Thomas, 'Industrial Development of the Llynfi, Ogmore & Garw Valleys', unpublished MA Thesis, University of Wales 1928

Philip R Björling, *Briquettes and Patent Fuel: Their Manufacture and Machinery Connected Therewith*, Rebman Ltd 1903

Botwell, Harold D and Geoffrey Hill, *Reservoir Builders of South Wales*, Industrial Locomotive Society 2006

British Coal, Iron and Steel: A Brief Survey of the Productions of Baldwins Limited, Burrow & Co. 1934

British Railways Western Region, *Margam Marshalling Yard*, c.1960

British Transport Docks Board, *Cargo Liner Services*, August 1965

Case, Albert Havelock, *Port Talbot Railways and Docks, General Information, etc. taken from a Paper read on the Occasion of the Visit of the Members of the Institution of Marine Engineers, September 1898.*

Chapman, Colin, *The Vale of Glamorgan Railway*, Oakwood Press 1998

Chapman, Colin, *The Ely Valley Railway*, Oakwood Press 2000

Cole, David, *Contractors' Locomotives*, Part I, Union Publications 1964

Croxton, Anthony H, *Railways of Zimbabwe*, David & Charles 1982

Day, ME, *The Engineers' Who's Who*, DMA Co. 1939

Edmundson, William, *The Nitrate King: A Biography of 'Colonel' John Thomas North*, Palgrave Macmillan 2011

Evans, A Leslie, *The History of Taibach & District*, Alun Books 1963

Evans, A Leslie, *Cwmavon Then & Now*, Port Talbot Historical Society 1992

Flint, Arthur John, 'Sir Robert Price, Bart., MP', in *Glamorgan Historian* Vol. 11, Stewart Williams nd

Granville, Neville, *Cefn Cribwr: Chronicle of a Village*, Stewart Williams 1980

Granville, Neville, *All Change at Cefn Junction*, the author 1998

Grindlay, Jim, *British Railways Locomotive Allocations 1948–1968, Part Six, Diesel & Electric Locomotives*, Transport Publishing 2007

Guest Keen Baldwins Iron & Steel Co. Ltd, ETW Dennis & Sons Ltd 1937

GWR Service Time Tables, South Wales Section, February 1866, reprinted by Dragonwheel Books 2004

Hadfield, Charles, *The Canals of South Wales and the Border*, David & Charles 1967

Haddock, K, *Giant Earthmovers: An Illustrated History*, MBI Publishing Co. 1998

Hanson, J Ivor, *Profile of a Welsh Town*, the author 1969

Harman, Fred W, *The Locomotives Built by Manning Wardle & Company, Vol. 3, Broad Gauge & Works List*, Century Locoprints nd

Harrison, Ian, *Great Western Railway Locomotive Allocations for 1921*, Wild Swan Publications 1984

Harvey, Charles E, *The Rio Tinto Company: An Economic History of a Leading International Mining Concern 1873–1954*, Alison Hodge Publishers 1981

Haws, Duncan, *Merchant Fleets No. 24: Britain's Railway Steamers: Western & Southern Companies plus French and Stena*, TCL Publications 1993

Higgins, Leonard S, 'John Brogden & Sons', in *Glamorgan Historian* Vol. 10, Stewart Williams 1974

Hill, Geoffrey, *Industrial Locomotives of Mid & South Glamorgan*, Industrial Railway Society 2007

Holcroft, H, *An Outline of Great Western Locomotive Practice 1837–1947*, Ian Allan 1957

Holding, David and Tony Moyes, *History of British Bus Services: South Wales*, Ian Allan 1986

Hughes, John Vivian, *The Wealthiest Commoner: CRM Talbot 1803–1890*, the author 1977

Hughes, Stephen, *The Brecon Forest Tramroads*, Royal Commission on Ancient and Historical Monuments in Wales 1990

Ince, Laurence, *The South Wales Iron Industry 1750–1885*, Ferric Publications 1993

Ince, Laurence, *Neath Abbey in the Industrial Revolution*, Tempus 2001

Industrial Rivers of the United Kingdom, T Fisher Unwin 1888

Jackson, PW (ed.), *The Letter-Books of W Gilbertson & Co. Ltd., Pontardawe 1890–1929*, West Glamorgan Archive Service 2001

Jarvis, Jason, *Pelenna Valley: A Pictorial History of Tonmawr and Pontrhydyfen*, Pelenna Community Council 1996

John, Arthur H and Glanmor Williams (eds), *Glamorgan County History, Vol. 5, Industrial Glamorgan*, Glamorgan County History Trust 1980

Jones, Edgar, *A History of GKN, Vol. 2, The Growth of a Business 1918–1945*, MacMillan 1990

Jones, Frank, *Mainline to Industry*, Lightmoor Press 1998

Jones, Gwyn Briwnant and Denis Dunstone, *The Vale of Neath Line*, Gomer 1996

Jones, Stephen K, *Brunel in South Wales, Vol. 2, Communications and Coal*, Tempus 2006

Jubilee of County Councils 1889–1939 (Glamorgan), Evan Brothers Ltd nd

Kelly's Directory of Monmouthshire and South Wales 1895

Lewis, DA, *A Cambrian Adventure: A History of the Iron Industry in Maesteg*, Goldleaf Publishing 2001

Lewis, David, *The Coal Industry in the Llynfi Valley*, Tempus 2006

Lewis, John, *Great Western Steam Rail Motors and Their Services*, Wild Swan Publications 2004

Locomotives of the Great Western Railway, Railway Correspondence & Travel Society
 Part 3, Absorbed Engines 1854–1921, 1956

Part 5, Six-Coupled Tank Engines, 1958

Part 9, Standard Two-Cylinder Classes, 1962

Part 10, Absorbed Engines 1922–1947, 1966

Part 11, The Rail Motor Vehicles and Internal Combustion Locomotives, 1956

Part 13, Preservation and Supplementary Information, 1983

Lyons, ET, An Historical Survey of Great Western Engine Sheds 1947, Oxford Publishing Co. 1972

Lyons, ET and ER Mountford, An Historical Survey of Great Western Engine Sheds 1837–1947, Oxford Publishing Co. 1979

MacDermot, ET, revised CR Clinker, History of the Great Western Railway, Vol. 1, Ian Allan 1964

MacDermot, ET, revised CR Clinker, History of the Great Western Railway, Vol. 2, Ian Allan 1964

Mackworth, Margaret Haig, Viscountess Rhondda, DA Thomas: Viscount Rhondda by His Daughters and Others, Longmans, Green & Co. 1921

Morgan, Alun, Porthcawl, Newton & Nottage; a Concise Illustrated History, D Brown 1987

Morgan, Richard, trans. A Leslie Evans, A History of Taibach to 1872, Port Talbot Historical Society 1987

Mountford, ER, A Register of GWR Absorbed Coaching Stock 1922/3, Oakwood Press 1978

Mullay, AJ, Railways for the People, Pendragon Publishing 2006

Nicholson, Tim, Take the Strain: The Alexandra Towing Company and the British Tugboat Business 1833–1987, The Alexandra Towing Co. Ltd 1990

O'Brien, James, Old Afan and Margam, the author 1926

Parry, Stephen, 'History of the Steel Industry in the Port Talbot Area 1900–1988'. PhD Thesis, University of Leeds 2011. http://etheses.whiterose.ac.uk/2591/1/parrystephen.pdf

Phillips, Martin, The Copper Industry in the Port Talbot District, Guardian Press 1935

Pike, WT, British Engineers and Allied Professions in the Twentieth Century, WT Pike 1908

Pocock, Nigel and Ian Harrison, Great Western Railway Locomotive Allocations for 1934, Wild Swan Publications nd

Port Talbot Docks, British Transport Docks Board 1966

Potts, M and GW Green, Industrial Locomotives of West Glamorgan, Industrial Railway Society 1996

Powell, Terry, Staith to Conveyor: An Illustrated History of Coal Shipping Machinery, Chilton Ironworks 2000

Price, MRC, The Gwendraeth Valleys Railway, Oakwood Press 1997

Protheroe-Jones, Robert, Welsh Steel, National Museums & Galleries of Wales 1995

Quick, Michael, Railway Passenger Stations in Great Britain: A Chronology, Railway & Canal Historical Society 2009

Rees, A, CRM Talbot and the Great Western Railway, West Glamorgan County Council 1985

Rees, Ronald, King Copper: South Wales and the Copper Trade 1584–1895, University of Wales Press 2000

Rhodes, Michael, British Marshalling Yards, Haynes Publishing Group 1988

Riden, Philip, John Bedford and the Ironworks at Cefn Cribwr, the author 1992

Sambrook, Chris, British Carriage & Wagon Builders & Repairers 1830–2006, Lightmoor Press 2007

Simmons, Jack and Gordon Biddle (eds), Oxford Companion to British Railway History, Oxford University Press 1997

Simnett, WE, Railway Amalgamation in Great Britain, The Railway Gazette 1923

Sites for Works at the South Wales Docks and Plymouth, GWR 1932, 1939

Slater's Directory of South Wales, 1859

South Wales Coal Annual, 1908, 1909–1910, 1917

Spender, JA, Weetman Pearson: First Viscount Cowdray, 1856–1927, Cassell & Co. 1930

Stacey, Claude (ed.), Men of the West, the author 1926

Toomey, Robert R, Vivian and Sons 1809–1924: A Study of the Firm in the Copper and Related Industries, Garland Publishing Inc. 1985

Tourret, R, GWR Engineering Work 1928–1938, Tourret Publishing 2003

Turton, Keith, Private Owner Wagons, Lightmoor Press

A Second Collection, 2004

A Fourth Collection, 2005

A Fifth Collection, 2006

A Sixth Collection, 2007

A Seventh Collection, 2008

An Eighth Collection, 2009

A Ninth Collection, 2010

A Tenth Collection, 2011

An Eleventh Collection, 2012

Vaizey, John, The History of British Steel, Weidenfeld & Nicolson 1974

Vaughan, A, A Pictorial Record of Great Western Architecture, Oxford Publishing Co. 1977

Walmsley, Tony, Shed by Shed, Part 6, St Petroc Infopublishing 2009

Watkins, Thos. C, 'Prize Essay on the Propriety of having a Railway from Aberavon to Mynydd-y Caerau, Cwmcorrwg & Maesteg', Aberavon Eisteddfod 1865

Who's Who in Cumberland and Westmorland, Who's Who in the Counties 1937

Who's Who in Wales, Western Mail 1921

Wilkins, Charles, The South Wales Coal Trade and its Allied Industries, Daniel Owen & Co. 1888

Wilkins, Charles, The History of the Iron, Steel, Tinplate and Other Trades of Wales, Joseph Williams 1903

JOURNALS AND PERIODICALS

Afan Uchaf, Journal of the Cymmer Afan & District Historical Society

Broad Gauge Society Broadsheet

Engineering

Heritage Railway

Historical Model Railway Society Journal

Industrial Locomotive

Iron & Coal Trades Review

Locomotive Magazine and Railway Carriage and Wagon Review

Model Railway News

Morgannwg, The Journal of Glamorgan History

Proceedings of the Institution of Civil Engineers

Proceedings of the. Institution of Mechanical Engineers

Railway & Canal Historical Society Tramroad Group Occasional Papers

Railway Archive

Railway Gazette

Railway Magazine

Railway News

Railway Times

Severn Valley Railway News

South West Wales Industrial Archaeology Society Bulletins

Transactions of the Aberafan & Margam Historical Society

Transactions of the Neath Antiquarian Society

Transactions of the Port Talbot Historical Society

Welsh History Review

Index